The Psychology of Media and Politics

The Psychology of Media and Politics

George Comstock
Syracuse University

Erica Scharrer
University of Massachusetts Amherst

ELSEVIER
ACADEMIC
PRESS

AMSTERDAM • BOSTON • HEIDELBERG • LONDON
NEW YORK • OXFORD • PARIS • SAN DIEGO
SAN FRANCISCO • SINGAPORE • SYDNEY • TOKYO

Elsevier Academic Press
30 Corporate Drive, Suite 400, Burlington, MA 01803, USA
525 B Street, Suite 1900, San Diego, California 92101-4495, USA
84 Theobald's Road, London WC1X 8RR, UK

This book is printed on acid-free paper.

Library of Congress Cataloging-in-Publication Data
Comstock, George A.
The psychology of media and politics / George Comstock, Erica Scharrer.
p. cm.
Includes bibliographical references and index.
ISBN 0-12-183552-9 (alk. paper)
1. Communication in politics. 2. Mass media–Political aspects. 3. Political psychology.
I. Scharrer, Erica. II. Title.
JA85.C677 2005
320′.01′4–dc22

2004030217

British Library Cataloguing in Publication Data
A catalogue record for this book is available from the British Library

ISBN: 0-12-183552-9

For all information on all Academic Press publications visit our Web site at www.academicpress.com

Printed in the United States of America
05 06 07 08 09 9 8 7 6 5 4 3 2 1

PREFACE

Our goal in this book has been twofold: to order several decades of research on media and political behavior within a communication framework, and to take into account social changes and recent research that lead to a perspective quite different from the wisdom of the mid-twentieth century.

We believe the media have a central role in modern politics. For this reason, we believe the field of communication has much to contribute to the understanding of political behavior. At the same time, the field of communication, here as elsewhere, is dependent on the data and analyses of many different fields and disciplines: social psychology, political science, sociology, and even cognitive neuroscience. We have colonized many sectors of these fields and disciplines, and we hope their citizens will forgive us for this appropriation.

We conclude that the media have a large, important, and distinctive role in affecting the political decisions of the voting public. This emphasis on the centrality of the media in politics is a major contribution of the field of communication to the understanding of political behavior. We hope this volume adds in a small way to that contribution.

ACKNOWLEDGMENTS

We owe a major debt to the many dozens of individuals who conducted the studies upon which we have drawn. We hope they will find our treatment of their work of interest (our optimistic side), and will not be too unhappy with the uses we have made of it (our pessimistic side).

We are grateful to David Rubin, Dean, S.I. Newhouse School, and Michael Morgan, Chair, UMass Amherst Department of Communication, for providing a scholarly setting, and to the S.I. Newhouse chair for financial support. We thank Marcia Wisehoon for a painstaking and thoroughly professional preparation of the final manuscript. We also thank Mary Deskiewicz, who was persevering and unfailing in processing the final-draft-but-one, and two graduate assistants, Yun Jung Choi, a demon bibliographic sleuth of the highest order, and Jack Powers, whose stalwart mastery of the Internet was invaluable.

We found several analyses to be particularly helpful. These key studies include:

Doppelt, J. C., & Shearer, E. (1999). *Nonvoters: America's No-Shows.* Thousand Oaks, CA: Sage Publications, Inc.

Hamilton, J. T. (2004). *All the News That's Fit to Sell.* Princeton, NJ: Princeton University Press.

Marcus, G., Neuman, R.W., & Mackuen, M. (2000). *Affective Intelligence and Political Judgment.* Chicago, IL: University of Chicago Press.

Mutz, D. C. (1998). *Impersonal Influence: How Perceptions of Mass Collectives Affect Political Attitudes.* Cambridge, UK: Cambridge University Press.

The Pew Center for the People and the Press. Various surveys of media use and political behavior, and especially *RetroPolitics: The Political Typology:* Version 3.0 (November 1999).

CONTENTS

PART I

Early Knowledge

CHAPTER 1

Conventional Wisdom

The notorious third-person effect has emerged over the past decade as a prominent paradigm for the examination of relationships between public opinion and the mass media following several years of obscurity. It was introduced by W. Phillips Davison in *Public Opinion Quarterly* in 1983, and refers to the inclination of people to assert that others are or have been or will be influenced by the stimuli presented by the mass media while they themselves remain beyond and—in their minds, the evidence suggests—above such manipulation. It has attained the status of a truism; the public is skeptical of the capability of others to resist the entreaties of the media but individuals generally are confident of their own ability to do so.

I. THE THIRD PERSON

The empirical evidence that attests to this phenomenon has five important characteristics. The first characteristic is a high degree of consistency among data collected by a variety of methods from different populations; the third-person effect replicates again and again. The second is its extension to behavior—it occurs not only in regard to the exertion of influence on opinion but in judgments of the degree to which the media are used constructively. The third is the documentation that the underlying rationale in some circumstances may lead to blaming the media for adversely affecting public thought and behavior. The fourth is the implication for public policy and media behavior: if such influence is so common, and thereby presumably so powerful, perhaps something should be done to constrain the media. The fifth is the prominent role of perceived social disparity in the alleged vulnerability of others, with the attribution of such an effect increasing as others are perceived to be less well educated, intelligent, or energetic and active in processing the messages of the media.

The evidence, of course, is not without attributes calling for commentary or requiring qualification. Most importantly, the data invariably represent what people are ready to reply when asked a question about the likely response of themselves or others to the media.

The typical circumstance is a survey in which a sample is asked, by questionnaire or interview, how they believe they or others typically behave in regard to some category of media content that might be expected to influence opinion or behavior. Examples include brand name advertising for products and services; news coverage of politics, public affairs, and controversial issues; political campaign advertising; and various types of entertainment that might be thought to affect viewers or readers, such as dramas that are violent (which might encourage aggressive behavior) or portray dishonesty and corruption in high places (which might contribute to loss of faith in government or business). Less often, a sample is asked about the likely effects of a very specific product of the media, such as a particular political commercial attacking an opponent or the news coverage of a particular event or series of events.

In either case, there are three important consequences. One is that we learn only what people are ready to say when asked a question in which they may well have scant interest and to which they very well may have given little previous thought. We do not learn what they might say or think after careful reflection. The second is that we learn nothing about the actual relationship between the effects of the media on the respondent and on others. We learn only what people have to say—and thereby, what they appear to think—about such effects. The third is that we do not learn what they would conclude after extensive public debate or argument over the influence of the media. We learn nothing of the possibly mitigating effects of heightened interest in and greater knowledge about media influence.

A. The Evidence

Nevertheless, evidence in behalf of third-person effects has been produced so consistently that there can be little doubt about the public's perception of the media: the media are powerful, although, as the evidence also shows, that power is seen as dependent on the vulnerability of their audiences. Third-person effects have been recorded among children (Henriksen & Flora, 1999), college students (Cohen & Davis, 1991; Perloff, 1989), and adults (Hoffner et al., 1999; Salwen & Dupagne, 1999); certainly display no geographical limitations; and have been produced by experimental methods in which subjects are asked to respond to the influence of particular stimuli such as advertisements or news coverage (Gunther & Thorson, 1992; Vallone, Ross, & Lepper, 1985), and by surveys in which respondents are simply asked for their opinions (Salwen & Dupagne, 1999).

They also have been observed for an extraordinarily wide range of topics, so that they easily escape the onus of being limited to one or a very few categories of possible influence. These include advertising, product commercials, and public service announcements (Brosius & Engel, 1996; Gunther & Thorson, 1992; Henriksen & Flora, 1999); news coverage, political campaigns, and commercials for political candidates (Cohen, Mutz, Price, & Gunther, 1988; Price, Huang, & Tewksbury, 1997; Price & Tewksbury, 1996; Cohen & Davis, 1991); news reports of violent events and violent television dramatizations (Hoffner et al., 1999; Rojas, Shah, & Faber, 1996; Scharrer, 2002); and a miniseries dramatizing the hypothetical defeat of the United States in a war with the once-evil empire, the Soviet Union (Lasorsa, 1989).

For example, Henriksen and Flora (1999) found both in a survey of about 570 seventh-grade pupils and in an experiment in which about 665 fourth-, sixth-, and eighth-grade pupils were presented with either cigarette or anti-smoking commercials that the children and adolescents said they believed other young people were more influenced by cigarette advertising than they themselves were. Cohen and Davis (1991) found in an experiment with about 100 undergraduates as subjects that those seeing a television commercial attacking a candidate they supported were more likely to believe that others were influenced than to attest to influence on themselves. Driscoll and Salwen (1997) found in a survey of about 600 adults that the respondents believed that others were more influenced by media accounts than they themselves were in judging whether O.J. Simpson was guilty or innocent. Hoffner and colleagues (1999) in a survey of about 250 adults found that they believed that others were more affected by television violence than they were themselves, and this held for both of the types of effects inquired about—aggressive behavior and the belief that the world is mean and dangerous.

Such perceptions embrace not only what the media do to cognitions and emotions (a likely component when judgments of criminal guilt and support for political favorites are involved) but also behavior in regard to media. Peiser and Peter (2000) found among a sample of 200 adults in southwest Germany that there was a tendency to perceive others as more likely to engage in less constructive modes of television use. Specifically, these adults believed that others watched more television, more often watched to avoid loneliness, more frequently viewed as a matter of habit, were more likely to use the medium as a means of escaping from problems, and were more likely to be seeking entertainment, while they perceived themselves as more often choosing programs purposively and as more likely to be seeking information about current events. In the language of Comstock and Scharrer (1999), others were perceived as engaging more in ritualistic viewing and as motivated more often by the desire for diverting escape while self-perception emphasized instrumental viewing and the motive to keep abreast of what was transpiring in the world.

B. Rationality

People on the whole tend to be quite rational in pursuit of the consequences of these perceptions. They hold the media responsible for distorting reality in certain circumstances, and in other circumstances, when these effects are thought to be harmful, they become more willing to censor the media. Both Vallone, Ross, and Lepper (1985) and Perloff (1989) found that those with highly partisan views—in these cases, pro-Israel and pro-Palestinian young adults—when shown exactly the same televised news coverage of controversial events open to some interpretation were likely to perceive the coverage as distorted, and that the distortions favored the opposing partisan view. This has become known as the *hostile media phenomenon*—the belief among partisans that media coverage better serves their opponents.

Salwen and Dupagne (1999) found in a survey of about 720 adults that belief in the influence on others of television violence, televised courtroom trials, and negative ("attack") political advertising in each instance was associated with the endorsement of imposing restrictions on the media. The same pattern has been reported by Gunther (1995) for erotica, by McLeod, Eveland, and Nathanson (1997) for rap lyrics, and by Rojas, Shah, and Faber (1996) for television violence. We term this the *media constraint phenomenon*—the belief that the solution to undesirable outcomes of media behavior lies in new rules, regulations, or statutes. Both follow logically from the belief that the media have a widespread influence on what people in general think and how they behave.

The key element responsible for the third-person effect is social disparity, but it has a number of dimensions, and among these is a central place for the enhancement or protection of the observing individual's ego. It is certainly easy to believe that a person who supports a political candidate will be fearful of the effects of attacks on the candidate's character, performance, or positions on issues and that a person with a strong stance on a particular issue will be sensitive to the possibility that news coverage contains elements unfavorable to that person's position. However, the root of these concerns in our view is not at all obvious. It is not the potential for an unfavorable outcome, although that is certainly present, but in both instances a crucial factor is the presumption that many other people are less well equipped to deal with the communicatory stimuli to which they have been exposed because they lack the requisite ideology to judge them accurately. The effect rests on the disparity between the observer and others.

The evidence in behalf of this broad proposition is striking and conclusive. First, there is the distinction that appears between others who are known or similar and others in general. The third-person effect, although present, was truncated among adults for "acquaintances" compared to "most others" (Peiser & Peter, 2000) and among children for "best friends" compared to "others" (Henriksen & Flora, 1999). The underlying basis, we infer, is not merely familiarity but the similarity in circumstances and background that is likely to lead to the same outlook and perspective. The result is a greater degree of trust, and thus such persons are believed to be better equipped intellectually and emotionally to make good judgments while others in general are believed to be less well equipped. Second, among adults the belief that one is knowledgeable about current events enhances the third-person effect. This enhancement is greater when the perceived knowledgeability pertains specifically to technical or legal issues of which many with some justification may be thought to be ignorant or uninformed (Driscoll & Salwen, 1997). Again, the implication is that others would be less able to make good judgments. Third, a major component of the social disparity upon which third-person effects are contingent among adults is the greater amount of media exposure that is believed to occur among those others perceived as more influenced by the media (Eveland, Nathanson, Detenber, & McLeod, 1999). Again, others are seen as functioning in an informational milieu—in this instance, greater media use—that leaves them less able to make good judgments.

There also is the considerable frequency of reports that responses that often would be judged to earn social esteem tend to elicit a first-person (or "reverse" third person, in the phraseology of some) effect, so that the third-person effect depends on the lower competence, control over impulses and thoughts, and cognitive command among those whose response is in question. Children and adolescents believe they are more influenced by antismoking commercials and less influenced by cigarette commercials than others (Henriksen & Flora, 1999), and among adults third-person effects consistently—if not invariably—have been found to be more likely for undesirable responses whereas first-person effects are more likely for desirable responses (Duck, Terry, & Hogg, 1995; Duck & Mullin, 1995; Gunther & Hwa, 1996; Gunther & Thorson, 1992; Hoorens & Ruiter, 1996). In this context, it is not surprising that a shift to the less invidious term *stimulated* from the manipulation-implying *influenced* in one survey attenuated the third-person effect for television commercials but not for television news (Brosius & Engel, 1996). Complying with the former (which is what the term *influenced* asserts) represents a nasty impact for a genre held in approbation and skepticism as to credibility by the public (Comstock & Scharrer, 1999) while *influenced* and *stimulated* are not so easily distinguishable in regard to desirability as responses to the news. Individuals are more likely to attribute wise, sound, and socially esteemed responses to themselves and responses that are otherwise to others. This was exemplified when a particularly suspect vehicle, such as the television commercial, was the source of ostensible influence. Finally, there are a number of surveys of adults in which those who are better educated are more likely to perceive third-person effects in others (Gunther, 1995; Rucinski & Salmon, 1990; Havice, Rosenfeld, Silverblatt, & Tiedge, 1991; Willnat, 1996), presumably because they would consider others less able to analyze critically what they encounter in the mass media—although the absence of an enhanced effect for those with greater education in some studies (Brosius & Engel, 1996; Driscoll & Salwen, 1997; Innes & Zeitz, 1988; Peiser & Peter, 2000; Salwen, 1998) warns that as a variable education may function irregularly.

The ego-defensive aspect of the third-person effect extends well beyond the mass media. It is not an expression of the social properties of the media but a fundamental bias of individuals that occurs with concrete regularity in regard to the media. This is amply demonstrated by Perloff and Fetzer (1986), who found in an experimental design that college students judged themselves and those close to them as less vulnerable to risks and harmful events, and this occurred with sufficient consistency to be repeated across 10 separate, distinct negative events. In accord with the principle of social disparity, the "average person" or "average college student" was seen as more vulnerable than the subject, closest friend, sibling, or same-sex parent. The third-person media effect is a specific instance of a general phenomenon, and rather than a prodigy of communication research is a borrowing from social psychology.

C. Hindsight

Benefiting from hindsight (for which 20-20 vision is the norm), we think there are two areas in which some wariness is called for. One area is education and the other is subject matter.

We believe some irregularities for education should be expected. Our reasoning is that the greater confidence in one's own judgments (compared to those of others in general) that would be expected to derive from greater education in some circumstances may be thoroughly undermined by the superior knowledge or the values induced by that education. For example, education might enhance third-person effects beyond what would be attributable to the relative superiority of the self in regard to television violence and television advertising. This enhancement would derive from the greater knowledge bestowed by education of the research on television violence and of marketing campaigns in which commercials seemingly played a significant role. In both cases, greater education would contribute to a rationale for the expectation of some influence.

This will not always be the case. For example, public service announcements promoting the use of seatbelts, cessation of cigarette smoking, voting, dietary changes, restraint from substance abuse, and financial contributions to socially (and often hugely geographically) distant charities—causes that have little promise of precluding or ameliorating any threat to the immediate environment of the audience member—are well known to have small, meager effects other than to inform a portion of the public that such campaigns are underway. Better-educated persons are much more likely to be aware of this, and therefore might be more skeptical of widespread third-person effects (while sometimes, when the cause is not an affront to intelligent self-interest, displaying the first-person or reverse third-person effect).

Greater education also may instill values that truncate a third-person effect. Thus, Salwen and Dupagne (1999) found that a belief in the harmful effects of television violence increased support for restraints on the media. This belief arguably would be more common among the better educated familiar with the research on the topic, but support for restraints would be undercut by the enhanced allegiance to freedom of expression associated with greater education.

Similarly, in addition to social desirability and the satisfaction of placing oneself in a superior position, personal welfare or self-protection may sometimes figure in first- and third-person effects. Two examples are shown by Salwen and Dupagne (1999) and Price, Tewksbury, and Huang (1998). The former found that belief in a mean world media influence—that violence in television entertainment and news promotes the perception that the world is mean and dangerous—was associated with a first-person effect ("me more than others") in the readiness to impose restraints on television news coverage, whereas the belief that such content increases aggressiveness heightened a third-person effect ("others more than me"). The latter found that college students believed themselves in greater opposition than others in general to the publication in a student newspaper of an advertisement denying the occurrence of the Holocaust. In each of these instances, there is arguably an element of social desirability and a display of moral superiority but there is also the benefit of living in an environment free from such troubling messages and images that at least partially may explain the first-person effects observed. Economists would call this an *existence value* (Hamilton, 1998)—a preferred state that enlists personal advocacy.

D. Central Elements

The central and overriding conclusion is that people in general perceive comparably greater influence of the media on others than they do on themselves, except under particular circumstances. These circumstances occur when an act connotes goodness or superiority, social desirability, or a more pleasant environment free of offensive communicatory stimuli.

This third-person effect pivots on the disparity between the observer and the observed. Attributes that place the self in a comparatively superior position for the seeking out and processing of communicatory stimuli govern the effect. Those who are observed—"others," "most others," "people in general"—are judged as less well equipped by talent, effort, and resources to be able to reach valid judgments about what they encounter in the mass media. Thus, outcomes for which a third-person effect have been recorded often include those that explicitly assign to others a decided vulnerability that escapes victimization only by the absence of dire consequences—buying products that aren't needed, letting the media do their thinking for them, and being distracted from worthwhile activities (Tiedge, Silverblatt, Havice, & Rosenfeld, 1991). As has been observed throughout the almost two decades since the introduction of the concept, there is at work a self-serving allegiance to the ego in the service of the third-person effect, with the observer invariably displaying greater perspicacity (Davison, 1983; Henriksen & Flora, 1999; Perloff, 1989).

The significance, from the perspective of the influence of the mass media (and in particular the news media) on public opinion and the voting public, is that individuals from their own perspective place themselves largely beyond the influence of the media. When influence is perceived as occurring, it is confined to morally good, socially endorsed, or environmentally beneficial judgments.

These varied data supporting the third-person effect are often interpreted, if sometimes only implicitly by the absence of any assertions to the contrary, as representing a perceptual bias. Individuals are credited with self-expertise. They are presumed to be right about themselves but wrong about others, most others, and people in general. The basis for this interpretation is that people can judge accurately the stimuli that affect their behavior. In fact, by the logic of mirror imagery, if they are right about themselves by extension they are wrong about others, because each of those others would repay the compliment by perceiving themselves as comparatively less affected than others in general.

The corollary is that proposed actions based on these perceptions of others are misguided, and would be better formulated if based on perceptions about the self. Media executives and their spokespersons often embrace this theme, arguing that the third-person effect is evidence of a stage falsely and dangerously set by public misperceptions for the imposition of guidelines, restraints, rules and standards, V-chips, or reforms in regard to television violence, media advertising, and news coverage of politics and public affairs. This attribution of expertise about the self strikes us as naïve. If it were accurate, we could abandon almost all of experimentation and much survey research in favor of simply asking people what influenced them.

On this point, the studies we have examined are largely mute. Accuracy of perception is ignored. Two exceptions are the experimental inquiry into the perceived damage done by defamation by Cohen, Mutz, Price, and Gunther (1988) and the survey of community standards for sexually explicit materials by Linz and colleagues (1991). In each case, the judgments attributed to others were harsher than the judgments offered by the experimental subjects or the survey respondents. Because the judgments of community members are the commodity at issue, the authors make a good case in these instances for a distorting bias; that is, many would argue, as they do, that community standards should equal the average of the judgments reached by the individuals that make up the community. In both cases, estimates of the opinions of others led to more restrictive judgments and thus were "wrong" by the criterion of what people in the community actually thought. For the most part, however, no criteria for judging accuracy are offered. If tacitly, the hypotheses of self-expertise and other-naïveté seem to be widely accepted. Thus, Salwen and Dupagne (1999) find "encouragement" in the resistance of the better educated to restraints on the media and Davison many years ago (1983) explored his creation as a cognitive sin.

As we begin to make clear in the next chapter, our view is somewhat different. We are skeptical of self-expertise. We similarly do not think that individuals are necessarily accurate about the views of others, although we have some doubts about the wrongness of "community standards" when compared to the sum of individual opinions. Nevertheless, one of the three central elements historically of a psychology of politics and media has been the stout belief on the part of individuals in their comparative immunity to media influence and their symmetrical stout belief in the vulnerability of others to such influence. The other two central elements are the degree to which public opinion and voting behavior conform to the perceived opinion, behavior, and expectations of others and the degree to which they are rooted in personal experience.

II. CONFORMITY

A wide variety of empirical evidence from research on public opinion, individual judgments made in the context of group decision making, and the responses of individuals to disconcerting requests made by persons exhibiting the trappings of authority seemingly points to the exertion of considerable power over the individual by the opinions, behavior, and expectations of others. Quite recent data derive from the spiral of silence hypothesized by Noelle-Neumann (1993; Glynn, Hayes, & Shanahan, 1997). Earlier widely cited and debated data come from the social psychological research of Sherif (1936, 1947), Asch (1951, 1952, 1956), and Milgram (1974; Blass, 2000b). Conformity, these data suggest, is the norm. The interpretation frequently extended to the decision making of individuals about public affairs and politics is that the perceived behavior of others often has a governing role.

A. Spiral of Silence

The spiral of silence was introduced more than three decades ago by Elisabeth Noelle-Neumann (1974), a prominent German pollster. The theory shouldered two enormous burdens: a recognition of powerful media effects when minor and limited effects had become the language of choice in the social and behavioral sciences (Baran & Davis, 2000; Littlejohn, 1999; McQuail, 2000), and the hypothesis that published polls can curb the expression of individual opinion when most pollsters defensively were asserting that polls merely recorded what representative samples said (Crespi, 1997). These impediments proved insufficient to bestow obscurity on the spiral of silence, and 16 years later one informed commentator (Kennamer, 1990a) declared it "one of the most influential recent theories of public opinion formation." We begin with its major dimensions, and then turn to the ostensible role of polls and news coverage, the conditions on which their influences are contingent, and the psychological mechanism that is said to be behind the disinclination under some conditions to speak out.

1. Major Dimensions

Noelle-Neumann (1974, 1984, 1993) proposed that individuals regularly survey their social environments for cues about the prevailing balance among contending viewpoints. This was said to be a "quasi-statistical" process by which individuals would reach an approximate but certainly not carefully deliberated estimate of the support for a particular position or political candidate. This estimate would be sensitive enough for a person to form an impression about which among contending viewpoints had the most support as well as which were rising or declining in public enthusiasm.

These estimates derived from personal experience, which the spiral of silence defined as conversations with others, the firsthand observation of events and symbols, such as political rallies, parades, and bumper stickers, and use of the mass media. The motivation for this quasi-statistical surveillance was ascribed to social survival—a desire to avoid being perceived by others as out-of-step, ill-informed, and as a consequence experience the unpleasant anxiety of feeling isolated from others. Thus, the spiral of silence would be set in motion by the attractiveness of being comfortably part of the social fabric.

This ostensible surveillance of public opinion becomes most intense when opinions are perceived as colliding. That is, when major issues are being debated, in times of crisis, and during elections when the first becomes ritualistically enshrined and the second is often seen by partisans as transpiring. The outcome of this motive to be one with others and the consequent quasi-statistical tracking of public opinion was hypothesized by Noelle-Neumann to be a willing suppression of the expression of opinion on the part of individuals who perceived themselves as confronting a growing majority with an opposite or different viewpoint. In turn, this would affect personal experience. The articulation of views in opposition to the majority becomes muffled or silent. Events and symbols representing the minority consequently are less often encountered. News coverage implies and polls report lowered support for the minority viewpoint. Thus, the spiral of silence holds that (a) those in the minority will curb the expression of their views, with (b) the result that the impression of public opinion resulting from the tripartite of personal experience—others, events, and media—will be distorted toward an overestimate of support for the majority and an underestimate of support for the minority. The "silence" is the consequence of finding oneself in the minority, and the "spiral" is the exaggerated effect on the judgment of the balance among conflicting viewpoints.

Noelle-Neumann (1984, 1993) advanced two kinds of evidence in behalf of her theory. One was the data from polls during closely contested German elections. She identified instances in which small shifts in voter support for the two leading parties in published polls, and consonant changes in the emphases of the news media, were followed by detectably reduced expressions of support in subsequent polls for the party now in the minority. The other evidence was made up of responses in various polls to questions such as the "stranger on a train" item. Respondents were asked whether they would be willing to discuss one or another controversial issue with a stranger they met on a train. Those who held views that seemingly were declining in public favor were consistently less willing to do so. Much later, Glynn, Hayes, and Shanahan (1997) would record in a meta-analysis covering 17 surveys in six countries with more than 9,500 respondents that there was a small but statistically significant correlation between perceived support for one's views and willingness to express them as hypothesized by the spiral of silence.

2. Polls and News Coverage

The spiral of silence assigns a central role to the mass media. They are the means by which the public is informed of the results of polls, which constitute an unambiguous articulation of the balance among contending viewpoints. News coverage is equally important. It is in regard to its emphases that the quasi-statistical process is seen as entering most forcefully. The amount of attention given to a partisan group, viewpoint, candidate, or political party signals its importance. Mode of coverage then is said to govern the perceived public support the group or person enjoys. Explicit declarations of approval, the degree of public favor implied by imbalances in the number and stature of those quoted as advocating one or another position, the journalistic framing of occasions as representing success or failure, the adept adjective ("harried," "triumphant," "subdued")—all these are presumably summed by the voter to achieve some sense of which viewpoints are in the ascendancy and which are in decline. In the case of television, camera treatment was said to have an influence by varying in the degree to which a candidate was portrayed as powerful, in control, able to command the attention of the public, articulate, informed, a convincing communicator, admirable and likable, and a man or woman able to lead.

Underlying political allegiances of the various media would shape coverage, but coverage also would be influenced by variations in public support for one or another contending viewpoint. Those perceived by the media as falling in public favor would be treated less favorably. The increasing reluctance to speak out would reinforce this trend. Personal experience would become largely dominated by polls and the mass media. What was encountered directly, by conversation and through observation, was said to be of comparatively small significance in most circumstances, and in the degree of expressed opposition to the majority presumably would be diminished by the same factors afflicting the observing individual.

A key element is the similarity in the emphases of news coverage across different media that commonly occurs. Everywhere (roughly speaking), Noelle-Neumann argues, the hypothesized quasi-statistical process engaged in by individuals usually is responding to essentially the same stimuli. With this condition met, the spiral would be set in motion. The ascendancy or decline of one or another viewpoint would be exaggerated. Thus, the theory hypothesizes a role for polls and the news media in which the latter are scurrying about to provide what they think are appropriate accounts of what is taking place without the entry of calculated bias, but reserves a subversive capacity for those instances in which some components of the media would trumpet a particular perspective in order to advance its public support.

3. Contingent Conditions

The spiral of silence is contingent on the presence of circumstances that would favor the curbing of the expression of opinion by those who perceive themselves in the minority. As Noelle-Neumann (1984, 1993) pointed out, such circumstances are not always present. Thus, the spiral of silence is a theory of situational factors, and the perception of facing an opposition that is growing stronger is insufficient to bring it into play.

Two factors on which the hypothesized spiral is contingent are the degree of publicly visible support for a particular viewpoint and the degree to which holding such a viewpoint puts an individual at risk in his or her relations with others. Noelle-Neumann (1984, 1993) specifically drew attention to the first. In our view, the second is a corollary.

When a minority position on an issue enjoys widespread attention from the media, and that attention includes argumentation on its behalf by individuals who are authoritative and prestigious, an individual taking that position will not feel the isolation necessary for the hypothesized spiral to occur. The reason is that the very public support, and the respect implied by the attention of the media, will legitimate the viewpoint despite its minority status.

Similarly, issues that have become institutionalized over time as the subject of widespread disagreement become less likely to be subject to a curbing of expressed support. Thus, we would not expect the death penalty to provide data in the United States supportive of the spiral of silence. Its opponents (and supporters) receive ample coverage in the media; include chiefs of police and penologists who manage prisons, religious leaders, and well-known and respected academics; and there is no shortage of publicly available argumentation for both sides. There is no reason for those who oppose the death penalty to falter in expressing their viewpoint even though they have become a minority.

The second factor represents the degree to which negative consequences may follow from the expression of a point of view. In the United States, the most prominent example during the twentieth century was the "Red scares" in which the identifying of individuals as sympathetic to communism led to a loss of job, occupational blacklisting, social ostracism, and harassment. When one side bears the banner of patriotism while the other carries the burden of disloyalty, subversion, and un-Americanism; when judgment can be called into question or motives impugned; or when a position can be marginalized as unacceptably radical, then the willingness to express support for the target of such vituperous rataplan will be sharply curtailed. Thus, added to the feeling of isolation, and giving it a frightful thrust, is the trespass into normatively unacceptable territory.

Our reasoning thus leads to a qualification in regard to institutionalized issues. Their exemption from the spiral of silence depends on the character of media attention. It must include sufficient argumentation by authoritative individuals with the consequent legitimization of opposition to the majority to supply the necessary social support. When there is an event that draws public attention and raises public passions, such as a particularly repellant crime in the case of the death penalty, an institutionalized issue may become subject to the influence of the second factor: it will fall victim to ideological vituperation, and the spiral will be initiated.

Most of the time, news coverage by the media and published polls will be the predominant source for the quasi-statistical process that is said to lie behind the spiral of silence. Ordinarily, personal contacts will be inadequate to counter their influence. This is partly because they will be diminished in opposition to the majority as part of the spiral, and partly because they will be neither forceful nor uniform enough in opposition to the majority. However, as Noelle-Neumann (1984, 1993) observed, there is one exception. That occurs when an individual is part of a network of others who are cohesive, loyal, and among themselves consistently express support for their viewpoint. Whether this expression of opinion extends beyond this inner circle to the stranger on a train would depend on the degree to which negative consequences are likely to result.

Thus, the spiral of silence essentially is contingent on two factors, although they may take different forms. The first is the absence of social support. The second is the severity of likely sanctions. As the former declines, or the latter increases, so too does the hypothesized probability of a curbing of expression and the initiation of a spiral of silence.

4. Psychological Mechanism

The psychological mechanism specified as responsible for the disinclination of those finding themselves in the minority on a controversial topic to voice their opinion is the avoidance of aversive feelings of aloneness and isolation. Noelle-Neumann (1984, 1993) was quite insistent that the motivation was the reward of being part of a larger social entity. People do not wish to seem out of step. They follow in the footsteps of others because this ensures a self-satisfying confidence in behaving correctly. Thus, the behavior is driven by a psychological need of the individual that finds sociological representation in the expression of opinion among large aggregates holding contending viewpoints.

This formulation by Noelle-Neumann goes somewhat beyond the hypothesis generated by impression management theory that individuals would avoid expressing minority opinions because they wish those with whom they are speaking to think well of them. Instead, Noelle-Neumann finds the key element in the importance of belonging, which presumably would be diminished by adhering to a perspective that is tumbling out of favor.

We know of only one instance in which this aspect of the theory has been empirically tested. Mohn (1991) surreptitiously obtained by an apparently unrelated questionnaire the viewpoints on two controversial issues of experimental subjects. The principal experimental treatment consisted of the dramatic presentation of overnight poll results indicating that their point of view now represented the majority or the minority. On one of the two issues, the Star Wars defense initiative of President Reagan, she obtained evidence of both a reduced willingness to express arguments in behalf of their point of view and increased scores on a psychological scale of need for affiliation as a consequence of holding a viewpoint now in the minority. Thus, there was a match both on the hypothesized spiral and the imputed psychological mechanism. Because the other issue was the death penalty, where we would not expect much in the way of spiral of silence effects, this finding gives some credence to Noelle-Neumann's formulation.

The theory does not directly address whether those who refrain from expressing their opinion change their views. Instead, it proposes that public opinion is affected by the consequent underestimation of the support for the position perceived as falling into the minority, with individuals more likely to adopt an opinion with growing than declining support. Some presumably would desert the position with weaker support, but effects would be more likely among those making up their minds and seeking the psychological surety of siding with a majority. However, self-perception theory (Bem, 1972; Eagly & Chaiken, 1993) directly predicts that individuals would become less committed to views they are disinclined to express. The rationale is that to some extent people infer what they think and feel from how they behave. In terms of the spiral of silence, this means that those who forego the expression of a viewpoint would become less firmly committed to it. Thus, there is some possibility that the spiral would function directly by reducing conviction, and indirectly by altering the perceived balance among competing viewpoints.

B. Sherif, Asch, and Milgram

Muzafer Sherif, Solomon Asch, and Stanley Milgram are household names within social psychology (Jones, 1998), enshrined as classics by every textbook (Korn, 1997; Miller, 1995). Their research remains central to the examination of the power of conformity in the behavior of individuals despite an astonishingly long history—more than 60 years in the first instance (Sherif,

1936), more than 45 years in the second (Asch, 1951), and more than 35 years in the third (Blass, 2000a; Milgram, 1963, 1965, 1974). Together, the three present a strong case for the lasting vitality of social and behavioral science when certain commanding elements are in place: a compelling paradigm, crafty and impeccable implementation, and outcomes bearing fundamentally on the way people in our culture behave.

1. Paradigms

The Sherif paradigm is almost always described as making use of the "autokinetic light" illusion (for brief but good accounts, see Jones, 1998; Mutz, 1998; and, Taylor, 1998). This reference to the apparently active, lively behavior of a light in motion identifies a perceptual error—a stationary light in a dark room will be seen as moving about, and thus the phenomenon has earned the label of a self-propelled light. Of course, the self in which the motion resides is actually the observer, which is the key factor in the Sherif paradigm.

Although the exact combination of the order of experiences and the number of subjects varied somewhat, there were essentially four variants:

1. The single subject alone
2. The single subject alone before joining one or two additional persons
3. The single subject alone before joining one or two additional persons and again alone
4. A group of two or three subjects followed by one or more of these subjects alone

In each variant, the subject or subjects in a series were asked to say when the light began its journey, identify its itinerary, and describe its travels. Occasionally, the other person or persons with whom a subject participated were accomplices of the experimenter who had been instructed how to respond; most of the time, they were simply other subjects offering their own judgments.

The Sherif paradigm called for decision making under conditions that varied in social makeup. The stimulus that was the subject of the decision making was unfamiliar and ambiguous, and the decision making occurred in settings that varied in regard to the participation of other persons. It permitted the examination of judgments made alone, as part of a group, and again alone after having participated with others in the making of such judgments. Thus, it provided an opportunity to examine the role of others in the reaching of judgments by individuals.

The Asch paradigm substituted for the errant light the announced judgments of a substantial number of other persons that diverged from the physical evidence being evaluated by an individual. The social setting in which decision making occurred, rather than a cooperative endeavor (as it had been with Sherif), confronted subjects with a two-stage process. There was first an evaluation of the physical evidence, followed by a decision of whether to publicly announce a judgment counter to the majority (for brief, good accounts, see Jones, 1998 and Mutz, 1998). In the Asch paradigm, the key factor was the conflict between individual experience and group decision making.

The decision making task in this instance was to choose which of three lines matched a fourth line in length. There was no ambiguity. Only one of the three lines was the same length as the fourth line. The other two clearly differed. The group in each case consisted of 4 to 16 and most often 6 to 9 people, with the lone subject the only one not following the earlier covert instructions of the experimenter as to how to respond. There were typically 18 repeated trials in one experimental session, with two major variants:

1. The consistent majority condition, in which the confederates of the experimenter unanimously would choose a line that did not match the fourth line on 12 of the 18 trials.
2. The diluted majority condition, in which one or more of the confederates would accurately match the lines on those dozen trials.

The single subject in each experimental session invariably announced the choice among the three lines after having heard the choices of the other participants; thus, the subject perceptually loyal to the properties of the lines sometimes stood alone when faced with making an announcement.

The Asch paradigm confronted an individual with decision making by a group that did not adhere to the physical evidence. There was no ambiguity in the properties of the objects. Judgments were public. The lone subject's announcement followed those of the experimenter's confederates, who varied from complete to somewhat diluted unanimity. Thus, the focus was on the response of a lone individual when faced with erroneous decision making by a group.

The Milgram paradigm substituted for the authority of the group the forceful prescriptions of the psychological experimenter, who demanded that the individual subject perform a series of increasingly distasteful if generically similar tasks. In the initial experiment, the model for many subsequent ventures by Milgram (1974) and others (Blass, 2000b), subjects were males between the ages of 20 and 50 recruited by a newspaper advertisement. Each subject individually was asked to assume the role of a teacher who would notify his pupil of errors by delivering progressively painful electric shocks. The ostensible purpose was to study the effects of punishment on learning. As the shocks escalated, the sounds of physical agitation and sometimes cries of pain representing distress and pleas for mercy became intrusive. The subject typically became increasingly hesitant to proceed beyond a threshold at which life seemingly might be threatened and intense pain certainly assured (for a thorough description, see Miller, 1986, and for an update, see Blass, 2000a). The key factor in the Milgram paradigm was the response of the individual subject when authoritatively assigned a task that was repugnant, ethically and morally questionable, and counter to the everyday norms of human interaction.

The victim, a confederate of the experimenter, was strapped in a chair and connected to electrical wires. The teacher was instructed to read a series of words to the student. For each one, the student supposedly would attempt to choose the previously learned correct match from an assortment of four. When the student erred, the teacher was instructed to notify him by delivering an electric shock. The shock generator had 30 switches, ranging from 15 to 450 volts, with a "mild" label at the lowest level and a "danger" label at about 400 volts, with some switches beyond the 450 level marked "XXX." With each error, the teacher was asked to increase the level of shock. There were several variants:

1. The baseline design, in which the student, located in another room and addressed by intercom, pounded on the wall at 300 volts and failed to respond to the stimulus word at 315 volts
2. Victim proximity, in which the student's locus was changed from an adjoining room to the same room and, in the most extreme case, to a position adjacent to the teacher who now faced the unsavory task of placing the student's hand on the shock plate
3. Experimenter distance, in which the supervisor's physical presence was reduced by giving instructions by telephone from another room
4. Legitimacy of the setting, in which the auspices and site were changed from Yale University to a private research firm operating out of a somewhat shabby low-rent office building in an industrial city
5. Gender of subjects, with later experiments including females as well as males

The lone subject often questioned whether it was proper to continue, usually citing the possibility of severe harm to the student. The experimenter was insistent that the experiment continue and that there was "no tissue damage" to the student, and he employed four progressively demanding prods that (as described by Korn, 1997) left the subject with only one option:

At the first sign of balking, "Please continue . . ."
Next, "The experiment requires that you continue . . ."
Then, "It is absolutely essential that you continue . . ."
Finally, "You have no other choice, you must go on . . ."

If the subject then failed to persevere, the experiment was halted (and the subject consigned to the roster of the nonobedient). There were, of course, no actual shocks.

The Milgram paradigm focused on the conditions under which individuals would engage in behavior that violated social norms. There was hardly any doubt that voltages of 300 and above were distressful to the student. The experimenter applied what one observer has called "extreme and unrelenting pressure" (Jones, 1998, p. 31) to gain the teacher's compliance. The subject matter, then, was obedience to authority and circumstances that might ameliorate it.

2. Implementation

The experiments of Sherif, Asch, and Milgram have not prevailed as landmarks in social psychology because they were technically superior to the experimentation of others but because the way they were conducted led to important conclusions. The design, in each case, fit the problem under investigation.

Sherif's subjects interacted together over a period of several days. The task they were asked to perform truly presented them with an ambiguous stimulus. It was an undertaking in which the decisions made by others might be helpful. Thus, the two major factors that would make the results meaningful were in place: the extended opportunity to draw on the opinions of others and the motive provided by ambiguity to do so.

Asch's subjects found themselves confronted by a quite different situation. The stimuli were unambiguous, so that perception unaccompanied by interfering stimuli invariably would lead to a correct choice. The interfering stimuli in this case were the prior judgments of a substantial number of other persons. These judgments were correct one-third of the time, so they were not devoid of verisimilitude. This situation offered group decision making that was not without credibility, and made conformity on the part of the individual subject unambiguous when it occurred and thus a tractable event for scrutiny.

The Milgram subjects found themselves asked to serve as an experimental assistant within a very confining set of circumstances. They were continually admonished to adhere to a rigid set of procedures. The experimenter, who usually wore a white lab coat, was unrelenting in his insistence that the subjects continue to deliver increasingly severe shocks. The shock generator, an enormous device by contemporary standards (for a photo, see Marsh, 2000, p. 151), extended an ominous credibility to the harm delivered, as well as to the scientific nature of the enterprise. Legitimacy and expertise—the scientist at work—thus combined to provide the circumstances to study the willingness of individuals to obey outrageous authority.

In each case, there was a sizable measure of what in social psychology is called *mundane realism*—a representation of events likely to be taken at face value and possessing the credibility of an occurrence that is neither more nor less than it seems to be (Aronson, Wilson, & Brewer, 1998). There were judgments to be made about what the experimenter (Sherif) knew to be the autokinetic light illusion. There was the matching of lines in face of what the experimenter (Asch) knew to be an often erroneous consensus. There was the delivery, in the context of the study of the effects of punishment on learning, of progressively severe electric shocks that the experimenter (Milgram) knew to be bogus. None represented an experience likely to be encountered in everyday life, but each presented a plausible task within the context of psychological research.

These are circumstances that would lead to unfeigned, honest responses that would permit inferences about human behavior in similar circumstances. A stimulus of uncertain properties and the availability of the opinion of one or more other persons (Sherif), group decision making that often seems to ignore the evidence (Asch), and a task imposed by the authority of legitimacy and expertise that is counter to the wishes of an individual (Milgram)—these are all part of human experience, although fortunately for most persons in descending order of likelihood.

3. Outcomes

The paradigms of Sherif, Asch, and Milgram are represented not only by their own experiments but by many dozens of additional experiments by those who followed their examples. Ironically, social psychology has been a field in which innovative research that makes stars of its originators leads to widespread conformity in applying the nascent paradigm (Jones, 1998). The outcomes of these experiments, taken together, present strong testimony in behalf of the influence of others on the judgments and behavior of individuals. They also variously offer evidence on the conditions under which such influence is likely to rise or fall.

Sherif's primary hypothesis was that human interaction leads to the development of norms that guide thought and behavior. The data were thoroughly supportive.

The judgments of when the light moved, in what direction, and how far by individual subjects acting alone were much more varied than when they were making judgments in the company of one or two additional persons. When an individual subject made judgments in the company of one or two additional persons after making judgments alone, the variation in the subject's judgments decreased and they came to resemble those made by the other person or persons. When an individual subject made judgments alone after having done so in the company of one or two additional persons the judgments approximated those that had been made in the company of one or two others.

This occurred whether or not the individual subject had made judgments alone before doing so in the company of one or two additional persons. These constructed norms also showed great vitality across generations of subjects. When naïve subjects replaced confederates (who, in this case, had guided the norm construction), they quickly adopted the established norm, and this norm adoption persisted for a remarkable five sets or generations of replacements (Jacobs & Campbell, 1961). Judgment then is a social product when the opinions of others are available and there is some ambiguity or uncertainty about the matter under evaluation.

Asch intended to focus on the roots of independence, and his paradigm was an opportunity to examine resistance to erroneous group decision making (Korn, 1997). He was certainly successful in creating a set of conditions that consistently produced wide variations on the part of individual subjects in their conformity to the errors expressed by the other participants.

About one-third of responses overall conformed to the unanimous but erroneous majority. About one-fourth of the subjects were consistently independent. About one-fourth conformed to the majority on two-thirds or more of the critical dozen trials. About three-fourths conformed at least once, but the most frequent response was a judgment independent of the other participants. When the majority was diluted even by a single dissident, the degree of conformity dropped very sharply. However, three unanimous confederates offering an erroneous decision were sufficient to produce as sizable an effect as 15 confederates. Unanimity or absence of deviance was the key. Subsequent debriefings indicated that the individual subjects experienced some alarm and tension when faced with the unanimous misjudgments of the rest of the group, wondered sometimes about their perceptual ability or comprehension of the instructions (perhaps it's the width of the lines), and often felt uncomfortable at voicing a judgment counter to the announcements of the others (Asch, 1956).

The emphasis in the interpretation of these outcomes in social psychology textbooks (Friend, Rafferty, & Bramel, 1990) and summaries of Asch's research (Moscovici, 1985; Ross, Bierbrauer, & Hoffman, 1976) generally has been on the ease by which dramatic instances of conformity have been elicited, although a few have recognized that there was a substantial amount of independence in the face of aberrant, unified opposition (Campbell, 1990; Mutz, 1998). There is nevertheless no question that when others in the vicinity voice judgments that unanimously depart from the physical evidence, the willingness of an individual to announce publicly a judgment that conforms to his or her perception can be subverted.

Milgram's intention was to demonstrate that an individual placed in the role of an agent under the supervision of someone exhibiting authoritative insistence in a setting bestowing legitimacy on the enterprise could be induced to inflict severe physical distress on another party. Thus the primary purpose of the experiments was to document the degree to which individuals under certain conditions would perform contrary to their own wishes and generally accepted norms. This is quite clear from his own words:

> There is a propensity for people to accept definitions of action provided by legitimate authority. That is, although the subject performs the action, he allows authority to define its meaning. (Milgram, 1974, p. 145).
>
> Men who are in everyday life responsible and decent were seduced by the trappings of authority, by the control of their perceptions, and by the uncritical acceptance of the experimenter's definition of the situation, into performing harsh acts. (Milgram, 1965, p. 74)
>
> I would say, on the basis of having observed a thousand people in the experiment and having my own intuition shaped and informed by these experiments, that if a system of death camps were set up in the United States of the sort we saw in Nazi Germany, one would be able to find sufficient personnel for those camps in any medium-sized American town. (On CBS's *Sixty Minutes*, March 31, 1979; quoted in Blass, 2000b).

Milgram offered two criteria for obedience: the percentage of subjects who would deliver the maximum level of shocks (450 volts) and the average maximum. In a typical baseline condition at the Yale University laboratories, the obedience rate was 65 percent with a 405 volt average maximum. With increased proximity of the victim, these figures dropped to 40 percent and 312 volts when the student was in the same room and to 30 percent and 268 volts when the teacher had to place the student's hand on the shock plate. Experimenter distance similarly reduced the obedience effect. With the reduction in the legitimacy of the setting, the figures declined to 48 percent and 312 volts. Most of the subjects were males between the ages of 20 and 50, but when females were used in the baseline design the obedience rate was the same and the average maximum shock level only somewhat lower.

By Milgram's criteria a substantial majority were obedient in the baseline design, and substantial minorities were obedient with an increase in victim proximity, an increase in experimenter distance, and a reduction in the legitimacy of the setting. Thus, there is a consistent willingness on the part of individuals to accept the dictates of a situation and the person in charge once they have willingly assumed the role of a participant.

Elisabeth Noelle-Neumann's spiral of silence and the social psychological research of Muzafer Sherif, Solomon Asch, and Stanley Milgram present a strong case for the influence of the thought and behavior of others on what an individual will say or do. Whether the specific issue is the willingness to express unpopular views, the formation of opinions and judgments, readiness to adhere to physical evidence in disagreeing with others, or submission to rather ruthless instructions, the evidence points to a considerable degree of conformity. The seeming implication for the decision making of the individual about politics and public affairs is that what others think, say, and do matters.

III. PERSONAL EXPERIENCE

The empirical documentation of voting patterns that began to accumulate after World War II—in what are often called the "classic" voting studies—makes a strong case for a substantial role for personal experience in the political behavior of Americans. This personal experience typically has been interpreted as contrasting in scope and power with what might be experienced and learned from use of the mass media. It thereby joins the immunity that individuals perceive themselves as enjoying from the influence of the media as a further indication that significant barriers—an "obstinate audience," in Bauer's (1971) classic formulation—render the media ineffectual in affecting the political allegiances, views, and judgments of the public.

The first of this evidence on a large scale came from the surveys of voters that have become looked upon as landmarks in the empirical study of political behavior: Erie County, 1940 (Lazarsfeld, Berelson, & Gaudet, 1948) and Elmira, New York, 1948 (Berelson, Lazarsfeld, & McPhee, 1954). At the time, they were regarded as opportunities to examine the various influences on the political decision making of voters with clinical accuracy.

There were some surprises. Despite the role of newspapers everywhere as the major means by which news of politics and public affairs was conveyed to the public, their sometimes anxiously anticipated endorsements (by candidates and supporters, certainly, but also occasionally by the public), and the well-established place of commentators and news discussion forums on radio (Kobland, 1999), the authors concluded that influence of the mass media was slight. What mattered most was personal history, which had its strongest expression in party allegiance. People repeatedly voted for the candidates of the same party.

Four out of five voters made up their minds before presidential campaigns began (Katz, 1971). This further insulated the individuals from external opinions, whether from media or associates. Maverick voters were not only rare but tended to fall into three categories. One group was made up of the politically unanchored, who were uncertain and undecided while usually uninformed and largely uninterested in politics, and who often in the end would not vote. We would call the second group the prodigals, who frequently reverted during the campaign from a choice different in party from those they had voted for previously. They strayed, but only temporarily. The third group was made up of those who persisted in their defection.

People usually discussed politics with those similar in outlook and perspective, and thus these experiences usually reinforced initial beliefs. Later research (Katz & Lazarsfeld, 1955) recorded that information from the media often was filtered through others. These "opinion leaders," as they were called, usually shared the same outlook and perspective as those with whom they conversed. The result was that most of the information reaching the individual ordinarily had a congenial and reinforcing cast.

The role assigned to personal history became even more prominent in political decision making with the apparently clear identification in the evidence on political socialization of the family as the major influence on children and adolescents (Hyman, 1959; Kraus & Davis, 1976). Political dispositions were not only typically stable, but were acquired during childhood from those looked upon with respect—parents. Thus, party allegiance usually had been established before the young citizen reached the age of enfranchisement. Growing attention to the role of rational behavior, with voters choosing candidates on the basis of their holding views on issues similar to those of the voter (Key, 1961, 1966) did not significantly alter the role ascribed to personal history. This was because the differences between the two major parties would act to ensure that the compatibility on issues between voters and their preferred candidates would continue the hegemony of party allegiance.

We argue, beginning in the next chapter, that this conventional and widely accepted view of the place of mass media in American voting patterns no longer holds. Nevertheless, to understand what has changed since the middle of the twentieth century, it is necessary to give a thorough reading to what at one time seemed immutable. We begin with the early evidence on political socialization. We then turn to party allegiance, social influence, and issue voting.

A. Political Socialization

The data from the 1950s and 1960s on the transmission of political values and political behavior to the young seemed to support a strongly linear and highly hierarchical process. The paramount role was assigned to the family (Braungart, 1971; Easton & Dennis, 1969; Hess & Torney, 1967; Hyman, 1959; Maccoby, Matthews, & Morton, 1954–55). The family was seen as exerting influence early, before the child gave much attention to other sources, and then continuing to do so as additional sources gained in relevance. The initial step was the arousing of political interest (Johnson, 1973), presumably in emulation of the interest in politics expressed by parents. Peers generally provided reinforcement because the commonalities of outlook traceable to neighborhood, region, and similarities in socioeconomic class usually would lead to children associating with other children whose parents were much like their own in political disposition.

School played a supplementary role, although the factual information and positive constructions invariably placed on such institutions as the presidency, the Congress, and the Supreme Court were thought to add importantly to the political outlook taking shape among the young (Easton & Dennis, 1969). Attitudes toward authority figures, such as the president, which typically were favorable if somewhat more idealistic than those held by parents (Greenstein, 1960), were a central part of this socialization and became well established by the years just prior to entry into high school (Hess & Easton, 1960).

As Kraus and Davis (1976) insightfully observe in their extraordinarily comprehensive (if sadly out of print) examination of the empirical evidence on the effects of mass communication on political behavior, the mass media largely were perceived as conveyors of events whose importance lay in their inherent characteristics and not in their construction or framing by the media or in the fact that without the media they would secure the attention of far fewer children and adolescents. Thus, the importance of the president, presidential election campaigns, and the first televised presidential debates between Kennedy and Nixon in 1960 were all interpreted as having some role in political socialization, and in particular in drawing the attention and interest of young persons to political events, but they were not seen as particularly representing phenomena attributable largely to the mass media (Easton & Dennis, 1969; Hess & Torney, 1967).

B. Party Allegiance

The single most forceful and lasting inheritance owed the family in political socialization was thought by many to be a preference for and at least a tacit affiliation with a political party (Greenstein, 1965; Hyman, 1971; Maccoby, Matthews, & Morton, 1954–55; Searing, Schwartz, & Lind, 1973). We see this process as having two aspects: the development of a philosophical outlook that would favor the candidates of one or another party because of their point of view, and a less ideologically grounded preference for any candidates bearing the label of a particular party (such as the yellow dog Democrat, who would vote for a yellow dog if he or she were on the party ticket). Thus, it is composed of both ideology and loyalty. This was construed to occur quite early in childhood as part of the process of creating an interest in politics, at least in terms of a disposition if not a well-thought-out position or articulable allegiance, and to remain for most unchanged in regard to partisan preference throughout adulthood.

The data on voting behavior in four of the five presidential elections between 1940 and 1956 (1940, 1948, 1952, and 1956) that entered the empirical literature after World War II were highly supportive of the major role for party allegiance among adults (Berelson, Gaudet, & Lazarsfeld, 1948; Berelson, Lazarsfeld, & McPhee, 1954; Campbell, Converse, Miller, & Stokes, 1960; Campbell, Gurin, & Miller, 1954). It was consistently and by a large margin the best predictor of the candidates for whom an individual would cast a vote. The empirical evidence seemingly supported four propositions strongly enough that they could be considered laws (Katz, 1971; Klapper, 1960):

1. Early decision making—A large majority of voters made up their minds before the presidential campaign began in earnest.
2. Party loyalty—Individuals cast votes for the candidates of the same party in election after election.
3. Regression to the past—About one out of five of the minority of voters who early in the campaign professed some likelihood of deviating from the party whose candidates they had supported in previous elections reverted during the campaign to their earlier preference.
4. Reinforcement from the mass media—The potential influence of the media in undermining party loyalty was undercut by the tendency of voters to choose media content congenial to their outlook, and this exercise of selective exposure presumably would be aided by selective perception by which uncongenial information would be reinterpreted so that it was more in accord with the beliefs and opinions already held by a voter, so that the media typically reinforced the political opinions of their consumers.

C. Social Influence

The empirical evidence from this period on the influence of associates, friends, and neighbors assigns them a prominent role that can be thought of as an extension of the family. That is, they largely reinforced beliefs and opinions bequeathed by earlier socialization (Berelson, Gaudet, & Lazarsfeld, 1948; Katz & Lazarsfeld, 1955). In certain respects, they governed the influence of the news, acting as interpreters of what appeared in the media then: newspapers, radio, and magazines.

As with the mass media, peers largely provided information that reinforced preexisting beliefs and opinions (McClosky & Dahlgren, 1959). In general, they shared both among themselves and with the individual, the same background and outlook. Communication between persons generally occurred within social strata and groups with established norms. Group norms, echoing often but also elaborating on and sometimes redefining those of the strata, were expected to lead to the rejection of messages that were contrary to them. These group memberships and allegiances—to unions, professions, clubs, neighborhoods, and (in the area of politics in particular) to political parties—thus functioned to maintain the status quo. Party allegiance was merely the foremost example of how affiliations with social groupings created barriers to changes in the political thinking of individuals.

The selective exposure that operated in the choosing of media to ensure that content was congenial attitudinally had its parallel in the inevitability with which those with whom one associated were similar in background and outlook. In both cases, the likelihood was reduced that viewpoints, and argumentation and information in support of those viewpoints, that were counter to presently held beliefs and convictions would be encountered.

The multistep process by which the messages of the mass media were filtered through the interpretations of others thus typically increased the role of social influence in maintaining the status quo. Most commented upon and probably most common was the two-step flow in which a person designated as an opinion leader—by those studying the phenomenon—served as a conduit and interlocutor for information and opinion collected from the mass media (Lazarsfeld & Menzel, 1963). Such leadership seldom exemplified a paternalistic hegemony over a variety of topics. Instead, it usually was topic specific (Merton, 1949). Possibly, greater access to the media (the conduit role) was joined by perceived expertise (the consultant role) in the elevation of individuals to opinion leadership.

Opinion leaders were found in all social strata and groups (Katz & Lazarsfeld, 1955). This had two important consequences. One is that opinion leaders almost invariably were similar in background and outlook to those to whom they passed on their impressions of the content of the media. The other is that they almost invariably coalesced with those to whom they passed on these impressions in the norms to which they adhered. In the case of politics and other topics, these data—selective exposure, multistep flow, similarities among those participating—were properly interpreted as largely representing discussions and exchanges between those of approximately like minds (Berelson, Lazarsfeld, & McPhee, 1954).

Sometimes, a preliminary series of exchanges were observed in which two or more persons exchanged impressions before they were passed on to those who, because they themselves did not consistently play a role in the relaying of what had been initially acquired from attending to the media, were considered followers (Berelson, Lazarsfeld, & McPhee, 1954); thus, the process usually represented by the two-step flow was sometimes a many-step flow. There also was a paradox in regard to learning about what had transpired without the addition of evaluation and judgment (Lazarsfeld & Menzel, 1963). The mass media played a larger role than other persons when what was being conveyed was merely information without interpretation about what had occurred—that is, knowledge of newsworthy events. Thus, the data began to hint that the media would have considerable influence under two conditions: when such knowledge was sufficient to sway opinion, and when personal sources were absent.

What at the time relegated such possibilities to the rare and unlikely was that the first seemed decidedly uncommon and the second appeared to be confined largely to those with a scant interest in politics and public affairs and thus those with a low likelihood of giving any attention to the news media. Neither certainly could be expected to occur with any frequency. The overall picture, then, was one in which social influence delimited the power of the mass media, provided reinforcement for the beliefs and opinions of the individual so that they would persist and prevail over the ideological competition, and served, within each network of individuals, to maintain a relatively stable perspective in regard to political outlook.

D. Issue Voting

The evidence soon began to point to an even more extensive role for personal experience. Personal convictions and beliefs about issues joined the broader ideological aspect of party allegiance to guide voters. Specific passions thus joined fundamental dispositions. The analyses of post–World War II elections by V. O. Key (1961, 1966) were particularly prominent in advancing this interpretation. The title of his posthumously published *The Responsible Electorate* was intended to emphasize the thoughtful sorting through of issues by voters in choosing among presidential candidates. Voters made rational choices, observable in the match in the empirical data between the views of the candidates for whom they cast a ballot and their own opinions.

Events experienced by voters were critical in Key's interpretation, and thus party loyalty seemingly was diluted by the issues that voters might employ in discriminating between the candidates. This perspective was seen by some (Kraus & Davis, 1976) as an enormous challenge to and essentially a refutation of the view that voting represented stable behavior traceable to political socialization, party allegiance, and personal experience devoid of influence from the mass media. However, upon closer examination it becomes clear that in fact it is quite compatible with such a viewpoint.

The choices of a rational voter presumably would reflect the three major influences on voter behavior set forth in the recent and masterful review of the social psychology of voting by Kinder (1998):

1. Material interests
2. Sympathies and resentments
3. Political principles

The first represents the endowments of class, race, gender, and age: what is in the best interests of an individual as a consequence of being blue or white collar, worker or professional; black, white, Hispanic, Asian, or otherwise identifiable as to ethnicity or national origin; man or woman; beginning to work, in midcareer, or facing retirement and its attendant medical and financial needs—pocketbook voting. The second represents the expression of dispositions toward others who may benefit from or be damaged by various social policies endorsed or opposed by candidates: affirmative action, welfare, Head Start, health care, Social Security, prescription drug policies—symbolic gesture voting. The third represents adherence to the ideology usually inculcated jointly with a preference for one or the other of the major parties by parents in the process of political socialization—ideological voting.

These three pillars on which rest the voting behavior and political actions of individuals do not, by themselves, stray from the governance of personal experience. They are the concrete expression of the cognitive legacies of political socialization, party allegiance, and social influence. Socialization, allegiance, and the influence of those with whom one associates would create the framework of values and loyalties, dispositions and preferences, and evaluations and judgments by which pragmatic interests, symbolic gestures, and the adoption of a particular political philosophy translate into specific opinions and votes.

The rationality of voters, then, could be readily interpreted as the consequence of personal experience. The challenge that issue voting seemed to offer to the stable, constrained, and norm-dominated behavior of individual voters thus was sharply forestalled by the very factors on which this voting was founded. The key elements were the political party and the ideology that led to a preference for one or the other of the two major parties.

Preference for and allegiance to a political party were products of upbringing dating back to childhood, the maintenance of which was dually located in the delimited influence of the mass media and the personal influence both of those who interpreted and passed on information and of those with whom one associated. The party embraced a catalogue of views that would be largely consonant with one another and would be in accord for the most part with the material interests, sympathies and resentments, and the political principles of most of its adherents.

The recognition of an important role for rational voter behavior in the form of issue voting did not at all immediately undermine the factors that had so clearly been at work in shaping voting patterns in the election studies that began to appear after World War II. Instead, the rationality of voters simply meant that considerable reasoning joined habit and that loyalty was under some constraint from ideology in determining the final decisions of voters when they entered the polling place.

Nevertheless, there were forces at work—primarily, stunning changes in the allocation of leisure time and use of the mass media associated with the introduction of television—that would somewhat change the balance among the factors influencing voters. The 1950s saw the widespread diffusion of television among American households. In 1960, the first of what eventually would become an American political tradition—televised presidential debates—occurred. By the 1970s, the data on personal experience as a predictor of voting behavior indicated that significant changes were taking place.

Two corollaries of issue voting that began to appear with greater frequency were the discriminating voting booth behavior of ticket splitting and a greater independence from party labels. Voters more often split their tickets among candidates from different parties (DeVries & Tarrance, 1972) and became more volatile in shifting between parties from election to election (Dreyer, 1971–72; Rusk & Weisberg, 1972). When voters hold candidates responsible for advocating views that they themselves favor, party labels over time become somewhat less decisive in influencing votes because parties are less flexible and ideologically athletic than candidates. A seeming consequence was a progressive rise in the proportion of the public eligible to vote who saw their primary political identification as separate from the parties—independents (Nie, Verba, & Petrocik, 1976).

The authority of factors other than ideology and issue voting nevertheless has not so much declined as assembled in behalf of revolutionary shifts among large blocs of the electorate. The factors comprising personal experience have not withered away. In contrast, they would become central in historically significant alterations in voting patterns that would take place during the last half of the twentieth century. Greater volatility certainly became a fact, but there were realignments that were equally striking in which voters with similar backgrounds in the aggregate moved from one party to another.

The most substantial of these instances was the transformation of the South from a Democratic bulwark to a Republican bastion with the success of Ronald Reagan in winning the support of white blue-collar workers. This realignment did not rest on the disappearance of the factors comprising personal experience apart from ideology and issues. In fact, it depended on them. It was on the shoulders of personal experience that Reagan was carried to victory.

Earlier socialization, the ideology that originally favored the Democrats, and social influence both furthered this realignment. The policy options and the philosophies of the two parties changed in the degree to which they were appealing and congenial to this large and politically important social stratum. With these changes, factors comprising personal experience were marshaled in behalf of a shift toward the Republicans.

The crucial question is whether this change is best interpreted as rooted in the shared experiences of a particular social grouping or should be attributed to newly independent political thinking, and we believe the first is by far the more plausible. The public adjusted to new realities. The party that best served material interests, sympathies and resentments, and political principles changed. Thus, the traditional forces identified in the early voting studies—socialization, party, and social influence—continued to exert force. With the new millennium only two dozen calendar pages away, Kinder (1998) in his social psychological analysis of voting concluded that they still exerted sufficient authority to be fundamental in understanding the process of political decision making on the part of the public in contemporary America.

IV. THREE PROPOSITIONS

This highly varied body of social and behavioral science research ranges over more than six decades, extending from the recent inquiries into the third-person effect and the spiral of silence to the pioneering work of Sherif in the 1930s on the role of social norms in the making of judgments about ambiguous stimuli. Its legacy has been considerable skepticism over the ability of individuals to act effectively on the basis of their political beliefs and convictions. While in many respects the individual appears to be insulated from the "impersonal influence" of the mass media—a term we owe to Mutz (1998)—the evidence points in a distinctly different direction when it comes to other people. Here, influence looms large. Moreover, even the media have some role in conveying what others are thinking or in creating impressions of which points of view are gaining or losing ground as exemplified by the spiral of silence.

Three propositions crudely but efficiently summarize the resulting wisdom:

1. Although the mass media are often central in the dissemination of news about what has transpired, their influence on the judgments and opinions of individuals is small.
2. Political dispositions are largely rooted in personal experience where socialization by parents, the resulting allegiances to one or another political party and ideological outlook, and the social influence of those with whom one associates play major roles.
3. There is a strong tendency to conform to the expectations of others.

When the conformity studies are combined with the data on the role of social influence in voting, the result often has been a cause of alarm. Individuals are seen as ignoring their own perceptions in deference to group opinion and as ready to violate humane standards of conduct when authority so demands (Blass, 2000b; Moscovici, 1985). It often has been remarked that if in the Asch paradigm so much could be achieved by so little (in the way of authority, expertise, and pressure), the potential for eliciting conformity when more forceful factors are in place (as many would say occurred in the Milgram paradigm) is enormous (Ross, Bierbrauer, & Hoffman, 1976). Most interpreters have sided with the late Richard Pryor in regard to vulnerability to manipulation: "Who you gonna believe? Me, or your lyin' eyeballs?"

We take a different view. We reject those three propositions as well as the alarmism over conformity. In regard to politics, public affairs, and the individual, we believe the evidence has been misapplied and misinterpreted, and the media have been misunderstood.

Necessary Corrections

Our three generalizations at first glance are enormously satisfying. Personal experience is the basis of thought and behavior. The news media keep us informed but largely unshaken in our beliefs and opinions. We take into account the views of others, even searching for hints as to what others judge the correct course. Nevertheless, we are safe from manipulation by such impersonal means as the mass media. Voting is rooted in the empirical bounty or bleakness we have economically and socially experienced. Childhood sets the stage for a lifetime of stable, essentially measured responses to public occurrences. The individual is at the center of the matter, while individualism in its more expansive guises—rashness, intractability, and radical solutions—is constrained.

Our generalizations, in fact, can be turned to the profit of almost any outlook. They seemingly depict democracy at work, with the family as a guiding force. People are informed and knowledgeable, but act judiciously in the light of public opinion. They also are quite consonant with a much darker view. The conformity perspective, represented by the repeatedly documented deference of individuals to the expressed views of others, has enjoyed a persisting vogue in social psychology for over a half century (Friend, Rafferty, & Bramel, 1990; Jones, 1998; Korn, 1997; Moscovici, 1985; Mutz, 1998), largely because the findings dramatically cast the individual as unable to refrain from governance by the preferences of others, and thereby legitimize the subject matter of the field—social influence. Similarly, the personal history explanation, where so much converges to ensure that the familiar path is not abandoned, has been equally resilient (if for a somewhat shorter period) (Chaffee & Hochheimer, 1985; Kinder, 1998), and to some extent for similar service to the field—it has reserved for the academic study of political behavior forces that take precedence over the events, personalities, and campaigns covered by journalists.

The third-person effect glides easily from the support of one to the support of the other. It presents individuals as highly vulnerable to exterior influence, although by the media rather than by others, while also offering evidence that individuals see themselves as insulated from unwished-for media effects. The subtle conflict between conformity and personal history, with the former predicting vulnerability and the latter insulation from external influence, is readily resolved if the role of peers and opinion leaders are seen as representing conformity.

Despite the sunny interpretations to which some of the data lend themselves, these data on the whole often have been seen as revealing weaknesses in the functioning of American democracy. Although for different reasons, the conformity perspective and personal history explanations challenge the view that individuals are able to think and act independently. The first places the blame on the individual's frailty in the face of opposition (Moscovici, 1985). The second questions the ability of the individual to respond to new information and changing circumstances (Chaffee & Hochheimer, 1985). Both challenge the moral vigor and rational judgment of the individual, which presumably are assets in forming opinions about public affairs and making voting decisions.

Our dissatisfaction with these generalizations rests not on their pliability in becoming aligned with an optimistic or pessimistic viewpoint, but derives from their departure from the realities of contemporary American political life. These dogs don't hunt so well any more, and in some respects never did. What became conventional wisdom has been rendered inadequate by three factors. The first is the ambiguities that plague the interpretation of the third-person effect; it lacks a home. The second is the misapplication of the conformity literature; with one exception, it is a poor fit for public affairs, and that exception is counter to the usual onus placed on conformity. The third is the historical changes in the party allegiance of voters and in the mass media beginning with the introduction of television in the late 1940s that have altered forever the role of personal experience; it's still important, but it matters less.

I. AMBIGUITIES

The problem with the third-person effect in regard to the influence of the media is that the data tell us nothing about the accuracy of individual perceptions. Davison (1983), to whom we owe the concept, did not directly address this issue, but in our reading, his implication was that people overestimate the influence of the media, and perhaps dangerously so in regard to the degree of power and responsibility attributed to them.

The subsequent research, where the stack of relevant journal articles now stands as high as a mailbox full of Christmas catalogs, confirms that the phenomenon occurs regularly and for a wide range of topics—understanding of the news, cognitive and emotional reactions to television dramas, the likelihood of emulating violent depictions, and being swayed by advertisements for political candidates and brand name products. When resistance or indifference to the media would be the more cognitively and affectively noble response, at least according to general belief, people consistently estimate that they themselves are less likely to be influenced by the media than are others. These judgments cast a wider net than affective and cognitive responses. They also extend to the use of the media, with people consistently asserting that, compared to themselves, others are less likely to use the media constructively: others watch more television, watch more often for escape in a ritualistic, habit-driven mode, and are less likely to seek news and information from the media.

This subsequent research also makes clear that the third-person effect derives to an important degree from ego defensiveness and a belief in the inadequacy of those not like oneself to cognitively process media content effectively. Media effects are anticipated among others when the outcome would carry some degree of social approbation, but when the outcome would be desirable, effects are often said to be more likely for oneself than for others. A prominent example is the belief among children and adolescents that others are more likely to be susceptible to cigarette advertising whereas antismoking announcements are more likely to have an influence on oneself (Henriksen & Flora, 1999). In turn, the third-person effect is enhanced as social distance between oneself and others increases, presumably because greater distance implies less knowledge and skill in responding to the media. This is exemplified by the finding that adults estimate media influence as greater for "most others" than for "acquaintances" (Peiser & Peter, 2000) and among children and adolescents for "others" compared to "best friends" (Henriksen & Flora, 1999). As we observed earlier, these are media-specific instances of a general psychological disposition toward perceiving oneself as less vulnerable to harm and victimization than are others (Perloff & Fetzer, 1986). Individuals flatter themselves, and perceive vulnerability as a function of the likely absence of the skills and abilities they themselves possess.

These data tell us that many people ascribe considerable influence to the media, and that they consider themselves comparatively immune to such influence. The one exception is made up of the many instances in which media influence would be socially desirable, and here effects are estimated as more likely for oneself than for others. The point on which the data are uninformative is the accuracy of these estimates. Surely a social psychologist reasoning within the context of Bandura's theory of social cognition (1986) would be unconvinced by the assertion of a parent or child that the child had been less influenced by violent portrayals than were other children. Similarly, an advertising executive looking at successful sales reports might be skeptical of little or no influence on the part of his or her latest campaign. The data document a disparity in perceived effects, but they fail to tell us anything about the direction of misperception. The data tell us neither about influence on others nor about lack of influence on oneself.

There is one circumstance in which the data seemingly step beyond these bounds. These are the cases in which expectations or judgments are offered about a community, and then compared with the views of the responding individuals. When these diverge, the tally of individual responses arguably would be a better representation of the views of the community than an estimate of its outlook. Specifically, the two reported cases have involved perceived standards for sexually explicit materials (Linz et al., 1991) and anticipated defamatory damage (Cohen, Mutz, Price, & Gunther, 1988). In both instances, the estimated community response was more stringent than the average tally for the individuals themselves. Linz and colleagues found that their survey respondents believed the objections of the community were greater than their own, whereas Cohen and colleagues found that their experimental subjects believed that others would be more affected by a derogatory news account about a locally prominent person than they were. The investigators are convinced the discrepancy should be resolved in favor of the tally produced by personal judgments on the grounds that it best represents the community. We are not so sure. The former (expectations or judgments about a community) calls for the invocation of standards and values in behalf of an abstraction—the community—that presumably would entail moral responsibility that goes beyond personal opinion. The latter (views of responding individuals) calls for an estimate of the risk of harm that quite plausibly, in the interests of fairness and protecting the maligned individual, would become more sensitive when estimating the response of the community. That the estimates are more severe is not surprising and does not render them inaccurate because they represent the invocation of an abstraction and allegiance to its more stringent demands. Thus, even here ambiguity persists and we can only say that there was a discrepancy between reports of personal opinion and estimates of community response.

II. MISAPPLICATION

The interpretation of the data on conformity has placed few boundaries on the circumstances in which influence could occur and largely has lodged in the source of communication the factors on which influence will be contingent (Cialdini & Trost, 1998). The conformity perspective decidedly offers a great deal of explanatory power for certain situations, but in our view these situations are far more limited than generally has been taken to be the case. They tell us very little about public responses to politically relevant information, and not a great deal more in regard to the formation and expression of political opinions. This is despite a great deal of hand-wringing on the part of public opinion researchers (Noelle-Neuman, 1993) and social psychologists (Moscovici, 1985) over the opposition the data ostensibly offer to the concept of a sensible, thoughtful set of citizens making independent judgments. Responsible is the misapplication of the data, as represented by unwarranted generalization beyond the contexts in which the data were collected, misinterpretations, and a stubborn ignoring of the limited pertinence of much of the data.

We do not quarrel with the scientific validity of any of the conformity paradigms. The spiral of silence and the work of Sherif, Asch, and Milgram have enlivened and enlightened the study of communication and behavior. All four have met the test of excellent science—the facilitation of research that has added to knowledge and theory about the way people behave. Where we dissent from many interpretations of the data is the degree to which these paradigms have been informative about the public sphere of psychology and politics.

A. A Closer Look

The spiral of silence has been the subject of extended controversy. Its inventor, Noelle-Neumann, has been accused of subverting democracy by arguing that people are incapable of independent thought (Simpson, 1996); the theory has been said to apply only to authoritarian regimes where the media are controlled and dissenting views may lead to punishment (Glynn & McLeod, 1985; Salmon & Kline, 1985); two psychological processes—selectivity (Kennamer, 1990b), and especially selective exposure and perception, and the false consensus effect (Marks & Miller, 1987; Mullen et al., 1985) in which people think that others share their opinions and convictions—would mitigate strongly against the theory; and some have concluded that any relationships between perceived public opinion, fear of isolation, and a disinclination to express a minority viewpoint have been too small for social significance

(Glynn, Hayes, & Shanahan, 1997). In fact, the meta-analysis of 17 published and unpublished surveys from six countries with about 9,500 respondents by Glynn and colleagues produced a very small but statistically significant positive correlation (Pearson $r = .054$, $p < .0001$) between perceived support and the willingness of the respondent to express his or her viewpoint to another person. Thus, the data seemingly hint that there is a consistent if very small spiral of silence operating.

The weakness of the evidence in behalf of the spiral of silence is not the small size of this correlation coefficient. The weakness resides in part in the absence of evidence based on what people do rather than what they say they expect they would do; the surveys only document a correlation between the expression of perceived support and stated willingness to voice an opinion. The weakness also resides in the lack of consistent and pervasive evidence for the various mental and social processes that the theory argues govern the spiral of silence. These processes include:

1. The continual quasi-statistical estimation by individuals of the opinion climate based on what they observe and what they encounter in the media
2. The discernment of shifts in popular sentiment among those who find themselves holding a minority viewpoint
3. Fear of social isolation or other sanctions as a consequence of expressing a minority viewpoint
4. The disinclination to express a minority viewpoint to neighbors and friends, strangers, and media representatives
5. The presence or absence of support for a minority viewpoint from an individual's circle of acquaintances, with support sharply decreasing the likelihood of reticence to express an opinion
6. The institutionalization of controversies, so that disagreement is socially recognized and different viewpoints easily can find supporters among prominent persons, moral authorities, experts, and the media

There is considerable support for the notion of a quasi-statistical surveillance of the opinion environment if we go beyond research on the spiral of silence. Robinson and Levy (1986 a,b) found in surveys that knowledge about the news often depends on interpersonal discussion, and this would certainly imply that one stream of information circulating by this means would be judgments about public opinion. Gunther (1998) experimentally demonstrated that favorable and unfavorable media depictions of an issue shift beliefs about public opinion, with support perceived as rising or falling as a function of favorable coverage. There is little reason to believe that the polls disseminated with such regularity by the media are not usually taken as accurate reflections of what the public is saying (Lavrakas & Traugott, 2000; Mann & Orren, 1992), although under some circumstances they may not be very good predictors of what the public will say or do, such as voting for a particular candidate, at a later point in time (Comstock & Scharrer, 1999; Crespi, 1989). In each case, individuals are reaching judgments about what others think either from what they experience or what they encounter in the media.

The correct discernment of the state of popular sentiment is another matter. Major (2000), in a large-scale survey of adults in two communities, found that news media use, belief in the influence of the news coverage on one's own opinion, and the seeking of information were all predictors of accuracy in identifying the majority viewpoint on four environmental issues: air pollution, drinking water purity, landfill scarcity, and toxic waste disposal. This is contrary to Noelle-Neumann's expectation that the media often lead to inaccurate assessments of public opinion. Furthermore, Major also found that interpersonal discussion was not a predictor of accuracy, which suggests that this particular diffusion process for quasi-statistical estimates is often inefficient. She suggests, based on data from school desegregation in Boston between 1973 and 1975 (Taylor, 1986) and the return of Hong Kong to China in 1997 (Atwood & Major, 1996), that estimates are more likely to be accurate for well-publicized issues—for which the environment would qualify in terms of long-term coverage although not short-term saturation (Comstock & Scharrer, 1999). The well-established false consensus effect (Kreuger & Clement, 1994; Marks & Miller, 1987; Mullen et al., 1985; Ross, Green, & House, 1976) further undermines support. False consensus—the belief that others think like oneself (thereby converting personal opinion to majority conviction)—is the antithesis of the spiral of silence. This bias (sometimes called a "mirror image" or "looking glass" perception) is so strong that in one instance a viewpoint held by only three percent of the population was believed by this small percentage to be shared by a majority (Fields & Schuman, 1976). In this particular case, the data represented approval of play involving black and white children in Detroit at the beginning of the 1970s, and this raises questions about the contribution of media coverage to accuracy of perception. Our resolution is to offer two hypotheses:

1. Media coverage of a topic or issue enhances the likelihood of having an opinion about public opinion.
2. Coverage of public opinion on a topic or issue, when accurate, increases the accuracy of estimates of public opinion.

Race certainly was in the news in Detroit; public opinion about interracial playing probably was not. Public opinion about the environment, school desegregation in Boston, and the return of Hong Kong to China probably were in the news; it was part of the story along with the topics and issues themselves.

The role of the accuracy of estimated opinion, of course, is a matter of circumstance. The theory holds that, when public opinion shifts, accurate perception of the emerging majority viewpoint will deter those holding a contrary view from publicly expressing it. The result is an underestimate of the strength of the minority viewpoint. However, the theory also holds that the same process will occur when there is a perception of a shift that is factually without grounds. Noelle-Neumann (1984) concluded that this is essentially what occurred in the 1965 German election. Polls showed the public about evenly divided between the two major parties. The polls then recorded a growing belief, ostensibly based on media coverage, that opinion was beginning to favor one of the parties. Belief in greater support predicted a greater likelihood of voting for the victorious party. In terms of the spiral of silence, this would have been attributable to the diminution of vocal support for the losing party, and particularly at the interpersonal level; the argument is that the belief preceded shifts in voting intention that stemmed from the diminished expressions of support. The consequence of the dual role of media accuracy—on the one hand, they provide factual information while on the other hand they distort public opinion and campaign momentum—is that on this point the theory hangs on the power of the media to overcome the false consensus effect, which seems limited to two circumstances: (a) when there is extensive coverage of public opinion on the issue or topic in question, or (b) when media coverage is slanted or biased, so that an observer would anticipate that public opinion would favor one outlook or another.

Fear of social isolation as the mediating factor gains some support from the Mohn (1991) experiment. She included among the questions posed to her subjects a psychological scale of "need for affiliation" and found an inverse correlation between willingness to express a viewpoint perceived as representing a minority and scores on the scale. Because this was an experimental design, the difference could be attributed to the treatment—the induced belief that the viewpoint was in the minority. This was a decidedly mundane conception of fear of isolation. Noelle-Neumann (1984) extended it to much more enervating risk of sanctions and social disregard:

> Slashed tires, defaced or torn posters, help refused to a lost stranger—questions of this kind demonstrate that people can be on uncomfortable or even dangerous grounds when the climate of opinion runs counter to their views . . . (T)hese . . . issues . . . involve real hazards (p. 56)

In this regard, the survey data give some comfort to the more severe Noelle-Neumann conceptualization. In the meta-analysis of Glynn, Hayes, and Shanahan (1997), it is tempting to turn to the data on willingness to voice a minority opinion to neighbors or strangers. Surely, one would think at first, neighbors should inspire greater fear of isolation because of their much greater opportunity to impose sanctions. A stranger is here now but soon gone. But because of similarity of background and circumstances, neighbors also might be perceived as more likely to share a minority viewpoint (when compared with the overall division of opinion in the larger society) and they also might be thought to be more tolerant of deviance among those they know. As a result, the "no difference" between the two is neither a mark for nor against fear of isolation. The greater recorded unwillingness to express such a viewpoint to representatives of the media is a different matter. Such reluctance is clearly compatible with a disinclination to be publicly identified as standing against the social tide.

Support for the hypothesized linkage between perceived public support and willingness to express a viewpoint publicly is weak on two counts. The first is that the magnitude of such an effect appears to be very small across topics and issues; the Glynn, Hayes, and Shanahan (1997) meta-analysis recorded only a minute correlation. The second is that this result, while representing a substantial number of respondents, represents only what people say they would do. The Mohn (1991) experiment where spiral of silence effects were demonstrated for the less institutionalized of two issues (the Strategic Defense Initiative, or Star Wars defense proposal) provides a superior type of evidence because it recorded what the subjects did when faced with the information that their viewpoint had fallen into disfavor. Unfortunately, experimental support representing actual behavior is a rarity.

Noelle-Neumann identified two groups who would be resistant to a spiral of silence: the "avant garde," who pride themselves on being different from and presumably ahead of the mainstream, and "hard cores," who are thoroughly committed to a position. These concepts combine a personality variable with the variable of social support, for presumably both categories of individuals would interact with others of like mind. There is ample support for the notion that willingness to express oneself in behalf of a minority position is enhanced by company. The data produced by the Asch paradigm repeatedly documented that the willingness of an individual to oppose dominant opinion increases with the number joining in (in this case, rising with the increase from one to three dissenters, then leveling off). Cialdini and Trost (1998), in their review of the literature on social influence, name a number of factors likely to be present in groups of like-minded individuals that promote conformity to their norms rather than those emerging in the society at large: unanimity of opinion, confidentiality of expression, and prior commitment. Thus, perceived support from a minority enhances resistance to the spiral of silence.

The institutionalization of issues is another circumstance that provides a buffer against a spiral of silence. Issues have three characteristics (Center & Jackson, 1995): (a) two or more opposing views; (b) emotional involvement on the part of a large number of people; and, (c) considerable concern that the resolution will affect either individuals directly or the functioning of society. If unresolved and threatening, an issue will be transformed into a crisis.

As an issue becomes recognized as a legitimate and enduring matter of controversy, prominent persons, moral authorities, experts, and the media variously become readily available to provide support for one or another position. The minority viewpoint is well reinforced by public expressions of concurrence. The issues on which the public focuses usually represent oscillations of media and public interest in a limited and persisting number of broad topics: health, education, social welfare, crime and terrorism, disaster, international relations, the economy, and the environment. Within these broad categories, one or another often quite specific issue or topic gains temporary prominence in the media or among the public. Center and Jackson (1995) proposed that issues typically are in one of four stages: (a) "latent," when circumstances are in place for an issue to emerge but public and media attention has yet to develop beyond the cursory; (b) "emerging," when media attention begins to focus on the topic; (c) "hot," when the topic is the subject of continuing attention and debate; and, (d) "fallout," when the topic fades from media and public attention, but there are often some residual consequences—perhaps a few newly prominent faces in the public sphere. Paisley (1989), after examining issue coverage over about 30 years, offered a similar classification, with attention to various issues (a) falling or (b) rising, and (c) sometimes reaching a peak of substantial attention before a fall, but added the category of (d) issues that remained relatively stable in attention—what we call institutionalized issues. The model proposed by Downs (1972) describes the typical cycle of media attention:

1. A triggering event gains media and thereby public attention.
2. Public concern grows and various initiatives, usually involving government, are proposed.
3. Public interest and, as a consequence, media attention declines.

The cycle ordinarily follows the sequence proposed by Maxwell McCombs for agenda-setting (Dearing & Rogers, 1996): the coverage of the triggering event arouses public interest, which the media exploit by providing additional coverage. As a result, the issue rises in the importance on the public agenda of social problems. These issues and topics will have public lives that range from a few days to several months and often several years.

When issues and topics are emerging, the likelihood of a spiral of silence is particularly great because people are making up their minds. They are seeking cues identifying the viewpoint that is seemingly right or correct, likely to be socially approved, and likely to bring personal satisfaction, and for all of these reasons what others are thinking may have an important role (Mutz, 1998). Public opinion, as perceived by the individual, confirms the majority conclusion (thereby tallying votes for the "correct" viewpoint), assures a greater likelihood of social approval (by identifying the majority), and suggests the most satisfying outlook (by providing confidence that one's viewpoint is widely shared). As issues and topics enter what might be thought of as their midlife of media and public attention, such effects become constrained by the continuing substantial number of spokespersons on either side.

There also are a few issues and topics that achieve a maturity in which they recurrently are given attention by the media, almost always in response to a triggering event, but that change very little in their form, arguments, or forces aligned one way or another. Three that readily meet these criteria are the death penalty, abortion, and gun control. Although the intensity of opinion may make many persons reluctant to voice their opinions casually or to strangers, there will be no spiral of silence in which the ostensibly minority viewpoint progressively is expressed publicly less often because of the high degree of support publicly available for both a pro or con position.

Our conclusion is that the processes on which the spiral of silence rests do not occur with sufficient frequency for the theory to describe a phenomenon that occurs with any regularity. There is not a great deal of support for several of the required processes. The implication is that most of the necessary conditions are not in place most of the time. In fact, evidence is strongest for processes that would mitigate a spiral of silence, such as the false consensus effect, the resilience to external influence extended by supportive associates, and complete or at least partial institutionalization of issues.

Nevertheless, we do believe that when the requisite circumstances occur a spiral of silence becomes quite likely. We would even expect that under conditions in which the elements that contribute to such a spiral were highly magnified, even the protective restraint of an institutionalized issue might be shattered. A horrendous crime, for example, might create a swell of support for the death penalty that would silence opponents. The incarceration of Japanese-Americans during World War II certainly drew little in the way of public criticism, although it is impossible at this juncture to say whether this constituted an underrepresentation of criticism or opposition. "Red scares" presumably intimidated individuals from voicing opinions that would be associated with leftist views, as exemplified by the career of Senator Joseph McCarthy in the early 1950s and the extended hearings of the House Un-American Activities Committee. These were occasions where deviance could (and for some, did) lead to palpable sanctions, such as blacklisting (prominent in the media and among entertainers), dismissal (especially among college and university faculty), and ostracism (by neighbors and colleagues). National sanctity is a powerful factor, as was possibly the case with the Japanese-Americans in World War II. Eveland, McLeod, and Signorielli (1995), for example, documented that people overestimated support for the Gulf War (with about 80 percent believing that "most" supported it, whereas the actual figure for the sample was slightly less than 50 percent). In times of conflict and threat, the media typically depict public opinion as supportive of government action and policy, as was the case with the Gulf War both at the national (Peer & Chestnut, 1995) and local levels (Reese & Buckalew, 1995), with television, the medium people most frequently turn to in times of crisis (Comstock & Scharrer, 1999), decidedly more fervent than major newspapers in depicting patriotic unanimity. More recently, the September 11 terrorist attacks on the World Trade Center and the Pentagon, while not silencing criticism by a few prominent individuals and some academics of the subsequent armed response by the Bush administration, certainly created a situation in which flying the flag and other indications of support were a course least likely to lead to some unpleasantness (such as a death threat). Within the week, about 90 percent of representative national samples said they supported military action, and about 70 percent said they did even if it meant a "long war with large numbers of U.S. troops killed or injured" (American Enterprise Institute for Public Policy Research, 2001). On a more subdued note, we would also point out that a spiral of silence may be confined to a specific community that experiences the necessary circumstances. For example, we suspect that support in early 2000 among Hispanics in Miami for returning the young refugee Elian Gonzalez to his father in Cuba would have been muted by the widespread local fervor to allow him to remain with relatives in this country. These instances all have several commonalities: an event or issue that exceeds normal boundaries in gaining attention, the involvement of the sanctity of the country or a community, the arousal of strong feelings and decided opinions, a clear majority as to the public mood, and the real possibility of punishment for a private citizen expressing a contrary view.

B. A Contrast

The Asch and the Sherif paradigms, along with that of Milgram, are often described as a progression in the study of conformity (Jones, 1998). In terms of genealogy, this is accurate. Asch drew on Sherif's earlier experiments, and Milgram emulated Asch but substituted implacable authority for unanimity (Cialdini & Trost, 1998; Jones, 1998; Korn, 1997). However, each also is quite distinct not only in conceptualization but in what can be learned. This is particularly true of the Asch and Sherif paradigms, which in their applicability to individual decision making about public affairs are at opposite poles.

1. Asch

The Asch paradigm fails to reproduce the circumstances under which political opinions are formed and political judgments expressed. In the paradigm, the individual is confronted with the judgments of others about a physical fact. When those judgments on the part of a group of almost a dozen are unanimous, there is a maximum degree of conformity on the part of the subjects. After hearing each of these individuals voice *in seriatim* an erroneous judgment, the subjects often contributed a final, concurring error. When even one member of the group deserted the majority, subjects became much more likely to report accurately, with as few as three desertions producing the maximum level of recorded accuracy.

These data convincingly demonstrate that many individuals will betray the evidence of their eyesight ("those lyin' eyeballs") when presented with the consistently contrary judgments of a sizable number of persons. When called upon, without prior training, involvement, or knowledge of the task (beyond the fact that detecting a difference in the lengths of the two lines and verbally identifying the longer one was well within the perceptual and cognitive capabilities of college students), many subjects repeated the falsehood they had heard rather than voice a view contrary to the unanimous group.

The conclusion that these data identify an unhealthy degree of conformity in the realm of public affairs and politics depends on three factors: (a) the degree to which conformity to group opinion was demonstrated, (b) the extent to which the responses of the experimental subjects parallel those of persons reaching political judgments, and (c) the simulation within the experimental setting of the social conditions under which political opinions are formed and political judgments expressed. In each case, the evidence is unconvincing.

There is no doubt that, by the measure of expressed opinion, many individuals conformed. However, the consensus of expert opinion on the Asch data has emphasized conformity at the expense of the frequency of the display of independence by the subjects. Conformity has been at the forefront of interpretation while independence in fact has dominated the data. For example, Friend, Rafferty, and Bramel (1990) examined 99 accounts of the Asch studies in social psychology textbooks published over a 30-year period and found a great deal of distortion in favor of conformity, which increased with the passage of time. Other analysts (Korn, 1997; Mutz, 1998) concur that the role of conformity has been exaggerated. There are three discrepancies between the popular interpretation and the actual data: the frequency of individuals conforming, the overall rate of conformity, and the necessity of unanimity. Although many subjects conformed on some trials, most subjects offered a correct judgment on one or more of the several trials. In fact, the majority of verbal responses across all subjects were accurate. Finally, unanimity among the confederates was an important factor that for many subjects achieved the status of a necessary condition. Even one defection was sufficient to lower substantially the likelihood of conformity, and as many as three defections rendered the remaining majority ineffective in imposing its view. Friend and colleagues reported that the actual rates across judgments were 33 percent errors (representing conformity) and 67 percent correct (representing independence), whereas more than half of the textbook accounts mentioned only the 33 percent error rate and fewer than one-fifth mentioned the rates for both errors and correct responses. Thus, the data on the frequency of individuals erring, the overall rate of error, and the near-necessary role of unanimity are convincing about the occurrence of conformity but not at all as to its predominance or universality.

Postexperimental interviews with the subjects raise another difficulty (Friend, Rafferty, & Bramel, 1990; Korn, 1997). Subjects were quite disturbed—the term "cognitively agitated" seems appropriate—when presented with reiterative falsehoods regarding what they could plainly see for themselves. They wondered in some instances about their understanding of the instructions. Could they have misheard or misunderstood? A few, indeed, decided that it was unlikely that everyone else was wrong, thus accepting that for themselves some eerie perceptual illusion must be operating. However, when faced with unanimous error many saw the situation as offering two options: to speak against the group by offering a correct judgment, or to agree with the group in the interests of social harmony without doubting that they had perceived the lines correctly. Often, then, the conformity recorded did not represent a shift in opinion but instead an artifice to satisfy the demands of the situation.

Finally, the circumstances invoked by the paradigm fail to simulate the social conditions in which political opinions are formed and political judgments expressed. The unfamiliarity and ideological neutrality of the task are an advantage in regard to registering sensitively the effects of hearing the erroneous opinions of others before offering a judgment; as Jones (1998) remarks, Asch is a fine example of the use of extreme circumstances (as contrasted with the "mundane realism" advocated by many; Aronson, Wilson, & Brewer, 1998) to produce valuable data. They nevertheless constitute a marked departure from the mundane realities of politics and public affairs. Usually, there will be familiarity with the topic. Often, there will be prior commitment to a party or a viewpoint. Preferences of party and ideology may be long-standing and not open to change. The assembly of a numerous chorus speaking serially one by one hardly parallels the day-to-day experience of most in regard to politics and public affairs. The Asch paradigm is akin to polling those seated on the aisle of an airplane, train, or movie theater and getting the wrong answer about the color of the upholstery. It has no parallel in everyday life. It is true that people often discuss politics and public affairs with those similar in background and outlook, but this is not at all the same as encountering a series of individuals who are unanimous in erring on a matter of observable fact. The social situation, then, differs on at least two counts from what ordinarily transpires: the stimulus being judged is unambiguous, whereas in matters of politics and public affairs there is often some ambiguity about the correct course for government policy, and the voices are unanimous in opposing the judgment reached by the individual, whereas in everyday personal exchanges about politics and public affairs there usually will be less certainty and some variability. These are circumstances wholly outside the ordinary. Aside from the expressing of a judgment, the Asch paradigm fails to simulate the realities of politics and public affairs in everyday life.

The data generated by the Asch paradigm tell us very dramatically that the individual faced by unanimous error on the part of a group is likely to react with cognitive agitation and perceptual caution. Social harmony very often takes precedence over expressing a correct judgment. Although sometimes the subjects became inaccurate because they did not believe that so many could be so wrong, more often they covertly retained confidence in their perception while publicly agreeing with the group. The data fail to convince on all three tests: the frequency of conformity, the parallel with individual decision making in regard to politics and public affairs, and the simulation of the social circumstances in which political opinions are formed and expressed. The data tell us that being alone in voicing even an obviously accurate judgment is not without psychological perils, and that a frequent but not predominant resolution is to feign agreement with the group. In this respect, they support the spiral of silence in the rare circumstance when there is unanimity of opposing opinion. Otherwise, the data do not transfer to our realm of interest.

2. Sherif

The Sherif paradigm stands in contrast. Like the Asch paradigm, it is very convincing in producing interpretable data. Unlike the Asch paradigm, however, there has been no history of misinterpretation, and a good case can be made for at least a modest degree of applicability to the realm of politics and public affairs. This greater applicability of the Sherif paradigm obviously does not rest on the stimulus used, the kinetic light illusion. Instead, it derives from two factors: (a) the ambiguity of the autokinetic effect, and (b) the social setting, in which the judgments of others can be called on in identifying the location and trajectory of the elusive light.

The Sherif and the Asch paradigms differ in at least three important ways. First, the Asch paradigm presented an unambiguous stimulus (the lines) whereas the Sherif paradigm employed the ambiguous (as to location and direction) autokinetic light. Second, the Asch paradigm aligned a large number of others in opposition to the subject and the Sherif paradigm made the subject a member of a small group seeking a solution to a problem in which the individuals had an equal voice. Third, the Asch paradigm confronted the subject with an array of opinion that was counter to a seemingly easy-to-make judgment; the Sherif paradigm invited the subject—who, with equal accuracy, could be called a participant from his or her own perspective—to join in the process of reaching a judgment of uncertain dimension. In each respect, the Sherif approximates more closely than the Asch paradigm the circumstances in which political opinions are formed and expressed.

The apparent movement of the light presented a stimulus for which there were no physical criteria—say, a benchmark or stationary object—by which to assess location and direction. This created a situation in which the subject had only one source for guidance: the judgments of others. The result was that the judgments of the subjects consistently paralleled those made by the other participants. Once a judgment had been made by the subject in the context of the group, the subject continued to adhere closely to that judgment even when later acting alone. The paradigm demonstrates neatly that when other standards—tradition, prior experience, a ready heuristic such as the sun sets in the west; that is, some sort of metric or yardstick—are absent, individuals will look to others for guidance. What we learn is that, in the absence of alternatives, social influence is likely to be a major source and resource for making a judgment.

This certainly does mean that under such circumstances people often will conform to the opinions of others, and so the Sherif paradigm is unambiguously relevant to the study of conformity. However, in this case the conformity does not represent a surrender to the views of others, but the quite rational use of social information when other bases for decision making are not present.

The parallels with the realm of politics and public affairs are clear. When candidates are unfamiliar, when issues are new or ill-defined, when the outcomes of a policy are uncertain, when the situation (as many would say was the case after September 11, 2001) is unstable with the possibility of calamitous events—all conditions often encountered in the public sphere—people often will turn to some degree to the opinions of others in making up their own minds. New candidates and third parties; tax, education, health, welfare, and other government policies; war and the response to terrorism represent instances where there is likely to be ambiguity about the best course or the eventual outcome. As a result, they are topics on which individuals are particularly likely to be influenced by the opinions of others.

Even so, the Sherif paradigm applies only to a very limited area of the public sphere. Often, the very ingredient that drives it—ambiguity—will be absent. Parties are known and candidates are familiar; ideology and party loyalty, along with earlier opinions, dictate support or opposition to candidates and policies. Thus, the Sherif paradigm is quite narrow in its application to politics and public affairs. It demonstrates the often major role of social sources when there is ambiguity, but does not support the widespread occurrence of conformity. Instead, it depicts individuals as quite rational, and confines the use of social sources to situations where other bases for opinion formation are not present.

3. A Difficult Case

The Milgram paradigm presents the strongest possible case for a general readiness to conform when faced with legitimized authority. This conclusion derives from the attributes of the paradigm and from the expectations that people—both experts and nonexperts on human behavior—seemingly had about how subjects would behave.

The paradigm calls for the subject to inflict punishment on the individual who takes the role of the learner in the experiment—punishment that was always painful, sometimes conceivably life-threatening, and repugnant to the subject. The subjects were ordinary persons, often but not always college students, who had no history suggesting that they were either particularly susceptible to the influence of an authority figure or especially ready to inflict pain and discomfort. The central influence on the subject was the authority of the experimenter, although apparently this authority assumed more than one guise. For example, Blass (2000a) had students familiar with the paradigm rate six different possible bases for the social power displayed, and the high scorer was identification with the experimenter, followed by the desire for approval. Four thought to be less important were (a) the knowledge that would be gained from the experiment, (b) the scientific validity of the enterprise, (c) the expertise of the experimenter, and (d) the implication of unpleasant consequences for the subject ("The experiment requires that you go on"). Thus, the personal qualities and professional standing of the experimenter take precedence over the scientific trappings, while undoubtedly benefiting from them. The modest reduction in conformity that occurred with the shift of the site from Yale University, an undeniably prestigious institution, to the offices of Research Associates of Bridgeport (Milgram's cover) in a seedy commercial building in an undistinguished urban landscape further testifies to the importance of the contrived persona of the experimenter and the interaction between the experimenter and subject. The evidence gained considerable credibility, and what one commentator (Blass, 2000b) repeatedly called "revelatory power" (pp. 38 and 44), from Milgram's report that both a group of psychiatrists and a group of Yale students underestimated obedience effects by huge margins (after hearing an explanation of the experiment, the psychiatrists and the students estimated compliance at less than one percent and about one percent, respectively). Milgram was so pleased by the apparently nonintuitive nature of his findings that he smugly remarked in regard to the psychiatrists,

"Indeed, I have no doubt that a group of charwomen would do as well" (Blass, 2000b, p. 44). The high rates of compliance are strong support for conformity under the specified conditions.

Although the Milgram paradigm could be interpreted as demonstrating that outrageous behavior can be elicited by the endorsement and insistent support of a person clearly responsible for what transpires in the circumstances (an interpretation offered by Milgram in his comment that the subjects surrendered their moral composure to the demands of the situation and his concept of agency in which the subject was relieved of responsibility because he or she was obligated to follow the instructions of the experimenter), the data also were interpreted by Milgram as demonstrating how authoritarian governments could induce "good people" to act reprehensibly and as an experimental analogue of the Holocaust in Nazi Germany. Thus, the claim has been made that the paradigm not only powerfully elicits compliance but also can be applied to the realm of politics and public affairs.

Milgram drew on the Asch paradigm (Korn, 1997), so it should be no surprise that a conclusion that the data identify an unhealthy degree of conformity in the realm of public affairs and politics depends on the same three factors: (a) the degree to which conformity was demonstrated, (b) the extent to which the responses of the subjects parallel those of persons reaching political judgments, and (c) the simulation within the experimental setting of the social conditions under which political opinions are formed and political judgments expressed.

There is no doubt that the first condition is met. In contrast to the Asch paradigm, a majority conformed in what we would take as the baseline condition—the learner in a separate room where he can be heard but not seen, the experimenter present beside the teacher. Even when authority was weakened by removing the experimenter from the scene, or the unpleasantness of the task increased by placing the learner beside the teacher, the rate of conformity was substantial.

The second and third conditions are a different matter. The Asch and the Milgram paradigms share the property of introducing unusual circumstances to study a supposedly common phenomenon—conformity to external influence—in the case of Asch represented by unanimous or majority judgment, and in the case of Milgram by the trappings of authority and legitimacy. Unlike Asch, the Milgram paradigm possesses mundane realism in that the circumstances do not depart wholly from what one might conceivably encounter in a scientific experiment. There is the psychologist in proper clinical attire, there is the laboratory, and there is the awesome device for delivering electric shocks. Nevertheless, neither a parallel with the reaching of political judgments by individuals nor a simulation of the social setting for the formation and expression of opinion is present. Unlike individuals conversing about politics and public affairs, the subject was unfamiliar with the experimental setting, had no prior experience with the task, and there was minimal opportunity for reflection. Norms, except for that of not harming another person, did not apply because for the subjects no standards had been established for this particular situation. The relationship established by the experimenter with the subject precludes discussion or debate ("You must continue"). The social situation, in which the subject voluntarily placed himself or herself under the authority of the experimenter who unremittingly exhorted compliance, had more in common with the Marine Corps training at Parris Island depicted in Stanley Kubrick's *Full Metal Jacket* than with an interpersonal exchange involving public affairs, politics, and government policies.

The key element in the paradigm is the relationship between the experimenter and the subject (just as the key element in the Asch paradigm was between the unanimous group and the subject), which hinged on the unfamiliarity with the situation and task, the authority of the experimenter and his insistence that the delivery of shocks be completed as instructed, and identification with and the desire for the approval of the experimenter. As with the Asch paradigm, the data record what can be accomplished by external influence under very unusual conditions. Ordinary realities were suspended; implacable authority was substituted.

The significance of the attributes of the paradigm is importantly underscored by their role in governing estimates of the likelihood of conformity. The original estimates of about 1 percent or less collected by Milgram were in response to a very general description without much detail (Blass, 2000a); the attributes essentially were ignored. When the descriptions were more detailed and thereby more informative of what actually transpired, the estimates increased markedly. Kaufmann and Kooman (1967) and Mixon (1971) informed individuals in considerable detail of the methods employed, with the former describing the procedures and the latter reading the "Methods" section from a Milgram (1963) experiment. They obtained estimates of the proportion of subjects who continued to deliver shocks to the very end (and thus, reached maximum voltage) of about 27 and 44 percent, respectively. In fact, Mixon found that he could vary the estimate of complete conformity from 90 to zero percent by altering the degree to which his description minimized or maximized the likelihood of the teacher evincing awareness that the learner was suffering serious damage. This suggests that a further avenue by which the experimenter exerted his authority was his insistence that no harm was being done (despite the evidence of the cries of pain and protest and the warning labels on the electric shock machine—lyin' ears joining lyin' eyeballs). Thus, estimates of obedience in the Milgram paradigm are highly dependent on the impression created by description of the attributes of the paradigm, and the revelatory power of Milgram's findings was an artifact of the vague (and thereby inaccurate) description that he chose to use. As the demands created by the experimenter become apparent, the bizarre becomes the expected.

We conclude that the Milgram paradigm is neither the stuff of totalitarian states, emboldened by secret police and military support and exerting control of the mass media, nor a representation of conformity as it might occur in the realm of public affairs and politics. The subject matter was not opinion and judgment. It was essentially surprise when faced with an unfamiliar situation and a dictatorial authority when alternatives—as a function of prior experience, norms, or support from others—were absent. The Milgram paradigm has little application in the public sphere. It applies to private transactions, such as occur within bureaucracies and military organizations, and even here its applicability would be restrained by the infrequency of unfamiliar situations. In our judgment, the Milgram paradigm adds little to the case for conformity in the realm of politics and public affairs.

III. RETHINKING THE PERSONAL

The evidence in behalf of a dominant role for personal history and experience in the forming of opinions about politics and public affairs requires reconsideration. However, the circumstances are quite different from those confronted by the spiral of silence and the Asch and Milgram paradigms. The conditions necessary for the appearance of the former are relatively rare; the latter two have scant bearing on everyday communication about politics and public affairs. In contrast, the data attesting to the importance of personal background established a set of concepts that remain important today for evaluating the effects of the mass media on political communication. Nevertheless, several factors call for a reweighing of the evidence.

The principal point at issue is whether the media remain decisively subordinate to the political socialization provided by the family, the party loyalty and ideological preferences that this socialization instills, the tendency to associate with like-minded individuals, and the reliance on certain of these individuals for opinion leadership. Certainly, these factors retain considerable power. Where they fail is in convincingly assigning a minor role to the media.

We have three quarrels with the interpretations inherited from the middle of the last century. The first is that the conceptualization of media effects, and particularly in the so-called classic voting studies, was so limited and narrow that it excluded the possibility of meaningful media influence. The second is that historical changes that make individuals more vulnerable to media influence—in the political allegiances of the population, the availability of the media, and the practices of journalism—are inevitably not taken into account by these early interpretations. The third is that the psychological processes that are likely to figure in any influence of the media are ignored.

A. Conceptualization

The conventional histories of mass communication research describe the replacement of a hypodermic needle model (which construed the influence of the media as analogous to the injection of a chemical substance with known properties into the bloodstream of an individual) of media effects by emphases on personal history, interpersonal communication, and the reinforcement of beliefs, opinions, and prejudices by the media (Bineham, 1988; Katz, 1996; Sills, 1996; Wartella, 1996). The hypodermic needle model, which posited very powerful effects in accord with media content, was fueled by right-wing demagogues using the radio to reach millions (such as Father Coughlin in the United States), the rise in Europe of totalitarian states that controlled the media (such as the Soviet Union and Nazi Germany), and the vigorous use by the Nazis of propaganda emanating from a government ministry. It ostensibly became less convincing with the production in the 1940s and 1950s of several works that preferred a view of distinctly limited and arguably even rare media effects. There were the surveys of voter behavior by Lazarsfeld, Berelson, and Gaudet (1944) and Berelson, Lazarsfeld, and McPhee (1954); the survey of consumer behavior by Katz and Lazarsfeld (1955); and the comprehensive summary of research results by Klapper (1960)—*The People's Choice, Voting, Personal Influence*, and *The Effects of Mass Communication*. The voting studies established the likelihood of the well-known two-step flow; specifically, in *The People's Choice* those who described themselves as opinion leaders in regard to politics and public affairs made greater use of the media to follow the presidential campaign than those who did not so identify themselves. *Personal Influence* extended the two-step flow, with information from the media disseminated by a select number of opinion leaders who also might reinterpret or evaluate that information, to consumer products, fashions, and movies; specifically, in these data those who were described as having had some influence on an individual in one or another of these areas proved to have greater access to the media than those who were not so described. Thus, the actual tracing of the path of influence confirmed the two-step flow that seemingly had appeared in *The People's Choice*.

The authors concluded that the direct effects of the media in politics and public affairs, consumer purchases, fashion, and entertainment choices were rare. Interpersonal communication was typically a necessary and often modifying intervening factor. In politics and public affairs, socioeconomic status and religion, which usually would be filtered through the family in the process of political socialization and the attendant building of party loyalty and ideological preferences, would also play a role in diminishing the likelihood of media influence.

These concepts were "packaged neatly" (Katz, 1996) or codified (Chaffee & Hochheimer, 1985) in the very limited effects model advanced in *The Effects of Mass Communication*. Klapper classified study outcomes as representing either conversion or reinforcement, with a third category of minor effects that were dismissed as essentially inconsequential. Conversion was a significant change in behavior or thought—a hypodermic needle outcome, although it might be confined to individuals with particular characteristics. The selective processes—in particular, exposure and perception, but also retention—made reinforcement much more likely. Klapper concluded that conversion occurred infrequently. He decided reinforcement was the typical outcome, with the media employed by an individual in ways that would amplify or at least coincide with existing beliefs, predispositions, and prejudices. The large role of interpersonal sources in acting as gatekeepers and reinterpreters of media content was seen as further delimiting the influence of the media.

Persuasion, attitude change, and the behavior of voters during presidential campaigns were particularly prominent in Klapper's analysis, as would be expected from the research available at the time, but he also covered other topics, such as the influence of the media on children. Reinforcement was the norm; what the individual brought to the media was more important than what the media conveyed to the individual. Klapper became the touchstone for those skeptical of media influence, and one of the most cited authors in communication research. He was a sociologist, and some credit *The Effects of Mass Communication* with effectively erasing the media from the research agenda of the discipline.

This limited-effects perspective, and particularly the survey data from the voting and consumer studies on which it seemingly rested, has been subject to intense criticism (Bineham, 1988; Bucy & D'Angelo, 2004; Chaffee & Hochheimer, 1985; Gitlin, 1978). Lazarsfeld and colleagues conceived of media influence as marketing effectiveness observable in short-term changes in thought or behavior (Gitlin, 1978). As Chaffee and Hochheimer (1985) report in their account of the beginnings of political communication research in the United States, this limited-effects model held that media influence was drastically circumscribed by the attributes of audience members and the characteristics of communication situations. The former included socioeconomic status, religion, and family background; the latter included the specifics of media depictions and accounts, the nature of the subject matter, its importance or relationship to the audience member, and the influence of interpersonal communication. Typically, the specifics of content were governed in their effect by these other factors, and media influence was consigned in size to "small" and in consequence to "unimportant."

Chaffee and Hochheimer offer an uncompromising corrective based on two dimensions:

1. The failure of the marketing analogy to incorporate important elements of the political environment.
2. The responses of the public to questions posed in the early voting studies about the role of the media.

They argue that the marketing perspective confined the criteria for influence by the media to far too narrow a range of outcomes. The two major ones were changes in voter thought or behavior—attitudinal dispositions or behavioral change. As a result, they conclude, Lazarsfeld and colleagues in *The People's Choice* and *Voting* excluded influence on beliefs and perceptions about what was transpiring politically; heightened or lowered interest in these occurrences; additional knowledge about political events that might stimulate reflection, evaluation, or political participation; and the weakening or the possible strengthening of beliefs, predispositions, and prejudices. Chaffee and Hochheimer thus shift the focus from changes in dispositions or behavioral intention to alterations of an individual's worldview. Knowledge becomes a major effect.

This is in accord in fact with the early data on the two-step flow, which indicated that media were preeminent in disseminating information about what had transpired. And this is precisely what the marketing perspective dismisses, and by that exclusion encourages a falsely confident indifference to media influence. Chaffee and Hochheimer further challenge Lazarsfeld and colleagues on their analysis and interpretation of data. They point out that the conclusions that reinforcement was preeminent and conversion rare were based on shifts between May and October, which would have ignored interspersed media effects on beliefs and perceptions. Zaller (1992) made a similar argument in a more general form—that net effects over a period of time, although important because that is how elections are decided, may overlook shifting, intermittent effects of the media on dispositions and intentions that occur during the process of public opinion formation. Chaffee and Hochheimer also observe that Lazarsfeld and colleagues ignore data in the Erie County study that would have encouraged a more generous assessment of the media's role. In this instance, before the arrival of television, more than two-thirds of the sample cited newspapers or radio as helpful in reaching a voting decision while fewer than one-half cited another person, such as a relative, business acquaintance, neighbor, or friend. When asked about a single most important source, more than one-half named either radio or newspapers but fewer than one-fourth cited another person. These findings are inconsistent with the preeminence assigned by authors to interpersonal factors. Finally, Chaffee and Hochheimer note that the two-step flow, well documented in that era, is inconsistent with an analysis that weighs each voter equally because it ignores the disproportionate reliance on the media of those who function as opinion leaders. Again, indifference to media influence seems unjustified.

If the vote as the outcome of significance in registering marketing effectiveness delimited the range of conclusions that might be offered about the influence of the media, the sites chosen seriously circumscribed the places and times to which the outcomes could be generalized. Chaffee and Hochheimer note that the places chosen to collect the data—Erie County, Ohio (*The People's Choice*) and Elmira, New York (*Voting*)—were politically stable communities with, compared to such urban centers as Chicago, Los Angeles, and New York, limited access to mass media and, more importantly, little in the way of competing interest and ethnic groups. This foreclosed the possibility of reflecting the functioning of the media in more volatile and contested areas, sites, and circumstances where increasing proportions of voters have come to reside. The adoption of the conclusions of these studies as laws governing American political behavior that would extend to other times and places was not merited—but that is essentially what took place.

The arbitrariness of Klapper's work is that it rests on a false dichotomy. The division of study outcomes into conversion, representing distinct changes in thought or behavior, and reinforcement, representing the amplification or at least maintenance of beliefs, predispositions, and prejudices, in effect erased from consideration two important outcomes. On the one hand, conversion excluded the consideration of the importance of shifts in thought or behavior insufficiently grand to qualify as a conversion. The labeling of these as minor removed them neatly from consequence. On the other hand, reinforcement soon became translated in the jargon of social science as "mere reinforcement," implying that the reinforcement of a belief, predisposition, or prejudice was of no consequence. In fact, it requires no imagination to see that many effects of the media falling beneath the threshold of conversion might be of consequence, and that the maintenance of beliefs, predispositions, and prejudices would be a sizable and significant feat for the media. Surely, the apparent belief on the part of Katz, Klapper, and Lazarsfeld that the media could only amplify or strengthen such dispositions, as reported by Katz (1996), constituted extraordinary faith in the selective processes and the motivation to avoid contrary or uncongenial information that would govern them, for the mass media ordinarily could not help but disseminate uncongenial as well as congenial information to the widely varied segments of their heterogeneous audiences. Again, even the data of the time are inconsistent with the preferred interpretation because they indicate that in the dissemination of information the media often bypassed opinion leaders.

B. Historical Changes

Our second set of objections is that historical changes have diminished any claim these generalizations of limited effects may have to contemporary relevance. Party membership and loyalty have declined (Chaffee & Hochheimer, 1985; Kinder, 1998; Nie, Verba, & Petrocik, 1976). The result is that political socialization has shifted from an emphasis on designating a preferred party to the inculcation of a set of ideological preferences. The latter removes much of the automatic link between personal history and voting choice, and opens the way for the media to have much greater influence in evaluating parties and candidates.

Over the same period, beginning in the early 1950s, access to the media increased enormously. By the 1952 presidential election, television was in one of three households. By the end of the decade, the medium would be in almost 9 out of 10 households, and by the end of the 1970s would reach its present near saturation level of 98 percent of households (Comstock & Scharrer, 1999). This produced a novel phenomenon—the availability of news in almost every household in the nation. Television regularly has covered the nominating conventions and presidential campaigns from the earliest primaries and caucuses, and quickly became one of the major means by which the public followed unfolding political events, and televised presidential debates changed from an extraordinary event (in 1960, when John F. Kennedy faced Richard M. Nixon) to a tradition. The significance of this is that television, with its visual coverage of events, attractive and highly credible news personnel, and commitment to making the news readily understandable (for how else could you attract the mass audience that television was seeking?) undercut the two-step flow and the opinion leader. Developments in the print media, while seemingly contributing to an increasing scarcity of news outlets, in fact were complementary. Although the number of urban dailies declined sharply, and time spent reading newspapers decreased precipitously (Robinson & Godbey, 1997), in regard to direct access by a substantial proportion of the public to the media these factors were countered by the wide readership of the three national newsmagazines (*Newsweek*, *Time*, and *U.S. News & World Report*) and the emergence of national newspapers distributed throughout the country (*New York Times*, *USA Today*, and the *Wall Street Journal*), with at least one (*USA Today*) possessing many of the cognitively unchallenging characteristics of television. The consequence is that the near-universal availability of print media further reinforced the process begun by television—the diminishment of the two-step flow and the opinion leader.

C. Journalistic Practices

The sporadic coverage of political figures and public affairs by non-news media, especially as the presidential electoral cycle turns toward the selection of candidates, brings exposure to politics for many in their audiences who would ordinarily ignore such subject matter (Norris, 2000). These extracurricular sources include daytime and nighttime talk shows, television with other primary emphases, such as MTV, and the many magazines that give some attention to presidential aspirants and a few controversial issues among their pages devoted to celebrities, fashion, crime, and rock and roll.

Journalistic practices have changed in ways that favor an influence on public opinion in the realm of politics. Television news has become much more obtrusive and self-referential in reporting on politics, with sound bites that give politicians the opportunity to address the public directly growing more abbreviated and the time allotted to commentators and analysts growing longer (Patterson, 1993). Television news in general gives much greater emphasis to bad news than good news (Comstock & Scharrer, 1999), but in the coverage of politics the media in general increasingly have come to focus on unfavorable imagery, possible wrongdoing, and self-interested maneuverings of politicians (Cappella & Jamieson, 1994; Patterson, 1993, 2002). Newspaper journalism has shifted toward longer stories in which the events experienced by individuals more often serve to exemplify social conditions or widespread malaise (Barnhurst & Mutz, 1997; Mutz, 1998). Polls have become ubiquitous throughout the media in the coverage of presidential campaigns, and the sole noteworthy change in newspaper reporting on such campaigns over the past century has been a substantial increase as newspapers began to compete with television in the attention given to the sportslike aspects of politics—who's winning, and by what means (Sigelman & Bullock, 1991). The increasing prominence of the media in interpreting events and the reduced exposure to the words of the politicians covered, the emphasis on the negative and unfavorable that may undermine political support and loyalty, the framing of thematic accounts that remove the ambiguity of social significance from the experience of individuals and bestow political meaning, the heightening of public involvement by the parade of constant personalities and intermittent crises, the increased attention to what the public is thinking about politicians and political campaigns that leaves individuals with few doubts about majority opinion and the popular acceptance or rejection of candidates—these are all developments in journalism that increase the likelihood that the information disseminated by the mass media will influence public opinion.

D. Psychological Processes

The third major source of our dissatisfaction is the absence of any attention to the psychological processes that might enhance and possibly shape the influence of the mass media. Of course, we are far more knowledgeable today about such processes because of the research of the past three decades. This somewhat excuses the early advocates of the limited-effects model but it does not redeem the model in regard to its contemporary applicability.

These processes often constitute biases that affect the accuracy of decision-making. For example, individuals typically are highly risk aversive, preferring to safeguard present well-being at the possible expense of forgoing greater future resources, and the media as a result of their emphasis on bad news are filled with unwanted consequences visited upon individuals. The interest of the media in the unusual, along with their tendency to focus on possible harm or damage rather than the actual likelihood or risk of suffering these consequences, give the media considerable power in creating alarm among the public (Comstock & Scharrer, 1999; Singer & Endreny, 1987). People tend to ignore base rate information about the frequency of an event or occurrence, such as unemployment, the homicide rate, or the winning of a huge financial prize in a Powerball lottery, and instead often base inferences (and sometimes subsequent behavior, such as staying home at night in the case of unsolved, possibly serial homicides or buying a pocketful of tickets in the case of Powerball) on exemplars, the detailed and frequently dramatic experiences of individuals that are a staple of the mass media (Borgida & Brekke, 1981; Kahneman, Slovic, & Tversky, 1982; Zillmann & Brosius, 2000).

At the same time, people may discount their personal experiences, those of their friends and relatives, and what is taking place in their immediate environment, in favor of information about what is taking place in the larger society. This is because the former, real and valid enough in regard to immediate circumstances, will be open to the possibility of being an exception attributable to unusual circumstances, while the latter will carry the verisimilitude of media reports unaccompanied by any means for independent verification (Mutz, 1998). Thus, personal satisfaction with health care, optimism over one's financial future, and skepticism about becoming the victim of a crime may be accompanied by ratings of health care, the economy, and crime rates for the country as a whole that are decidedly more negative. The principle of personal and local exceptionalism deprives personal experience of its force. In these cases, the media take precedence over personal experience.

Then, there are the ubiquitous public opinion polls. Individuals, when lacking other bases for decision making, such as party loyalty, ideological preferences, or factual information (which in many cases is elusive and difficult to interpret, such as what might be expected of the economy or the Dow Jones), may draw on them in attempting to satisfy the three motives for taking into account the opinions of others: reaching a correct decision, gaining the approval of others, and enjoying vicarious reward by identifying with the successful or more popular side. On the other hand, when data on public opinion are unavailable and there is no ambiguity that might be resolved by turning to the opinions of others, a distinctly different phenomenon may occur—the false consensus effect in which people conclude that others share their viewpoint (Fabrigar & Krosnick, 1995; Gunther, Christen, Liebhart, & Chia, 2001; Marks & Miller, 1987; Mullen et al., 1985). Here, the failure of the media to convey accurate information about public opinion becomes a factor.

These psychological processes that enter into individual decision making constitute a prima facie case for an influence of the mass media on public opinion about politics and public affairs. They join the narrowness of the conceptualization of media effects and the historical changes in the availability of media, party allegiance, and journalistic practices in diminishing the pertinence of the limited-effects model.

In early accounts of the development of mass communication research, the limited-effects model often was presented as a corrective based on empirical evidence to the hypodermic needle model (Bineham, 1988; Delia, 1987). This supposed succession misrepresents the sequence of paradigms. Except perhaps for the study of propaganda, as exemplified by the works of Lasswell (1930, 1935) and Doob (1950), there was no advancement or presumption of a hypodermic model by social and behavioral scientists. The early voting studies by Lazarsfeld and colleagues, although certainly proposing a decidedly different perspective, made no reference to a hypodermic model. Even in the area of propaganda studies, such powerful effects were offered as speculation and a possibility because empirical data were confined to the content analysis of the symbols employed in propaganda (Chaffee & Hochheimer, 1985). Chaffee and Hochheimer (1985), Schramm (1997), and Wartella (1996) all conclude that research antedating the limited-effects model regularly drew on intervening and contingent variables. Two examples are the now famous Payne Fund studies in the late 1920s of the influence of motion pictures on children and adolescents (Charters, 1933) and the World War II experiments on the effects of propaganda films (with titles such as *Why We Fight*) on American soldiers (Hovland, Lumsdaine, & Sheffield, 1949). In both cases, variables such as perceptions, predispositions, past experience, and social environment had important roles in the analyses along with, in the case of the children and adolescents, age, gender, and parental influence. They are typical of earlier research. Schramm was so bold as to assert that he knew of no informed person who had entertained a hypodermic needle perspective. The limited-effects model, then, was not a corrective although it was certainly correctly applicable to certain limited circumstances.

IV. OUR INTENTIONS

We intend to focus on the psychology of media and politics, by which we mean the various ways in which individuals, and by extension groups and social strata, make use of the mass media in reaching conclusions about public affairs. The most obvious outcome of such conclusions is voting. However, we are interested in the broadest possible range of responses to public events, including the forming of opinions, disinterest, and nonparticipation as well as participation in the political process. We will begin with the media, for they are the major source of information about public affairs that compete with personal experience, the two-step flow, and opinion leaders. We will then turn to the vast potential audience for information disseminated by the media, and we will attempt some distinctions about the makeup of this audience in terms of interest, involvement, ideological affiliation and party preference, and likelihood of voting. However, we are not interested solely in the precipitation of voting choices but in the larger and more varied uses the public make of the media. This endeavor leads us directly to the effects of the media on political thought and behavior, where we will spend considerable time on the two major means identified by Mutz (1998) in her pioneering *Impersonal Influence* by which the depictions and accounts in the media influence the political decision making of individuals: the stories, descriptions, and impressions conveyed by the media about what people beyond one's immediate locale are experiencing and are thinking. Finally, we extend the concepts, principles, and processes, psychological and social, beyond politics to two other topics in which the media arguably play a large role: consumer behavior and socialization.

PART II

Press and Public

CHAPTER 3

The New Media

One of the major changes in American political life in the twentieth century was the expansive development of the mass media and, as a consequence, the emergence of the media-based presidential campaign. It is difficult to picture a contemporary campaign for a high-profile public office that does not employ the media to attempt to persuade, inform, inspire, and mobilize voters. Surely such a campaign would be doomed to obscurity and, ultimately, failure. In the modern world of politics, potential voters are reached in their vehicles by radio reports of campaign visits and speeches; in subway cars, buses, and trains by newspaper reports of the latest standings in the polls of candidates, and by overhead advertisements for candidates and ballot issues; in their living rooms, bedrooms, and kitchens by television advertisements, reports on the morning or nightly news, and newspaper accounts; and at their desks by Internet web sites created by the candidates or designed to cover the campaign. This montage omits the no-longer novel political appearances on talk shows and MTV election coverage; the weekly devotions and ruminations of the newsmagazines; direct mail and unsolicited (and sometimes somewhat disguised) telephone promotions; and the enormous array on the Internet of established, traditional news outlets in addition to Internet-only content sites. The extent of the influence of the modern media on the strategies of politicians and political hopefuls and their intrusiveness in the daily lives and decision making of potential voters are difficult to overstate.

Admittedly, the media are not the only source of information, persuasion, and even entertainment about political affairs. Some voters still turn to parents or other family members for guidance in their political views and activities.

Others look to the church or synagogue. Still others have their opinions shaped by their peers: friends, bosses, and coworkers. A few will become opinion leaders, dispensing authoritative judgments and commentary to a small number of acquaintances.

It is fathomable that a very small number of voters base their political analysis and decisions on firsthand encounters with candidates, relying on personal observations of campaign speeches and whistle stops more than on mediated accounts or interpersonal discussions. Yet, in every one of these varied scenarios, the presence of the media is still felt. In politics, media are the basis for interpersonal exchange. In effect, they have for most of their audiences a monopoly on events, and it is on events that political fortunes turn. Even conversations with others and one's own personal observations are inevitably shaped by the information received about and from the candidates via the media. Media coverage of the political scene provides the lens through which political affairs are viewed, regardless of whether the media are a sole source of information or whether information gleaned from media exposure is accompanied by other sources. Largely,

> The pictures we have of politics are not the products of direct involvement but are perceptions focused, filtered, and fantasized by a host of mediators—the press, entertainment programming on television, movies, popular magazines, songs, and group efforts in election campaigns . . . (Nimmo & Combs, 1983, p. 2).

The contemporary news media have a tight hold on the reins of American politics, dictating the pace, the form, and the content of the election.

This is not a viewpoint that would once have had any credibility among those familiar with the research on media and politics. As we have seen, the large-scale voting studies following World War II and relying on public opinion data collected in the manner of pollsters, although analyzed with much loftier ambitions and greater curiosity and sophistication, led to the almost universal conclusion among political scientists, sociologists, and social psychologists that the media played a small and subsidiary role in presidential elections and, by implication, in elections for other important offices (Berelson, Lazarsfeld, & McPhee, 1954; Campbell, Converse, Miller, & Stokes, 1960; Campbell, Gurin, & Miller, 1954; Lazarsfeld, Berelson, & Gaudet, 1944).

I. THREE FACTORS

Three factors are largely responsible for the ascendant role now assigned to the media. The first factor is the critical reexamination of the paradigm employed by these early investigators that assured a highly circumscribed role for the media (Chaffee & Hochheimer, 1985). Persuasion, measured by the elevated and highly demanding standard of changing the electoral choice of a voter, was at the forefront of criteria for assessing media influence. Party allegiance (a major factor then that still retains some of its importance), prior voting history, and the views of friends, family, and coworkers were credited with influence when conversion from one candidate to another did not occur. The shaping of political opinion, and the rise and fall of degrees of support, were largely ignored. With the media confined to the background, data that would suggest a different or larger role often were neglected—such as substantial proportions naming the media as figuring importantly in their choice at the polls.

The second factor is the diminution of parties as the chief factor in determining the choice of most voters. Over the past five decades, the proportion of voters who declare themselves as independents has increased substantially. Ticket-splitters who shift between the parties for the various offices on a ballot rather than voting a straight party ticket have become more common, and switching parties from one election to another in the choice of presidential candidates (and candidates for all other offices, for that matter) has become more frequent. Uncertainty over the candidate of choice, marked by switched leanings and doubt until the final week of the campaign, once confined to a very small minority of voters, has become a regular if not invariant feature of presidential races for a sizable proportion—if still a decided minority—of voters (Comstock, 1989; Comstock & Scharrer, 1999). One consequence is that the role of personal history as exercised through the inculcation by the family of the superiority of one party or another has become far less important. The same can be said of coworkers, friends, and family; they, too, are no longer so certain in their allegiance to a party, and as a result they are no longer so consistent or in unison in voicing support for one party or the other. This process has been abetted by the prominence of issue voting in which voters are persuaded by the themes of one or another presidential candidate rather than the ideological history of a party. The implication of these varied shifts in voter orientation and behavior is that voters have become more dependent on the coverage provided by the media of campaigns and politically relevant events, and more susceptible to the particular frames, emphases, and spin employed by the media they use.

The introduction of television is the third factor. This progeny of the second half of the twentieth century, whose schedule ironically is so thoroughly dominated by entertainment (Comstock & Scharrer, 1999), has been associated with and is sometimes a major contributor to significant changes in the role of the media in politics. Television first entered American homes in the late 1940s. By 1960, 87 percent of households had sets. This phenomenal popularity would lift that figure to 96 percent over the next decade and by 1980 the ceiling of 98 percent would have been reached (this is apparently the practical limit to television's saturation of society). Its first major political appearance occurred in the 1952 presidential election when about one out of three households had a set. The party conventions were televised for the first time to large audiences, and large numbers of viewers had their first introduction to political commercials (Cranston, 1960). Both, of course, have become permanent fixtures with stunning consequences.

The televising of the conventions essentially opened their doors to public scrutiny in a way that went far beyond the scribbled communiqués of print journalists, with the result that the parties increasingly came to understand that they must not fail to make a favorable impression on the American public. Woe clearly befell those who failed at this task, as exemplified by the 1968 Chicago Democratic convention with its clashes between anti–Vietnam war protestors and Mayor Daley's police and the freewheeling 1972 Miami convention of the same party where the nominee, George McGovern, flouted accepted practice and political wisdom by not bothering to give his acceptance speech in prime time. Whatever else they may have retained of their past (and the widespread adoption of caucuses and primaries to select candidates would convert them from deliberative judges of candidate credentials and suitability to tent shows stamping approval of the candidate who arrived with a majority of delegates), conventions forever after became showpieces with orchestrated parades, demonstrations, and speeches designed to flatter the party and eventually the nominee.

With the commercial, television changed things in another way. The commercial, impossible to gauge as to its moment of appearance on the screen and essentially too brief to flee, overcame the filters by which many people protected themselves from political information—in some cases, any information about politics, and in other cases, information contrary or somewhat tangential to their views. This had been easy enough with print media (excepting the occasional billboard and bumper sticker), but with television was no longer. Television would eventually account for more than three-fourths of campaign expenditures in major races, and the correlation between expenditures on television commercials and vote totals became hard to ignore. This stealthy entry into the homes of the electorate was accompanied by the inclusion of political coverage in the nightly newscasts, whose format, like the unexpected scheduling of political commercials, made the stories, by the nature of the design of television news, always short and brisk, hard to avoid. Television brought politics to the hearth.

One of the most significant contributions of television was to expand greatly the potential reach of the media. It readily overcame deficits in literacy and by its presence in almost every household had the potential to render irrelevant the norms and habits that would dictate whether newsmagazines or newspapers were read. Thus, television became the medium of choice when something of moment occurs (Comstock, 1989), and television news joined newspapers as a consistent component of the media followed regularly by those who consistently attend to the news (Patterson, 1980). This potential reach, of course, applies to every geographical entity: nation, state, and congressional district. It is seldom exercised because only about half the adult public follows the news regularly (Patterson, 1980), but this previously unprecedented reach does become mobilized on rare occasions such as the terrorist attacks of September 11, 2001.

Television also brought a different kind of storytelling to the news, thereby widening somewhat the proportion of the public that could understand to a reasonable degree the events that were transpiring. Television has been accused of simplifying stories, which it surely often does, but this same tendency, accompanied by appealing visuals and informative graphics, and managed by plain-spoken and attractive anchors of both sexes, also makes stories interesting and comprehensible to those who would find them opaque and without drama in print (Graber, 2001; Neuman, Just, & Crigler, 1992).

Before television, print news too often pursued the dramatic or attention-getting storytelling angle in covering political events. The Lincoln–Douglas debates of 1858 certainly were not dependent on television, but they were the focus of intensive media coverage and editorializing and, as has been the case with television, the two seekers of the Illinois Senate seat hardly would have engaged in them without the expectation of substantial media attention (Kraus, 2000). Moreover, as also has been the case with televised presidential debates, much of the media's attention was given to dramatic exchanges, gauging the winner, and the more colorful and personal aspects of the encounters (Kraus, 2000). Nevertheless, it is the medium of television that has made debates between presidential candidates a fixture of modern elections. These confrontations are thought to be enormously important by the public, figure importantly in the decision-making processes of voters (by their own account) although only rarely resulting in an individual shifting from one candidate to the other, and despite diminishing audiences (by the standards of early debates) remain a centerpiece of each campaign because they are subsequently covered assiduously by all the media: television, radio, newsmagazines, and newspapers (Comstock & Scharrer, 1999).

Those three factors—the paradigm, the diminution of parties, the new medium—which represent how we think about media influence, social changes, and new technology, constituted a revolution in the political role, conceived and actual, of the media. Personal history, with its fortifications of family socialization, party allegiance, and like-thinking friends, coworkers, and family, took a large step backward. Events of the day strode to the forefront. Television, of course, is not as dominant a news medium as public opinion would suggest. Large majorities name it as the source of most of their news (probably because television connotes the big, dramatic, and sometimes threatening events that most people define as news), but in actuality more people will see a newspaper than a television news program in any two- or three-week period and more people who follow the news regularly will do so by reading newspapers than by watching television news (Comstock & Scharrer, 1999; Lichty, 1982; Patterson, 1980; Robinson, 1971). The significance of television is not that it dominates media use but that it reached the portion of the public eager for news and vulnerable to political advertising at a time when the barriers to influence abbreviated by the term *personal history* were in retreat. It stands with newspapers and newsmagazines as one of the three major means by which the public follows politics and politically relevant events. The emergence of CNN and, later, C-SPAN, CNBC, MSNBC, and Fox News, simply augmented the array of choices that make it more likely that a viewer can find a congenial news source just as the proliferation of print media has made it more likely that a reader can find a similarly congenial source (Norris, 2000). This earlier revolution, which embraced both the means of dissemination and the content of the news, is now being followed by another revolution that appears likely to have more to do with dissemination than with content, although there surely will be some different content and possibly a few reached by content they otherwise might have missed, but adds the important element of candidates being able to mobilize support by direct contact with voters and financial contributors: the Internet.

II. First Things

Although the connection between media and politics seems especially close in the contemporary arena, the two have been inexorably linked throughout this nation's history. In the United States, the media have functioned as a political institution since colonial times (Cook, 1998; Starr, 2004). Initially, newspapers—weeklies of four pages with circulations of a few hundred (the first successful daily did not appear until 1784)—observed a genteel neutrality and a deference appropriate to a colonial enterprise toward government, which was an arm of Great Britain. By 1720, however, they had become forums for public debate, with newspapers functioning as common carriers for all points of view, and beginning in about 1765, with the enactment of the British Stamp Act, they shifted toward partisan opposition to the British (Starr, 2004). The latter was the date of enactment of the British Stamp Act, which imposed a tax on newspapers, resulted in a two-to-one ratio of voices in behalf of the Revolution.

In the first decades of the nation's existence, many newspapers and political newsletters were directly funded by or otherwise overtly aligned with political parties or other ideological organizations, although in some cases this was merely a matter of declared allegiance without the exertion of party control over journalistic practice, and some papers maintained political neutrality. Reporting news and public events with an admitted, open political bent was nevertheless the norm from the birth of the United States until the latter half of the nineteenth century, and until the emergence of the penny press newspapers reached small and local audiences. The links with government went far beyond ties between parties and newspapers and the partisan outlook of many papers. They included a wide range of financial support, although some of it was disguised, and a set of conditions favorable to the prospering of the press. The state and federal governments both paid newspapers to publish newly enacted laws for public instruction, and there were printing contracts for documents and forms. These payments underwrote other, overtly partisan activity as well as journalism in general, and printing contracts naturally favored enterprises and newspapers favorable to those in power (Cook, 1998; Starr, 2004). The allotting of printing contracts as a reward to politically supportive presses, including newspapers, continued for decades until, in response to scandals over the awarding of contracts and the handling of funds, the bipartisan establishment of the Government Printing Office (GPO) in 1860.

Then there were the important subsidies by the Post Office, which helped many newspapers survive and extended their reach into the countryside. The major pillar was negligible postal rates, accompanied by a special case of free distribution. Low postal rates were crucial, because many papers, while quite local in their emphases and circulation, nevertheless had subscribers in substantial proportions well beyond the range of hand delivery or personal purchase. The benefit of the subsidy was augmented by a policy of establishing postal routes even when they would not be self-supporting. By 1828, less than four decades after the Post Office Act of 1792, Congress had authorized 2,476 new postal routes, all of which would not only serve citizens with personal mail, and serve commerce with catalogs, but would also assist newspapers in gaining subscribers (Starr, 2004). The Post Office thus promoted newspaper circulation. The special case was another type of subsidy: free postage for the exchange of issues. This gave each newspaper a steady supply of newsworthy information that could be incorporated in its own coverage, and thereby reduced the costs of journalism. A single newspaper would receive several hundred issues weekly (Starr, 2004).

These factors combined with a broad array of other circumstances highly favorable to the development of communication (Starr, 2004). Among these were the widespread availability of common schools; a consequent market for school texts that contributed to the health of the printing industry; increasing levels of literacy that ensured a welcome reception for the products of the presses, including religious publications, political tracts, and lurid accounts of crime; and the eventual interpretation of the First Amendment that made the right to publish freely the law of the land (Starr, 2004). Together, these forces amounted to a governmental and societal policy of cheap print, free expression, and journalistic abundance.

The relentless pursuit of scandal associated with public figures traces back even further in history, with the first newspaper published in America in 1690 alluding to an extramarital affair being conducted by the King of France (Stephens, 1989). Thomas Jefferson was subjected to various assaults on his character in rival party newspapers. Indeed, many political figures regularly were subject to attack by newspapers subsidized by their opponents due to the conjunction of news source and political party that began in the George Washington era and continued until the increasing size and diversity of urban markets led to the success of the penny press (Starr, 2004). Covering politics with a game or sports metaphor to emphasize who was ahead and who was behind has been traced back to the 1830s when Jackson introduced rallies and party conventions, and the allure of the spectacles that they create, to political life (Patterson, 1993). Because newspapers were openly partisan well into the second half of the nineteenth century (Starr, 2004), they vied against one another to promote the qualities of their favored candidates in the hearts and minds of the public, thereby extending the metaphor from the coverage of politics to the conduct of the press.

Most historians agree that the birth of the penny press traces to the founding of the *New York Sun* by Benjamin Day in 1833 (Sabato, 1991). The partisan model of the press that had been the norm faded in the face of the lure of new urban markets and the new technology in the nineteenth century that allowed for mass production of newspapers. These technological developments began to have a major influence in the first quarter of the nineteenth century. They included remarkably faster cylindrical and rotary presses, manufacturing techniques that made paper less expensive, and stereotyping (in which molds were employed to reproduce pages of type, eliminating the need to reset or keep type standing). Other factors encouraging the rise of mass-circulation newspapers included the population shift to cities, which created a new mass audience, and the settling of the American West, which created a market for news that could be said to be of national significance (Bennett, 1983). Still, with the founding of the penny press the great urban newspapers still lay somewhat in the future because at that time only 4 percent of the population lived in cities of 25,000 or more. Thus, the *Sun* and its noted rival, James Gordon Bennett's *Herald,* were harbingers rather than instant transformations. The overt link of a newspaper to one party or one political leader, the prior model, limited the size and scope of its potential circulation. On the contrary, economics, which previously had favored the security of close and partisan ties to a political party, now began to favor impartiality and objectivity so that a mass audience could be wooed without alienation or complaint and a large readership cutting across ideological inclinations could be pursued (Bennett, 1983; Patterson, 1993; Schudson, 1978).

The transition was sufficiently accomplished by 1861 so that Abraham Lincoln determined that his administration would not be linked to a particular newspaper (Sabato, 1991). However, the shift toward an independent press would continue until the turn of the century (Table 3.1). Daily circulation in the nation's 50 largest cities grew from 1.4 to 8.3 million over these decades, with the proportion representing newspapers that claim political independence increasing from 26 to 53 percent.

Although open partisanship in the news coverage of most newspapers was now in the past, the pursuit of outrage continued in the form of muckraking, and public figures from all parties and political leanings were equally at risk for this unwanted attention. The journalistic ideals of objectivity and accuracy were far from firmly in place as some newspaper publishers only exercised their newfound power to attract massive audiences. Scandals involving political and public figures were often salaciously reported and were frequently scant on facts.

TABLE 3.1 Political Independence of the Press, 1870–1900 (Fifty Largest City Dailies)

	Number of Papers	Total Daily Circulation	Percent Papers	Percent Circulation
1870				
Democrat/Republican	155		87.1	74.3
Independent	23		12.9	25.8
		1,384,560		
1880				
Democrat/Republican	161		64.2	44.4
Independent	85		33.9	55.2
		2,427,730		
1890				
Democrat/Republican	170		54.0	46.3
Independent	138		43.8	53.3
		5,518,160		
1900				
Democrat/Republican	161		50.2	46.6
Independent	152		47.4	53.0
		8,275,020		

Adapted from *All the news that's fit to sell: How the market transforms information into news*, by J. T. Hamilton, 2004, Princeton, NJ: Princeton University Press.

Muckraking and "yellow journalism" waned as profits for newspapers grew and their publishers became prestigious citizens with a desire for respectability and, conceivably, a disinclination to harm the reputations of their fellow prominent citizens (Sabato, 1991). World War I, the Great Depression, and World War II also helped quash the press's penchant for yellow journalism and lust for scandal, as did the Depression-beset administration of Franklin Delano Roosevelt. Indeed, Sabato (1991) observes that the respectful distance the press kept from potentially scandalous stories about FDR, refraining from emphasizing illness, poor health, or his estrangement from his wife, was a journalistic standard that held for 40 years—that the private lives of politicians should remain untouched by the news media unless they affected performance in office.

The ideal of objectivity in reporting developed from a number of forces. In 1848, the Associated Press was born, along with the novel idea of distributing and selling standardized versions of prominent stories to newspapers everywhere. Technology quickly affected syntax. The use of telegraph wires to transmit the news resulted in a "simplified, standardized reporting format—something that could convey a large amount of information in the most economical form" (Bennett, 1983, p. 79). Thus, the construction of news stories around who, what, where, when, and why—the pervasive "five W's" of journalism education—ensured that the most important elements of an event would be transmitted, allowing less room for the embellishment of yellow journalism and defining the news with a narrative structure that would endure.

In the 1950s and 1960s, the press was still largely avoiding the reporting of scandalous stories that pertained to the personal lives of public figures. Members of the press appeared to make a conscious decision not to pry into John F. Kennedy's extramarital affairs and the public drunkenness of members of Congress and other public officials. Furthermore, though their actions pertaining to Vietnam and Watergate were certainly well scrutinized by the news media, various transgressions in the personal lives of Presidents Johnson and Nixon were seemingly off limits for journalists (Sabato, 1991).

When did private matters become perceived as fair game for investigative reporting? Sabato (1991) pinpoints Senator Edward Kennedy's role in and later response to the Chappaquiddick tragedy, the psychiatric problems of Senator Thomas Eagleton, and, of course, the Watergate scandal as the defining events that changed the press's orientation toward the private lives of public figures: Chappaquiddick because it effectively ended the presidential hopes of Ted Kennedy, a huge story that joined the personal and political; Eagleton, because widespread ignorance of his mental health record let him slip onto the Democratic ticket as George McGovern's running mate (and unraveled McGovern's liberal mantel of defying the mainstream when he removed

Eagleton); and Watergate because it involved the holder of the highest office in the land in a series of clandestine capers to damage opponents and an elaborate scheme to launder campaign contributions to thwart the laws governing political contributions (and thereby promote the agenda of the Republican Party on both the ideological and financial fronts). From then on, journalists largely have taken the position that private issues and topics beyond the limelight can importantly affect public life, and therefore are legitimate topics of news coverage. Never was this new standard more apparent than in the highly drawn out and extensively reported scandal involving President Bill Clinton and White House intern Monica Lewinsky.

The press in the United States has always closely followed and even attempted to shape politics. What began as overt partisanship in the treatment by newspapers of political candidates shifted with the ability to mass produce and mass distribute newspapers. It gave way, first, to sensationalized muckraking and yellow journalism and, then, to the pursuit of objectivity and accuracy. Negativity and an adversarial tone in covering candidates and political figures, as well as the occasional pursuit of scandal, were early themes that would robustly persevere in future relations between the press and politicians. This is best exemplified in the "focus and discard" process that marks presidential primaries (Comstock & Scharrer, 1999; Patterson, 1993). The front runner, the major challenger, and new entrants receive intensive scrutiny, and past dishonesties, ambiguous curriculum vitae, plagiarism, adultery, emotionality, and past alcohol or drug abuse are gifts the journalist offers to the public to see if one or another is enough to retire the candidate from the roster of contenders. Thus, the media act as hurdles that must be overcome before the benefits of popularity and the appeal of a political platform can be enjoyed. The framing of a political election as a race or a game that was also evident early would continue to characterize media coverage. In fact, the so-called "horse race" aspects of presidential campaigns have become prominent in all media, but especially in television where the metaphor matches neatly with the narrative utility of men or women facing challenges (Comstock & Scharrer, 1999; Graber, 1988). The commercial imperative of news media in the United States in which outlets are expected not just to perform a service by informing the public but also to contribute positively to the parent company's bottom line was established quickly. It would only become intensified in subsequent years. Thus, the coverage of politics as sport is a product of the appeal of this type of coverage and its usefulness in assembling a large audience for a newspaper, magazine, or television channel (Hamilton, 1998).

The value of objectivity serves as a useful illusion for the press (Schudson, 1978). On the one hand, it serves as a heuristic credo for maintaining a professional aura in the newsroom. On the other, it serves two exemplary purposes in the relations of the press with the public (Comstock & Scharrer,

1999). The means by which objectivity is ostensibly achieved—the checking of facts, interviewing of multiple participants or witnesses, the avoidance of accusatory language, and the insistence on two or more sources for controversial stories—all provide protection to and shield the media from criticism and rebuke by the public and from lawsuits by offended individuals. It also vigorously asserts the continuing claim that the news coverage of a news outlet can serve a public varying in its views, and thus can pursue with greater possibility of success a profitable mass audience.

Objectivity, however, is probably best thought of as a useful heuristic rather than a state that can be achieved. If we think of news coverage as having three dimensions, we could probably agree as to whether the behavior of a medium in a specific instance met these criteria (Comstock & Scharrer, 1999). The three dimensions are accuracy, by which we mean adherence to fact and identifying uncertainties; inclusiveness, by which we mean the full coverage of facts favorable to one or another of the various sides or perspectives in a controversy; and, fairness, by which we mean the roughly equal treatment of opposing sides, candidates, and parties when a correct or preferred resolution is ambiguous (this criterion acknowledges that sometimes one or another side has distinctly less merit). These constitute objectivity once coverage has been initiated. However, there is a crucial fourth dimension. Only selected stories are covered by the media, and one outlet may pursue one or another theme or topic that is ignored by another outlet. The news is not a blank slate upon which events are writ, but a construction of reality where organizational needs, personal judgments, and events meet in setting the day's stories (Comstock, 1989; Shoemaker & Reese, 1991; Tuchman, 1978). News values, on which many news workers will agree, at best provide a general guide but, except at the national level of disasters, strikes, crises, wars, assassinations, and some aspects of presidential politics, are not determinative. For example, the intrusion of news policies promoting the pursuit of audience satisfaction lead local television stations to vary wildly in their coverage of murder, rape, and violent crime (Hamilton, 1998). Objectivity, then, is less of a servant than a slogan when it comes to the content of the news.

The same concerns ennobling objectivity led to the divorce of editorial commentary from news coverage. This duality has long besieged the media, and each medium in turn has had to develop standards distinguishing news from opinion as a strategy to protect itself from charges of bias in the former while often retaining the right to express a point of view in the latter. The solution that has emerged for newspapers ostensibly confines opinions to the editorial and "op-ed" pages and the columns of clearly identified commentators (which in some cases may be scattered throughout the paper). The commercial model did not end partisanship and support for candidates and parties but attempted to deflect them to a more confined arena. The four terms of FDR amply demonstrated that a charismatic political figure could triumph without the editorial support of the nation's newspapers, for a majority consistently opposed Roosevelt and urged voters to cast their ballots for his rivals. However, editorials are not mere exercises of the ego either, as Robinson (1974) documented in his analysis of poll data from five presidential campaigns in which there were modest but detectable increases in the vote for candidates supported by local newspapers. Radio is far less sharp in this demarcation, with some widely disseminated newscasters crafting their stories in a decidedly opinionated way. Still, there has been a definite struggle to keep the two separate, with CBS a pioneer in the pre–World War II years in forbidding "commentary" (which would be only opinion) and welcoming "analysis" (presumably based on facts), and the networks in general both before and after the war using panels of commentators to avoid the appearance of a single editorial viewpoint (Kobland, 1999). Television has taken a similar path, with comment confined to the broadcast (or cable) equivalent of newspaper columnists and panels known for their ascerbic exchanges. Networks and local stations have scrupulously avoided the appearance of editorializing by restricting analysis to the expert elucidation (presumably based on facts) of events such as elections, plane crashes, cult murders, upcoming trials, and terrorist attacks. The separation is inevitably imperfect; the very selection of a story for coverage inescapably introduces material that may be more or less favorable for one or another point of view, political party, or candidate.

III. CONTEMPORARY MEDIA

The first half of the twentieth century can be characterized as the adolescence of the mass media, with newspapers commanding huge circulations and with television first appearing as a potential competitor in the late 1940s. Television became prominent as a news medium in the 1950s, and by the early 1960s had become in the minds of a majority the primary source from which they received "most of their news" (Roper Starch, 1995). Increasingly, people named television as their primary news source; by the mid-1990s almost three-fourths were naming television and only 38 percent were naming newspapers, an advantage of about two-to-one. Television had markedly expanded the options for seeking out information about politics and campaigns. Decisions about whether to vote, and which party or candidate to support, now drew on the easily accessible and generally easy to understand medium of television along with the two staples of print journalism: newspapers, with their great detail and daily updates, and newsmagazines, with their narratives placing the news in historical context (Neuman, Just, & Crigler, 1992).

A. Logic of Television

In the 1996 election, when Dautrich and Hartley (1999) asked a panel of about 500 randomly selected voters about their sources of information on the campaign, four out of five responded that the news media were their primary source, compared to fewer than one out of 10 who cited "conversations they had with others." Conversations had once been considered the most important among sources of political information (Berelson, Lazarsfeld, & McPhee, 1954; Kraus & Davis, 1976; Lazarsfeld, Berelson, & Gaudet, 1948), with opinion leaders who translated, interpreted, and conveyed what they took from the media to a circle of friends and coworkers being especially important (Katz & Lazarsfeld, 1955). Television was part of a revolution in political communication that moved the mass media a much more central place. Reporting specifically on daily sources, 72 percent listed television, 60 percent newspapers, and 51 percent radio as the medium to which they turned for news of the campaign. The authors concluded that "for better or worse, Americans experience campaigns through the lens of the news camera, the pens of the journalist, the mouths of radio talk show hosts, and, increasingly, the information superhighway" (Dautrich & Hartley, 1999, p. 6).

The transformational power of the medium of television is of paramount importance to the study of media and politics. Television was not just a new medium that entered the media landscape neatly without disturbing the prior occupants. Rather, the characteristics of the medium led to its immense popularity and rapid diffusion as a source of news and entertainment and irrevocably changed the forms of other, preexisting media (Comstock & Scharrer, 1999). In the realm of politics and beyond, "the logic of television has increasingly become the logic of all mass media" (Nimmo & Combs, 1983, p. 26). The format and structure of the news as presented on television has altered the format and structure of the news as presented in newspapers and newsmagazines, giving way to uncluttered open designs, color photographs and other visuals, and encapsulated articles that recount issues and events in fairly dramatic, storytelling fashion. Their transformational power is exemplified by the national newspaper *USA Today*, which mimics television not only in its brief stories and conspicuous graphics but network television in targeting a national audience; the magazine *People*, which adapts the spirit of the late night talk show to the printed page; and the substantial increase in which newspapers devote space in presidential campaign coverage to who is winning or losing (the "horse race"), previously a specialty of network news (Figure 3.1).

In nationally representative public opinion polls that have been conducted since the 1950s, one can track the growing domination of television as a news source in the minds of Americans. The 34 percentage point difference between those citing television and those citing newspapers as their primary source of

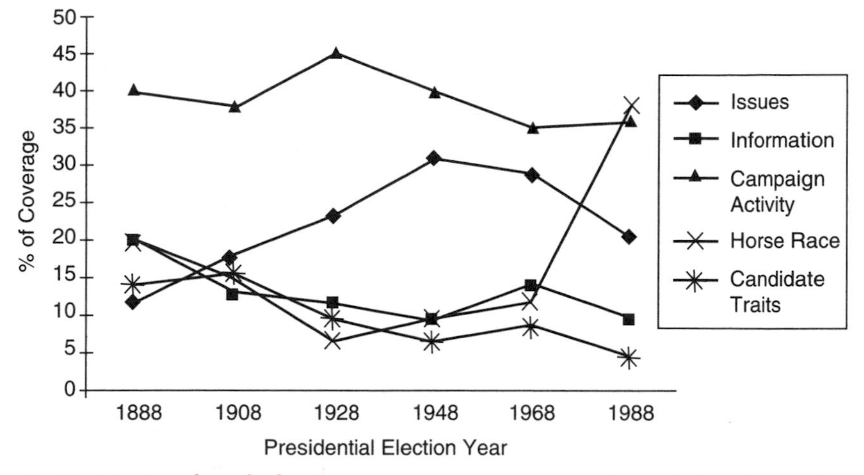

FIGURE 3.1 Presidential election coverage in newspapers, 1888–1988. Adapted from "Candidates, Issues, Horse Races, and Hoopla: Pesidential Campaign Coverage, 1888–1988," by L. Sigelman and D. Bullock, 1991, *American Politics Quarterly, 19*(1), pp. 5–32.

news in 1995 had grown regularly and consistently in favor of television over time. Indeed, the gap increased by 8 percentage points from 1992 to 1995 (Roper Starch, 1995). Television news is also given higher scores among the American public for its credibility, with 51 percent citing television news as the most credible source when confronted with conflicting information and 31 percent citing newspapers (Roper Starch, 1995). The high marks for the credibility of television news in our view is attributable to three factors: the personable and seemingly trustworthy newscasters (Newhagen & Nass, 1989); the use of authoritative visuals that attest to factuality such as reporters live from the steps of the Supreme Court or in the foreground of a burning building or crime scene tape (Graber, 1990; Tuchman, 1978); and the immediate and brief character of the reporting, which largely precludes the late-breaking events that undermine newspaper accounts and minimizes the possibility of errors (Comstock, 1989).

Polls accurately reflect what people say in response to a question, but what they say they do and what they actually do may be quite different. What people say about television as a primary source is ample testimony to the importance they accord to the medium and to the connotative meaning they give to the concept of news. Decades ago, Robinson (1971) recorded that a majority in a national sample of over 2,000 respondents cited television as their primary news source, yet more than half recounted in their media use diaries that they had not actually seen any portion of a network evening newscast in the previous two weeks. On any given day, three times as many respondents read at least part of a newspaper compared to those who saw at least part of a network evening newscast. The same pattern existed in the late 1980s, with daily readership of newspapers across the United States around 100 million compared to less than 40 million audience members for the evening news on ABC, CBS, and NBC (Comstock, 1989). It persists today, with the combined audiences for the network evening newscasts at about 30 million, and would not be changed much by including morning magazine programs and specialized news channels because their audiences are too modest in size and overlap too much with the audiences for the network evening newscasts to make a significant difference (Comstock & Scharrer, 1999). Newspapers remain a staple among the portion of the public that follows the news.

The discrepancy between opinion and behavior regarding the primary news source of the American public leads to two important conclusions. First, when respondents are asked about their number one news source, they are likely to envision high-profile, breaking news incidents rather than the more mundane daily surveillance of events and of life's minutiae. Since television news is by far the preferred choice during crises and highly significant news stories, as seen in the dramatic temporary increases in ratings for CNN and other cable news networks when events of this caliber are unfolding (Dayan & Katz, 1992), this connotative element favors television in respondents' reports (Comstock & Scharrer, 1999). Significantly, national politics is one of the realms in which television news is especially salient because of its visual imagery that focuses on the candidates (Bogart, 1989) and the prominence of election stories in four-year cycles on the television news agenda. Second, newspapers remain a very important medium, and especially so for politics. Certainly, the amount of time each day that the American adult spends with a newspaper has declined more than 60 percent from the mid-1960s when it stood at 21 minutes (Robinson & Godbey, 1997), but circulation has not declined as dramatically. Furthermore, much of newspaper coverage, with its greater detail, extensive quotes, background material, sidebars, and texts of important speeches, is not at all redundant to television news coverage, and presumably for these reasons it is the medium most preferred by those most likely to participate actively in politics by voting, attending a meeting, or writing a letter to the editor or a public official (Putnam, 2000).

Use of news media is highly correlated with age, and the data clearly suggest that part of the reason is a generational effect. More than 50 years ago, Schramm and White (1960) pioneeringly collated data on the demographics of newspaper reading. Education and socioeconomic status, as they are today, were clearly positive predictors of use of newspapers. Age was a much more modest predictor, with those aged 20–29 fewer than 4 percentage points behind the next category and those aged 50–59 registering only 2 percentage points higher than those aged 60-plus—in effect, hardly any relationship at all. The Pew Center biennial survey of the national news audience, using a representative sample of more than 1,000, produces strikingly different results for the year 2000. About two-thirds (67 percent) of those 50 or older reported that they watched television news the day before, compared with 44 percent of those younger than 30, and 51 percent of 30- to 49-year-olds ("Internet sapping broadcast news audience," 2000). Similarly, 58 percent of those 50 or older reported reading a newspaper the day before, compared to 29 percent of those younger than 30, and 43 percent of 30- to 49-year-olds.

The role of age in going online for information depends on the particular use (Table 3.2). These Pew Center data identify overall use (Internet, web, e-mail) as strongly and inversely associated with age (Hamilton, 2004). Similar patterns occur for sports and entertainment. Nevertheless, news in general, and the topics of politics and health and science, display no marked association with age (although for political news, females aged 18–34 and males aged 35–49 are somewhat more likely to be users). Thus, age has little to do with use of the medium for news but quite a bit to do with which topics are of interest, with sports and entertainment particularly popular among younger age groups—which largely accounts for their greater online activity for these topics and greater online use in general (see Hamilton, 2004, Tables 3.3 and 7.1).

During the 2000 presidential campaign, 18 percent of Americans reported that they had gone online for elections news, up from only 4 percent in the 1996 presidential election ("Internet election news audience seeks convenience, familiar names," 2000). In the 2004 presidential election, 21 percent reported the Internet was one of their main sources of news, and when

TABLE 3.2 **Age, Gender, and Internet News Use**

		Percent					
		Females			Males		
	Total	18–34	35–49	50+	18–34	35–49	50+
Access Internet, web, e-mail	54	71	63	28	72	59	40
Of those going online							
At least 1–2 days per week for news	61	55	51	51	70	68	67
Political news	39	38	29	33	42	48	42
Entertainment news	44	57	41	35	54	35	27
Health/science news	63	66	67	71	60	58	60
Sports news	42	31	23	26	68	52	46

Adapted from *All the news that's fit to sell: How the market transforms into news*, by J. T. Hamilton, 2004, Princeton, NJ: Princeton University Press.

asked whether they received any news from the Internet, 41 percent reported in the affirmative ("Moral values: How important? Voters like campaign 2004, but too much 'mud slinging,'" 2004).

This pattern has two significant elements. The first is a distinct difference by age cohort in use of more traditional news media, including television. This finding is quite compatible with earlier data suggesting somewhat less interest among the younger cohort (under 30) in public affairs than was the case several decades ago (Comstock, 1991), with the exception of those events or occurrences of either particular interest or particular pertinence, such as violent events, sports, or issues that directly affect these younger individuals. The reduced use of more traditional media is countered by greater use of newer media, such as the Internet. The second element is the documentation that the means of news dissemination are undergoing a second revolution.

Thus, the burgeoning number of available news options creates a scenario in which the audience is further splintered and subgroups are accommodated variously by preferred media. One likely outcome for some, as Bimber and Davis (2003) point out, will be the exercise of greater selectivity to avoid discordant views. The huge diversity inherent in the Internet ironically will promote for some a narrowing of the range of views reaching them. Substantial numbers of Americans remain true to their local or regional newspaper, but the audience for newspapers has lost ground in all but the older age brackets. Nevertheless, television is likely to retain its preeminence as a news medium both by its prominent use and its perceived dominance as a source. This is because the Internet is better at present as a substitute for print media, and any visual coverage it can present will often have been recycled onto the small screen from television. Thus, the strength of the Internet is as a secondary medium of dissemination for well-established print and televisual media (Norris, 2000). These media are likely to dominate the Internet, far overshadowing (although unable to completely crowd out) independent voices, upstart innovative ventures, and rogues (Davis, 1999). They alone have the resources in their well-trained, efficient staffs and their in-place logistics of news gathering, along with occasional stars of journalism, to present an array of stories of sharp quality and comprehensiveness that on the whole will be familiar to and respected by users. The Internet will increase access to these media, providing users with a wider array of choices from which to select those that are ideologically congenial.

One of the great strengths of television news is its use of visuals. This is a narrative resource of great power, and we cannot see it supplanted by printed paragraphs, however transmitted. (The high-speed Internet access and latest computer processors necessary for the smooth, uninterrupted playing of video news footage from web sites are currently enjoyed by only a relatively small proportion of Americans.) We particularly do not see the displacement of local television news by the Internet, because its pleasures reside in the visual depiction of events in the local community with a certain reverence for celebrities, sites, and customs (the annual fair, the new mayor, the Greek festival, and the photo of the day in bucolic San Diego—with the latter frequently accompanied by mirthful comments about the snow and ice in the Northwest should the season be winter).

Though data collected over the past few decades has generally accorded national and local news with equal public favor (Comstock & Scharrer, 1999), the survey in the mid-nineties by Smith et al. (1997), which asked a representative national sample of more than 3,000 for evaluations of the news media on a variety of dimensions, reported unexpected enthusiasm and admiration for local news. The Internet as a news medium, then, is likely to be confined to information, which implies that its role will be greater for political news and sports (injuries, scores, entries and results at Santa Anita), as well as the most popular of television staples, the weather, rather than events, human interest, and news coverage in general. The other great potential for the Internet in politics is the new power it extends to politicians and parties to communicate directly with voters. The flexibility of web pages gives the self-interested communicator much greater latitude than print and television, which can exclude as well as include, and direct mail, which is slow and rigid in attention to events. The Internet offers not only a means of reaching voters directly, but a comparatively dramatic means of mobilizing support both in terms of votes and financial contributions. It will probably further diminish the roles of the two major parties by helping charismatic candidates communicate directly with supporters and build financial bases with many small rather than a few large contributions. Outsiders who are opposed by the party apparatus have won nominations before (George McGovern in 1972 is an example), but the Internet has the potential to make this more likely.

We are skeptical of the interpretation of Tolbert and McNeal (2003) of their National Election Study (NES) data for 1996 and 2000. They conclude that access to the Internet and online election news increased the "probability of voting" (by 12.5 and 7 percent, respectively, for the two media). The national samples are big enough (*N* = about 2,000), and representative. We acknowledge that the persistence of a greater probability of voting after statistical controls for socioeconomic status, partisanship, attitudes, use of other media, and aspects of the political environment eliminates some of the influence of self-selection. However, we are struck by an improbable circumstance: these increases occurred without any observable effect on turnout and without attracting attention from the antennae of the media.

Our own interpretation is that in these early days of the Internet and online news, those who would use these sources would be those with a particular interest in a given subject matter. In this case, that subject matter is politics and these same individuals would be more likely to vote (thus, the positive correlation between Internet and online use and voting). This is in accord with the general principle that Internet and online activity follows uses for earlier, traditional media rather than strutting out in new directions (Flanagan & Metzger, 2001). Surely, for most of these individuals the benefits of the Internet and online news would have been modest—the news is just quicker, more convenient, and more up-to-date.

Our reasoning nevertheless leads us to reserve judgment for when the Internet and online news become more available. Those previously lower in use of the news might then gain the advantage of access to major newspapers and specialized sources. Some small positive influence on voting then becomes conceivable; even so, we wonder why these persons would turn to the Internet or online news when they have ignored the easily accessible available sources of television and newspapers. What certainly would constrain any such effect of greater access to information is the comparatively low levels of political interest that are unlikely to be overcome by access to this new technology, because they have persisted in the past in the face of accessible media.

Campaign web sites are a very specialized arena. Bimber and Davis (2003) examined their audiences in the 2000 election by surveys and experimental designs. Those who patronized these sites were of higher socioeconomic status and had much greater interest in politics than the average citizen, and about four out of five were committed to a candidate. Use of campaign sites was infrequent compared to attending to the campaign in other media; only about 15 percent of adults saw a site compared to about 80 percent who paid "some" or more attention to the campaign in one or another medium. The principal motive for visiting a site was recreational ("browsing" was number one among the reasons named for visiting a site), but there also was quite frequently a search for information. For national candidates, who usually have received considerable coverage of personal characteristics, most often sought was information about positions on issues. However, for candidates in state-level races, who typically receive far less coverage of any sort, the most sought for information was on personal characteristics: background, achievements, family. This is testimony to the legitimacy of the presumption by the media of interest in such information by the public, and to the validity of Hamilton's (2004) argument that it is the least intellectually taxing aspects of political campaigns that are most attractive to the public. Nevertheless, there was a small minority of uncommitted voters seeking information about positions on issues, a modest amount of cross-site visiting (for example, about 16 percent visited both Bush and Gore sites, although this would include those checking out the opposition as well as comparison shoppers), and minority party sites receive a substantially higher proportion of visitors seeking information than those of major party candidates. Presumably, such information would be helpful to voters making up their minds, and particularly that about minority party candidates who receive much less coverage by the media in general. Nowhere in the data of Bimber and

Davis was there any evidence of campaign web site influence on voter turnout or voter choice. This further convinces us that it is unlikely that the Internet—although admittedly these data are confined to campaign web sites, with about 80 percent of the visits to the partisan sites of candidates—at this juncture promotes increased political participation through voter turnout.

The Internet is in its infancy in politics. Estimates from a nationally representative sample of households with children (Roberts & Foehr, 2004) in the late 1990s placed Internet connections at about 40 percent of households, with connection, as would be expected, positively associated with higher socioeconomic status. More recent figures show that approximately 60% of those 18 and older have at-home Internet access (Statistical Abstract of the United States, 2003) and high-speed, broadband Internet access is used by 48 million American adults from home (Pew Internet and American life project, 2004). We expect the political role of the Internet to expand with increasing access among households, greater familiarity with what it offers, and web sites that are easier to navigate and more attuned to the interests—and, in some cases, passions—of users.

B. Competition and Dissatisfaction

Increased competition clearly has an enormous and still-growing role in the ways media outlets of all types cover politics. In television, the nightly newscasts of the original three broadcast networks no longer compete only with each other but also with Fox, CNN, and other cable news channels, local television news that often now incorporates national stories, and the proliferation of entertainment programs available at the same time through cable and satellite transmission. Newspapers face a situation in which readership is declining, ownership is often concentrated in a conglomerate with multiple media holdings, and fierce competition no longer occurs from other newspapers in the same locale—now largely vanished—but from television, national newspapers, and the Internet, which will deliver coverage from well-known magazines and distant or national newspapers along with a mix of upstart and novel sources.

The financial health of newspapers has been affected by a number of factors. These include population shifts from certain parts of the country to others (e.g., from the Northeast to the South and Southwest) and from city centers to the suburbs. The former has undercut the reading public for some papers while significantly expanding it for others; the latter has brought about vast increases in the costs of getting papers from printing plants to readers and greater time lags between freshly printed news and delivery to the reader. Other adverse developments include the rising cost of newsprint; the lack of personal relationships between retail entrepreneurs who might advertise and newspapers as chain stores have grown; and the sociological changes that have altered the composition of the American household and loosened ties between individuals and their surrounding communities and thus the governance and civic aspects of those communities as contrasted with the entertainment, sports, shopping, and employment opportunities they offer (Bogart, 1989; Putnam, 2000).

Heightened competition has created a paradoxical situation in which news organizations both vie to distinguish themselves from others by uncovering "the big scoop" in the political realm (breaking a news story that no other organization has reported) and at the same time frequently become one of the "pack" in reporting the same stories as their competitors. The ironic juxtaposition of competition and the cooperation of "pack journalism" was dissected in Timothy Crouse's *The Boys on the Bus*, an account of the group of reporters who traveled together for several weeks at a time to cover the 1972 presidential candidates. The chummy quarters of the pack in that intimate setting, as well as the use of pool reporters in general in reporting on everything from elections to the recent war in Iraq, allows for a sharing of experiences and good will—and occasionally of notes—that generates homogeneity in news accounts. In less close-knit situations, pack journalism occurs through the modeling of "elite" news sources, such as the *New York Times* or the *Washington Post*. Journalistic history suggests that when a political story makes the pages of these elite news sources, smaller newspapers and other news media outlets will usually follow suit and report on the same story. Pack journalism, then, sets in out of fear of failing to cover what will become the next big story and therefore appearing noncompetitive to the audience (Nimmo & Combs, 1983). The result is that the search for the original story that stuns readers or viewers and embarrasses the competition is largely confined to the elite media, although in those situations where public interest is high and news sources abound—as was the case in Los Angeles with the O.J. Simpson murder trial—almost every conceivable outlet will be breaking a story at one time or another.

The contemporary scene features a staggering increase in the diversity of television channels along with the wide availability of a variety of print media in all but the smallest and most remote communities. These outlets, in addition to the great amounts of entertainment they provide and the many personal interests they serve, produce a wide assortment of news formats able to appeal to viewers and readers varying widely themselves in educational background, political interest, and cognitive ability.

With a heightened emphasis on commercial viability, the scandalous scoop, the packaged and easily scanned news story, and the eyebrow-raising status of the horse race are appealing practices for all news media attempting to attract audiences. The conventional view is that the decline of newspapers and the continuing prominence of television constitutes a net loss in the quality of political coverage given attention by readers and viewers. However, several authors offer a distinctly more optimistic interpretation (Graber, 1997, 2001; Neuman, Just, & Crigler, 1992; Norris, 2000). Coverage of high quality is said to be still widely available, and certainly sufficiently so for anyone who wishes to seek it out. Television makes many stories more understandable, and certainly more interesting than would occur for many print accounts, and does so especially for the less cognitively adept and skilled who would be less able to envision the events described by newspaper prose as exciting or interesting. The wide variety of media makes it possible for many more people to encounter political coverage. The argued consequence of the glass-is-half-full authors is that the new media landscape offers more coverage and greater access to politics for a greater diversity of readers and viewers.

We are inclined to agree, on the grounds that the "net loss" argument confounds the ideal with the practical. Ideally, media would be demanding of their audiences, and insistent in the depth and breadth of their coverage, but in fact large numbers of media consumers choose undemanding over more demanding fare whether it is entertainment, sports, or news (Goodhardt, Ehrenberg, & Collins, 1987; Hamilton, 1998, 2004). Nevertheless, the competitive milieu ensures that the fist of economics commands the table. Sabato (1991) makes the point succinctly: ". . . (C)ontemporary corporate managers of print and broadcast media are closely attuned to the contribution each outlet makes to the overall profit or loss of a company. Ratings and circulation increasingly matter . . ." (p. 56). The route of television during the second half of the century as it reached maturity as a ubiquitous medium and became a factor in elections at every important level—gubernatorial, Senate, House, but especially the presidency—was marked out by the search for profits. This is the case for most media in a commercial, capitalist culture where private enterprise plays a dominant role (Bogart, 2000). The significance is that news values and the ideal of informing the public are tempered by the need to serve the economic interests of the particular outlet in surviving, which means that news must have popular appeal (Hamilton, 2004; Himmelstein, 1994)—a positive factor in providing an incentive to make political stories interesting but less positive in providing incentives to avoid controversy, mollify the politically powerful, court a favorable public impression and generally favor news that is thoroughly palatable. The result is that the news is not only constructed to be as interesting as possible, so that viewers and readers will enjoy attending to it, but tailored by media outlets to fit the audiences they have or wish to attract. The coverage of hard news by television rises and falls at the local level with signs among the audience of interest in such topics, as indicated by the per capita sales of newsmagazines (Hamilton, 2004). Network evening news, whose most diligent viewers are those over 50, attempts to lure the young adult females aged 18–34 who occasionally watch, who are of particular value to advertisers (and young adult males in the same age bracket, who are less sought after by advertisers), by covering issues in which they are known to be interested, such as gun control and education (Hamilton, 2004). This tailoring—chasing the audience, in more colorful terms—is particularly pronounced in television news, where every viewer will have an equal chance to see every item. Newspapers can be read more selectively than television news can be viewed, and so can meet the challenge of appealing to particular audience segments by including items that other segments can ignore without losing interest in reading the paper (Hamilton, 2004).

Palatability and competition, of course, are not entirely compatible. The latter triumphs with a scoop—which may risk inaccuracy—and revelations—which may risk offense—while the former makes residence with the status quo and the conventional. The penalty has been some signs of disenchantment and diminished confidence among the public. The Pew Research Center's survey of approximately 1,500 randomly selected adults found that only about one-third (35 percent) of Americans agreed that the press "usually get the facts straight" in early 2001, down from 55 percent in 1985 ("Terror coverage boosts news media's images," 2001). About one-third also viewed the press as "too critical of America" (36 percent), said the press "hurt democracy" (32 percent), and judged the press as "immoral" (34 percent) in early 2001. All of these figures represent increases since 1985 but the most marked was the jump in those deeming the press "immoral," up 21 percentage points. In contrast, as the title of the report asserts, news media coverage of the events of September 11, 2001, received very high marks by the public and led to a marked rally in favorable opinions of the press, evident in data collected in November of 2001.

The degree of the public's satisfaction with the news media's handling of elections was at least temporarily weakened by the controversies surrounding the 2000 presidential election. The Pew Research Center's nationally representative poll of more than 1,000 voters the weekend after the election suggests that the public was quite satisfied with the media's performance during the campaign ("Campaign 2000 highly rated," 2000). Seventy-five percent said they had learned enough about the candidates to make a choice, 62 percent found the debates helpful, 46 percent thought there was greater attention to issues, and 46 percent thought there was less mudslinging in the coverage than in the previous campaign. Election night was another matter. Sixty-nine percent expressed anger or disappointment with the premature call that Bush had won the election. About half (52 percent) believed the inaccurate declaration that Gore had won Florida may have influenced voters in other parts of the country. About the same number (53 percent) endorsed the statement that the media had too much of an influence on the election. Despite the favorable evaluations of campaign coverage registered on some dimensions,

39 percent graded the news media with a "D" or an "F" for their handling of the election.

The polling problems, miscues, and rush to judgment that led the television networks to change their minds repeatedly about who was the next president in 2000 led to an even greater debacle in the election of 2002 ("Voter news service: What went wrong?" 2003). The principal difference was that the lower profile of the contests—for governor, Senate, and House—made it possible for the media to hide what one account called a "perfect storm" from the public. The members of the Voter News Service (VNS) consortium—ABC, CBS, NBC, Fox, CNN, and the Associated Press—had decided after 2000 to completely revamp the computer-based projection system. One of the features was intended to collect exit poll data from 30,000 observers with a voice recognition system. Data pools were to be combined for more ready access. Projections were to be instantly available, and would use past voting patterns for comparison. Almost nothing worked, despite estimated expenditures of between $10 and $15 million. The voice recognition system regularly cut off callers before they could complete their data input. Past election data were not available. The projections were starkly wrong. For example, the computer early had Erskine Bowles leading Elizabeth Dole for the North Carolina Senate seat, and the margin grew as the day progressed. Alas, Dole won by almost 200,000 votes. The programming was inept, the system had not been thoroughly tested, and the divisions of authority among the participants had led to ineffectual implementation. As the storm subsided, the media quietly dissolved VNS. In the future, they will rely more on their own polling, data supplied by the Associated Press, and because of the benefits of cost sharing, perhaps new cooperative endeavors. The lessons are that technology is severely limited by the human talent that puts it to work, and that the failures of the media largely escape public notice except for those that are extraordinarily prominent.

The public's rating of Election Night coverage rebounded in 2004, according to a national sample of over 1,200 respondents ("Moral values: How important? Voters like campaign 2004, but too much 'mudslinging,'" 2004). Just over half (52 percent) said news organizations did "a good job," 22 percent rated them "fair" and more extreme judgments were less widely held (17 percent called the performance "excellent" while eight percent called it "poor"). These ratings were largely the same for Bush and Kerry supporters.

C. Hostile Media

Substantial proportions of the American public find the news media somewhat politically biased. This has been true throughout the past century, as data on television from the 1970s and 1980s attest (Bower, 1973, 1985). What has changed is the degree of the perception of bias and its far more prominent location at one end of the political spectrum (Table 3.3). In the mid-1990s, 62 percent of a nationally representative sample of more than 3,000 described the news media as having either a liberal or a conservative slant when covering politics (Smith, Lichter, & Harris, 1997). Those television data from the 1970s and 1980s put the comparable figure between 20 and 30 percent. Perceptions of political bias in the more recent data were dependent on the political ideology of the respondent; more respondents who identified themselves as conservative perceived a liberal media bias than vice versa (Smith, Lichter, & Harris, 1997). This result represents a change from past data that have shown approximately equal perceptions of media bias on the part of those who label themselves conservative, liberal, or middle-of-the-road (Bower, 1973, 1985).

Indeed, essentially the same pattern of a perception of a liberal bias continued for coverage of the 2000 presidential election, with somewhat more respondents believing that Al Gore received a more fair news treatment than George Bush. Of the respondents surveyed by the Pew Research Center, 65 percent said the news media were fair to Bush and 74 percent said they were fair to Gore ("Media seen as fair, but tilting to Gore," 2000). A key difference in opinion emerges, however, according to political party affiliation. Only 48 percent of Republicans saw the news media as being fair to Bush, whereas 72 percent of Republicans viewed the news media as being fair to Gore. No such discrepancy occurred for respondents identifying themselves as Democrats—the same percentage of Democrats, 75 percent, reported that the news media were fair to Gore and fair to Bush. A similar pattern appears for the question about which

TABLE 3.3 Political Ideology and Perceptions of Bias

	Political Philosophy of Respondent			
How would you describe the views of the media on most matters having to do with politics?	Total	Liberal	Middle of the Road	Conservative
Sample size (*N*)	3,004	760	1,008	1,173
Respondent said	Percent of respondents			
Liberal	43	40	30	57
Middle of the road	33	34	47	19
Conservative	19	21	16	21
Don't know	5	6	6	3
Refused to say	—	—	—	1

Adapted from *What the People Want from the Press*, by T. J. Smith, S. R. Lichter, and L. Harris and Associates, 1997, Washington, DC: Center for Media and Public Affairs.

candidate most journalists seemed to be "pulling for." Of all respondents, 23 percent perceived journalists to be pulling for Bush and 47 percent perceived them pulling for Gore. Of those identifying themselves as Republicans, only 12 percent perceived journalists to be pulling for Bush and two-thirds (67 percent) perceived them pulling for Gore. In contrast, the Democrats were nearly equally split, with 36 percent perceiving journalists to be pulling for Gore and 30 percent perceiving them pulling for Bush.

Members of both parties largely agreed that media coverage of politics is swayed by the views of journalists, with 86 percent of Democrats and 90 percent of Republicans agreeing that "political views influence coverage" ("Media seen as fair, but tilting toward Gore," 2000). These figures have increased since 1992, again suggesting a trend toward increased suspicion of partisan bias.

One conclusion to be drawn from these data is that most Americans believe the ideal of political neutrality in election reporting is largely a myth rather than a reality. Indeed, data from the same source (the Pew Research Center) collected in 2004 found 31 percent of respondents believed the press was unfair to candidate Kerry and 40 percent thought the press was unfair to candidate Bush ("Moral values: How important? Voters like campaign 2004, but too much 'mudslinging,'" 2004). Yet, the differences that emerge according to political party should not be ignored. In recent data, Republicans more than Democrats perceive that news media are hostile to their own political interests. These data identify a particular sensitivity on the part of conservatives and Republicans (a substantial proportion of which are conservatives) to their treatment by the media, a product of the intense ideological enthusiasm at the present time among conservatives, and they suggest that the rhetorical strategy (Robinson & Sheehan, 1983) on the part of Republican leaders to decry the "liberal news media" has been successful.

We interpret this pattern as representing the "hostile media phenomenon" (Comstock & Scharrer, 1999). This concept first appeared in an experiment by Vallone, Ross, and Lepper (1985) in which identical tapes of ABC, CBS, and NBC news coverage of the Middle East were shown to pro-Arab and pro-Israeli groups. Each side pointed the finger of benefit at the other, perceiving the media as hostile to their partisan interests. The pro-Arabs perceived the media as favoring Israel; the pro-Israelis perceived the media as favoring the Arabs. More informed individuals on both sides were more likely to perceive bias. This contradicts the popular view among news personnel that the better informed are more likely to perceive the media as fair because they will understand better the subject matter. Not so, when passions run strong. Instead, knowledge increases perceived hostility because it enhances the ability to perceive distortions. Perloff (1989) later replicated this effect experimentally with pro-Israeli and pro-Palestinian subjects. The patterns we have just seen in the data of Smith, Lichter, and Harris and the Pew Research Center perfectly fit the hostile media phenomenon. Those who label themselves as conservative today are particularly conscious of their partisanship, have particularly forceful allegiances to their ideals, and have inherited from long-standing complaints about the liberal biases of the media a heightened sensitivity to media portrayals.

D. COLLECTIVE TO INDIVIDUAL

Presidential politics has been converted from campaigns in which the two major political parties shared prominence with the media to nearly pure media campaigns in which the conventions of journalism, and particularly those of television journalism, are dominant (Patterson, 1993, 2002). One of the key factors contributing to the increase in the power and prominence of the media's role in politics is lower levels of partisanship on the part of the American public (Wattenberg, 1996)—so much so that the media now occupy the role that the political party had enjoyed in guiding voter opinion and support (Dautrich & Hartley, 1999). For example, the three-study analysis of Comstock and Scharrer (1999), drawing on the research by Bartels (1993), Holbrook (1996), and Domke and colleagues (1997) that together present data from more than 150,000 respondents and variously cover five elections, make a strong case for media influence on the perception of issues, candidate image, support for a candidate, and the intention to actually vote for one or another presidential aspirant. Trends identified earlier (DeVries & Tarrance, 1972; Nie, Verba, & Petrocik, 1976) have continued to appear in more recent National Election Studies (NES) data (Wattenberg, 1996). These (NES) data demonstrate a near-linear decline in party identification from the 75 percent of Americans who considered themselves either Democrats or Republicans in 1952 to the 61 percent who so labeled themselves 40 years later in 1992. Not only has identification decreased, but strength of feelings about political parties has declined as well. In the NES data, only 13 percent of Americans described their feelings toward the parties as neutral in 1952, whereas in 1992 the figure was 32 percent. Furthermore, oscillation voting by casting a ballot for candidates from different parties from election to election has increased. In 1952, NES data revealed that only 29 percent of voters reported that they had ever voted for a Republican presidential candidate in one election year and a Democratic candidate in another. In 1996, Dautrich and Hartley (1999) found that a full 63 percent had done so.

The decline in voter identification with political parties stems in part from the decline in party power. The presidential candidate nominating procedure has undergone reforms that have shifted the power to advance the nomination of a candidate from party machinery and party professionals to the voting public. This has occurred through sweeping changes in the way the delegates who vote at the nominating conventions are selected (Patterson, 1980). Between 1916 and 1968, fewer than one-third of national convention delegates were elected through primaries. More than two-thirds were chosen in state conventions that were largely controlled by party leaders. However, in 1968, efforts to reform the process in behalf of greater voter participation triumphed. In 1972, about 50 percent of the delegates were chosen in state primaries and by 1976 that figure had increased to 70 percent (Ranney, 1977). In addition, most of the states that do not hold primaries hold caucuses that are much freer of party control than were conventions because participation is not as restricted. In many states, it is possible for a voter to participate in whichever primary or caucus he or she chooses regardless of past party membership or declared party affiliation. The result is that the role of the political party in the choosing of delegates has dwindled, opening the door for more open and less predictable outcomes via the primary and the caucus. The news media's coverage of the primaries has established them as the normative means of choosing candidates (Rubin, 1980). Serious candidates have no choice but to appeal directly to voters to secure the nomination, and to use the media—rather than the political parties—to attempt to secure a favorable position in the nominating process.

The political party's role in the election process declined while the capabilities of the modern media grew. Until television had near-saturated American households and its political coverage had achieved considerable sophistication in news gathering and reporting in the early 1960s, the parties remained an advantageous way for candidates to reach voters through party-organized canvassing and by appealing to party loyalty (Patterson, 1980). The options available to a candidate for using the news media as a means of advancing a campaign in the early to mid-twentieth century were limited by the geographically constrained distribution of newspapers that made reaching a national audience laborious and difficult, and the infancy of television news, which in its earliest years relied heavily on the same wire services and other sources as print news and featured only very short reports on candidates. In 1963, however, the television networks introduced their 30-minute nightly newscasts that remain in place to this day, and since then coverage on the nightly network news has become a major goal of presidential aspirants due to its national audience and opportunity to feature candidates in full dimension—videos and sound bites combining to convey an impression of a person rather than a representation in print or photo. In the meantime, changes in the way newspapers operate led to a renewal of their political prominence. Wire services, exemplified by the Associated Press founded in 1848 by six New York publishers, had since the middle of the nineteenth century made it possible for newspapers to present news from afar, and national campaigns for the presidency were certainly among the topics in which these services specialized. However, faced with the competition from television, newspapers gave their major political coverage a more personal and aggressive stance by beginning the now common practice of assigning reporters to travel with candidates. This enlarged the reportorial frame from the local to the region and the nation. In addition, the consolidation of newspapers into chains offered these reporters a far wider stage. Thus, competition led to the supplementation of the wire services by more vigorous political reporting. The consequence was enhanced distribution of election news (Patterson, 1980).

The shift from an emphasis on a collective (the party) to the individual (a candidate) plays perfectly into the strengths of television and its ability to personalize the news and foster a sense of intimacy and connection with viewers (Hart, 1999). For example, seeing the candidates on television news has the same effect as conversations with friends, family, and coworkers—both increase confidence of the voter about his or her tentative choice (Lucas & Adams, 1978). With the weakening of the push and pull of the political parties and the simultaneous ascendance of the news media led by television, the logic of television prevails once again. In a climate in which disenchantment with both major parties is on the rise and many members of the public believe the parties are no longer significantly different from one another, the candidate as an individual, rather than as a representative and spokesperson for a party, emerges. In this setting, television fits the needs of both candidates and the public.

Party loyalty bestows stability and predictability that has been increasingly absent in presidential elections. There is no longer certainty about the base of party-oriented support at the polls (although it will certainly be there in some magnitude), the transmission of loyalty to a party across generations, or the role of newly presented information merely reinforcing prior party ties, as had largely been the case in the past (Berelson, Lazarsfeld, & McPhee, 1954; Converse, 1966; Fiorina, 1981; Jennings & Niemi, 1983; Lazarsfeld, Berelson, & Gaudet, 1948). What results is an expanded role for the news media:

> Today, however, because of the weakening of partisanship, the vote is less predictable and more volatile. It also is more sensitive to short-term influences, such as an election's issues and personalities, which are transmitted largely by the media. Voters' evaluations of the candidates are now based more heavily on what they learn through the media during the campaign. Correspondingly, the candidates' fates depend more heavily on their media coverage (Patterson, 1980, p.6).

E. Horizon

The top national news stories of the day typically are closely followed by only about half of the public, and for most stories the proportion is much less. Often these stories have little to do with politics, and concern sensational crimes (such as the Washington, DC–area sniper attacks, and Columbine school shootings), natural disasters, or airline crashes.

We make these estimates from the proportions of people saying they have closely followed particular stories in the periodic Pew Research Center surveys of the public's attention to the news and from the percentage saying they typically follow the national news closely. Those who do in the future are likely to use the Internet more and the traditional media, including television, less ("Internet sapping broadcast news audience," 2000). The Pew Research Center's biennial survey of the national news audience—using a nationally representative sample of over 1,000 respondents—shows that in the year 2000, one in every three Americans accessed the Internet for news at least once per week, up from one in every five in 1998. A small but substantial number—15 percent—reported going online for news every day. During the same time period (from 1998 to 2000), regular viewing of network news fell from 38 to 30 percent and regular viewing of local news dropped from 64 to 56 percent. Interestingly, cable news viewing seemed unaffected by Internet news use, remaining fairly stable over the period. This is not a surprise. Media with much smaller audiences usually will be less vulnerable to alternative means of dissemination because their users will have chosen them for their particular features. More popular outlets are more often chosen for convenience, and will be supplanted when more convenient outlets become available. As we argued earlier, this trend is likely to continue as the Internet sees greater usage generally, the technology that delivers news by this means becomes easier to use, content becomes more compelling, and younger cohorts who presumably will be more likely to use the Internet enter the news audience. However, the Internet as a news medium will be dominated by the three great media already in place: the broadcast and cable networks, the newspapers, and the newsmagazines (Davis, 1999; Norris, 2000). Thus, the shift has much more to do with the means than the content of the news.

The Goods

I. **Under the Magnifying Glass**
  A. Status
  B. Scandals and Missteps
  C. They're Off!
  D. Sound Bites
  E. Bias
  F. Civic Disenchantment
II. **On the Shelves**
  A. Election Day
  B. Advertising
  C. Debates
III. **Narrative and Normalization**

The news media have been subjected to numerous criticisms for their political coverage. These include negativity, an emphasis on the horse race instead of the issues, the foreclosing of access by politicians to the public through the sound bite (and the intrusive glorification of those representing the media), and the framing of stories in ways that alienate voters and heighten their skepticism of the motives of politicians and perceptions of bias (Bucy & D'Angelo, 2004; Cappella & Jamieson, 1997; Lichter, Rothman, & Lichter, 1986; Patterson, 1993, 2002; Sigelman & Bullock, 1991; Smith, Lichter, & Harris, 1997). We begin our close examination of this coverage with these emphases in everyday campaign and political journalism, and then turn to three staples of political content: election-day coverage, political advertising, and presidential debates.

I. UNDER THE MAGNIFYING GLASS

Patterson (1993) documents several of these trends in the handling of presidential candidates by the media in his *Out of Order*. One trend is greater scrutiny of candidates leading to marked increases in negativity in coverage. Patterson traces this shift to the defining experiences of journalists while covering the Vietnam War and the Watergate scandal. In both cases, information was withheld and outright mistruths were advanced by high-ranking officials. A newfound wariness has since characterized reporting on political leaders. This is evident in the data Patterson collected from over 4,000 stories in *Time* and *Newsweek* covering major party presidential candidates from 1960 to 1992. Evaluative statements of the candidates made by reporters in the stories were 75 percent favorable in 1960 and only 40 percent favorable in 1992.

A. Status

Favorability of news coverage is related to the competitive status of the candidate. Patterson (1993) identifies four possible positions of candidates during the presidential primaries and caucuses. Each typically triggers a distinct response by the press. When polls indicate that a particular candidate has been gathering increasing support, this "bandwagon"—at least in the short run until frontrunner status is achieved—is usually reflected in favorable coverage. In this situation a candidate meets the definition of a good, dramatic story by having emerged from the pack in terms of popularity and prominence. The typical result is favorable attention. Conversely, the candidate seen as "losing ground" has a double-edged sword with which to contend. The bad news of his or her position in the polls, also the subject of news coverage, is usually coupled with unfavorable treatment by the news media. Somewhat similarly, those identified as "likely losers" based on polls shoulder increasingly unfavorable coverage. The drop in favorableness is not as dramatic as it is for those "losing ground" because they do not typically have as far to fall, but it is nevertheless substantial. Finally, the "frontrunner" usually attracts somewhat mixed coverage, favorable in terms of his or her advantageous position but unfavorable in scrutiny of the tactics and strategies involved in achieving and attempting to maintain the lead and of personal and political credentials (Robinson & Sheehan, 1983). This is the focus and discard process discussed earlier in Chapter 3.

One advantage of frontrunner or likely contender status is that those positions are sure to generate substantial amounts of attention in the news. For example, after the 1976 New Hampshire primary in which Jimmy Carter emerged as the leader for the Democratic nomination, his photo was on the cover of both *Time* and *Newsweek* and he received three times as many newsmagazine story lines and four times as much newspaper and television coverage as the other Democratic contenders combined (Patterson, 1980). There were also temporary increases in coverage of the other Democratic nominee hopefuls after primary wins in other states. The media shift attention from one frontrunner and set of leading challengers to new frontrunners and challengers in accord with polls and the results of primaries and caucuses (Comstock & Scharrer, 1999). Future success is likely to be contingent on media coverage, and media coverage is a function of past success or eminent promise; the media are gatekeepers for the access to the public of candidates, and the key to the gate is popularity. The news media, and especially television with its special studio sets and logos declaring election coverage, and articulate commentators (who, by election day, will have become quite familiar), have established the caucuses and primaries as central to election coverage because those contests meet the qualifications of newsworthiness and exemplify the narrative structure of the ideal news story: conflict with a resolution. The result has been the earlier initiation by several months of intensive news media attention to a presidential race, and the lengthening of presidential campaigns.

The media's power to give shape to electoral contests by choosing the stories to report and the frames by which they are cast constitutes considerable authority. A race requires a field of competitors, and the media contribute early by identifying likely prospects. Later, emerging contenders, frontrunners, those losing ground, and likely losers are depicted. The coverage goes to the candidates in the more advantageous positions, so that the voices of opponents become muffled. These contributions by the media take place within the parameters established by events, which sometimes will be surprising. The media influence but cannot control electoral events; they can with certainty only exploit them. The reporting of a loss of momentum and a consequent perception on the part of the public of dwindling popularity can render a deathblow to a campaign. Nimmo and Combs (1983) discuss the creation by the media of a hierarchy of likely success.

> Because a melodrama is a simplification of complexities, the imperative demands that, if there are a large number of candidates entering the contest for a party's nomination, they must be narrowed, or winnowed, down quickly. Otherwise the plot line is confusing; audiences may be lost. To anticipate how the winnowing will go, the news media rely on a number of indicators—opinion polls, assessments by experienced politicians and observers, the status of each candidate's campaign organization, who is supporting whom, the size of the contenders' financial war chests, even the amount of coverage the media themselves are giving respective candidates (p. 55).

B. Scandals and Missteps

Scandals and controversies unveiled in the course of the campaign also contribute to negativity of coverage. Patterson (1993) distinguishes between "policy problems" covered in the news—topics that have to do with "how the government should act"—and "campaign controversies"—those that have to do with "how the candidate should act" (p. 146). Controversies discovered and brought to light (typically by journalists themselves) during the campaign comprised around 30 percent of issue stories in *Time* and *Newsweek* from 1960 to 1972, but grew to approximately 50–60 percent from 1976 to 1992 (Patterson, 1993). At the same time, issue stories focusing on policy problems decreased. The press tends to jump on gaffes and missteps (from Jimmy Carter's "lust in my heart" to Dan Quayle's spelling error and Bill Clinton's sexual dalliances), thrusting those topics onto the agenda with some force. Additional past studies have found a similar trend toward focusing attention on campaign misdeeds and away from policy issues (Clancy & Robinson, 1985; Lichter, Amundson, & Noyes, 1989).

This proclivity of the press was memorably described by Sabato (1991):

> . . . (T)he news media, print and broadcast, go after a wounded politician like sharks in a feeding frenzy. The wounds may have been self-inflicted, and the politician may richly deserve his or her fate, but the journalists now take center stage in the process, creating the news as much as reporting it, changing both the shape of election-year politics and the contours of government (p. 1).

The frenzy occurs when multiple press outlets pursue a scandalous revelation or an unfortunate gaffe. There is a surfeit, and arguable excess, because the topic remains on the news agenda at the expense of other, often more significant, stories and the damage done to the individual in hindsight often will seem unjust in magnitude. Examples of scandals past range from the insensitive and offensive (e.g., the reference to New York City as "hymietown" by Jesse Jackson in 1984) to the tragic (e.g., the drowning of a campaign aide in the company of Senator Edward Kennedy off Chappaquiddick Island).

Scandals do often attract the attention of the public, so it is understandable that they would be attractive to journalists. Although the behavior involved is often rather commonplace, these scandals teeter into the spotlight on the grounds that they represent the violation of norms to which the well-known and prominent are supposed to adhere. What raises questions about the performance of the press are the types of scandals thought to be fair game—many are highly personal and private in nature and presumably unrelated to job performance—and the ways in which the scandals are pursued by dogged reporters (Sabato, 1991). Many journalists defend the hyper-scrutiny of candidates as a necessary strategy to cut through the spin of events provided by campaign managers and public relations professionals. Yet, this seems to miss the point because it is not the products of political spin that are at issue. As Jamieson and Waldman (2003) argue, many journalists extend the role of watchdog, standing vigilant to check the power of the government and fight against corruption, to the role of amateur psychologist, attempting to bridge the distance between public persona of candidates and their private selves.

Attention to Al Gore's stoicism or Bill Clinton's "appetites," then, results from reporters' "psychological profiling that seeks patterns in these private and public moments and from them draws inferences with a broad brush" (Jamieson & Waldman, 2003, pp. 24–25), while at the same time failing to make convincing links to performance in office with the foibles they have exploited.

C. They're Off!

The most striking observations Patterson (1993) makes about the news media's treatment of politicians concern the reliance on framing the political process as a game or a horse race. He recounts several anecdotes documenting stark differences between the policy-relevant content of stump speeches by candidates followed by policy-related questions from members of the live audience and the ensuing news media coverage. Consistently, the media ignore the information on the positions held by candidates and the concerns of potential voters in favor of the current standings of candidates in the race toward election. In explaining why the news media emphasize the sprints, stumbles, and second winds that candidates experience en route toward victory or defeat, Patterson points to the conventions of news gathering and reporting that are steadfastly held by journalists.

> The first fact of journalistic life is that the reporter must have a story to tell. . . . The news is not a mirror held up to society. It is a selective rendition of events told in story form. For this reason, the conventions of news reporting include an emphasis on the more dramatic and controversial aspects of politics. . . . The game is always moving: candidates are continually adjusting to the dynamics of the race and their position in it. Since it can almost always be assumed that the candidates are driven by a desire to win, their actions can hence be interpreted as an effort to acquire votes. The game is thus a perpetually reliable source of fresh material (pp. 60–61).

Television employs the game or horse race metaphor more frequently than the other news media (Graber, 1997). One reason is that most television news stories are short (average of 90 seconds) and need to be straightforward and simple because the audience member is attending at a pace dictated by the reporter or anchor rather than reading at his or her own pace and reviewing when necessary what has already been read (Patterson, 1980). Television also is typically more interpretive and less descriptive compared to newspapers, and for essentially the same reason; the brevity of the stories do not give viewers the same opportunity as those reading much longer accounts in newspapers of making their own interpretations (Patterson, 1980). However, framing an election story with the qualities and figures of speech of a game or a race is a fairly common practice in every news medium (Graber, 1997).

The language of election coverage is thoroughly wedded to the lingo of the racetrack, as the journalist Paul Volponi has pointed out ("Track Talk," 2003). A surprise winner is said to have pulled an "upset," which derives from Man o' War's sole lifetime loss to Upset in the 1919 Sanford Memorial at Saratoga. There is always a "frontrunner" (although no "speed horses"), a "field" of candidates, and contests are often described as "neck and neck" and "coming down to the wire." A candidate unlikely to win (but not without interest to the media because of the possibility of an upset) is a "dark horse." This term joins *upset* in having a distinguished etymology. It is attributed to Benjamin Disraeli who in 1831 remarked, "a dark horse, which had never been thought of, rushed past the grandstand in sweeping triumph." There is even a "bounce," although it has the opposite meaning in the two jurisdictions (in politics, it refers to the gain in popularity for a candidate that usually follows immediately upon a party's nominating convention; at the track, it refers to a sudden regression after a particularly good performance, and derives from the arcane practice of the Ragozin sheets of using larger numbers to represent poorer performances—so that, when graphed, a lesser performance appears as an upward bounce).

The shift toward a dramatically more frequent emphasis on the game of the presidential race and away from a central position for policy-oriented stories is apparent in Patterson's *Time* and *Newsweek* data. They depict a decided increase in use of game or horse race frames, with twice as many such stories in 1992 compared to 1960. At the same time, stories framed toward policy issues decreased from 50 percent in 1960 to less than 20 percent in 1992. We have already seen the same trend in newspapers for game or horse race coverage, and the same data show a decline in issue coverage since the late 1940s (Sigelman & Bullock, 1991). Another recent analysis, investigating sources used in coverage of governor's races in 15 daily newspapers, found experts commenting on the horse race (such as pollsters) appeared about twice as often in news stories than experts commenting on the issues (Freedman & Fico, 2004).

D. Sound Bites

A simultaneous and related shift in television news coverage of politics is seen in the shrinking size of the sound bites of political leaders. These are the occasions when the news carries excerpts from their actual words. Often, but not always, these excerpts are accompanied by video footage of the individual. The sound bite has been a frequent target of criticism. The sound bite certainly exemplifies the tendency of television news to reduce potentially complex and multifaceted statements to a small number of words and phrases that may or may not represent the whole. The shrinking length similarly represents the intrusiveness of a medium, but in a different way—here, television usurps the politician's role of spokesperson and substitutes the medium's own commentators. When covering appearances and speeches, television now more often speaks for politicians rather than allowing them to speak for themselves.

Defining a sound bite as a "block of uninterrupted speech by a candidate on television news" (Patterson, 1993, p. 74), Hallin (1992) found in samples of the three network evening newscasts over six presidential elections beginning in 1968 that sound bites of the candidates became progressively and dramatically shorter, falling from 43.1 seconds to 8.9 seconds. Adatto (1990), examining the entire universe of evening newscasts by the three networks for 1968 and 1988 found a similar decline from 42.3 seconds to slightly less than 10 seconds. A similar length of 10 seconds was recorded in another content analysis of 1992 election coverage ("Clinton's the One," 1992). In both of these election years (1988 and 1992), reporters and anchors spoke for 6 minutes for every minute that the candidates spoke for themselves in the form of a sound bite ("Clinton's the One," 1992). A parallel trend has occurred in newspaper coverage (Stempel & Windhauser, 1991). Patterson (1993) recorded the average length of a continuous quote from a candidate in front-page *New York Times* stories in 1960 at 14 lines compared to 6 lines in 1992.

Patterson offers three reasons for the diminishing size of the sound and print bite. First, candidates have changed the ways they campaign in light of the central role of the news media, and particularly television. They have attempted to play to the cameras and, by extension, the American public, by consciously conveying an image by way of a forceful, readily quotable statement. Second, the prestige associated with the journalism profession has contributed to a larger role for the journalist. As some journalists (Woodward and Bernstein, Walter Cronkite, Dan Rather, Peter Jennings, Tom Brokaw, Barbara Walters) became celebrities themselves, journalists became players in and not just observers of the political process, often interpreting the news rather than reporting it. Finally, the rising centrality of news stories based on polling has pushed out other election-oriented content. These arguments, though formulated largely to apply to television, also apply to some degree to newspapers. The parallel between trends for television and newspapers suggests that, while the particular characteristics of the medium of television probably played a role, another factor is a general trend in the news media to shift toward thematic, interpretative narratives and away from description confined to what has transpired (Barnhurst & Mutz, 1997; Mutz, 1998).

Polls have certainly had an influence on election coverage in all media, and they encourage the game or horse race frame by providing scores. In the 1970s, many prominent news organizations began conducting their own polls or teaming up with commercial polling companies (e.g., Gallup, Harris, Roper Starch, Yankelovich) to gather and report poll results (Mutz, 1998). Since then, the prominence of polls in both television and newspaper coverage of elections has become greater and references in newspaper coverage have become more frequent (Traugott, 1992). For example, stories that pertained to polls comprised 10 percent of the total amount of election coverage in 1980 (Stovall & Solomon, 1984). Eight years later, poll stories accounted for 53 percent of *Washington Post* and 37 percent of *New York Times* election stories during the month of October (Ratzan, 1989).

E. Bias

The most vocal and widely publicized advocate of the view that the media are dominated by liberals was Richard Nixon's vice president (until he was indicted for misuse of funds while he was Maryland's governor), Spiro Agnew. However, empirical evidence in behalf of such a view traces to data collected by Lichter, Rothman, and Lichter (1986). They surveyed persons employed at major media organizations in the Northeast, and found that 54 percent classified themselves as liberal compared to 17 percent who classified themselves as conservative. A few years later, Weaver and Wilhoit (1992) in a national survey of those working for news organizations found that 44 percent classified themselves as Democrats compared to 16 percent who classified themselves as Republicans, a partisan distribution more skewed toward the Democrats than was the case among the American public as a whole. These data justifiably elicit concern among those who consider themselves as conservative or Republican, and raise the question as to whether these dispositions translate into biased political coverage.

Although public opinion research has revealed that significant numbers of Americans perceive a partisan bias in the news, systematic analysis of news content has not consistently documented such bias. Analyses of negative and positive emphases in news coverage of the 1968, 1972, 1980, 1984, and 1996 presidential elections found the vast majority of coverage was neutral in tone, and when valence was present typically it was fairly equally divided between the Republican and the Democratic candidates (Domke et al., 1997; Hofstetter, 1976; Robinson & Sheehan, 1983; Smith & Roden, 1988; Stevenson, Eisinger, Feinberg, & Kotok, 1973). D'Alessio and Allen (2000) quantitatively aggregated the outcomes of 59 individual empirical examinations of media bias spanning presidential elections from 1948 to 1996, using the techniques of meta-analysis (Hunt, 1997). This is the single most impressive record on bias because of the range of elections, multiple number of databases, and the inclusion of three types of bias (all variants of our concept of "fairness"): (a) "gatekeeper," or selection of stories about one or another party; (b) "coverage," or the amount of attention devoted to one or another party; and, (c) "statement," or favorability toward one or another party. They found "no significant biases" for newspapers, "virtually zero" biases for newsmagazines, and only "small, measurable, but probably insubstantial" coverage and statement biases for television network news (p. 133).

However, there are exceptions to the overall pattern. The frontrunner bias leads to greater coverage of the leading candidate—which may or may not be beneficial, depending on whether it incorporates greater proportions of scandalous material—and this is particularly pronounced in primaries. Campaigns also are not always equal in newsworthiness, which again is ambiguous as to benefit because greater coverage might result from more success at manipulating the media or might represent the fruits of scandalous activity. For example, Domke and colleagues (1997) examined over 12,000 stories between March 10 and November 6 from television newscasts and newspapers and found that in the 1996 campaign, both Clinton and Dole received slightly more favorable than unfavorable paragraphs and their ratios of favorable to unfavorable coverage were nearly identical. The exception to the pattern of equality was that Clinton received more news coverage—estimated at 27 percent more than Dole—probably attributable in part to his frontrunner status (Robinson & Sheehan, 1983; Ross, 1992) and in part to his seizing upon themes that had greater resonance with public concerns (Comstock & Scharrer, 1999). In this case, the greater attention to Clinton in news coverage constituted an advantage for his campaign.

Thus, the data do not give much support to the view that political coverage has been consistently biased in a liberal direction at the level of the presidency, and in the instance of presidential elections. However, it would be naïve to believe that these allegiances and self-descriptions on the part of individuals would not affect a number of important aspects of news gathering, such as the topics thought to be of interest and thus the content (more accurately, the components) if not the slant of the news. Of course, the ability to translate one's own political penchant into news stories is likely to be curtailed by editors, publishers, owners, and other members of the newsroom's organizational hierarchy.

The news media are biased toward bad news. This is reflected in more stories that are negative than positive of almost every type, and a majority of television news directors at local stations believe that negative events are generally more newsworthy than positive events (Comstock & Scharrer, 1999). We certainly agree that negative and positive events are hardly symmetrical in their implications for individual or social welfare. The sun rising is nice; the failure of the sun to rise would be a calamity. An increase of 100 in the Dow Jones, unrealized, is decidedly pleasing, but a decrease of 100 lowers the level at which shares can be redeemed; a door has been slammed shut. The media follow this principle during presidential campaigns. Campaigns occur in a world of trouble and misery. Graber (1987) industriously recorded all the television news headlines—the announcement of the forthcoming story—between Labor Day and election day in 1984 on ABC, CBS, and NBC. Half of the stories about events in America and abroad were categorized as bad news—death, pain, harm, suffering, threat. Only 17 percent qualified as good news. This negativism constitutes a trend that is hard to blame on the decline and fall of order in the world. Patterson (1993) records the shift since World War II: positive coverage of presidential candidates, once in the majority, has decreased and negative coverage has gained an increasing majority.

F. Civic Disenchantment

Finally, there is the concern that news coverage promotes lack of faith in government and politicians, skepticism about their motives, and at the extreme, a disinclination to participate by voting or otherwise becoming involved with politics (Cappella & Jamieson, 1997; Moy & Pfau, 2000; Patterson, 2002; Putnam, 2000). The mechanisms by which this is said to occur are varied, but one common element is that television is at the forefront. Nevertheless, most of the arguments apply to the media in general, although television generally exemplifies their concrete appearance. First, the media frame politicians as greedy, ambitious, and interested in success at winning or retaining office rather than pursuing policies on principle or in behalf of public benefit. The game and horse race metaphors delicately part company here, with the former representing stories about the strategies, tactics, ploys, and spin devised to achieve success and the latter covering reports of actual success in primaries, caucuses, and polls. Second, the pursuit by the media of inconsistencies, mistakes, and ineptitude reduces the confidence of voters in the competence of elected officials. Third, the focus on transgressions of a moral or sexual nature confounds the personal with the political, with the opprobrium of the former transferred in the public mind to the latter. Fourth, the rise of television as a medium of attention has been accompanied by a substantial decline in the use of newspapers, and newspaper use historically has been a strong predictor of political participation. Finally, the lure of television as a home-based source of entertainment has been one of many factors—generational changes in values, the toll of long work hours and the frequent need for both a husband and wife to work, and urban sprawl that has led to long commutes and the cloistering of much of the population in homogeneous enclaves without much civic life—that purportedly has resulted in a disengagement from community, organizational, and political life.

The problem with these arguments is that they collide with a persistent fact of the past six decades: use of the media for news consistently has been a positive predictor of political participation, and this includes attention to television news (although attention to television news has been a weaker predictor of political participation than attention to newspapers). Of course, such positive correlations at a given moment or over the short span of a political campaign do not preclude the possibility that the media over much longer time spans turn some people off politically rather permanently while remaining the focus of attention for those who retain interest. After all, it would be unreasonable to anticipate that those interested in politics and expecting to vote or write letters to the editor or an elected official would fail to follow the news, because for most that would be the primary source of politically relevant information.

In our view, the most informative data on the question of media use and civic disenchantment are those of Moy and Pfau (2000). They conducted content analyses of the treatment by a variety of news media and talk shows of such institutions as Congress and the presidency in the mid-1990s. At the same time, they surveyed almost 1,300 adults about their media use and attitudes more closely representing lack of faith, skepticism, and disenchantment with politics than a disengagement from or disinclination to participate in political life. In the content analyses, they found (as one would have suspected) that political talk radio and entertainment television talk shows were much more negative in their depictions than traditional media such as newsmagazines, newspapers, local television news, and network television news, although these were often negative in their depictions, too. In examining the public opinion data, these investigators controlled statistically for the use of other media when examining the evidence about a particular medium. This produces a pure, if in practice unrealistic, measure of the association between use of a medium and attitudes. They found that use of newsmagazines and newspapers was positively associated with favorable attitudes about institutions. Results for network news were somewhat mixed, but for the most part the pattern was one of negative associations between use and favorable attitudes—network news viewers generally thought less favorably of these institutions. These viewers also apparently liked what they saw, because viewing was positively associated with favorable attitudes toward the news media. In contrast, use of local television news generally was associated with favorable attitudes toward institutions. Watching newsmagazines and entertainment talk shows was associated with favorability toward the news media. However, viewing entertainment talk shows was associated with negative attitudes toward institutions. Political talk radio produced an anomaly—despite the pronounced negativity compared to traditional news media, substantial negative associations between use and favorable attitudes did not appear, thus giving comfort neither to the hypothesis of influence nor to the hypothesis of self-selection.

Interpretation of these data is not straightforward. The authors lay out a case for causation based on the dual pattern of information about content and information about associations between use and attitudes. The problem with this argument is that the pattern of negative content is so widespread that any association of use with negativity could be interpreted as causal. Our view is strengthened by the failure of the most negative of media—political talk shows on radio—to be associated with negative public opinion. We reach a conservative (although admittedly inferentially cowardly) conclusion:

1. These data—admirable in their comprehensive coverage of the content of many media and a wide range of public institutions (which we did not single out because we are interested in the most general pattern)—are highly consistent with the criticisms of the mass media, including the tendency of the media to glorify themselves (we refer here to the associations of media use with favorability toward the media).
2. These data do not make a consistently convincing case for causation because too often the explanation of selective attention by those with the attitudinal dispositions in question is an equally plausible explanation. Three examples will suffice: (a) those more favorable toward the news media may more consistently watch network news because it provides easy and inexpensive access to an undertaking they admire and find interesting and perhaps exciting; (b) those with more favorable attitudes toward institutions may read newsmagazines and newspapers more often because their dispositions provide a motive for seeking out news about these institutions from media that require greater cognitive effort and greater expenditure of time but also provide greater detail and more thorough and varied accounts; and, (c) the failure for the expected negative associations to appear for political talk radio apparently occurs because of the undercutting role of expertise about these institutions (which their listeners apparently have in ample measure), which implies that the listeners drawn to this medium begin with dispositions that remain untouched by the media experience.

II. ON THE SHELVES

News organizations, like supermarkets, must assemble and dispense a large assortment of goods that, however varied when taken one by one, fall into a few broad categories and, like supermarkets, to do so they rely on routinization of tasks and the division of activities into a few recognizable formats (Altheide, 1976, 2002; Fishman, 1980; Gans, 1979; Tuchman, 1978). Even a topic as significant, broad, and multifaceted as politics is attended to in the news in a finite number of ways. Much of such news media attention occurs through coverage of politicians and candidates: poll, primary or caucus results, campaign speeches, scandals or campaign missteps, or election day itself. Additional attention occurs through political advertisements and scheduled political debates. Each of these forms of news media attention to politics has been the subject of a massive amount of analysis. We review only the most enduring of scholarly observations, with an emphasis on the critical themes we have outlined. Nontraditional and nonnews formats have increasingly become visible venues for candidates to demonstrate that they have a sense of humor and are down to earth—such as appearances in 2000 of both George W. Bush and Al Gore on talk shows and the late-night shows and the saxophone artistry of Bill Clinton eight years before—but we focus on traditional news media. Our reason is that these other venues, while colorful and amusing, amount to a minute portion of media time devoted to politicians and candidates—although they may play an important role in making a new figure more familiar to the public (Comstock & Scharrer, 1999).

Much of the news coverage of elections has been discussed in terms of two conceptually distinct, yet in practice overlapping categories of content. These are image and issues. Stories (or elements within stories) pertaining to image have to do with the character of the candidate, the candidate's style or appearance, personal life, and personality. Stories having to do with issues describe a candidate's platform (policies and priorities if elected to office), positions on controversial or timely topics (such as abortion or gun control), and record of prior voting or public service. Despite much concern voiced by critics, news stories tend to contain more issues-based than image-based elements, in both newspapers (Sigelman & Bullock, 1991) and television (Paletz & Guthrie, 1987). However, even when issues-based stories appear in newscasts, only about 1 in 10 provide a rationale or background information on candidates' stances on issues (Rudd & Fish, 1989).

Issues-related and image-related stories are typically outnumbered by stories that pertain to the election itself, including stories that feature poll results regarding the level of public support for the candidates and stories about the relative health of candidates' campaigns. Polls often lead television newscasts, with about half of poll stories appearing as the first or second story (Keenan, 1986). The amount of subsequent coverage in the news that a candidate receives is a function of his or her status in the race (Comstock & Scharrer, 1999; Johnson, 1993). This certainly occurs in the primaries (Patterson, 1993), but there also is evidence that it occurs during the election itself (the Clinton–Dole race of 1996, which we just discussed, is an example). The frontrunner usually gets the most media attention (Halpern, 1996; Robinson & Sheehan, 1983; Ross, 1992) while third-party candidates and those behind in the polls usually get less attention.

There has also been an increase in recent years in news stories about political commercials used by individual candidates (Kaid et al., 1993) as well as a growth in the number of stories about media coverage of politics (Johnson, Boudreau, & Glowacki, 1996). What is represented mostly by this meta-coverage—coverage about coverage—and stories about the election as a whole rather than about individual candidates is a self-indulgent role for the news media as an active participant in the election process rather than an impartial purveyor of information (Patterson, 1993). The exception are those stories that cover the development of campaign themes and media advertising blitzes, and the design of particularly misleading commercials, which might serve some voters as inoculations against manipulation as well as providing information (possibly useful in the voting booth) about the scruples of the candidate and party involved. One consequence of meta-coverage crowding out other stories is a diminished opportunity for voters to learn the specific positions on issues of the individual candidates that would be helpful in arriving at an informed voting decision.

The candidates themselves certainly attempt to control news media coverage of the campaign, and with some success. They schedule campaign speeches and visits to historic sites, factories, hospitals, shopping malls, symbolic Main Streets, or other locations, and they employ staffers who are frequently in contact with members of the press. Modern campaigns of any significance from the House to the presidency are now organized around the strategic use of information—its deployment and spin in media coverage and the use of polls about the reactions of the public to plan future initiatives of the candidate (Stonecash, 2003; Strachan, 2003). This is the "new politics" discussed more than 30 years ago by Mendelsohn and Crispi (1970) as the conjunction of television, polls, and the quick analysis of the latter's data by computer for planning media strategy, with the important difference that in their time these new politics were confined to the presidency and they now permeate the system. One sure way to ensure news coverage is for one candidate to attack another, since such an attack carries the newsworthiness of the conflict element of a good story (Jamieson & Waldman, 2003).

A. Election Day

Our discussion of news coverage on election day requires attention to the confusion and controversies swirling around the 2000 election. Using exit polls conducted as voters left polling places but reporting, as usual, before the votes were fully tallied, the news media committed a series of errors. Television was perceived by the public as the villain because it was reporting live, but much of the responsibility lay with the VNS, which represented a consortium of television and print media. Gore at first was declared the winner in the swing state of Florida. Later, Bush was declared the winner. As more votes were tallied, it became apparent that the election was too close to call. Soon, there was the incompetently designed ballot in one area that produced many hundreds of votes for Pat Buchanan that were intended for Gore. Television sets were on in 15 million American homes when the election was called for Bush at 2:20 A.M. At 3:50 A.M., when the call was taken back by the newscasters, 8.5 million homes had their sets on (Jamieson & Waldman, 2003).

The language used by the anchors on the major television networks during and after the process represent the variety of postures assumed by the networks. They included certainty, doubt, exasperation, and apology (Jamieson & Waldman, 2003). For example, Tom Brokaw commented on NBC, "I think I indicated earlier we don't just have egg on our face, we've got omelet all over our suits at this point. . . . We awarded Florida erroneously at one point, and came back, and managed to make everything equal by awarding it erroneously a second time." Democrats argued that the false reports hurt Gore's chances and Republicans argued that they hurt Bush's chances among those voters who had not yet cast their ballots before the confusion began. Projections and exit polls had long been blamed for influencing those who had not yet voted, particularly on the West Coast where the number who had not voted would be greatest. One argument was that knowledge of the likely winner would discourage supporters of both candidates from voting; another was that expectation might assert a bandwagon effect for the likely winner. Never before, however, had the medium circulated essentially false reports. In the 36 days that followed, the news was populated by stories of hanging chads in the recounts, the misaligned ballot that transferred votes from Gore to Buchanan, new polls to determine who the public thought should be declared president, and ultimately the Supreme Court decision. The news media largely used the frame of chaos and continuing uncertainty, and many thought the Bush campaign was more successful than the Gore campaign in inviting the media to focus on some angles over others (Jamieson & Waldman, 2003).

There are two issues here. One is the behavior of the television news organizations. The other is the possible effects on those who had not yet voted.

It is clear in hindsight that the television networks were too quick to call the Florida race when they did not have sufficient data for the interpretations they offered. Their unanimity was partly attributable to the pack journalism syndrome of not wanting to be late with the story, but it was made inevitable by reliance on the same pool of data and the expertise supplied by VNS. The creation by the news media of a cooperative endeavor had been a wise move economically, but journalistically it proved disastrous. The problem, then, was twofold. The urge to break the story betrayed the news media into error, and reliance on a common set of data and experts led them into duplicating each other's errors. However, there is no way to be sure that additional polls independently conducted for different news organizations would have detected the error. This is because we cannot be sure that the VNS data were the product of sampling variability. It is entirely possible that the data may have represented a systemic bias in the replies of respondents that would have shown up in poll after poll. Thus, the only fault of which we can be confident is the rush to interpret data unsuitable for interpretation.

The evidence is quite clear about effects on those who have not yet voted. The principal allegation has been disproportionate loss in turnout for the losing candidate. The party would then be hurt by the reduced vote for their candidates for lesser offices. Data, in fact, suggest scant influence (Fuchs, 1966; Lang & Lang, 1968; Mendelsohn, 1966; Tuchman & Coffin, 1971), although admittedly they were collected in electoral circumstances far less dramatic than those of Florida in 2000. Only between 6 and 12 percent of those yet to vote typically learn about a likely winner. The pattern of voting for those voting before and after the dissemination of such information has been about the same. The pattern for those voting in the East or Midwest, who voted before such information was available, and those voting in the West, where it would have been more frequently encountered, also has been about the same. This has been true both for turnout and switching between candidates. The strongest possible estimate of influenced voters would be 1 percent (Comstock & Scharrer, 1999).

The Florida fracas may have raised many doubts about the electoral system, and particularly the accuracy with which votes are tallied. It may have led to some disillusionment over the lack of clear rules by which disputed elections are adjudicated (although polls would indicate that a majority of the public thought the Supreme Court was just the right ticket for settling matters, despite the almost inevitable bias of the court toward one or another of the major parties). It probably did not much influence voting elsewhere. First, the small proportions reached by such information would limit effects, although it is certainly possible that the closeness of this particular election would have led to greater interest in and as a result somewhat wider dissemination of such information than the instances in which the evidentiary data were collected. Second, two key assumptions are unlikely to be met (Tannenbaum & Kostrick, 1983). These are the assumptions of (a) little or no interest in other races and the (b) disproportionate lowering of turnout for the candidate expected to lose. Third, the increasing practice of ticket splitting would mitigate any detriment to the party of the losing candidate.

B. Advertising

Political advertising, another salient media format, constitutes the primary reason why campaigns for political office are inordinately expensive in the postmodern era (Goldenburg & Traugott, 1987; Morris & Gamache, 1994). Most of the expenditures go to television. Political commercials, constructed with visual and political expertise by professional production teams and members of the campaign staff and carefully placed in particular media markets to address specifically targeted audiences, are very pricey. This creates a situation in which only those with access to large amounts of money can run for major office. In 1992, for instance, Bill Clinton, George H. Bush, and Ross Perot spent a combined $133 million on media buys for political ads (Devlin, 1993). Even those with sufficient personal wealth to attempt a run at a major office must also rely on the whims and favors of wealthy donors. Incumbents typically garner more financial support than challengers, and thus have an advantage beyond name recognition and a record in office. In 1996, for example, Clinton outspent Dole by $20 million (Devlin, 1997).

Analysis of the content of political commercials reflects the fluidness and dynamism of a particular campaign. They are created to initiate or respond to issues and topics that surface during the campaign. The candidates enter with a strategy and an agenda. However, they must be flexible because they cannot perfectly predict either the behavior of their opponent(s) or events. Incumbents and challengers tend to differ in the topics and themes they choose to emphasize. Based on data collected from nearly 600 candidates for seats in the House in 1982 and 1990, Tinkham and Weaver-Lariscy (1990, 1995) concluded that incumbents tended to call attention to voting record, service to constituents, and prior accomplishments, whereas challengers focused on issues and not-so-admirable personal attributes of their opponents. Incumbents play to their strengths, which include high name recognition and a past record of service. Challengers try to overcome their usually weaker initial posture by chipping away at these advantages or by engaging in personal attacks (Comstock & Scharrer, 1999).

In the 2000 election, 6 out of 10 voters reported that they had seen ads for each of the two major candidates by the end of the first week of October ("Media seen as fair, but tilting to Gore," 2000). Use of commercials in the 2004 election began at an unprecedentedly early date, months before nominating conventions, so exposure to commercials by the beginning of October possibly was even greater. The Midwest in 2000 appears to have been the region most heavily targeted by the candidates' placement strategies, as this section of the country had the largest number of respondents—approximately 70 percent—who reported having seen Gore and Bush ads. Voters awarded each of the candidates similar grades for their ads. Just over one-third (39 percent for Gore, 36 percent for Bush) assigned a score of A or B. Slightly more respondents perceived Bush to be more critical of Gore than Gore was of Bush. Four out of 10 voters said that Bush had been "too personally critical" of Gore, whereas 29 percent reported that Gore had been "too personally critical" of Bush ("Media seen as fair, but tilting to Gore," 2000). In 2004, almost three-quarters (72 percent) said the Bush and Kerry campaigns featured more "mud-slinging" than campaigns in years past ("Moral values: How important? Voters like campaign 2004, but too much 'mudslinging,'" 2004).

As with news coverage, political commercials can be described in terms of their relative attention to issues or image, and their negative or positive messages. Shyles (1984) found in a study of 140 commercials from the 1980 presidential campaign that the most frequent topics covered in image-oriented commercials involved altruism, competence, experience, honesty, leadership, personal characteristics, and strength. Among the most frequent topics covered in issues-oriented commercials were record in office, domestic policies, the economy, energy, foreign policy, and national security/the military. In both cases, these are the staples from election to election.

Commercials usually are constructed differently depending on whether they emphasize image or issues. Image ads typically use endorsement by prominent others, still shots of the candidate, fast transitions, and music. Issue ads most often feature the candidate in formal attire, directly speaking into the camera. The former typically are small narratives reminiscent of documentary film and product commercials, with the frequent use of testimonials; the latter often are straightforward advocacy designed to gain approval or acceptance of a proposition. Negative advertising is used more frequently in close races (Hernson, 1995) and by challengers than incumbents (Kahn, 1993). In fact, the overall pattern of the use of positive appeals more often in successful races is largely a product of the electoral advantage of incumbents and strong candidates rather than an indictment of effectiveness of negative appeals (Comstock & Scharrer, 1999).

C. Debates

Televised presidential debates between candidates represent a rare opportunity for an extended, long-format view of the candidates and fuller explanation of their campaign platforms and stances on issues. They also allow for judgments of character and image to be made as the press and audiences alike observe the candidates for warmth, sense of humor, confidence, and other qualities. However, effects on public opinion and public impressions are likely to be greater for issues than for images. This is because the former usually remain only murkily perceived by the time of the debates—a circumstance partly attributable to the media attention to the character and personalities of the candidates and the emphasis on the horse race—whereas the latter usually develop early in the campaign as one of the first things about which political impressions form, and this is facilitated by that same attention of the media to the character and personal attributes of candidates (Comstock & Scharrer, 1999).

Yet, despite the uniquely long platform, what typically emerges in debates is one or two "defining moments." These reign supreme in how the debate is recounted in the immediate analyses of television news commentators and in subsequent news accounts. They also come to symbolize the debate in memory, just like a short phrase sums up an entire song or the name of a character evokes a novel. The defining moment sometimes occurs when a comment of one debater is quickly and wittily dispatched by a short, and often humorous, remark. Sometimes it occurs when a question has an unexpected edge. And often it occurs when a candidate makes a mistake. The strong emphasis of journalists on such one-liners and dramatic moments establishes these occurrences as defining or "decisive" moments in the debate (Clayman, 1995; Jamieson & Waldman, 2003). Three examples are "You're no Jack Kennedy" by Lloyd Bentsen in the 1988 vice presidential debate with Dan Quayle; Bernard Shaw's question in that same year to Michael Dukakis as to whether he would think differently about the death penalty if his wife Kitty had been raped and murdered; and Gerald Ford's mystifying comments in 1976 that many took as suggesting he thought of Eastern Europe as not under Soviet domination. Jamieson and Waldman (2003) argue convincingly that these defining-moment remarks are not always "off the cuff" but are prescripted to gain the attention by the press. This was certainly the case with Bernard Shaw's question, and it fits Ronald Reagan's "I am not going to exploit, for political purposes, my opponent's youth and inexperience" to Walter Mondale in 1984 and his "There you go again!" to Jimmy Carter in 1980. In addition to focusing on quotable highlights, subsequent news coverage also tends to emphasize physical presence or demeanor, and characterizations of performance (such as nervousness, confidence, displays of anger) rather than the substance of issues and proposed policies (Kraus, 1979; Sears & Chaffee, 1979). About two-thirds of the public will be exposed to commentary or some form of news coverage following a debate (Atkin, Hocking, & McDermott, 1977). Nevertheless, postdebate coverage is a critical element in the public's understanding of what took place. These analyses and accounts play a crucial role in the public's beliefs about a particular encounter (Elliott & Sothirajah, 1993; Kraus, 2000; Lowry, Bridges, & Barefield, 1990). The comments of the political experts and veteran journalists immediately following a debate affect interpretations about what was important and who won, and sometimes the impression among debate viewers of who fared better will change as the media's interpretation becomes widely disseminated and, in most instances, accepted.

The audience for televised presidential debates continues to dwindle, thereby enhancing the importance of postdebate analysis on the part of the news media. Of the 20 debates on which Nielsen Media Research has collected data between 1960 and 2000, the five lowest-rated debates all occurred during the 1996 and 2000 presidential election campaigns. Since the 1960 encounters between John F. Kennedy and Richard Nixon in which about 60 percent of homes with television were tuned to the debate, there has been an almost perfectly linear trend downward to the most recent figure of 26 percent of homes with television watching the final debate between George W. Bush and Al Gore in 2000 (Jamieson & Waldman, 2003). The exception to the downward trend occurred with the novelty of a three-candidate debate in 1992 with the addition of Ross Perot (Comstock & Scharrer, 1999; Kamber, 1993). The shrinking debate audience is largely attributable to two factors. First, the novelty has become tarnished and the excitement diminished. At first, they were perceived as highly unusual opportunities to catch a rare, extended glimpse of the candidates. Now, they have become *de rigueur* and are perceived as more mundane than extraordinary. Second, the near-captive audience that once existed is no more. When the three original networks dominated television schedules, viewers had few other choices than to tune in to the debates on one of the networks. Today, viewers have dozens of viewing options in the typical household and even in those markets without cable there will be numerous options (including, almost certainly, a popular movie or two, which has become a favorite tactic of independent stations during the debates).

Public opinion regarding political debates between (or, occasionally, among) presidential candidates is largely favorable. Sixty-two percent of a nationally selected group of respondents in both 2000 and 2004 reported that they found the debates helpful in arriving at voting decisions ("Campaign 2000 highly rated," 2000; "Moral values: How important? Voters like campaign 2004, but too much 'mudslinging,'" 2004). However, in another poll in 2000 at about the same time, only 29 percent of voters said the debates would matter in terms of shaping their vote and 60 percent said that by the time the debates were aired they had already made up their minds ("Lukewarm interest in presidential debates," 2000). Still, a declaration by almost one-third of the public that the debates figured in their decision making constitutes a major educational contribution to the electorate by the media. Independents (38 percent) were more likely than Democrats (27 percent) or Republicans (25 percent) to indicate that viewing the debate would influence their vote. At the same time, public opinion polls reveal that interest in debates was unenthusiastic. In 2000, for instance, only 43 percent reported that they were very likely to watch the debates, compared to 67 percent in 1992, and 55 percent in both 1984 and 1988 ("Lukewarm interest in presidential debates," 2000). More than one out of five said they were unlikely to watch the debates in 2000 (22 percent in 2000, 8 percent in 1992, 17 percent in 1988, 16 percent in 1984). This certainly demonstrates that the closeness or uncertainty over the outcome of an election does not ensure high attention to the debates, but whether these data should be interpreted as a commentary on this pair of candidates or the debates as an institution is moot. Interestingly, despite being more likely to agree that viewing the debates would influence their vote, independents displayed less interest in watching the debates than did Democrats or Republicans ("Lukewarm interest in presidential debates," 2000). We tentatively interpret this as an example of the roles of motive and function. Those who see themselves as aligned with a party perhaps have greater motive to take an interest in the debates while independents perhaps are more likely to think the debates might be useful because for them party alignment had not made a decision unnecessary. About 9 out of 10 respondents usually report that they watch debates to learn about the issues, whereas three-fourths report watching to evaluate the candidates as individuals (Comstock, 1989). We can conclude at this time that presidential debates have become pro forma and often are received with only passing interest by much of the public.

The achievement of institutional status by presidential debates has made debates a frequent feature of elections at every political level, from the local to presidential primaries and caucuses. Many of the elements are the same. Candidates with the greatest disadvantages have the most to gain and the greatest incentive to engage in a debate. More advantaged candidates find it difficult to refuse to debate, either because of the tradition of past debates or fear of signaling arrogance or indifference to the public. The first in a series will usually attract the largest audience because of the curiosity and interest that will be satisfied for some by the initial encounter. The first also will have the greatest influence on public belief and opinion because of the larger audience and the formation of initial impressions that usually will not encounter any subsequent reasons for change. Image may have a somewhat more prominent role among outcomes during the primaries and caucuses because it will not be as firmly established as for the final presidential contenders. However, the biggest difference is the close adherence to an established structure in presidential debates. Because of the high stakes, presidential debates are the product of extended negotiations. Challengers generally argue for a larger number of encounters, to increase the likelihood of scoring gains. Incumbents prefer fewer debates, to minimize the likelihood of losing status. The same pattern would hold for debates at lower levels, with those with the most to gain the least risk averse. However, the most distinguishing feature below the level of confrontations between the nominees is that debates are more freewheeling, rules are fewer or more vague, and last-minute changes, unheard of when the two presidential candidates face off, sometimes occur (Comstock, 1991; Comstock & Scharrer, 1999).

III. NARRATIVE AND NORMALIZATION

W. Lance Bennett (1983) neatly summarizes the treatment of politics by the news media with four concepts: personalization, dramatization, fragmentation, and normalization. News stories attend closely to the characteristics and actions of the key individuals involved in the election, capitalizing on the dramatic tensions and conflicts that arise. They fragment potentially complex topics by providing disjointed accounts. They ensure the continued popular acceptance of the American political system by giving legitimacy through attention and publicity—the normalization process—to the two-party alignment, elite officials in the administration, and prominent politicians and media-centered campaigns.

The focus on a game metaphor and horse race frame of winning and losing and the attention paid to potential scandal reflect the striving of the news media to personalize stories. Bennett (1983) explains, "the personalization of the news is accomplished primarily by building stories around human actors. . . . The human focus may be interesting, but it often obscures the most important features of events, most notably, the workings of political processes, power relations, and economic forces" (p. 8). Political elections are characterized more by the images, characters, and personalities of the major candidates involved than by detailed accounts and explanations of their positions.

Bennett (1983) also points to political news reporting as highly contingent upon dramatization, providing an account of events that is structured around a narrative that includes conflict (principally among those personalized individuals), action that rises and falls, and a resolution or definitive ending. The problem that arises from such a focus is that each story containing those narrative threads is reported in isolation from other stories, eliding the connections that could be drawn among event-driven accounts and ignoring structural causes, history, and long-term consequences. Societal focus is vanquished by the construction of narrative. Furthermore, when dramatic action becomes the measure of success of a news account, the role of the journalist expands to include the embroidery, detail, and exaggeration of popular fiction, and interpretation becomes as necessary as the conveying of fact, a trend that Patterson (1993) documents in the dominance of commentary by journalists over quotes from political candidates.

News reporting on politics is often fragmented. Elements of the story sometimes are taken out of context and often are compressed into a pared down, easily comprehended construction. Television news "often sacrifices length and detail in favor of pace, change of scene, and personalization. . . . Similar fragmentation effects are achieved in newspapers jumping back and forth between interviews, actors, scenes, factual information, and plots" (Bennett, 1983, p. 19). This is particularly so at the local level (where national as well as local politics will receive some attention) when station policy dictates an "eyewitness action" format (Hamilton, 1998). The fragmentation and abbreviation of elements within a story can confuse the audience and leave readers and viewers with less information than is necessary to understand what is taking place. Furthermore, as exemplified by the dramatization of events, fragmented stories are reported as independent from one another, thereby making it difficult for those readers and viewers to draw links among events and issues. Indeed, Bennett notes that the overwhelming tendency is "that the news slate is wiped clean each day" (p. 20). The task of remembering and making connections among news stories on the same topic is left to the audience. Few news outlets reporting on politics provide a scaffold for audiences' knowledge about politics and public affairs—an important element for public understanding of the news (Neuman, Just, & Crigler, 1992).

Political reporting serves to normalize the sociopolitical status quo, bestowing the canons of inevitability, justice, and hallowed procedure. It provides a central place for "official" sources from the administration to reify the political power they enjoy (Bennett, 1983). The vast majority of sources invited to comment and contribute to the news occupy official positions in local, regional, and national power structures, from those elected to local school boards to members of the President's cabinet. There is certainly the pursuit of personal scandal and the unceremonious unveiling of skeletons in the closets of public officials, but there is a simultaneous disinclination to severely challenge governmental action, whether to go to war or to enact a tax cut.

CHAPTER 5

Heterogeneous Faces

The enormous amount of attention given by the news media to politics and political figures implies a public with a great interest in and a huge appetite for such information. Interest and appetite in fact describe only a modest proportion of the public. The news media avidly woo readers and viewers, but with each story about politics and public affairs that receives some degree of prominent, continuing, serial coverage they must settle for about a half of the public at best and often, at worst, for about one-fourth (our estimate is based on the Pew Research Center's rolling polls of public attention to current stories in the news). Most Americans behave in accord with Down's (1957) well-known principle of rational ignorance, in which the likelihood of affecting any given governmental policy is so remote that there is little incentive to be well informed. Politics is assigned comparatively low salience by most Americans. This is exemplified in low voter turnout, the dominance of two parties each encompassing a broad range of views rather than several fractious and ideologically differentiated partisan factions, and the discomfort stimulated by extremists of every disposition among many Americans. Politics for many does not arouse great fervor—most of the time (Neuman, 1986; Neuman, Just, & Crigler, 1992).

The resolution of political issues depends on debate and conflict. Issues and topics are placed on the public agenda by events, advocacy groups, and prominent political figures. Often, these function in tandem, with unpredictable events used by advocacy groups and political figures to further the policies they support. Resolutions contend for endorsement. Public opinion takes shape. Elections are held. The president and Congress now contend over implementing a much smaller range of options. This process in the United States is stratified, with the responsibility to participate actively delegated to a comparative few volunteers and professionals by the many (Almond & Verba, 1989a, 1989b; Berelson, Lazarsfeld, & McPhee, 1954).

These few are those actively involved in political parties, advocacy groups, and social movements. In our view, they also include those who closely follow public affairs and the journalists who make this possible through news coverage, commentary, and analysis. One consequence of these circumstances is that most people most of the time are woefully ignorant of political matters such as the names of elected officials, pending legislation, and proposed reforms (Neuman, Just, & Crigler, 1992). The media have a crucial role in this process of resolving disagreements and discord. They are the means by which the contending entities—parties, politicians, advocacy groups, social movements, and commentators—attempt to win public support. By default, it falls to the media to orchestrate coverage of elections that will arouse interest and mobilize voters. It also falls to the media to supply sufficient information for voters to have confidence in their ability to make a choice. As we have seen, the pursuit of the former by horse race coverage and personalization, while not wholly inconsistent with the latter (public opinion about and the personal qualities of candidates are not irrelevant to voter decision making), also does not fully serve the prospect of choice where the positions of candidates on issues would have a prominent role.

I. OUR MODEL

We turn now from the performance of the media to the public that attends to the media. We attempt to identify several broad groupings that represent distinct orientations toward politics and the media. Responses to the media vary by these groupings, and they become an important factor for understanding how the media function politically. In particular, they are important for assigning a correct place to the electoral cycle in voter mobilization and for understanding the weight in the system of the latent or nonvoter. The core of this system is a set of norms for political behavior that preclude violent disruptions such as a coup d'etat. This stability allows for the correction of publicly perceived errors of policy and direction without threatening the mechanisms by which these were achieved. The penalty for loss of the public's faith is temporary banishment from power—and only partially since either party will remain well-represented in Congress. In our view, this is the mindset that underlies the success of the American system. It is the subscription by huge majorities across most of the political spectrum to the belief that the transfer of power is always by legitimized means. The consequence is that the electoral system can be quite imperfect in the solutions voters arrive at without imperiling its short-term efficiency or long-term stability. This is often phrased as a "belief in democracy." This strikes us as a misperception, because the essential element is not the conviction that the people rule but that there are rules that cannot be broken.

A second characteristic that distinguishes the system is its reliance on the mobilizing of participation within the cycle of elections. Americans pay little attention to presidential candidates—in the sense of whom they want in the White House—until after Labor Day. There is then a shift upward in interest following the months of coverage of the primaries and caucuses and the nominating conventions that is visible in the increased numbers who express interest in campaign coverage.

Writings about the electoral process, whether scholarly or journalistic, tend to endorse one of two heuristics: the monolithic public or the normative voter. In the former, the attention is given to an aggregate that can be personalized as if it were an individual. The public is spoken of as having low interest or being woefully ignorant in regard to civic knowledge, as we have. In the latter, the voter is characterized as an individual using the variables that differentiate the aggregate public. Questions address the consequences for voting of gender, race, age, and socioeconomic status. These are both useful perspectives. The outcome of an election undeniably represents an aggregate decision by a public that embodied certain leanings and preferences, and whose actions may or may not represent the climax of long-term trends or the initiation of important changes or realignments. Voters certainly vary as a function of gender, race, age, and socioeconomic status. The key element that often goes unremarked is that the public is heterogeneous in a quite orderly way. The result is that we can substitute for the monolithic public and normative voter the concept of diverse publics.

Our principal concern is to identify the factors on which different responses to the media's coverage of the electoral cycle are dependent. The monolithic public is particularly inept for this task because it ignores the possibility of differences. The normative voter serves better, but is quite awkward in directing attention to a series of variables—gender, age, ethnicity, religion, or socioeconomic status—with each operating in isolation from the rest. Our alternative is to identify major clusters within the public. We think these clusters represent the best way to describe the public for our topic, the psychology of media and politics, because they retain the property of aggregation that is so fundamental to political analysis and at the same time differ in response to the news media's coverage of politics and in the likelihood of voting or otherwise participating in politics.

We will draw on three sources: (a) studies of those who do not vote, whom we initially call "dropouts" (e.g., Doppelt & Shearer, 1999; Patterson, 2002), (b) the many sources of data on the variables that affect dispositions toward politics and voting (e.g., Kraus & Davis, 1976; Roper Center, 1997; Smith, Lichter, & Harris, 1997), and, (c) analyses that segment the voting public into groups based on responses to measures of political and social beliefs and party preferences (Pew Center, 1999). We readily acknowledge that our breakdowns are only approximations of reality. Our goal is not to offer definitive typologies but to identify in concrete and realistic terms the substantially different responses of segments of the public to the same information environment.

We begin with the dropouts. We then turn to the pool of likely voters. Next, we examine the electoral cycle and the important role of the media in orchestrating participation in the political process, including voting. We then return to nonvoters, but this time focus on an important subset whose interests and media behavior make them potential participants. Finally, we turn to the preeminent role of interests and motives in guiding political and media behavior.

II. DROPOUTS

The turnout in the United States for presidential elections currently stands at about 50 percent, a decided decline from the approximately 60 percent who voted in the five elections between 1952 and 1968. This is not unprecedented. Similar figures were recorded for 1924, 1928, 1932, and 1948. It is also not beyond change—the three-way race between Clinton, Bush, and Perot in 1992 brought out 55 percent. The 2004 presidential election drew nearly 60 percent of eligible voters (Adair, 2004), a surge likely explained by the confluence of pressing issues affecting candidate choice, including terrorism, the war in Iraq, and sensitive social issues such as gay marriage. And declines have been somewhat exaggerated by the shift in voting age from 21 to 18, for as McDonald and Popkin (2001) point out, rates in fact have been close to flat since 1972. Nevertheless, turnout in the United States is the lowest in the world among functioning democracies.

The stereotype of the nonvoter encompasses several variables: little interest in politics, low knowledge about issues and political figures, low use of news media, and a distrust of politicians and political parties. These all certainly make an appearance, but they are, as a package, too simplistic and only part of the story.

The best available data are those presented by Doppelt and Shearer (1999). They draw on a telephone survey of 3,233 adults 18 years of age and older living in the continental United States. About 1,000 were identified as likely nonvoters. Nonvoters are much more likely to be younger, to be black or members of other racial minorities, to have fewer years of education, and to have lower incomes (Table 5.1).

The data, obviously, are not as fully representative as one would like. The forthcoming presidential election produced slightly fewer voters than nonvoters whereas the survey produced voters at a ratio of greater than two to one. There are three suspects: the rather high likelihood that the response rate for nonvoters would be significantly lower than for voters because the same variables that are correlates of nonvoting are also predictors of nonresponse to

TABLE 5.1 Profile of Nonvoters (in Percentages)

N =	Actives (288)	Disenchanted (250)	Know-nothings (146)	Disconnected (177)	Alienated (121)
Gender					
Male	46	50	33	50	48
Female	54	50	67	50	52
Age					
18–32	48	46	33	29	26
30–44	32	35	38	36	35
45–64	17	16	15	22	24
65 and older	3	3	12	11	14
Race					
White	74	65	74	65	71
Black	12	11	11	19	14
Other	13	24	13	15	15
Education					
Less than high school	8	24	22	14	26
High school graduate	37	40	41	36	41
Some college	32	24	20	26	22
College graduate	23	13	16	25	11
Income					
Under $30,000	40	55	52	44	63
$30,000 and over	55	39	32	48	29

Note: Percentages may not add to 100% due to rounding and the exclusion of those who refused to answer

Adapted from *Nonvoters: America's no shows,* by J.C. Doppelt and E. Shearer, 1999, Thousand Oaks, CA: Sage.

surveys, and especially the variables of minority status, low income, and fewer years of education; the use of the telephone, which would exclude not only those without phones but those whose work schedules would keep them away from home during normal calling hours; and the possibility that some classified as voters exaggerated their voting record and intent to vote to give more socially desirable responses. We recite these in what we judge to be the descending order of influence. The important point is that the presence of those of low income, fewer years of education, minority group status, and younger in age is almost certainly somewhat underrepresented among the nonvoters.

Based on a cluster analysis (a statistical procedure that identifies groupings relatively homogenous in their responses), Doppelt and Shearer single out five types of nonvoters. We have renamed several of the groups, relabeled a number of variables, and reordered them by newspaper reading, a major predictor of political interest and participation (Doppelt and Shearer used size of the group), to better serve our purposes (Table 5.2). "Volunteer" represents service with a charity or nonprofit group; "officials care" refers to the belief that officials care what people like the respondent think; "locus of control" refers to the belief that people control their destiny (with the percentage representing those who think they do not; that is, higher numbers represent lower belief in control of life's outcomes); "efficacy" refers to the belief that who is elected makes a difference; "salience" refers to the belief that issues in Washington

TABLE 5.2 Beliefs and Behavior by Nonvoter Typology

Percent of Total	Actives (29)	Disenchanted (18)	Know-nothings (14)	Disconnected (27)	Alienated (12)
Volunteer	70	58	54	59	49
Newspaper	53	52	19	0	2
TV news	58	62	39	35	49
Officials care	53	25	27	24	22
Locus of control	28	43	41	47	51
Efficacy	66	39	30	36	34
Salience	79	57	48	52	51
Good opinion					
Republicans	63	37	1	40	32
Democrats	63	52	0	60	34
Congress contact	30	28	15	10	16

N = 1,001

Adapted from *Nonvoters: America's no shows*, by J.C. Doppelt and E. Shearer, 1999, Thousand Oaks, CA: Sage.

affect the respondent; and "Congress contact" refers to writing, telegraphing, or otherwise attempting to make the individual's viewpoint or complaint known to a member of Congress.

There are three major conclusions. The first is that not voting does not always signify an indifference to public affairs or involvement otherwise in community activities. This is apparent from the high media use scores for the actives and disenchanted, and the substantial percentages for volunteer work for all the groups. The second is that nonvoters are not a homogeneous group. This is quite clear merely from scanning across the rows in Table 5.2 where differences in percent for one or more of the columns are often considerable. The third is that slightly over half—the know-nothings, disconnected, and the alienated—fit the stereotype of the nonvoter quite well. They are low in daily newspaper use (to the extent of 2 and zero percent in the case of the alienated and disconnected), low on efficacy, salience, believing that people control their own success, and in attempting to contact a member of Congress, and two are low in their favorability toward the two major parties (with one, the know-nothings, apparently not knowing enough to voice an opinion).

The disconnected and the disenchanted are quite similar attitudinally. However, they differ sharply in their use of the news media, with the former paying no attention to newspapers on a daily basis and only about a third regularly watching television news while more than half of the latter attend to newspapers daily and almost two-thirds regularly watch television news. The former would be less likely than the latter to be aware of, and therefore less likely to be influenced by events covered by the media or the emphases of the media in covering those events.

The group that stands apart from the others is the actives. They are rivaled only by the disenchanted in their regular use of newspapers and television news, and on attitudinal measures they are much more positive about government than any other group, scoring highest on whether officials care, efficacy, salience, and favorable opinions of the two major political parties. They also have the strongest ranking by far on locus of control (scoring 13 percentage points lower than the next lowest group in the proportion agreeing that success is outside an individual's control) and, while the rates for community volunteer work are substantial for all the groups, the actives record the highest rate.

These groups differ across four dimensions. One is attentiveness to public affairs through the news media. The alienated, disconnected, and know-nothings score particularly low here, leading to little expectation of attention to politics except possibly during presidential election campaigns. The second is beliefs and attitudes concerning salience, efficacy, dispositions of officials, and locus of control. All but the actives are comparatively skeptical that government matters, that individual politicians can make a difference, that officials care, or that people can exert control over their lives. The third is favorability toward the major parties. Here, the know-nothings and the alienated present the extremes of least favorable evaluations whereas the actives present the most favorable and evaluations equally positive for both parties. The fourth consists of demographics: education, income, race, and age. These are all important descriptors of the ways the nonvoting groups differ from one another.

The data make a strong case for a psychological as well as a sociological component as factors in nonvoting. Sociological components, of course, include both personal and systemic factors, with the former including low education, poverty, and lower age, all predictors of nonvoting, and the latter represented by difficulties in registering, actually voting, or both. Nevertheless, as Doppelt and Shearer illustrate through interviews with nonvoters, beliefs also play an important role, so that systemic repairs will make only modest differences in turnout.

The Doppelt and Shearer interviews, along with statistical summaries of the survey responses, provide a profile of each group and justification for our labels. The alienated are distinguished by low education (only 11 percent have graduated from college), low income (70 percent made less than $30,000 a year), and are extremely pessimistic about the effectiveness of political action. The disconnected are similarly low in education and perceived efficacy of political action but are much younger (81 compared to 62 percent below the age of 45). A majority of know-nothings are women who were only somewhat better off financially than the alienated (52 percent made less than $30,000 a year) and almost as young as the disconnected (73 percent under the age of 45); their distinguishing feature is their reply, "I don't know," in response to knowledge and opinion questions. In sharp contrast, the disenchanted are well informed about politics, following public affairs closely in the news media, are comparatively well educated (25 percent had college diplomas) although similar in income to the know-nothings (52 percent made less than $30,000 a year) but attitudinally very hostile to politicians; as Doppelt and Shearer comment, it is not lack of information but dislike of the people and activities that make up political life that sets them apart. Finally, the actives resemble the disconnected in age, but are better educated, have much higher incomes (in fact, are quite likely to be professionals) and have beliefs and attitudes that extend considerable importance to political action (scores for efficacy, salience, officials caring, and favorability toward the two major parties are the highest of all the groups, and they believe in the capacity of the individual to make a difference in his or her success rather than suffering as the pawn of events beyond his or her control).

The profile for the actives identifies them as what we would term "rational instrumentalists." They think the outcome of voting is very important but that their vote will not make enough difference to matter, analogous to the rational ignorance proposed by Downs (1957) to account for the indifference that many display toward policy issues—the likelihood of influencing a decision is disproportionately small when compared to the costs in time and effort of deciphering the most judicious course. However, their beliefs and their close following of the news make them potential voters when crises seemingly arise or certain proffered policy options seem particularly odious or onerous. As Doppelt and Shearer comment, these nonvoters "view their vote as a negative tool to be used to fix a political problem or change a bad situation rather than as a measure of civic responsibility" (pp. 27–28).

III. PARTICIPANTS

The voting population is even more diverse. The typology developed by the Pew Research Center (Pew Center, 1999), using the same sort of cluster analysis but with a nationally representative sample of almost 5,000 adults age 18 and upward, led to nine groups that participate in politics (Table 5.3). They can be arrayed by partisanship: three have a greater affinity for (in fact, in the case of what Pew labeled the "staunch conservatives," total loyalty to) the Republican party, four prefer the Democratic party, and two cannot be said to favor either party (and were assigned the label "independents").

TABLE 5.3 Typology of Voters

Political Alignment	Estimated Percentage of Voters*
Republican Groups	
Conservatives	12
Moderates	13
Populists	11
Democratic Groups	
Liberals	10
Social Conservatives	16
New Democrats	10
Partisan Poor	10
Independents	
New Prosperity	10
Disaffecteds	8
	100

N = 5,000

*Size of group weighted by prior presidential election (1996) turnout.

Adapted from *Retropolitics: The political typology, Version 3.0* (Survey report), Nov. 11, 1999, Washington, DC. Pew Research Center for the People and the Press.

Nine comparatively homogenous groups pose a considerable challenge for description. Our solution is to treat them by the three arrays: Republican (Table 5.4), Democratic (Table 5.5), and Independents (Table 5.6).

Seventy percent or more of each of the three Republican groups consider themselves to be GOP adherents, with all the rest labeling themselves as independents who say they lean toward the Republican Party. The same can be said of three of the four Democratic groups: 70 percent or more say they are Democratic adherents among the social conservatives, new Democrats, and partisan poor, with the remainder labeling themselves independents who say they lean toward the Democrats. The greater independence of the liberals appears to be more a matter of esteem for the concept than the expression of pragmatic neutrality, for while only 56 percent identify themselves as Democratic adherents with the remainder saying they are independents who lean toward the Democratic Party, 92 percent who voted in 1996 cast their presidential ballot for Bill Clinton.

A. Republicans

The Republican groups otherwise vary considerably in makeup (Table 5.4). All three are predominantly white, but the large majority of the conservatives (we drop the "staunch") are male whereas an only slightly smaller majority of the populists are female. The conservatives stand out for their financial success, distrust of government, and values that are antisocial welfare, antigay, pro-life, pro-military, and indifferent to environmental issues. Six out of 10 regularly use the Internet. They follow the news regularly and attentively, and read newspapers and listen to the news on the radio more than any of the remaining eight Republican-Democratic-Independent groups. They are also among those most likely to vote, with 85 percent having done so in the preceding presidential election.

The distrust of government of the conservatives is well exemplified by their political view of the government as wasteful, with 82 percent agreeing with this response compared to only 33 percent for the moderates and 64 percent for the populists. Similarly, 62 percent agree that elected officials don't care what they think, compared to a scant 29 percent for the moderates and an even more hostile 66 percent for the populists.

The moderates depart from the conservatives in being quite positive in their beliefs about government and in their concern for environmental issues. Like the conservatives, they are self-defined patriots, and are pro-military, pro-business, and have little concern for the poor. They are financially satisfied, well educated, and have the largest percentage of Catholics across all nine groups. They are above average in Internet use (58 percent), average in media

TABLE 5.4 Republican Groups

	Conservatives	Moderates	Populists
Sex			
Male	65	50	40
Female	35	50	60
Age			
Under 30	10	23	14
30–49	40	40	50
50–64	23	18	18
65 and older	26	18	16
Race			
White	95	94	91
Black	1	2	11
Other	7	11	2
Education			
Less than high school	7	9	16
High school graduate	29	36	43
Some college	29	23	24
College graduate	35	31	16
Family income			
Under $30,000	16	23	34
$30,000 and over	70	63	52
1996 Presidential voter turnout	85	77	72
Media use			
Newspaper	64	52	49
Network nightly news	45	42	35
Internet	59	58	42
Views on issues			
Favor giving president fast track authority	22	43	35
Favor requiring abortion consent for minors	86	86	79
Favor increasing the minimum wage	44	75	84

Adapted from *Retropolitics: The political typology, Version 3.0.* (Survey report), Nov. 11, 1999, Pew Research Center for the People and the Press, Washington, DC.

consumption, but pay attention to politics and are highly knowledgeable about politics. They were also much more approving of Clinton's performance than the other two Republican groups, with 44 percent approving compared to 31 percent for the populists and 16 percent for the conservatives. Thus, it is not surprising that the moderates were more divided than the conservatives in support for the Republican nominee in the previous presidential election, with only 65 percent voting for Dole compared to 86 percent for the conservatives.

The populists are strong in religious faith (42 percent are white evangelical Protestants), take conservative views on issues they perceive as having a moral component, and are rather insular in being distrustful of those different from themselves. They are less well educated and less affluent than the other Republican groups. They favor social welfare to help the needy, and believe that corporations have too much power. They are lower in Internet use (42 percent) than average, average in media consumption, but low in political knowledge and even more divided than the moderates in their support for the Republican nominee in the previous presidential election, with only 51 percent of those voting supporting Dole.

These profiles make several important points. The Republican Party harbors at least three major elements, each in many (but not all) ways different from one another, and two of which offer the prospect of occasional defections. The party inevitably is constantly in a state of marshaling its resources to maintain the loyalty of implicit voters, and its most supportive element, the conservatives, constantly face the paradox of ideological fervor and commitment and the need sometimes to compromise in the interests of electoral success. Equally important for our particular interests, these elements will differ in their responses to the news media, and these responses will vary as the media transit the unvarying landmarks of the continually cycling events that occur from one presidential election to the next. Populists, because of lesser attention to politics and lower knowledge that will inhibit their ability to incorporate new information (Comstock & Scharrer, 1999; Neuman, Just, & Crigler, 1992), will pay the least attention to the media between campaigns. Moderates, in contrast, are knowledgeable about politics and follow political news closely although they will be somewhat constrained in doing so by their average amount of attention to the media. Both will be vulnerable to defections as a consequence of the information received and images depicted, but these effects largely will be confined to the campaigns among the former while among the latter they more often will have their roots in what is encountered between campaigns. Conservatives, on the other hand, typically will pay more attention than either the populists or moderates to the news media between campaigns but their commitment to their ideology, along with their political knowledge, will fortify two defenses against changes in attitude or behavior: counterarguing, and the ability to explain or justify events not entirely commensurate with their point of view. As a result, defections from the Republican Party will be rare.

B. Democrats

Although four out of five liberal Democrats assert they are independents (although admittedly leaning toward the Democrats), more than 9 out of 10 voted for the Democratic candidate in the previous election (Table 5.5). They are the best educated of any of the nine groups, with 50 percent having college degrees. They support gay rights, are favorable toward pro-environment issues, and in general support liberal causes. They are the least religious of any of the nine groups, and the most sympathetic toward the poor, African Americans, immigrants, and the women's movement. These are the quintessential "L's." They are average in use of news media, but above average in Internet use and more than 40 percent get news online. Most live in urban areas, and many

TABLE 5.5 Democratic Groups

	Liberals	Social conservatives	New Democrats	Partisan poor
Sex				
Male	47	47	42	34
Female	53	53	58	66
Age				
Under 30	27	14	23	16
30–49	41	38	36	40
50–64	20	25	19	22
65 and older	12	21	20	20
Race				
White	80	80	71	52
Black	11	16	21	39
Other	16	13	21	22
Education				
Less than high school	5	18	15	22
High school graduate	18	44	34	46
Some college	27	21	27	19
College graduate	50	16	23	12
Family income				
Under $30,000	24	29	31	60
$30,000 and over	62	56	56	31
1996 Presidential voter turnout	76	76	77	77
Media use				
Newspaper	55	58	54	51
Network nightly news	37	53	46	39
Internet	70	44	53	32
Views on issues				
Favor giving president fast track authority	55	50	61	52
Favor requiring abortion consent for minors	51	81	71	71
Favor increasing the minimum wage	96	91	89	89

Adapted from *Retropolitics: The political typology, Version 3.0* (Survey Report), Nov. 11, 1999, Pew Research Center for the People and the Press, Washington DC.

(compared to other groups) patronize the arts: ballet, opera, and theater. They are the most knowledgeable politically of all the groups, but are only average in electoral turnout.

Social conservatives are quite different in every respect except for their support of Democrats, with more than 8 out of 10 who voted supporting the Democratic candidate in the previous election. They are highly religious, patriotic, intolerant toward gays and immigrants. A majority describe themselves as "working class," and many follow professional sports (no arts patronage here). They are less educated than the liberals, but a majority read a newspaper regularly and there are more regular viewers of network evening news than in any other of the nine groups. They are labor union supporters and skeptics of big business. Average in political knowledge and average in turnout, four out of five say they follow political news closely.

The new Democrats constitute the group that was the most satisfied of all with the Clinton presidency. More than 9 of 10 who voted in the previous election supported the Democratic candidate. They are sympathetic toward African Americans, the poor, and immigrants, but less so than the liberals. They are fairly well educated, have middle incomes, and almost 6 out of 10 are women and 1 out of 5 is black. Concerned about the environment, accepting of gays, and union supporters, they watch newsmagazine formats on television and specialized cable news channels such as CNN more than average. They are average in political knowledge and turnout.

The new Democrats have the second largest number of African Americans. The largest number (39 percent) occur among the partisan poor. This is a group in which voter registration is among the highest for all groups (equaled only by the Republican conservatives). Religious and hostile to big business, they support civil rights and the women's movement. They are strong supporters of welfare and other government programs to help those in need. They are not very well educated, have low incomes (4 out of 10 make less than $20,000 a year), and two-thirds are female. Half attend Bible study or prayer group meetings. About one-fourth regularly watch daytime talk shows, and the fewest of any group (32 percent) use the Internet. They are average in voter turnout but strong in Democratic support, with more than 9 out of 10 voting for the Democratic candidate in the previous election.

The four Democratic groups present a spectrum of views surprisingly similar to those among the Republicans. We find moralistic conservatives (social conservatives), moderates by another name (new Democrats), the disaffected who display considerable political activism (the partisan poor), and an ideologically committed group whose members often reject party labels while overwhelmingly voting Democratic (liberals). It is easy to discern parallels with the three Republican groups, the populists, moderates, and conservatives. Moralistic judgments, positive views of both business and governmental action, and ideological commitment variously mark the elements that make up both parties. What seemingly sets the Republican and Democratic groups apart, besides the differences in partisan allegiance and the very different perspectives of the ideologically committed (the conservatives and the liberals), is the recorded greater likelihood of defections among the Republicans. However, our judgment is that this is not structural, but simply a matter of the popularity of the two candidates in the previous election. Clinton was very popular; Dole was not. The defection rate is a function of the enthusiasm of those who lean toward one or the other of the two major parties for the particular candidate nominated by the party. These Democratic groups, like those within the Republican Party, will respond somewhat differently to the news media. Social conservatives are particularly high in use of the news media, and so we would expect more influence from events between presidential campaigns. These effects will be somewhat truncated among liberals and new Democrats by their only average attention to news media. The partisan poor are outside the range of the media except possibly during periods of national crisis or presidential campaigns; the media would play a very limited role in their political thinking.

C. Independents

The two groups comprised largely of independents are quite different from one another (Table 5.6). The new prosperity independents are comparatively well educated (almost 4 out of 10 have a college degree), are well off financially (almost one-fourth earn $75,000 a year), and a sizable minority think of themselves as Republican (21 percent). In the previous election their vote was almost evenly divided between Clinton (28 percent) and Dole (25 percent), with Perot receiving a sizable share (16 percent). The disaffecteds are not well educated (8 percent have a college degree), lower in income (about three-fourths make less than $50,000 a year, and more than one out of four describe themselves as "poor"), and only about 15 percent think of themselves as either Democrats (8 percent) or Republicans (6 percent). In the previous election, they overwhelmingly voted for Clinton (33 percent) but gave Perot more votes (16 percent) than Dole (10 percent).

The new prosperity independents were quite satisfied with what had taken place in the United States. They are on the whole a liberal, cosmopolitan group that is both favorable toward protecting the environment and pro-business. They are tolerant on social issues and accepting of homosexuals (with slightly more than half having a friend, colleague, or relative who is gay), and they are quite sympathetic toward immigrants but not so much so toward African Americans and the poor. They are largely unreligious (only about one out of

TABLE 5.6 Independents

	New prosperity	Disaffecteds
Sex		
Male	55	52
Female	45	48
Age		
Under 30	28	20
30–49	42	50
50–64	17	17
65 and older	12	10
Race		
White	91	85
Black	4	8
Other	12	11
Education		
Less than high school	5	19
High school graduate	30	48
Some college	26	23
College graduate	38	8
Family income		
Under $30,000	19	49
$30,000 and over	57	33
1996 Presidential voter turnout	69	59
Media Use		
Newspaper	59	46
Network nightly news	38	38
Internet	75	40
Views on the issues		
Favor giving president fast track authority	39	38
Favor requiring abortion consent for minors	67	76
Favor increasing the minimum wage	73	86

Adapted from *Retropolitics: The political typology, Version 3.0* (Survey report), Nov. 11, 1999, Pew Research Center for the People and the Press, Washington, DC.

eight attend church regularly), with many pro-choice in regard to abortion. They are almost evenly divided between men (55 percent) and women (45 percent). They are above average in use of news media, with 6 out of 10 reading a newspaper regularly. They also use the Internet more than any other group (75 percent), and more than 40 percent regularly go online for news. They are politically knowledgeable, but average in voter turnout.

The disaffecteds had the lowest voter turnout of the nine groups. They are distrustful of everything and everyone in public life—politicians and political parties, government, and business corporations—and they are very unhappy financially (71 percent say they often "don't have enough money to make ends meet"). Fairly young, with about half between the ages of 30 and 49, with the most single mothers of any group except the Democratic partisan poor, they are hostile to gays and to immigrants. One out of five regularly watches daytime television talk shows. They are low in political knowledge.

These two groups lead to markedly different expectations on the role of the media. The new prosperity independents are high users of the news media, and by their status as independents will be seeking information to guide political decision making. This will produce continual processing of political information both between and within presidential campaigns. These voters are particularly sought after by the parties. They are particularly attractive to Republican campaigns, because the ratio of Republicans to Democrats is four-to-one (with a total of about one out of five thinking of themselves as Republicans), and their openness to persuasion is indicated by one of the two largest proportions voting for Perot (16 percent, the same as the disaffecteds). The disaffecteds are open to influence, as evidenced by that vote for Perot, but they are less attractive to campaigners for two reasons: they pay little attention to the news media and so are difficult to reach at any time, and they have the lowest voter turnout rate of the nine groups.

IV. ELECTORAL CYCLE

The news media pay continual attention to politics. However, attention rises every four years with the approach of the presidential election. This is the electoral cycle. It has three components:

1. A series of events that unfold with regularity every four years
2. Unexpected occurrences
3. Shifting public attention to politics

A. Regularity

The emergence of a winning candidate ends the electoral cycle. This ordinarily occurs by dawn of the day following the election, but as 2000 demonstrated, unexpected occurrences can extend it for more than a month. Each electoral cycle is marked by the same stages. The press and the voters proceed with the orderly procession of a sports season: preseason games, early results, the emergence of issues and contenders, key games, the playoffs, and finally a decisive selection of the champion. This is a product neither of the affinity of the press for sports imagery and metaphors nor the penchant of the public for contests of drama and triumph, but of the existence of regularly scheduled elections. Once they are in place, the press responds with coverage that inevitably attends to events that are structurally similar—in the sense of occurring at about the same point between elections and having basically similar properties from election cycle to election cycle—although usually differing considerably in their particulars.

Every presidential election is followed by speculation, rumors, and prognostications about the members of the cabinet. In 2000, this occurred in tandem for the two candidates, each of which advanced teams for a new administration. During the campaign, candidates generally do not announce their choices, largely because of the risk of expanding the range of topics on which they can be attacked. Now, the inauguration is only eight weeks away and the "honeymoon" that presidential electoral victors are said to enjoy—a period of greater than ordinary support from citizens and Congress—will benefit from an impression of decisiveness and respected cabinet members (Colin Powell was an excellent example of adding political value to an administration through appointments).

The inauguration is a symbolic event that will draw extensive coverage. However, it has no more political significance than the similarly well-covered Fourth of July celebrations. The State of the Union address to Congress is another matter. Symbolically, it places the president in the position of receiving a warm welcome from members of both parties. The president's political agenda is paramount. The address will set forth the priorities that the president will advance during the coming year and in part the criteria by which the president will be judged. It will make concrete the administration's intentions, serve as a banner assembling applause for the goals and priorities set forth, and supply the standards by which commentators, columnists, and editorial writers will judge (at least to some degree—the president's responses to unexpected events also will play a role) the administration's success. One major imprint of the State of the Union address is the agenda of topics during the coming months that the press will cover, and these emphases in turn will lead the public to attribute greater importance to these topics (Wanta, 1992; Wanta & Foote, 1994).

The next inevitable and protracted phase focuses on the relations between the president and the Congress. This has three aspects. The first is the success of the president in gaining approval of the initiatives he advocates. These vary with each year, but invariably include the reform of one or another domestic institution in which the federal government plays a large role: taxation, welfare, defense, education, health, labor relations, corporate behavior, or campaign finance. The second is the behavior of Congress, including the divisions within each party, the relations between the controlling party (which may or may not be the same as the party of the president) and the minority party in the House and Senate, and the passage or postponement of major legislation. The third is the public's ratings of the president's performance, collected by serial opinion polls. These are taken as indicators of whether support for the president is rising or falling, and as harbingers of the reelection of the incumbent or his successor as the party's nominee if the president is at the end of the two-term limit.

The media diligently cover the activities of the president. These will include meetings with foreign dignitaries at the White House or Camp David, ceremonial signings of successful legislation proposed by the president, press conferences, and travels abroad. These generally help maintain support for the president, but the determining element is drawing the attention of the public to events favorable to the president that are also perceived by the public as significant. We draw here on the data of Simon and Ostrum (1989), who examined public approval of the president in conjunction with 35 years of presidential speeches. They found that on average televised speeches in prime time were followed by increases in approval. They also found that when events clearly positive or negative for the president occurred close to a televised speech or announcement of major foreign travel, approval rose or fell whereas these activities by themselves had little if any effect. Thus, the two key factors are salience of the president in his (or her) official role and decidedly favorable events to which that salience draws attention. Good things are not enough; there must be a symbol that attracts the attention of the public.

There tends to be a teeter-totter relationship between the approval of the president and the public's evaluation of the media (Comstock & Scharrer, 1999). The media ordinarily take a somewhat adversarial role, with negative reports and stories outweighing favorable news in both emphases and quantity. When the approval ratings of the president are high, the public's evaluation of the press declines. When the approval ratings are low, the evaluation of the press rises. Thus, the popularity of the president coincides with disdain for the press, and a lack of enthusiasm for the president coincides with greater popularity for the press. However, it must be acknowledged that these ratings of the press compared to other institutions (such as "business" and the "military") have consistently over the years been among the lowest, so that for the press these shifts represent oscillations around a very modest average (Lipset & Schneider, 1983). The press's treatment of the 2004 election, for instance, was graded an A or a B by only 33 percent of those in a large national sample ("Moral values: How important? Voters liked campaign 2004, but too much 'mud-slinging,'" 2004).

The second year is similar to the first, with one major exception. We now approach the midpoint of the presidential electoral cycle that is marked by the off-year election of representatives, senators, governors, and other officials. This election is taken as a gauge both of success so far and the prospects for the next presidential election. Conventional wisdom predicts some loss of seats for the majority party in each of the two houses. The questions are how great a loss and over which issues. The most clear-cut and dramatic of the possible scenarios is control of both the House and the Senate by the party of the incumbent president who is ceded the nomination to run for reelection. In this case, the midterm elections become a referendum of the acceptability of the president's performance. Small, expected losses will signal a president in a formidable position. Large-scale rejection of the president's party in the two houses will signal storm clouds for the president.

The second half of the electoral cycle continues the drama, but with two important differences. There will be a sharp focus on the prospects of the president for reelection unless the two-term limit has been reached and on the struggle within the opposite party to gain the nomination. Relationships with Congress will now be stories within the story, subordinate and interpreted in terms of these two sagas. If the president has reached the two-term limit, the focus will be on the selection of a successor (often the vice president) and that successor's chances for success.

The news media now embark on one of their most important historical roles. They announce to a public highly differentiated in its interest in politics the initiation of the campaigns to elect a president. The earliest caucuses and primaries are preceded by coverage of the maneuvers and strategies of the candidates. The president, if running for reelection, will be assured of the party's nomination. The candidates for the opposing nomination will engage in a series of debates. The president will usually remain aloof, basking in the attention achieved from the media by the role of president. Among opponents, the early caucuses and primaries may or may not confirm the expected frontrunner, will surely lead one or more candidates to abandon the race, and may present the public with a surprising contender. Neither Jimmy Carter nor Bill Clinton could be said to have been early favorites for the Democratic nomination.

The first phase of the coverage of the struggle for the presidency formally begins with the first caucuses and primaries and concludes with the nominating conventions. Because so many delegates pledged to one or another candidate will have been chosen by caucus or primary, the conventions have become ceremonial events bestowing the mantle on the chosen one and only the high points—major speeches and particularly colorful demonstrations—are covered live by television. This is in contrast with the gavel-to-gavel coverage that once was network practice (and a matter of journalistic pride), and reflects the shift of the conventions from the deliberative (in terms of picking a candidate) to the ceremonial and the greater competition for viewers with increasing numbers of channels available. Nevertheless, the television coverage, which focuses on the nominee and visibly displays the enthusiasm within the hall aroused by the nominee, results in a typically transient boost in the public's favorability toward the nominee (Campbell, Cherry, & Wink, 1992; Holbrook, 1996). This has come to be called a convention "bump" or "bounce" and is usually largest for the first convention (and is likely to be greatest for a comparatively new face about whom opinions have not become stabilized).

B. The Unexpected

Unexpected occurrences fall into three categories, primarily distinguished by the degree to which they dominate the news and assume some stature in the public mind. We think of them as (a)the specifics that define everyday conflict, success, and failure in politics; (b) significant events that lead to a response by the president or a presidential candidate; and (c) large-scale events that dominate the news, occupy extended attention by the president or a candidate, and are a focus of public interest and concern.

The first includes the daily shifts in the sands of political fortune: votes lost in Congress, shifts in the economy, protracted struggle over a presidential appointee, a Supreme Court ruling with widespread implications such as abortion or civil rights, rises or falls in the public's rating of the president's performance, and standings in the polls en route to the fall election. These are the standbys of coverage that draw little or modest public attention and are quickly replaced by more recent events. Only occasionally is there more lasting significance, such as the success or failure of a major reform that will come to symbolize the effectiveness of the president or a Supreme Court decision that changes the boundaries of public policy.

The second is represented by singular events that elicit a newsworthy response from the White House or a candidate, with the result that media attention is more protracted and extensive: a terrorist attack on a United States embassy, the confinement of United States military for violating the territory of a neutral country, harsh disagreements with allies, or vocal questions about the record of the president or vice president regarding military service or conflict of interest. Then there are the charges and countercharges of the campaign that the contenders never ignore. These typically draw more attention from the media than those daily shifts in the political sands, and often more attention by the public, but usually they too are comparatively transient passages.

Large-scale events are a somewhat different story. Like all matters newsworthy, they eventually will be replaced by other topics. However, their residence on the nightly news, the front pages, and in the newsmagazines is likely to be lengthy, and they may define eras and decide the fate of presidents and policies: the Vietnam war, the civil rights struggle, the war against terrorism, or the invasion of Iraq. These events establish the context of public life, often invade private life, and frequently divide the country. They remain in the news for months and years. The first and second categories are symptoms of underlying conflict and discord; the third represents those conflicts in full regalia.

The electoral cycle assimilates these unexpected occurrences with ease because of the orderly, scheduled scaffolding of elections. Each political year is different, in the same sense that every movie or novel of a particular genre is different; in the same sense of those genres, each year of the electoral cycle repeats every other year falling in the same place in the 4-year sequence.

C. Shifting Attention

The public is not quite ready to pay attention yet except for those who regularly follow politics. Opinion at this time, while certainly measurable as the many polls that will appear in the press make clear, is highly unstable. The candidate seemingly favored by the public will enjoy his or her role, but it often will not last. Meaningful opinion, in the sense that it represents intent to vote for a candidate and has been reached after some contemplation of the alternatives, for many will wait until after Labor Day. Opinion almost certainly will still fluctuate, but it is becoming more stable. It also becoming more valid because it more frequently represents what voters would do were they to cast a ballot on the day they respond to a poll, although these intentions certainly may change.

The press largely pursues two themes: the strategy and tactics of the opposing candidates, and the likelihood of victory or defeat as measured by the opinion polls. The debates between the presidential candidates (and to a far lesser extent, the vice presidential candidates) will receive close attention, with the debates serving as educational for many voters in regard to issues despite their reputation for contributing mostly to the images of the candidates (Comstock & Scharrer, 1999). Much of the attention of the media and public, however, is on who is perceived as the winner. This often is influenced by the judgments of postdebate commentators and polls (Kraus, 1988). Whatever they may have concluded individually, most of the public very quickly will acknowledge that one or the other fared better, on the basis of the media coverage of the debates.

The social function of the press is much grander. Here we distinguish between the actions of the media and the ends they serve. The news media are the means by which the public is mobilized to participate in politics by voting on Election Day. This occurs through the arousal of interest, the renewal of partisanship, and the activation of hitherto latent loyalties. The media create an arena of public discourse. They participate in the winnowing of contenders and they give an incumbent some advantage by the coverage extended to the presidency. But they also importantly turn the attention of the public to the business of choosing a leader. Other topics become subordinate to the contest for president, which is now foremost on the public agenda.

V. NONVOTING

The act of nonvoting does not necessarily represent either ignorance of public affairs and politics or alienation from the political system. Among the dropouts, the actives—whom we have labeled rational instrumentalists—make this clear. They follow political events closely, think political decisions by those in power make a difference, have a high regard for the efficacy of the individual in determining his or her destiny, and have a comparatively favorable evaluation of both political parties. These dispositions represent a readiness to vote when circumstances are perceived by the actives as calling for intervention, and the possibility of support for either of the two major parties. Importantly, they pursue these interests and dispositions by regularly following public affairs and politics in the news media. This use of information means that what appears to be indifference masks calculated surveillance.

We think these rational instrumentalists also offer an example of a distinctly contemporary development in American politics. This contemporaneity rests not on historical uniqueness, for what we are observing is hardly a novel disposition toward voting, but on its embrace by so many. The actives think of voting as a contingency called into action by the threat of unacceptable risk or the perceived need for remedy. They apparently believe they are able to make these judgments by monitoring the news media. The media are the key element that renders their political stance sensible from their perspective. This stance depends on two assumptions that in fact apply to all voters:

1. The media are essentially valid in the agenda of issues they help set for the public and politicians, the descriptions they provide of the experiences of distant others, the state of public opinion, and the circumstances and importance of the unusual (and sometimes alarming) events to which they call attention.
2. The individual will be sufficiently free of common errors of inference to reach a satisfactory and satisfying reasoned decision based on the information disseminated by the media.

What sets the rational instrumentalists apart is that they do not look upon voting as a civic responsibility. Instead, they see their civic responsibility as represented by the necessity of following public affairs in the press. They are also open to arguments from a variety of political perspectives—which makes the media particularly important as the major source of such viewpoints—and they believe in both political and personal efficacy. Their catholicity of potential political action is reflected in their comparative favorableness toward both major parties, and their expectations of effectiveness are testified to by their beliefs that Washington decision making matters and people have considerable control over their lives.

There is an obvious psychological aspect that manifests itself in their attitudes toward voting. However, the search for causes should not stop with how people think. The more significant question is, why do so many think that way? We believe that the psychology, with its twin dimensions in this case of information seeking and reserving the act of voting as a last resort, is rooted in structural changes in American society. Our argument draws on Gerth and Mills (1964), who assigned social structure a role in the construction of personality. The psychology of the individual in this instance in part is the consequence of social change. The actives—a substantial group of about 30 percent of dropouts—think as they do, and decline to act as they could, because of the transformation of American society. They imminently may do as they do because of their attitudes but they have those particular attitudes largely as a consequence of the circumstances—the emerging social structure of America in the last half of the twentieth century—in which they live.

A. Social Structure

Robert Putnam (2000) has prominently advanced the thesis that, beginning in the mid-1960s, there has been a decline in America in civic engagement. By civic engagement, he means channels of personal participation: writing letters to the editor and to elected officials; attending city council and school board meetings and the gatherings of associational organizations; participating in volunteer activities (which may or may not have a political aspect); taking part in focused activities, such as those of a union, church, club, or political party; and voting. Since the beginning of the twentieth century, these kinds of participation had been on the rise in America, marked by the founding of ever more voluntary associations (as exemplified by the Goodwill Industries in 1901, the Boys Clubs of America in 1906, and the American Legion in 1919), a phenomenon that began with the founding in 1871 of the National Rifle Association and in 1872 of the Shriners. Each of these organizations had its particular focus and agenda, but they shared the goal of making a positive contribution to the society. In the 1960s, membership in almost all associational organizations began to decline (with the descent for some, such as the American Legion, beginning earlier), including the Kiwanis, Jay-cees, Elks, Lions, League of Women Voters, Parent-Teacher Association, and many others (Putnam, 2000, pp. 440–444). A similar decline in union membership began somewhat earlier, in the mid-1950s, and the decline in membership in associational organizations was paralleled by declines in church attendance (somewhat mitigated by immigrant groups, primarily Hispanics), and declines in club memberships.

This pattern of disengagement was paralleled by downward shifts in political participation: writing letters, attending meetings, and voting. The broader argument is that there has been a decline in what Putnam terms "social capital," defined as the benefits that accrue from human interaction. More specifically, in an early article he described social capital as the " . . . features of social life—networks, norms, and trust—that enable participants to act together more effectively to pursue shared objectives" (Putnam, 1995, pp. 664–665) without the same aura of constructive goals that would come to characterize his later use of the term (e.g., *Bowling Alone*, Putnam, 2000). This contrasts with the benefits of educational or human capital (e.g., training and knowledge), and economic or physical capital (e.g., worldly wealth and resources), although as critics have pointed out the boundaries are sometimes indistinct (Foley & Edwards, 1997). This human interaction takes two distinct forms. One is formal, as represented by membership and participation in associational organizations and participation in the activities of unions, churches, clubs, or political parties. The other is informal, as represented by the everyday conversations that transpire over dinners together, at chance meetings, and before and after competitive sports (such as league bowling). Two outcomes of human interaction in both formal and informal settings are particularly beneficial to both society and the individual: the opportunity to discuss issues and problems of public concern, from local zoning and schoolyard bullying to distant wars and the national deficit, which constitutes a potential step toward their resolution as public opinion becomes more focused, crystallized, and thoughtful; and the potential of direct help to individuals in search of jobs, information about training and education, health services, and other opportunities, by making available to them the information possessed by social networks.

Our particular interest is in voting and other forms of political participation. In our view, the social changes that Putnam presents as responsible for the decline in social capital play a large role in the development of a disposition toward politics in which voting is an option to address risk or impose remedy. Central to this shift is the patronage of the media as a means of civic surveillance and substitute for voting as an expression of civic responsibility. This outlook remains in the minority, but it represents a substantial and probably growing proportion of the electorate, as exemplified by the large proportion of nonvoters who fit the profile of the actives. We think this political outcome is the case whether or not Putnam is correct about the decline of social capital and its consequences, which include a lower quality of civic engagement, poorer resolutions of public issues and problems, and a citizenry less able to satisfy its personal needs. This is because Putnam's larger argument requires not only changes in American society, and a decline in social capital, but also two additional circumstances: that social capital has the benefits he describes, and that the decline has been sufficient to reduce those benefits. Our argument requires neither. We propose a narrower link between structural changes and dispositions toward political participation. Thus, we are not at all concerned when the data do not support all aspects of the hypothesized beneficence of social capital, such as the usefulness of social contacts in finding a job (Mouw, 2003). Similarly, we are not particularly concerned with whether it is more useful to employ James Coleman's conceptualization of social capital, which located it as a property of social structure, or Putnam's later version, which puts more emphasis on the attributes of individuals who make up a social system (Edwards & Foley, 1998; Foley & Edwards, 1997), although our own argument focuses exclusively on social structure. We are not endorsing Putnam's theory of social capital. Instead, we are applying a portion of that theory to voting and political participation, and we will argue that one outcome of the shifts in social capital proposed by Putnam is (a) participation in politics through media use because the act of voting has become less attractive, and (b) the use of the vote by informed citizens as an act of remedy or redress rather than one of civic responsibility.

There are five structural changes enumerated by Putnam as responsible for civic disengagement that we would apply to voting and political participation. They are: generational change in both values and behavior, urban sprawl, work pressures, and two aspects of the medium of television—the arrival of the first television generation, and the subsequent centering of activities in the home where several hours of television use typically occurs each day.

There is considerable justification for believing that one of the most engaged civically of all American generations were the veterans returning from World War II. They crowded the universities and colleges under the G.I. bill (the first author remembers the registration line snaking around the buildings for what seemed like miles at the University of Washington in 1950), learning about how society worked as well as acquiring professional and job-related skills that would serve them well in their participation in civic life. They joined organizations and associations that had agendas for the alleviation or redress of deficits and problems as well as the serving of particular personal interests. They attended meetings. They ran for office. They participated to an unparalleled degree in civic life. Succeeding generations did not share the same zeal for involvement (in part, because of the four remaining structural changes). These cohorts gave more emphasis to career, the home, privacy, and personal liberty. Personal values nevertheless would increasingly favor a democratic environment, with tolerance and a respect for differences in matters of race, religion, sexual orientation, and ideological expression becoming more prominent (Schudson, 1998).

Other shifts in values were not quite so salutary. Trust in government declined, with indices in national polls between 1980 and 1997 dropping in response to congressional scandals, negative economic perceptions, and concerns about crime (Chanley, Rudolph, & Rahn, 2000). National surveys registered an increase in materialism, with increased percentages stipulating more money, better clothes, more expensive cars, swimming pools, and worldly goods in general as necessary for "the good life." Conversely, endorsement of abstract values emphasizing society, such as patriotism, declined (Putnam, 2000). Personal trust in others also noticeably declined. Reciprocity—the belief and practice that generosity or trust will be self-benefiting in the long run when the deed is returned—became less common. Rudeness and indifference toward rules increased, as reflected in the ignoring of traffic signals, uncomplimentary gestures toward other drivers, and road rage. Thus, civic responsibility became less valued.

Urban sprawl takes a toll in a number of ways. Time spent commuting alone in a car is incompatible with the interaction on which social capital depends, and commuting is often measured in hours per weekday rather than minutes. Shopping is done in large impersonal stores scattered about among independent malls where meeting friends is unlikely. Communities are often gated, walled, and without sidewalks so there is little contact with neighbors. The grating rumble of the garage door quickly seals off the homecoming commuter. These homes are usually much alike in size, style, and cost, and are largely occupied by people who are much like each other in jobs, income, age, ethnicity, and education. Putnam gives eight examples: Jewish, white, black, upper-middle class, middle class, child- and family-focused, and retiree communities. The outside world and new experiences are shut out (which, admittedly, some would say is exactly the idea). Identity with a community and concern for its problems are nonexistent, although there may be considerable pride in the place in which one lives; commuting, shopping, and neighborhood geography are responsible, and the home owners association often takes the place of local government as the site for community involvement. Thus, urban sprawl not only reduces the time available for civic pursuits such as voting, but the human interaction and community involvement that would encourage voting.

The upscale luxury malls that some see as newly vital centers of suburban life (K. Starr, 2004)—the palaces of shopping and loitering—in no way counter these circumstances. The same applies to the defiantly postmodern entertainment panoramas that civilize (and sanitize) urban spaces, such as L.A.'s Universal City Walk. There are not enough of them, but more tellingly neither alleviates the absence of community. The malls certainly are uplifting, in the sense that entering the lobby of the Peninsula Hotel in Hong Kong makes you feel better (there are worse experiences than admiring in the chrome and glass canyons of a mall a display of Breitlings between a Burberry's and a Barney's), and the calculatedly vibrant architectural gazebos of the panoramas are pleasant enough, but the social intersections on which community involvement, civic participation, and social capital depend are largely absent. People have a good time in these places, and good times are valuable. Nevertheless, while the vicarious experiences of the coasts of luxury and safe passage on a safari through city life are gratifying compared to the ugly reflection of futility presented by lesser, ill-outfitted venues, they do not compensate for or resurrect the lost element—regular contact with others.

What often has been labelled the "New Urbanism" (K. Starr, 2004) is only a somewhat different proposition. Intended specifically to address suburban dislocation by three emphases—mixed use (residences, shopping, and employment), a diverse population (both ethnically and socioeconomically), and pedestrian friendliness (welcoming sightlines and vistas, parks and lagoons, pleasant streets)—the problem is quantitative rather than qualitative. However successful, only a miniscule proportion of the population will ever participate in the experience.

Work pressures further delimit the time available for civic activity. The downsizing of corporations and the instability of businesses over the past decade becloud the occupational horizon, and often longer hours are required for an employee to maintain his or her equity. Families that depend on two-parent incomes do not have the luxury of one parent volunteering time and effort. Single parents are under even greater pressures. This same uncertainty means that fewer people stay in the same job or division within the same company for much of their working lives, diminishing the frequency and depth of workplace interaction outside of job-related topics. The use of part-time employees, temporaries, and independent contractors further reduces the opportunities for workplace interaction. These factors mean that whatever interaction with others occurs at work is unlikely to compensate for the interaction with friends and neighbors that now occurs less often—those conversations over dinner, at chance meetings, and before and after sports.

The television generation—those who grew up for the first time with an operating set delivering three (and sometimes more) channels of entertainment and news to the household each evening—saw the home expand from the center of lived life to become the center of entertainment and diversion (undermining the movie theater, bowling alley, and minor league sports) and eventually of information. They became used to the idea of the home as the center of all activities. In addition, in the words of Robinson and Godbey (1997), "Television is clearly the 800-pound gorilla of free time. . . . " Television reduced their use of many other media, such as magazines, movies, and radio (although, at first, not newspapers, presumably because they served informational needs not satisfied by television, but by the mid-1970s newspaper reading too was suffering declines), and activities that would bring them into contact with those outside the household, including community activities (such as fairs and holiday celebrations) and religious observances (Comstock & Scharrer, 1999; Robinson & Godbey, 1997; Williams, 1986). These shifts all pointed to the allocation of time and attention that once was directed toward friends, neighbors, and others in the community as now centered on television and within the home.

Television enters again in its widespread and increasing role as a focus of entertainment and information in the home. The average amount of viewing by individuals is 3 hours and 14 minutes a day, or 22 hours and 38 minutes a week (Comstock & Scharrer, 1999). It is clear that those who watch greater amounts of television are less likely to vote; there is a consistent negative correlation between viewing and voting (Bedy, 1996). They are also less likely to join clubs and organizations, write letters to the editor or to elected officials, give speeches, attend church, and otherwise participate in activities with others (Putnam, 2000). Total use of television is extraordinary, although often attention is divided between the medium and some compatible task. Nevertheless, television as a background activity rather than the primary or secondary activity is a small minority of all viewing (Comstock & Scharrer, 1999). Household viewing is at an all-time peak, which is particularly remarkable given the declining size of households (meaning that individuals are viewing more). Use of the television set is further extended by the VCR and DVD. In-home theater systems mark a development in which the appeal of television as a center of home entertainment and information has placed it in competition with other major family expenditures, such as vacations, automobiles, and remodeling—a phenomenon represented by the increased share of communication expenditures as a proportion of gross national product (GNP) in Western countries (Comstock & Scharrer, 1999). In the short run, as we have argued elsewhere (Comstock & Scharrer, 1999), television represents the way people allocate the time they have that is not assigned to school or work and sleep, and the dropouts apparently had plenty of time that could be spent with television (or there wouldn't be that negative correlation). However, in the longer run television surely reinforces a home-centered life, with its endless entertainment, and undemanding access to information.

There is no doubt that attending to the news is a positive correlate of voting and other political participation (Comstock & Scharrer, 1999). This association has been stronger for newspaper reading than for viewing television news, but it has been positive for both. Thus, the negative association between viewing and voting by implication traces to entertainment and sports. In fact, there is a negative association between nonnews viewing and various measures of civic engagement (Moy, Scheufele, & Holbert, 1999; Shah, 1998). This kind of viewing would buffer individuals from public affairs and politics, with occasional (and sometimes accidental) news viewing allowing them to (barely) keep up with events. Immersion in the media and the ignoring of politics and public affairs join hands.

Those who detect some signs of a "virtuous circle" (Norris, 2000) would be correct. This is the proposition that use of media for public affairs information, participation, and trust enhance each other. Use of news media facilitates civic engagement, including voting, as does social interaction with others in a context that promotes political discussions. However, the concept of a circle (presumably unbroken) does not quite do justice to our state of knowledge. Trust enhances the likelihood of political participation, but acts of participation have an even stronger relationship with trust (Brehm & Rahn, 1997; Moy & Scheufele, 2000). People apparently take away positive impressions of others when they work with them in common cause.

Conversation has been considered a key element in political behavior since the classic voting studies in which interpersonal exchange seemingly trumped media influence and mass media content was disseminated through opinion leaders (Berelson, Lazarsfeld, & McPhee, 1954; Katz & Lazarsfeld, 1955; Lazarsfeld, Berelson, & Gaudet, 1948). Recent data give it an even larger presence that further supports the preeminence of the media in modern political life (Scheufele, 2002). When frequent users of serious news (from whatever print or television outlets) are compared, the predictability of political participation by news use is much greater among those who converse regularly with others about politics. In addition, those who currently function as opinion leaders in the classic sense of attending to the media more than the average and passing on their judgments to others are particularly likely to possess attributes associated with social capital: news use, social engagement, and social trust, which in turn further civic engagement (Scheufele & Shah, 2000). Thus, media are the currency of politics, and interpersonal involvement with others, rather than countermanding any possible media influence, in fact supports and facilitates the exercise of influence—at least in terms of participation—by the media.

There is an additional factor to which we would give particular prominence in the case of voting. This is the rise of the pseudo-association. As Putnam points out, the associational aspect in which members meet, discuss, and participate in activities has been replaced by professional lobbying, a struggle to sway public opinion using a campaign staff, the media, and direct mail, with a distant headquarters, usually in Washington, DC. Each has a central cause and an agenda, but a "member" does not interact with others. The "grassroots" is a populace whose members are anonymous to each other. They are linked only by writing checks to the same account. The Sierra Club is an example. It is prominent, credible among organizations working to protect the environment, but its successes and failures, and its very persona, take place in the media except for a chosen few at its core. Not for everyone is lunch in the redwoods. Like many other organizations ostensibly promoting the public interest, it is not a site of human interaction but a depository of financial contributions. In our view, this has two consequences for voter turn out: (a) it reinforces a norm of noninvolvement, and (b) more importantly, it provides political efficacy without personal political activity in regard to outcomes exclusive to the media, much as the rational instrumentalists participate in politics by their knowledge and the option, usually unexercised, of voting. (The recent form of political participation via e-mail listserves and messages sent to politicians and policy makers en masse by such organizations as MoveOn.org clearly employs the media as a means of political organizing but also creates a virtual rather than a face-to-face community.)

These factors have left millions (about one out of seven of those eligible to vote if we take the conservative stance that only the actives have been affected) employing media as a means of political participation.[1] Historically, partisan political socialization was at first diminished (reflected in the increase in independents), followed by the socialization to vote (because fewer parents were doing so). The decline in social capital means that an additional component of personal history that would encourage voting has been diminished—interaction with others. The changes in values and attitudes, the lack of interaction with others, the isolation of urban sprawl, the pressures of work, the centering of activities in the home, the decreases of membership in associational organizations, and the declines in active organizational participation, result in a different understanding of responsible political participation.

The entry of the increasing isolation of social and occupational life into the political sphere has had two consequences: the media more often are the primary means of political participation, and voting has become more frequently viewed as an exception rather than a responsibility of citizenship engaged in regularly. Our readings of the classic voting studies of the 1940s and 1950s tell us that the media have always been important despite the emphases of their authors (and especially Lazarsfeld and colleagues) on interpersonal influence and personal history. What is different now is that the media become not only sources of information about what is transpiring but also, for many, the means of thoughtful participation and a force that only sometimes will trigger the option of voting.

B. Economics of Voting

The constraints placed on voting by the structural changes in American society (which, in our view, are more certain than a broader erosion in social betterment attributable to a decline in social capital) have changed the way many think about the act of casting a ballot. Those who see a moral imperative believe voting is a personal responsibility; it is necessary baggage for a good citizen. Those who favor the authority of democracy argue that everyone should make known his or her judgment; a high turnout by definition is good. Others emphasize neither moral obligation nor the workings of democracy but

[1]The Doppelt and Shearer survey probably somewhat overrepresents the actives among nonvoters because the same factors that make them "active" would lead to a higher response rate; However, any exaggeration would be insufficient to render them less than a substantial proportion of the public.

the personal value of registering an opinion; every vote counts. These are normative judgments in which an "ought" figures prominently. These viewpoints at once ignore the social context of modern American voting, which is made up of the structural changes that for some make voting less likely, as well as the conditions that in fact render the comparatively low turnout in the United States—by the standards of history and other countries where open elections are regularly held—quite functional for democracy.

We see four fundamental parameters in the United States that characterize the act of voting:

1. The right to vote is irrevocable (barring conviction for a felony) so that the dropouts can enter the arena at any time.
2. Voting has concrete costs in time and effort that cannot be fully alleviated by reforms in the registration process.
3. Voting has informational costs because voter choice would be meaningless (and, if random, probabilistically self-canceling) if it were not based on reasoned judgments about policies and proposals, and this applies even to a candidate of the party usually preferred (we point to the concerns over the "wings" of each of the two major parties that occupy so much of the media's coverage of politics).
4. The rewards of voting, which essentially have remained unchanged, have become less appealing.

The potential voter usually is faced with two opposing candidates, each representing one of the two major parties. The potential voter may well prefer one or the other. The potential voter nevertheless faces two questions: Would the election of the less preferred candidate be sufficiently detrimental to his or her interests—whether defined in terms of benefit to society or personal gain—to make voting worthwhile? Is there confidence enough that the more preferred candidate will perform as expected? In sum, are risk or remedy at play, and are we certain of our preferences? In the American political system, with a substantial proportion of independents, two major parties each embracing diverse viewpoints (liberals, conservatives, and a center), and shifting loyalties between parties from election to election, the answer often will be "No."

From the perspective of the potential voter, this is not the abandonment of responsibility, an indifference to democratic participation, or carelessness in exercising judgment. It is rational behavior.

The dilemma facing the potential voter is exacerbated by the fallacy of accountability. Presidents and other politicians are held accountable for their actions. This is particularly so when the media focus on the particular policies in dispute (Mutz, 1998). Media attention helps place issues on the public's agenda, and the combination of personal experience (e.g., unemployment) combined with media attention (e.g., the economy is bad) is particularly powerful in mobilizing opinion. This is the inevitable course of politics. However, it is an imperfect and imprecise process in which ambiguity is more certain than certainty.

The crucial distinction is between execution (the potential sin of commission) and consequences (failure or success). Policies initiated long ago are often blamed or praised for recent failures or successes. A recent initiative may be too new to show its eventual promise. Actual changes in conditions may not be adequately or accurately reported by the press, so that there may be a lag between events and valid public judgment. New proposals can be judged only by their likely outcomes. The result is that presidents and other politicians can be held accountable fully only for what they do but only imperfectly and imprecisely for what they accomplish.

VI. SEARCHING FOR INFORMATION

The American public can be roughly divided into two groups: a small collection of individuals interested and engaged in political affairs, and the majority of others whose involvement—psychological and behavioral—is confined to major decisions with lasting political implications, such as presidential elections (Almond & Verba, 1989a, 1989b; Neuman, 1986). The latter group monitors rather than takes great interest in political news most of the time and increases their engagement when the electoral cycle calls upon them to consider casting a vote for prominent offices or on major public issues. The former are keen news audience members, with high levels of exposure and attention to the news as well as considerable stores of prior knowledge regarding political affairs. Marcus, Neuman, and Mackuen (2000), drawing on their expertise in political scholarship, estimate that between a third and a half of the public give "some frequent attentiveness" to news of public affairs and politics, although this would be far more than those who consistently engage in such attentiveness (although quite in line with our estimate from the Pew data of those attending closely to any particular story) and would vary from person to person with the topic (not everyone interested in politics will want to follow the sexual dalliance of a president, and not everyone interested in that sexual dalliance will care about free trade).

A. Media and Voting

The role of the news media is instrumental for both groups, although different for each. The minority of the highly involved attend to news about politics and public affairs closely and use the information reported in the news to bolster, refine, and elaborate on their prior knowledge and opinions (McLeod & Becker, 1974; Neuman, Just, & Crigler, 1992). Many among the majority use the media to participate in major elections armed with a sufficient amount of knowledge about the candidates (Comstock & Scharrer, 1999). They desire to learn from election coverage and the media messages disseminated by candidates, and they are somewhat successful.

Mere exposure to news media leads to knowledge of candidates and campaign issues (Chaffee, Zhao, & Leshner, 1994; Zhao & Chaffee, 1995), yet learning is enhanced when audience members are motivated to thoughtfully process rather than passingly attend (McLeod & Becker, 1974). Among those incidentally exposed, "knowledge gains . . . would be much less than the gains for those attending with interest" who have "cognitive schema well attuned to the political events" (Comstock & Scharrer, 1999, p. 216). News media use also has been shown to facilitate voting decisions in presidential elections (Bartels, 1993; Chaffee & Frank, 1996; Domke et al., 1997; Holbrook, 1996). The same pattern holds for other high-profile races receiving extensive media coverage: for governor, Senate, House, and even hard-fought local contests. The effect is enhanced by a large role for television that is only sometimes present outside of presidential campaigns (for example, in Arnold Schwarzenegger's 2003 campaign for the California governorship) but often absent with coverage of other races confined largely to newspapers. Thus, the purposive seeking of political information via news media exposure heightens returns to the political system, including the acquiring of knowledge about the election, key players, principal issues, and increased likelihood of voting.

The bulk of Americans become aware of impending political decisions of importance through the media and (subsequently) direct their attention strategically toward news media. Their motive is to arrive at a reasoned, informed voting decision. This instructional role gives the news media a central place in the electoral process.

Favorable coverage predicts increases in support for a candidate. Voter support expands and contracts in accord with the valence of news coverage. As we have seen (Chapter 4), in presidential contests this holds for primaries and caucuses as well as the election. In the 1996 Clinton–Dole race, Domke and colleagues (1997) found that a composite measure of the favorability of television and newspaper coverage predicted public opinion in regard to issues and images, as well as vote intention. In three earlier elections—1984, 1988, 1992—Holbrook (1996) found that campaign events, where public knowledge depended on media coverage whatever an individual's imminent source, predicted opinions about issues and images as well as support for the candidates. Bartels (1993) in the 1980 election found that the exposure of individuals to newspaper and television coverage separately predicted perceptions of issues and images, with the relationship stronger for television than for newspapers. The data demonstrate that the public uses political news to make judgments, which means the media can manipulate the public as well as serve its informational needs.

In addition to instructing the public about the electoral process, candidates, their stands, and campaign events, news media use can make it more likely that individuals will vote. Support for the news media's role in facilitating participation comes from studies from three regions in the United States. Among 400 voters in Toledo surveyed before the 1988 Iowa caucus, partisans reported paying greater attention to television coverage than independents, but independents who did follow the campaign on television and who also had keen interest in the campaign became particularly likely to vote (Smith & Ferguson, 1990). Presumably, these independents were seeking information, and would have been less committed to voting than the partisans; media had an enabling role. Kennamer (1990a) studied a group of Richmond, Virginia, residents and found that following the campaign on television among independents was associated with voting in the general election whereas among the entire sample, following the campaign by reading newspapers was the strongest media use predictor of voting. In either case, motivated attention to news media was propitious. In the 1996 presidential election, Pinkleton, Austin, and Fortman (1998) found that use of media to gain political information by Washington state voters predicted a greater likelihood of voting as well as a higher estimation of political efficacy. Negative attitudes about media coverage were associated with lower use of the media for political information, thereby identifying a subset of the sample who appeared to be cynical or distrustful about news attention to political affairs. Other researchers have discovered that some members of the public are disenchanted with both the state of politics and with news media performance (Cappella & Jamieson, 1997; Chan, 1997). These individuals would have modest motivation at best to learn from political coverage and little desire to cast a vote, and their exposure to election news would be primarily incidental and therefore not strongly instructive. This describes three of our five blocs of dropouts—the exceptions being the actives and, to a lesser degree, the disenchanteds.

B. Commercials as Instruction

Viewing political commercials has also been associated with learning about the campaign and the candidates. This media format is unique to election periods and therefore possesses both the novelty and relevance to capture audience members' attention. Commercials have been compared in instructional efficacy to other media formats that are typically longer, such as news coverage or televised debates. In such comparisons, political commercials fare surprisingly well considering how short they are and in light of accusations that they focus too heavily on image rather than issues. For instance, Patterson and McClure (1976), in a sample drawn from Syracuse, New York, in the 1972 election, found that exposure to political commercials resulted in greater knowledge of candidate's issue positions than exposure to television news. As with news coverage, however, Zhao and Bleske (1995) determined that differential effects occur depending on whether there was mere exposure or close attention. Using a sample of over 300 randomly selected residents of North Carolina, they found that exposure to commercials predicted more accuracy of knowledge and equal confidence in knowledge compared to exposure to television news. The advantage for learning from political commercials grew when they distinguished between attention and exposure. Both accuracy and confidence in knowledge about the candidates were more strongly associated with attention to political commercials than attention to televised news stories. In a comparison of learning from political commercials with learning from viewing a televised debate, Just, Crigler, and Wallach (1990) demonstrated the ability of issue-based ads to influence not just the acquisition but also the retention of information. Eighty percent of their sample was able to recall the position of a congressional candidate after seeing an issue-based commercial, whereas only 30 to 50 percent recalled various issue positions after viewing a debate.

At the aggregate level, the analysis of the 2000 presidential election by Benoit, Hansen, and Holbert (2004) is particularly instructive. This is because of the large National Election Study (NES) sample (N = 1,807), the nationally representative inclusion of voters from across the country, and the reflection in the data of actual campaign events. They divided their respondents into three groups: those from seven "super"-battleground states (Michigan, Missouri, New Mexico, Oregon, Pennsylvania, Washington, and Wisconsin), where the amount of political commercials was particularly high; 17 battleground states, where the amount of political commercials was substantial; and, nonbattleground or captive states, where the likelihood of victory or defeat was considered so certain that expenditures on advertising were comparatively modest. This analysis thus takes advantage of the logic of the Electoral College, in which victory delivers the total votes for a state regardless of the size of the majority or plurality.

As would be expected if commercials have an instructional role, knowledge of the stands of the candidates on issues and the salience of particular issues in preferring one candidate or another were greatest in the super-battleground states, and greater in the battleground states than in the captive states. These outcomes are particularly convincing because they occurred after statistically controlling for the influence of eight variables: age, gender, education, engaging in political discussions, and use of the media—national television news, local television news, newspapers, and radio. Thus, they represent the independent and net effects of commercials.

The authors somewhat ruefully observe that the Electoral College may have a dysfunctional role by shielding voters in captive states from information; we are inclined to label these outcomes as benefits for voters in the super-battleground and battleground states on the grounds that there is no criterion or norm for the proper and necessary amount of information for a wise voting decision. Personally, we believe that the election of a president who does not win the popular vote as well as triumphing in the Electoral College is displeasing—for the voters, the nation, and our system of government. In any case, the analysis of Benoit, Hansen, and Holbert documents that political commercials deliver information, and that this information goes beyond that obtained from the news media and from discussing politics with others.

We conclude that political commercials can be informative, especially when truly attended to rather than peripherally experienced. However, Zhao and Chaffee (1995) provide a reminder to avoid the dramatic conclusion that political commercials always outscore other media formats in informing the public. Zhao and Chaffee analyzed data drawn from national samples of respondents across six campaigns and found that news viewing was a more consistent predictor of knowledge than exposure to political commercials. We have two explanations for the disparity. First, not all studies distinguish between exposure and attention, yet this is an important factor. It is possible that the formulaic nature of televised news results sometimes in less attention compared to more novel and dramatic political spots. Second, the specific attributes of the media formats are likely to be major determinants. Not all political ads and not all television news stories about politics are instructive, informative, or particularly likely to attract and hold attention. The data point convincingly, however, to the potential for both commercials and news stories to inform the audience about candidates and issues.

Negative political advertisements represent a distinct category of persuasive attempts, and have been the subject of considerable controversy. These "attack" ads focus on the opponent, and malign his or her political credentials, character, or stands on issues. Political consultants frequently argue that campaigns organized around an advance and destroy strategy can be very effective (Lau et al., 1999)—especially if the attacks begin early and the campaign is well financed. The opinion of professional persuaders is supposedly particularly accurate in regard to what does and does not work because their careers are dependent on their ability to induce compliance (Cialdini & Trost, 1998). Several years ago (Comstock & Scharrer, 1999), we concluded that a group of experiments, because they permitted causal inference, demonstrated the effectiveness of negative or attack political commercials. For example, Garramone, Atkin, Pinkleton, and Cole (1990) exposed

372 students to either negative or positive political commercials. They found that exposure to negative commercials had greater effects on liking for the candidates, perceived strengths of the candidates, and knowledge about the candidates than exposure to positive commercials. Similar results were reported by Pfau and Burgoon (1989), Pinkleton (1997), and Tinkham and Weaver-Lariscy (1993). Survey research indicated that negative appeals were generally not well liked by the public, but the experimental record seemed to support effects on evaluations of candidates. Some commentators (Jamieson, 1992; Patterson, 2003) cast attack ads with the negative emphases of political news coverage as a factor alienating voters, with some risk of backlash against the sponsor because of the public's well-known distaste for such appeals (Jamieson, 1992).

However, the meta-analysis by Lau and colleagues (1999) leads us to revise this judgment. The finding that experimental designs did not produce results different from survey designs militates strongly against the possibility that outcomes might vary with research design. They examined 117 correlations between exposure to negative print and television appeals drawn from 51 separate studies. They found no consistent evidence of superior or inferior effectiveness, no consistent evidence of greater or lesser dislike, and pertinent to our earlier interpretation, no significant effects for televised negative appeals.

We cannot quarrel with the conclusion of the authors that the empirical record gives no support to the view that negative political appeals are particularly effective—so much for the judgment of the professional persuaders. However, there remains a question of the homogeneity of the appeals examined. They took the reasonable step of using the classification of the original investigator. This does not rule out the possibility that certain production and presentational features are crucial, although it does mean they would have had to escape the notice of the original investigators.

The record in actual political contests is clearer, although interpretation is not. The best data, because they cover such a large number and variety of electoral circumstances, are those of Tinkham and Weaver-Lariscy (1990, 1995) who asked nearly 600 candidates for the House to report on the frequency of their use of negative ads and compared that estimate to the percentage of the vote each obtained. There was a consistent negative relationship between use of negative ads and the number of votes received. We interpret this as indicating that negative ads are used more often by those in a weaker position, such as challengers or those trailing in the polls. Negative ads are strategies frequently embraced by candidates who face many obstacles to success, including incumbents who will benefit from prior commitment of supporters as well as greater voter familiarity (Gigenrenzer & Goldstein, 1999; Lau, 2003). Thus, the electoral efficacy of attack ads is clothed in ambiguity. There nevertheless is no doubt that negative appeals are sometimes part of effective campaigns, no doubt that a majority of voters express dislike of them, and that an aggregation of empirical results displays no consistent pattern of either particular effectiveness or ineffectiveness.

There also have been experimental comparisons of image versus issue ads (Kaid, Leland, & Whitney, 1992; Pfau & Burgoon, 1989; Roddy & Garramone, 1988; Thorson, Christ, & Caywood, 1991). Issue ads consistently have proved more effective by measures of recall or candidate evaluation. However, these comparisons usually involve students as subjects and thus don't represent adult voters. We could not venture beyond the interpretation that students believe issues are the more appropriate course for political campaigns.

C. Issues and Debates

Finally, as we argued earlier, televised presidential debates have an instructional role, particularly in regard to issues. Viewers who regularly follow a series of debates are particularly likely to use information about the positions of the candidates on issues in making voting decisions (Dennis, Chaffee, & Choe, 1979). Viewing one or more debates stimulates reflection on and discussion of issues (Atkin, Hocking, & McDermott, 1979; Becker, Pepper, Wenner, & Kim, 1979). Viewing one or more debates also increases knowledge of issues and the stands of the candidates (Comstock & Scharrer, 1999; Drew & Weaver, 1991; Friedenberg, 1997; Lanoue, 1991; Zhu, Milavsky, & Biswas, 1994). Indeed, a recent meta-analysis of the effects of viewing presidential debates in the United States (Benoit, Hansen, & Verser, 2003) shows that—regardless of study design and the use of student versus nonstudent samples—debate viewing significantly affected issue knowledge, perceptions of candidates' characters, vote preference, and issue salience (an agenda-setting effect). The findings from the meta-analysis suggest the first debate in a series is a stronger predictor of vote preference than subsequent debates. No other differential effects according to the position of the debate in a series were found. Thus, subsequent debates retain their impact on learning and forming impressions of candidates and important issues.

However, these knowledge gains are quite modest as a result of changes in the audiences for debates and the limited amount of novel information supplied by debates. The huge increase since the Kennedy–Nixon debates of 1960 in number of channels available means that viewers have many other options when debates are broadcast. The resulting smaller audiences include larger proportions of the politically interested and informed. These viewers with high interest in the campaign gain less in knowledge from debates than those with lower levels of interest (Patterson, 1980). This reverses the usual pattern where prior knowledge facilitates the incorporation of new information (Neuman, Just, & Crigler, 1992). The reason is that, for the highly informed and interested, the debates present little that is new while high interest in the campaign nevertheless predicts close attention to debates.

VII. INTEREST AND MOTIVE

Different media perform different functions in informing the public about politics. Local and state politics receive the greatest amount of coverage in newspapers rather than on television, and newspaper use among the public is, indeed, a predictor of voting in local and state elections (Kennamer, 1987). Television, on the other hand, is most frequently turned to for national elections and is listed by most voters as their primary source for coverage of presidential campaigns (Bogart, 1989; Mendelsohn & O'Keefe, 1976). It also can play a large role through political commercials as well as news coverage in drawing attention to major contests for Senate and governor. Newspapers typically outperform television news in informing the public in political communication research (Martinelli & Chaffee, 1995; Patterson, 1980; Stamm, Johnson, & Martin, 1997; Vincent & Basil, 1997). Television news viewing is somewhat greater than newspaper reading among those with less education; nevertheless information acquisition from each is substantial (Comstock & Scharrer, 1999; Neuman, Just, & Crigler, 1992). Furthermore, television is the preferred news source among young adults, who increasing do not regularly read newspapers (Comstock & Scharrer, 1999; Robinson & Godbey, 1997). These varied differences in media use take place within the general framework in which those who attend to the news with some regularity typically use all media to some degree while those outside this news audience attend only sporadically to the news, and usually only when there are threatening and compelling events, such as war, a terrorist attack, or election eve in a presidential contest, and in these cases they turn primarily to the most accessible medium, television (Comstock & Scharrer, 1999; Patterson, 1980).

Different media also differ according to the time at which they are most influential. The period within the electoral cycle in which the media present information plays a part (Holbrook, 1996; Patterson, 1980) because interest and attention change and because particular types of information vary in relevance at different points in time. The primary and caucus season and the nominating conventions are pivotal times for television news because the public is just beginning to form impressions of candidates and the visuals broadcast convey information that can be formative in shaping conceptions of image and in learning of issues (Holbrook, 1996; Patterson, 1980). The first debate offers a singular opportunity for television influence because the audience is usually larger than for subsequent encounters and the early position in the campaign increases the likelihood of affecting impressions and knowledge (Hollander, 1993; Sears & Chaffee, 1979). Political commercials are especially influential among the undecided in the final stages of the campaign, as Election Day approaches and those planning to vote but uncertain of for whom they will vote will be attempting to close in on a decision (Bowen, 1994).

A number of factors affect the degree to which individuals obtain political information from the media. Characteristics of individuals are consequential. The motivation to learn and reflect on the information provided (Perse, 1990) predicts greater consideration of electoral options. Interest and involvement in politics (Neuman, Just, & Crigler, 1992; Patterson & McClure, 1976) predicts greater attention to political coverage. Level of prior political knowledge (Rhee & Cappella, 1997) governs the ability to incorporate new and sometimes subtle or complex information into existing schemas. Strength of support for one candidate or another (Bowen, 1994) decreases the likelihood of a change in allegiance and the frequency of late decision making, and increases attention to a campaign. Attributes of the media themselves—credibility, use of visuals, clarity and ease of comprehension, appealing angles or frames—are heeded when individual audience members select media for the purpose of acquiring information about campaigns (Bogart, 1989; Martinelli & Chaffee, 1995; Mendelsohn & O'Keefe, 1976; Norris, 2000; Patterson, 1980; Stamm, Johnson, & Martin, 1997; Vincent & Basil, 1997).

The two paramount factors in the relationship between information and voting nevertheless are interest and motive. Interest assures the media generally of audiences, and in the case of politics largely explains the positive correlations between use of news media and participation. Those interested in politics attend to the media because the media are the sole comprehensive source of politically relevant information. The media in modern life in America are an essential link between the citizen and politics—they provide knowledge, signal novel and threatening events, and lead to judgments, and in these ways encourage participation. The events reported in the news may lead to assimilation, in which they become incorporated into present impressions; may become anchorages, in which they are taken as standards of right or wrong or greater or lesser significance that will be applied more broadly; or may lead to corrective action, as occurs when cognitive responses are accompanied by emotional reactions that signal the presence of risk or the need for remedy (DeCoster & Claypool, 2004; Marcus, Neuman, & MacKuen, 2000). But they also make it ever more feasible for the individual to make voting contingent on electoral circumstances while still maintaining a deep and ongoing interest in public affairs and political events. Nonparticipation for many becomes information based, and the media are the primary sources of political information. Among the dropouts, this stance is best exemplified by the actives.

Motive now becomes the central element. The potential voter is faced with a choice, usually between two candidates but sometimes among several. The likelihood of voting becomes a function of the rewards minus the cost weighted by the likelihood that the vote in question will affect the outcome (Hamilton, 2004):

$$\text{Voting } (f) = \text{rewards} - \text{costs} \times (\text{expected influence}).$$

As Downs (1957) has so convincingly argued, the final term is essentially zero. The rewards can be construed as a collection of positive thoughts and emotions:

Rewards (*f*) = satisfaction in behaving as a good citizen
social approval from others registering support for a candidate or ideology
participation in a social ritual.

Costs similarly can be construed as a collection of inconveniences and ambiguities:

Cost (*f*) = time consumed by registering
time allocated to going to the polls
effort to collect information
anxiety over error in decision reached.

Motive derives from the expectation that voting or otherwise participating in politics will lower risk or facilitate remedy and the personal satisfactions of voting. For many individuals, the decision not to vote is quite rational, for it is as much based on reason as the actions of those who do vote (DeLuca, 1995; Lupia, McCubbins, & Popkin, 2000).

Those who don't vote represent a collective force of considerable power. In fact, if the actives alone turned out in proportions resembling those who vote regularly, overall turnout would be well above 70 percent and entirely in line with what one would have expected given the positive correlation between education and voting and the dramatic rises in educational levels during the latter half of the past century. Motive at any time may send present dropouts to the polls.

Our model, of course, applies to both voters and dropouts. The important differences among the various types of dropouts is that the rewards and costs vary considerably. For the alienated, the rewards will be pitifully small. For the know-nothings, information costs are extremely high and the rewards, without the knowledge necessary for a reasoned decision, illusory. The Republican conservatives and liberal Democrats, in contrast, find that the differences in expected outcome well repay voting. Yet, there is an important nuance here exemplified by the terms *rational behavior* and reasoned *decision making*. All voters and dropouts are rational and reasoning in the sense that their behavior serves their needs. However, only a certain kind of dropout—represented primarily by the one out of six eligible voters who fit the profile of our rational instrumentalists—can be thought of as calculatedly accepting the economics of voting as the proper way for a citizen to behave. The significant factor, then, is not the logic of the economics, but the emergence of a new type of responsible citizen: prepared to act but only when necessary.

Some (Patterson, 2002) have expressed the fear that high levels of dropouts imply that this potential might be transformed into support for some demagogic movement or charismatic despot. We are skeptical of a threat from the politics of peril and precipice, but we do agree that high turnout by a citizenry that is well informed and stable in ideology mitigates against such outcomes. However, realistically we think the danger is small.

First, those most likely to be drawn to voting in a particular election from the population of dropouts are those least likely to be attracted to a scruffy movement or demonic candidate—those who follow the news, are well-informed, and think favorably of both parties, as exemplified by the actives. Second, the attention to the mass media required to draw other dropouts to an unsavory campaign would probably not be able to overcome the messages of the many sources advocating more established parties and candidates. Here, lack of interest deters radical motive. The sole exception would be the disenchanteds, who follow public affairs closely and whose hostility toward politicians might be overcome by a messianic, charismatic figure. Third, the deep-rooted distrust of Americans in general toward ideologues and extremists would constrain such perilous responses. This is a factor that would mitigate any vulnerability of the disenchanteds. In fact, the research on the knowledge gap (Gaziano & Gaziano, 1996; Rucinski, 2004; Tichenor, Donohue, & Olien, 1980) says crises and the perception of a special interest promote the spread of knowledge. Interest, if aroused, will lead to better information and more informed choices. We thus do not see the less knowledgeable panicking over events and rushing down a superhighway of unsound policies. Instead, we see them as addressing their panic by greater knowledge, often obtained from the media, and thereby entering the ranks of participants as informed voters.

PART III

The Collective Self

Using the Media

Despite some fragmenting of the mass audience (because of the increasing diversity of media available, and particularly of television channels) and specialized targeting of publics (because of direct mail, special interest magazines and newspaper features, and the Internet), the mass media provide the main means of transmitting messages regarding politics and public affairs to potentially large and heterogeneous groups of audiences. Individuals respond to those messages in myriad ways, ranging from outright dismissal or complete lack of attention to careful consideration or undiminished persuasion. Audience members differ according to their level of interest in, knowledge about, and attentiveness to political affairs at various times throughout the electoral cycle, and therefore select and attend to messages in a variety of ways.

The now-famous studies addressing the influence of pretelevision media on political decision making assigned a modest role to radio and newspapers, dwarfed in size and significance by the impact of previously held beliefs (Klapper, 1960) and the influence of others in one's social network. The data from the voting studies conducted in Erie County in 1940 (Lazarsfeld,

Berelson, & Gaudet, 1948) and in Elmira, New York, in 1948 (Berelson, Lazarsfeld, & McPhee, 1954) were interpreted as pointing to a limited role for media in shaping voting behavior (Chapters 1, 2, and 3). Scores of studies since—examining newspaper accounts, political commercials, televised debates, television news stories, Internet sites, and other media formats—have found convincing evidence of media influence on political information, views, and behavior. Such a relationship is often moderated by additional factors, but is also often significant (statistically and colloquially) nonetheless. Now, about 60 years since the issue was first investigated using social scientific tools and methods, political communication scholars and specialists are confident in their claims that audience members use the media in a variety of ways that contribute to the shaping of their political knowledge, attitudes, and behavior.

The primary ways in which the public employs media information for political purposes include such pursuits and processes as knowledge acquisition, the formation of attitudes about candidates and issues, and voting or other forms of political participation. Our central tenet is that the public uses the media continually to serve political ends, although this use is often at variance with the model of the ideal citizen seeking out information, analyzing it, and reaching a carefully reasoned decision about a policy or candidate. Public use of media for political purposes manifests itself in five important respects. As we have just seen (Chapter 5):

1. Individuals monitor the media for signs that important decisions are called for, as exemplified by the national electoral cycles, and then search the news media to acquire information that facilitates participation.

In addition:

2. Individuals use the media to identify pertinent issues and topics, as well as potential presidential candidates, as exemplified by agenda setting.
3. Individuals rely on the media to inform them—through polls, analyses of public sentiment, and reports of protests, rallies, and demonstrations—of what others think, which under some circumstances influences their own judgments.
4. Individuals rely on the media to convey the lived circumstances of others, an activity in which the media often supplant firsthand experience but risk the choice of inaccurate exemplars.
5. Individuals use a dual surveillance system, in which cognitive processing of not particularly arousing stimuli relies on habitual responses, whereas judgments focused by emotional arousal more often involve a review of alternatives and are open to changes of mind about candidates, parties, or position on an issue.

I. TOPICS, ISSUES, EVENTS, AND PEOPLE

Many discussions of the news media's role in setting the public's agenda—the topics, issues, events, and people to which the public imputes varying degrees of importance or salience—begin with Cohen's (1963) conclusion that the media are more successful in telling members of the public what to think about rather than what to think. Indeed, this is a useful and legitimate orientation to the basic premise of the theory of agenda setting—a premise that has received convincing support since its first empirical test in 1968 (McCombs & Shaw, 1972), although the theory also has evolved in important ways over time.

The same idea was proposed more than a decade earlier by Lazarsfeld and Merton (1948), but Cohen merits his place in social science history not only because of the felicity of the juxtaposed concepts ("what to think" versus "what to think about") but because he drew on empirical data: interviews with journalists and government officials about foreign policy. However, it would remain for McCombs and Shaw (1972) to collect data representing the general public and everyday use of the news media and thereby initiate a major sphere of communication research. From the vantage of the individual audience member, the theory holds that the news media, as the primary source of information about local, regional, national, and international issues and events, function as both filter and alert system. The filter—the gatekeeping function of the press—canvasses events and developments to determine which best satisfy news values and therefore merit placement among the reported news stories of the day. The audience member is presented with a distillation in a series of selected stories. The alert system announces that by the very nature of inclusion in the news these are things that matter, and the relative emphases of the media will amplify or mute the perceived importance of those selected occurrences. We have found it useful (Comstock & Scharrer, 1999) to describe agenda setting by three dimensions: research questions, process, and attributes (Table 6.2).

The first test of the theory of agenda setting was conducted with a random sample of undecided voters (because they would be less likely to be committed to the priority of an issue based on party preference and therefore would be more susceptible to media influence) in Chapel Hill, North Carolina, during the 1968 presidential election campaign (McCombs & Shaw, 1972). The paradigm—carried over in many but not all of the subsequent studies of the theory—was twofold. One element was a survey that asked respondents to name, in their opinion, the most important issues of the day. Those issues, ranked according to percentage of respondents naming each, formed an estimate of the public agenda. The second element was a content analysis of four local newspapers, the *New York Times*, two television network evening newscasts (CBS and NBC), and two newsmagazines (*Newsweek* and *Time*) to determine the frequency of news stories carried in each outlet that pertained to each issue raised by respondents. These results comprised the news agenda. The agenda-setting function of the press found support in calculations showing a significant correlation between the items included in the news agenda and the issues listed in the public agenda, explained by the researchers as a transfer of salience from the news to public views.

These were only correlational data not properly open to causal interpretation, although the authors argued in behalf of the influence of the media on the public's agenda. However, we think (Comstock & Scharrer, 1999) they had a good case:

> . . . (I)n retrospect (and in accord with Occam's razor) the original argument of McCombs and Shaw attains considerable credence because it would require uncanny sensitivity to public nuance for the media to follow opinion to such a degree, whereas the likelihood that media attention would guide opinion requires no such miraculous intervention (p. 197).

Over 350 studies of agenda setting have been undertaken since the Chapel Hill data were collected (Dearing & Rogers, 1996). The evidence is supportive of the agenda-setting effect in election years as well as at other times, on a national scale as well as locally, among not just undecided voters but general populations, and within the United States and beyond (McCombs & Reynolds, 2002). An initial critique of the inability to establish causal order in agenda-setting research was rectified by the use of experimental methodology to determine that news media exposure did, indeed, cause fluctuations in the public's agenda (Iyengar & Kinder, 1987a, 1987b). A meta-analysis of 90 empirical studies of agenda setting sets the mean correlation between news agendas and public agendas across research inquiries at +.53 (Wanta & Ghanem, forthcoming). Individuals look to the news media to determine the topics and events they should be concerned about, inferring that only important matters find their way to newspapers, newsmagazines, and newscasts and setting their own stated priorities of issues accordingly.

A. New Features

There has been considerable elaboration of the theory over time. Individuals' need for orientation (Tolman, 1932, 1948) has proven to affect the influence of the media on an individual's agenda. People vary in whether they find news items personally relevant and in the amount of prior knowledge and experience they have about topics. These two factors, relevance and uncertainty, comprise an individual's need for orientation, which in turn, has been found to predict agenda setting. Low degrees of relevance (e.g., a story from a distant locale) and of uncertainty (e.g., an emergency room nurse reads a story on the frequent occurrence of household injuries) decrease the impact of news media in setting an audience member's agenda. In the first case, individuals may remain unconvinced of the importance of the news item because they find it personally irrelevant. In the second, they would be unpersuaded by the news media of the importance of the issue because they already would be aware of its significance.

The relationship between need for orientation and agenda setting is important in a political context. Undecided voters close to the time of a presidential election such as those surveyed in the Chapel Hill study (McCombs & Shaw, 1972) are likely to have a high need for orientation and are therefore more susceptible to an agenda-setting effect (Weaver & McCombs, 1978). Conversely, the typically small group of exceptionally well-informed individuals who follow politics closely at the same point in time are likely to be less susceptible to an agenda-setting influence from news stories on political issues because they have a low need for orientation.

Agenda setting, of course, is a cyclical process and owes only a modest debt to real world events. Issues, events, and persons rise and fall in media attention and thus on the public agenda. There is often little correspondence between the attention of the media and real world indicators of issues. Funkhouser (1973a, 1973b) documented this for several topics, including the war in Vietnam (Figure 6.1). Other examples are drug abuse and crime. Food shortages in

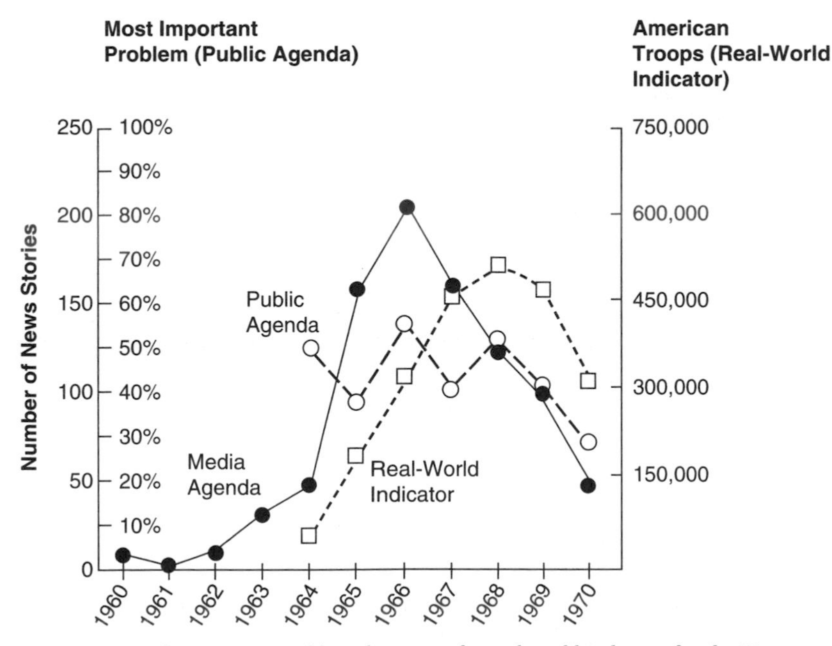

FIGURE 6.1. Media attention, public salience, and a real world indicator for the Vietnam war (Adapted from *Agenda setting*, by J.W. Dearing and E.M. Rogers, 1996, Thousand Oaks, CA: Sage; "The issues of the sixties: An exploratory study in the dynamics of public opinion," by G. R. Funkhouser, 1973, *Public Opinion Quarterly*, *37*(1), pp. 62–75; and "Trends in media coverage of the issues of the sixties," by G. R. Funkhouser, 1973, *Journalism Quarterly*, *50*, pp. 533–538.)

Ethiopia and Brazil were equally serious, but the former became a major news story in the United States and the latter did not (Dearing & Rogers, 1996). The media play to the expectations of reader and viewer interest. When redeemed by audience attention, stories are pursued. At some point, the possibilities for continuing coverage diminish. New events and issues appear. Media attention shifts. So too will the public's agenda.

Although there is certainly a pervasive tendency for individuals to discount personal experience as a measure of the state of the nation—whether the issue is what people are thinking or what people are experiencing—in favor of media accounts, firsthand experience does enter into the agenda-setting process (Comstock & Scharrer, 1999; Dearing & Rogers, 1996). First, individuals will give some weight to what they have seen or heard from others in evaluating media accounts. The distinction here is between obtrusive and unobtrusive events. Circumstances that dramatically impinge on daily life cannot be ignored, and will not be countered by media reports to the contrary in the formation of impressions about what is transpiring in one's immediate environment. Two examples are gasoline shortages and epidemics. Lines at local gas stations and quickly organized regiments of hospital beds are hard to ignore whatever the media may say. The agenda-setting power of the media is thus dependent on nonintrusive events that do not occasion dramatic local displays.

Historically, newspapers have scored more consistently as predictors of the public's agenda than television news (Comstock et al., 1978). This is partly a consequence of the early concern of agenda setting with a comparison of the public's imputations of importance with the emphases of the media. Newspaper emphases, enunciated by headline size and placement on the front page, are much easier to discern than those within a half-hour newscast with 15 to 16 items. Television news viewers comparatively are somewhat more passive, and would less often make the necessary discriminations (Wanta & Hu, 1994). In two circumstances, however, television may be more powerful. One is when the medium is far more prestigious, as in the case of a comparison between a small city daily and a network news program (Williams, Shapiro, & Cutbirth, 1983). The other is when television coverage is particularly intense, with a large number of stories within a short space of time (Brosius & Kepplinger, 1990). In both of these cases, television becomes more likely than newspapers to set the public's agenda. In the second instance, greater newspaper and newsmagazine coverage is likely to follow what we have called "spotlighting" by television (Comstock & Scharrer, 1999). The corollary is that the contribution of the media to the public's agenda will increase when television newly adds to the attention given a particular topic (Schoenbach, 1991; Trumbo, 1995). Finally, early research indicated that in election campaigns newspapers required four to six weeks before the emphases of coverage became reflected in the public's agenda (Wanta, 1997; Winter & Eyal, 1981).

More recent data make it clear this lag is circumstance bound. Topics can appear almost immediately on the public agenda when an event is dramatic enough (and given the requisite media attention); terrorism rose to the top of the public and political agendas with September 11, 2001. Extraordinary events dissolve the rules.

Recent research on agenda setting also has found that not only do news media have the ability to transfer the salience of a topic to audiences, they also have the ability to bring to the foreground the specific aspects that will govern thinking about that topic. The influence of the news media is not limited to the importance and relevance of issues, events, and people, but extends (as seems obvious in retrospect) to specific aspects of those issues, events, and people. In so doing, the agenda-setting function of the press goes beyond the confines expressed in Cohen's (1963) juxtaposition and affects what individuals think about the items in the news. The ability of these aspects (the "characteristics and properties," in the words of McCombs and Reynolds, 2002) emphasized in the news to affect what members of the public call to mind when they think of issues, topics, events, and people is called the second level of agenda setting.

Second-level agenda setting is immensely important in the political realm. News reports often focus on particular properties of candidates, events, and issues, especially in the medium of television in which constraints on time and an emphasis on simplicity largely eliminate the possibility of presenting multiple aspects within a single story. Exposure to news accounts results in individuals using those aspects made salient as a conceptual heuristic. For example, the characteristics of candidates given attention by the media affect voters' images of those candidates (Becker & McCombs, 1978; King, 1997; Kiousis, Bantimaroudis, & Ban, 1999; McCombs, Llamas, Lopez-Escobar, & Rey, 1997). Because news accounts are often the only source of information that members of the public can access about candidates, they become instrumental in determining what individuals think about candidates.

These second-level agenda-setting effects involve three concepts, each of which represents a different mode of salience. Attributes represent simple properties of candidates and issues that are reported by the news media and for some members of the public will affect evaluations. Example: X has behaved unethically; I disapprove. Framing represents the angle, theme, or justification for coverage (Gitlin, 1980), and often implies positive or negative evaluation within the coverage itself. Example: World trade protestors destroy a Seattle store; I disapprove. Priming represents the introduction of topics that imply greater or lesser favorability through audience members' associations of new information with related ideas (Iyengar, 1991; Iyengar & Kinder, 1987a, 1987b). Example: Social security is in trouble; Democrats will best protect it. This is an example of "issue ownership"—certain issues favor the Democrats or Republicans because each party has a different set of priorities established in the public mind by their histories (Ansolabehere & Iyengar, 1994; Petrocik, 1996). Agenda setting inevitably introduces an evaluative component because attributes, framing, and priming are often not neutral. Salience of this sort affects dispositions, and salience is guided in large part by the emphases of the news.

B. Priming the Key

Priming is the key concept on two grounds. First, it has been used to denote the seemingly inevitable effects of the emphases of the news media on evaluations of public figures. Second, it is a general process by which attributes and framing become involved in evaluations of issues, events, and people (Kinder, 2003). Attention leads to priming. Its extent, character, and shape will derive from the associations that are invoked and retrievability from memory of logically related cognitions and feelings. The stimulus belongs to the media. But so, too, do the responses, because they will be weighted toward availability, and this will be partly governed by the emphases of the media encountered earlier and especially those that seemingly represent drama and conflict and will be recalled vividly. As McCombs and Reynolds (2002) explain: "The link between agenda-setting effects and the subsequent expression of opinions about public figures or other objects is called priming. . . . Rather than engaging in a comprehensive analysis based on their total store of information, citizens routinely draw on those bits of information that are particularly salient at the time they must make a judgment" (p. 14). The news agenda provides the cues that citizens utilize in their political evaluations of candidates and issues because that agenda makes those cues salient and cognitively accessible (in the forefront of the mind) to audience members.

Two exemplary research studies illustrate priming in the evaluation of public figures. In one, National Election Study data collected when the Iran-Contra scandal broke are analyzed by Krosnick and Kinder (1990). The impact of the opinions of individuals about the scandal and U.S. policies in Central America increased in assessments of President Reagan's performance after widespread news coverage of the scandal. In the other, a survey of Oregon residents by Wanta and Chang (1999) found that for those respondents who reported that President Clinton's sex scandal involving Monica Lewinsky was an important issue, evaluations of the president were negative. Conversely, among those who gave priority to his issue positions, evaluations of President Clinton were positive. Both cases are examples of the interplay among news reports, public opinion, and the political judgments that ensue.

The final major shift in agenda-setting research has been increased attention to the question of how and by whom the news agenda itself is formed. Interest turns away from the relationship between news and public agendas to the forces and factors that shape the news agenda. In so doing, "the media agenda became the dependent variable whereas in traditional agenda-setting research, the media agenda was the independent variable, the key causal factor shaping the public agenda" (McCombs & Reynolds, 2002, p. 12).

A comprehensive model of the forces that operate in forming the news agenda is articulated by Shoemaker and Reese (1991), who discuss levels of influence that array in concentric circles ranging from the most micro- to the most macro-based. The most microscopic level of influence on media content is the individual level; that is, the influence exerted by the single reporter or editor, which includes deciding on stories to cover, selecting angles, and writing and editing. Personal feelings, tastes and preferences, values, opinions, and professional training influence content at the individual level. The media routines level focuses on the standard procedures used in gathering and disseminating news. Chief among the influences found at this level are news values such as deviance from the norm, sensationalism, prominence, proximity, timeliness, conflict or controversy, human interest, and impact on audience members or society as a whole (Comstock & Scharrer, 1999). Next is the organizational level, focusing on the impact of policies, managers, and owners of the organization in which the media content is produced. The next level, the extramedia level, has to do with elements and factors external to media organizations, including news sources, advertisers, and the audience. Finally, the ideological level is the domain of institutions and values that constitute the social context in which news gathering and reporting take place, such as (in the case of the United States) capitalism, individualism, and democracy.

The extramedia level is frequently brought into discussions of agenda setting because it encompasses the desire of key policy makers (such as the president) to attempt to prevail upon the public's agenda themselves, using the media as a platform for doing so. The role of high-level governmental officials in shaping the news media was investigated by McCombs, Gilbert, and Eyal (1982), who studied President Nixon's State of the Union address in 1970 and the subsequent issues that were covered in two network newscasts, the *New York Times*, and the *Washington Post*. They found that 15 of the issues raised in the speech found their way onto the news media agenda in the month that followed. The power and prominence of the office of the president is an external force that clearly has the authority and command to shape the news agenda.

C. President, Media, and Public

There has been considerable attention to the interplay between the president, major media, and the public (Comstock & Scharrer, 1999; Dearing & Rogers,

1996; Wanta, 1992; Wanta & Foote, 1994). The data are consistent with the "agenda building" concept proposed by Lang and Lang (1983) in which an agenda emerges to which the president, the media, and the public all contribute. We call this a meta-agenda because it stands apart from but overarches the initial agendas of the three contributors.

Wanta (1992) examined the relationships between the agendas of *CBS Evening News*, the front-page stories of the *New York Times*, the president (by way of speeches and policy statements), and the public (when nationally representative samples were asked to name the country's number one problem). He covered 34 polls over almost two decades from 1970 to 1988, and examined media and presidential agendas over the preceding and subsequent four weeks. The research question was the predictability of one agenda by another.

The results disclosed considerable variation and no particular ascendancy for the president, the media, or the public (Table 6.1). Most of the correlations were positive and substantial. This favors the interpretation that each to some degree influences the other. Thus, the media and the president sometimes respond to the concerns of the public and at other times the public and the president respond to the concerns of the media, and at still other times the public and the media respond to the concerns of the president.

Wanta and Foote (1994) identified the issues on which presidents are most likely to influence media coverage. They analyzed news stories during the first 80 days of the first Bush administration on ABC, CBS, and NBC. Significant associations appeared between topics addressed by the president and media coverage for international issues, social problems (education, environment, poverty, crime), and social issues (abortion, censorship, gun control, patriotism/flag burning). None appeared for the economy, probably because coverage is dictated by a wide range of sources: economic indicators, the stock market, and the Federal Reserve Board. Changes in the two agendas often occurred simultaneously, presumably because of the readiness of the media to respond to presidential initiative. There was what we have called "issue seizure" (Comstock & Scharrer, 1999), with the president influencing coverage of the topics to which these major media ordinarily would pay little attention (in this case, foreign affairs and patriotism/flag burning). For social issues, there was some evidence of the media influencing the president. Thus, there is specialization in the agenda-building cycle, with the president looking to the media for guidance on public concerns and the media following the president in regard to national interest and acknowledging his newsworthiness when he takes up novel topics (patriotism/flag burning).

The media collectively influence judgments of salience because of their high degree of consonance in coverage (Comstock & Scharrer, 1999; Dearing & Rogers, 1996). Even at the national level, media may differ in their coverage because of differences in the expectations about reader and viewer interest,

TABLE 6.1 Presidential, News Media, and Public Agendas

Percent correlations significant at $p < .05$ when prior agenda of one source is used to predict subsequent agenda of second party

President	President → *New York Times*	*New York Times* → President	President → CBS	CBS → President
Nixon	50	63	25	0
Ford	80	100	80	80
Carter	50	25	38	13
Reagan	77	77	69	54
Overall	65	65	60	40

President	President → Public	Public → President	*New York Times* → Public	Public → *New York Times*
Nixon	50	75	75	75
Ford	40	40	100	60
Carter	63	50	88	100
Reagan	77	77	100	69
Overall	62	65	91	76

President	CBS → Public	Public → CBS
Nixon	50	75
Ford	100	80
Carter	88	100
Reagan	69	54
Overall	83	83

Statistical control for association with other party: President as control*

					Earlier Coverage as Control	
President	*New York Times* → Public	Public → *New York Times*	CBS → Public	Public → CBS	Public → *New York Times*	Public → CBS
Nixon	63	75	50	50	25	50
Ford	60	20	60	40	0	0
Carter	50	25	50	88	13	25
Reagan	15	8	23	23	8	8
Overall	41	29	47	53	12	23

*Contribution of President or earlier coverage by same media statistically eliminated.

Adapted from "The Influence of the President on the News Media and Public Agendas," by W. Wanta, 1992, *Mass Communication Review, 19*(1/2), pp. 14–21.

differences in relative advantage (the visuals of television versus the extended and detailed coverage of print; the inverted pyramid of newspapers versus the dramatic narrative of newsmagazines), and differences in journalists' opinions about the merits of discretionary items. At the local level, news media may differ extravagantly as they pursue different visions of an advantageous and desirable position in the marketplace (Hamilton, 1998); every market has at least one "eyewitness action" news station that chases violence and crime and largely ignores issues of public policy, government, and education. Nevertheless, as we shift toward major stories the media become more alike in what they cover, and they usually adopt largely the same frames because frames result from the expression of universally accepted news values.

Neuman (1990) documents the phenomenon of consonance in coverage by examining news treatment of 10 topics for periods ranging from 5 to 27 years in the *New York Times, Reader's Guide to Periodical Literature* (which covers magazines), and the three original networks (ABC, CBS, and NBC). Coverage was similar for all three types of media, although television displayed an occasional divergence from the print media.

The reasons are that the media use similar means to collect the news, which result in similar judgments about what is newsworthy, and they compete with one another so one medium seldom ignores what other outlets are carrying. Prominent persons and issues are assured of coverage in all media. For less-prominent persons and issues, the media will match coverage to ensure their competitors do not gain an advantage. Certain elite media, such as the *New York Times* or major television news organizations, will serve as guides for other outlets. This emulation rests on successfully meeting the expectations of readers and viewers. When they fail to show interest, most media will abandon the story even if an elite outlet continues to give it coverage.

This intermedia agenda setting entailing the use of one news outlet (usually a well-respected one such as the *New York Times* but sometimes any competing outlet) in the formation of the agenda of another, fits within the media routines level of the Shoemaker and Reese (1991) model. The phenomenon of pack journalism (Chapter 3) is testament to the long-standing practice of news organizations to monitor coverage in other outlets. Past research has marked the outlet-to-outlet path of news on topics that range from pollution in the Love Canal (Mazur, 1987) to rates of illegal drug use (Reese & Danielian, 1989) and from the *New York Times* to various other outlets. The intermedia agenda setting (or agenda building) role of the Associated Press has also been tracked (Whitney & Becker, 1982). Thus, the news agenda of any given outlet is affected by other outlets that it deems either elite models of professional excellence or local competitors for audiences and advertising dollars.

We identify six principal attributes of agenda setting (Table 6.2):

1. There is considerable consonance among the media in what is covered as a consequence of competition and similarities in news gathering.
2. Expectations of audience interest have a fundamental role, because they lead the media to depart from real world indicators of the significance of a topic in catering to that interest.
3. Issues rise and fall on the public's agenda as a consequence of media attention rather than real world signs of urgency or significance.
4. Salience is constructed by individuals largely based on media coverage because of the wide and authoritative sweep of media surveillance, although personal experience sometimes will have a role.
5. A triggering event occasionally has a central role, such as attention by the president, coverage by the *New York Times* or other highly prominent news organizations, or an extraordinary occurrence given wide media play.
6. Certain topics are generally excluded from extended coverage and thereby the public's agenda, such as the environment, science, and medicine, unless there is a triggering event (the Exxon *Valdez* oil spill, the Nobel Prize, a SARs outbreak).

We offer several conclusions in regard to the public's use of media for political decision making. First, the news media open up the range of issues and topics beyond personal observation and experience that individuals will consider. Second, by virtue of their inclusion in the news, the issues and topics that receive emphasis in the news media will assume a position of relative importance among audiences. The gatekeeping function of the press and the formation of the news agenda translate into a view of the social and political world that is largely shared by members of the public. Third, although general patterns predominate in agenda setting, individual differences—and particularly the need for orientation—often moderate outcomes. Finally, the salience that is transferred from news to the public includes properties and characteristics that affect public evaluations and attitudes—what to think—of issues and of public persons, and those attributes are decisive in the formation of political judgments and evaluations.

II. ANONYMOUS OTHERS

One of the qualities of the news, as exemplified by agenda setting, is that it gives the individual audience member a glimpse beyond the confines of his or her own views and personal experiences. Diana Mutz (1998) writes convincingly about what she terms "impersonal influence," one variant of which is the ability of the news media to influence individuals by conveying the

TABLE 6.2 Three Dimensions of Agenda Setting

Questions	Process	Attributes
Are associations observable between media attention and the importance assigned by the public to issues and topics?	Changes in emphases of media are followed by shifts in the public's imputation of importance to issues and topics.	Mostly, the same issues and topics are covered by different media.
Do shifts in media attention precede changes in the salience of issues and topics? Do changes in the public salience of issues and topics precede media attention?	Importance of a topic and its attributes are both affected, with the latter often constituting the basis for evaluative judgment.	Media attention is often independent of statistical indices of topic importance.
What personal attributes predict a correlation between media attention and the importance assigned to an issue or topic?	Public interest sometimes precedes coverage, with the media agenda set by the public.	Topics rise and fall on the public agenda as a consequence of media attention.
Do issues and topics differ in the likelihood of an association between media attention and public salience?	Crises (such as war) dictate media attention and are assured of salience.	Salience is a social construction; individuals variously combine personal experience, the impressions of others, and media coverage.
Do the media differ in the associations observed between attention given an issue or topic and the importance assigned them by the public?	Always available dislocations (political scandals, health risks, environmental threats, international strife) depend on media attention for salience.	Increased salience is most likely when the White House is involved, there is *New York Times* coverage, or there is a highly prominent event.
	What the public finds interesting guides the media in issue and topic selection.	Certain issues and topics seldom receive extensive media attention and are rarely prominent on the public agenda.

	Obtrusive topics are more affected by personal experience than by media attention.
What is the particular role of television in the associations observed between media attention and the importance assigned issues and topics by the public?	Some topics are resistant to influence because they are perceived as fixtures.
What factors influence the attention given issues and topics by the media?	Topics vary in amount of media coverage required, with shifts in salience sometimes dependent on exceeding a threshold.

Based on *Agenda Setting*, by J. W. Dearing and E. M. Rogers, 1996, Thousand Oaks, CA, Sage; "The evolution of agenda-setting research: Twenty-five years in the marketplace of ideas." by M. E. McCombs and D. L. Shaw, 1993, *Journal of Communication*, 43(2), pp. 58–67; and "The threshold of public attention," by W. R. Neuman, 1990, *Public Opinion Quarterly*, 54, pp. 159–176.

impressions of aggregated others through reports of public opinion polls. Individuals tend to assign that type of information—gained through use of media and unlikely to be acquired otherwise (despite some of the claims in behalf of the spiral of silence)—some significance when making political (and other) judgments. This significance derives from three factors: acknowledgment of the authority of the media, recognition that interpersonal networks may not adequately reflect what others are thinking, and the belief that what others think is not irrelevant to reaching a correct and satisfying decision.

We would somewhat relax the definition of impersonal influence set forth by Mutz, and substitute a qualification of the communication channel by which it takes place. She confines impersonal influence solely to information about the opinions of others that is conveyed directly by the media—that is, by impersonal sources—and not other people. We understand the rationale—to focus clearly on impersonal sources (and we appreciate the scientific nicety of a precise definition). However, we think this purity is achieved by the abdication of realism. If the crux is what a person believes about opinion, then the proximal source should not be a factor on which exclusion or inclusion of phenomena is based. The distal source remains the media. This is particularly so for seemingly factual information that is being relayed from the media in interpersonal exchange and does not necessarily have the evaluative, attitudinal, or persuasive properties of perspectives rooted in partisanship. We prefer to think of types of information—factual accounts of the opinions and experiences of others versus interpretive judgments—and distinct originating channels—the media and the interpersonal.

In contemporary society, most of the information that individuals acquire no longer rests entirely or for most even primarily on firsthand experiences. Philosophers and sociological observers alike have heralded a change that began in the nineteenth century in which "indirect associations" with others, often facilitated through communication technologies, have supplanted to a substantial degree personal and communal relationships (Mutz, 1998; Starr, 2004). "Associations" (rather than relationships) is intentional to signify the anonymous nature of such transactions. Everyday economic exchanges provide a good example. Shopping occurs via catalog and phone call or through Internet use and need rely no longer on face-to-face interactions.

The media evolved in the same general pattern. The national markets for goods and services made possible by the postal system and a transcontinental railroad network and the increasing use of both financial credit and paper money created incentives for national advertising to occur via newspapers and magazines (Mutz, 1998). The news media quickly evolved into a national system in the nineteenth century (Cook, 1998; Kielbowicz, 1989; Starr, 2004). The Associated Press provided an information network that vastly expanded the dissemination achieved by the exchange of local newspapers. Postal subsidies for newspapers were joined in the 1850s by subsidies for magazines and books. Newspapers, and later magazines, provided a growing population—expanding westward, congregating to a greater degree in urban environments, and increasingly diverse in ethnicity because of immigration and the trek northward of southern blacks (Starr, 2004)—with news not just from the local arena but also from national and international realms, thus widening the scope of one's view beyond personal and interpersonal experience. Movies immediately sought national audiences, and in their nickelodeon days before World War I frequently dealt—in 10- to 30-minute formats—with current issues of economic disparities, social injustices, and the burdens of sweatshops and child labor and did so from both politically conservative and liberal perspectives (Starr, 2004). The advent and diffusion of the electronic media further strengthened the nationalized nature of media. Individuals in diverse locations could receive news from far-flung places seemingly effortlessly through the airwaves rather than with the accompanying constraints of physical delivery of print media (Mutz, 1998). In modern times, the conglomeration of ownership of news media outlets continues to ensure a national focus, often to the detriment of the heterogeneity in content across outlets that comes from in-depth and frequent reporting on the local community (Bagdikian, 1987).

III. WHAT OTHERS THINK

The media devote quite a bit of attention to reporting on mass opinion. One explanation for the media's reliance on public opinion polls is the journalistic ideal of objectivity, a standard that was developed fairly early if pursued somewhat erratically in the history of media (Chapter 3). Conveying the collective opinion of generalized others supports the pursuit of objectivity on the part of the journalist who is seemingly acting as a mere channel for the transmission of the data. Who can quarrel with *USA Today*'s report that a plurality names lamb as their least favorite meat? (Goat was not an option.) Data gathered from large-scale surveys and analyzed using statistics have an aura of science or at least specialized technology that lends legitimacy and authority to the news. The allure of the poll for the news media is also due to the expression of outcomes in unambiguous tallies and figures. There also is evidence to suggest that polls are generally successful at capturing the attention of members of the news audience (Robinson & Clancey, 1985). We suspect this frequently is as much due to their form—easily processed bits of information frequently presented using graphs in an inset box, or by superimposed visual—as to the significance ascribed to them by the public.

These are, of course, somewhat illusory attributes. Quite apart from question wording, the order of questions, the representativeness of the sample, and the timing of the survey—all potentially subjects of controversy—the decision to conduct a poll on a particular issue is hardly neutral politically. Polls call attention to topics, and the options offered define public opinion. Subtleties may be ignored or emphasized. Public opinion on prominent issues (abortion, the death penalty, marijuana in medical treatment, mercy killings) can be depicted as pro or con or delineated in gradations of qualifying circumstances and mitigating conditions. Polls at this level are the province of editors and news directors, and become weapons as well as servants of the press in establishing the public's agenda (which will now include the tallies of public opinion).

News media coverage of the opinions of others is also facilitated by a trend in content uncovered by Barnhurst and Mutz (1997). In their study of over 2,000 news stories in the Portland *Oregonian*, the *Chicago Tribune*, and the *New York Times* from 1894 to 1984, they found over time an increase in reporting of events beyond the local arena, in length of news items, and in amount of analysis of events. Barnhurst and Mutz see these as indices of thematic, contextualized, more detailed interpretive reporting. Results of public opinion polls fit within the first and third trend, extending beyond the local as well as the specific who, what, where, when, and how of events.

This is a journalistic shift, as Mutz argues, that would operate in concert with other social forces—postage rates, conglomerates, the formulating of most policies that seriously affect people at the national or state rather than the community level—to expand the role of impersonal influence. However, the influence of television on these changes in newspapers should not be underestimated. The increases in length of stories and attention to analysis in the Barnhurst and Mutz data, for instance, are most precipitous after the diffusion of television to most of the American public had occurred. Underlying these shifts, then, is most likely the necessary adjustment of newspapers to the competition of television, substituting for visual drama, brief accounts, and personable anchors and on-scene reporters, much greater detail, context, and interpretation (Neuman, Just, & Crigler, 1992).

Exposure to mass public opinion does not necessarily lead neatly to the shifting of individual opinions to align with the collective (Comstock & Scharrer, 1999; Mutz, 1998; Chapters 1 and 2). The spiral of silence, the third-person effect, the impact of exit poll results on subsequent voters, and the strength of momentum in the polls in predicting candidates' ultimate success all offer opportunities for presumed or perceived knowledge about public opinion to affect individual opinion and behavior. All encompass substantial bodies of data and potentially represent a form of what Mutz calls impersonal influence. Four major themes sum up the evidence. First, the magnitude of any effect of exposure to collective opinion is typically quite modest. Second, shifts in individuals' opinions toward or away from the collective depend on the strength of the original position and the amount of information one has about the topic, with shifts toward the collective most likely in the cases of little information and weak prior commitment to an original position. Third, the assignment of considerable weight to poll-derived expectations of political candidates' chances for success is most likely for little-known candidates. Finally, candidate momentum in the polls is most important during primary season in which voter information is low and uncertainty about candidates is high. Even then, popularity in the polls may not translate into victory as the collapse of the Howard Dean campaign in 2004 demonstrated.

Mutz (1998) offers a three-part conceptualization that resembles our own analyses by giving major weight to political involvement, use of the media for political information, and political knowledge. A small group of highly involved individuals often will use what they can learn of public opinion to ensure that their votes will have an effect. They will try to confine choices to contenders, or to candidates for whom a vote seemingly makes an ideological statement. These are the strategic voters. A somewhat larger but also fairly limited number of low-involvement individuals will use mass opinion as a consensus heuristic (Lau, 2003), moving their own opinions toward those of the collective with little reflection or cognitive processing. Collective opinion in these instances is perceived as more likely to be correct, as enjoying social approval and thereby normative, and providing some satisfaction by identifying with the majority. These are the bandwagon passengers, but they will usually not pass the turnstiles until after Labor Day or until collective opinion becomes discernible and presumably stable. The majority of individuals are seen as moderately involved in politics, and their use of public opinion information is dependent on their cognitive processing of the reasons underlying those opinions. Within this group, individual opinions may shift either toward or away from collective opinion, depending on the thoughts and arguments brought to mind. They neither chase nor flee public opinion; instead, it is a stimulus that generates cognitions. These are the typical American voter. They attempt to be rational with limited information and processing skills (with lack of prior information impeding processing of new information) and, at the same time, "compensatory," in the jargon of decision-making theory (Lau, 2003), by giving some weight to all known factors.

Mutz (1998) tests these assertions one by one with considerable ingenuity and methodological versatility. The overall pattern supports strategic activity by the highly involved, use of the consensus heuristic is employed when knowledge or commitment are not high, and the moderately involved elaborate on information—in this case, poll data—producing thoughts that may supply reasons to change or continue support of a candidate.

To confirm that highly involved individuals use poll information to participate strategically, she examined the timing of monetary contributions from individuals to campaigns using the 1988 presidential primary data generated by the Federal Election Commission. Contributing to a campaign was taken as a sign of high involvement. She aligned those data with content analyses documenting horse race fluctuations in stories of candidates gaining or losing ground. Thus, we have shifts in apparent support and potential shifts in contributions among the highly involved. The evidence points persuasively to two prominent patterns. One is hesitancy-based giving, contributing only when the viability of the candidate is on the rise. The other is loyalty-based giving, contributing when viability is declining in order to maintain or jump-start the campaign. The candidates who are the most ideologically distinct would be more likely to have loyalty-based supporters who will give money to help sustain the candidate even when success is dwindling (e.g., Jesse Jackson, Pat Robertson). Less ideological candidates would typically draw hesitancy-based giving (e.g., Michael Dukakis, Jack Kemp). The two distinct strategic maneuvers appeared. More ideologically distinct candidates drew increased contributions when their popularity faltered. For mainstream candidates, contributions rose or fell in correspondence with popularity. The loyalists backed their ideological favorites because each represented views not found among other candidates. Among the loyalists, ideas mattered more than victory; among the hesitants, victory for the preferred party was paramount. Thus, the data support strategic political behavior among the highly involved.

The use of the consensus heuristic among those low in involvement was examined using a representative national sample that was asked to evaluate an unknown potential candidate for Congress on the basis of short vignettes. These differed by the candidate's issue position and the amount of ostensible public support. After reading the vignette, respondents were asked to list their thoughts pertaining to the candidate or the issue and then voice their level of support for the candidate or the issue. When the vignette reported that public support for the candidate was high, respondents listed slightly more positive than negative thoughts pertaining to the candidate. When low public support was reported, many more negative than positive thoughts were listed. Support for the candidate was similarly affected. Negativity and positivity of listed thoughts was modestly predictive of the judgments of the candidate. The same pattern occurred in regard to issues, but only when individuals had low to moderate (as contrasted with high) commitment to the issues. Thus, with an unknown candidate and when issue commitment is not high the consensus heuristic comes into play.

The hypothesized tendency of those moderately involved in politics to engage in cognitive elaboration of public opinion poll data was explored in an experiment embedded in a national survey. Mutz labels this "the 1992 Democratic primary experiment." Subjects who (a) self-identified as

Democrats and (b) viewed the decision to support a party nominee as moderately important were exposed to polls showing varying public support for primary candidates. In a thought-listing task, the direction of the public opinion cues (high support or little support for the candidates) did not relate to the production of negative or positive thoughts about candidates; exposure to the public opinion data thus did not directly affect respondent support. However, those exposed to public opinion data listed more thoughts, as hypothesized, about candidates than those in a control group condition who were not exposed to such data. This demonstrated that the polls did influence thinking about the candidates. In addition, among these moderately involved voters the level of reported support affected the kind of thoughts produced. Low reported support generated more counterarguing. Positive or high reported support generated more supportive arguments. On the whole, then, the data gave some credence to the cognitive elaboration interpretation of public opinion influence. That is, among those moderately involved politically—who would comprise a substantial proportion of the public—the influence of poll data depends on the thoughts generated. Support of candidates was no more likely to align with public opinion than to oppose it; the direction of support depended on the thoughts brought to mind by the public opinion data.

Thus, neither the Asch nor the Sherif paradigms (Chapters 1 and 2) apply in a straightforward way to impersonal influence in politics. Everyone does not conform to the opinions of others, and not everyone uses public opinion to gauge the normative or socially approved choice in an election. Only among the politically least involved does public opinion have such a role. Among the highly involved, it serves as a basis for strategic behavior. Among the moderately involved, what counts is the thoughts generated, which may lead to decisions that are contrary to or consistent with public opinion.

The American public rationally employs rather than conforms to information about collective opinion. For most individuals, an irrational shift in the direction of the known opinions of others does not occur. The consensus heuristic is supported only when individuals have very little information on which to base support for candidates and issues (such as for the unknown congressional candidate). In the real world, such a situation would be confined to local elections, perhaps some House or state contests, and presidential caucuses and primaries, rather than prominent national decisions. It would also be further constrained by the low likelihood of ill-informed individuals voting. For presidential elections, the majority of individuals will fall within the moderately involved category. They will use impersonal information in an active rather than passive way. When there is knowledge, new information about public opinion will trigger reflection that may or may not lead to a change in opinion, depending on those thoughts—which will be a function of stored information, the value accorded majority opinion, and the accessibility of these factors (e.g., they're finally recognizing he's right; that savings and loan deal is catching up; he's a hero but maybe that's not the real story).

IV. EXPERIENCES OF OTHERS

The experiences of others—the achievements and challenges that mass collectives face as they navigate the social world—are an important part of the impersonal influence that is enacted through the public's use of mass media (Mutz, 1998). Such experiences are important in the realm of politics because they shape the priorities that individuals believe political decision makers should hold as well as the policies that they expect them to implement.

A. Collective Definitions

Mutz (1998) argues that impersonal influence can outweigh personal experience in the formation of political judgments, contending that "collective public definitions of problems typically have a greater influence on American politics than aggregated individual ones" (p. 8). This conceptualization asserts that what people judge about society will not always be the equivalent of the aggregation of individual opinions, and that the former (the collective experiences reported about others) will have more influence than the latter (the aggregated experiences of individuals themselves). However, it is demonstrably the case. One of the reasons behind impersonal influence is that individuals tend to compartmentalize information. One set consists of what they have gleaned through their own experiences. The other is made up of descriptions of the experiences of collective others. Individuals contrast their everyday lives with the large-scale, macro-level realms represented by societal segments based on ethnicity, gender, and age (social group identities), special circumstances (the disabled, blind, or terminally ill), and geography (cities and town, regions, states, and the nation). The result is a schism between individual experiences and social knowledge. Individuals tend to assign greater political value to social knowledge because it is representative of what is transpiring beyond one's immediate circumstances.

Collective experience offers a serious competitor in what are usually thought of as arenas where personal allegiances, individual experience, and interpersonal networks have strong roles. Mutz (1998) offers three examples: the qualification (or diminution) of party loyalty and partisanship in forming opinions on issues, sociotropic decisions that give weight to the greater good, and the discounting of the experiences of interpersonal networks. Party loyalty and partisanship, while a pervasive and strong factor in the formation of political dispositions, are susceptible to qualifications in the face of national experience.

Positions on political and social issues are often more complex than a vote of confidence for or against the current administration based on party (Conover, Feldman, & Knight, 1986; Mutz, 1992). For example, approval or disapproval of the Bush administration's actions in Iraq is likely to be based on more than whether the individual shares Bush's Republican affiliation.

The weight of personal experience in forming political dispositions is often superceded by impersonal influence. The expected link between one's own state of being and support for particular candidates or policies (e.g., I've been laid off, so I won't support the president for reelection) does not always occur. This is because individuals view their own experiences as highly individualized and explainable by particular circumstances rather than general malaise. These experiences are treated as unreliable indicators of conditions affecting the larger collective. As a result, there are only modest correlations between personal experiences (and those of relatives and acquaintances) and perceptions of collective experience (Kinder, 1981). Indeed, although information acquired from interpersonal networks (relatives, acquaintances, etc.) often shapes judgments and perceptions it is also subject to the same discounting as personal experience. This information does not clearly or consistently convert to political views or societal-level judgments. Explanation by unique factors and forces (e.g., I was laid off because I live in a depressed area; my brother-in-law never liked that job) results in the dismissal of personal experience in favor of reports of collective experience.

Personal experience does enter in a more subtle way. The political environment, represented by displays of support, such as signs in front yards, bumper stickers, and door-to-door canvassing, can create an atmosphere that testifies in behalf of one or another candidate or party, and such environmental cues of social approval have been shown to translate into heightened support from those already favorable to a candidate or party (Huckfeldt & Sprague, 1995).

Interpersonal networks are important sources of social influence, but they will be subordinate to media sources in assessing the state of public affairs and civic currency. On some topics, such as the likelihood of becoming the victim of a crime, they are likely to have a profound influence (Tyler, 1980, 1984). They are also likely to be an important means for the dissemination of the same information carried by the media; for information about local conditions and the experiences of friends, neighbors, and acquaintances; and as a source of maintaining or building interest in public affairs and politics, and thereby facilitating political participation. The question is one of authoritativeness. Accounts of a local robbery or mugging are highly credible about the state of the neighborhood and personal risk, but less so as indices of conditions in the city or across the nation (Mazur & Hall, 1990; Tyler & Lavrakas, 1985). Again, the bias toward explanations based on the particulars of a situation leads to the discounting of the significance of the experiences of social networks.

Nevertheless, interpersonal networks can act as a powerful extension of the media. As Rogers (2002) points out, an event displayed in the media may depend for large-scale influence not only on its transmission by interpersonal sources but also on the cognitive and affective emphases supplied by personal interaction with others. His primary example is the more than tenfold increase in calls to a national AIDS hotline the day after Magic Johnson's November 7, 1991, announcement at a press conference that he was HIV-infected and retiring from professional basketball. The two elements responsible were extensive, immediate news coverage and widespread conversations about AIDS and about Magic Johnson. Rogers offers two other examples. The *Challenger* disaster on January 26, 1986, was followed by very high levels of public attention as a consequence of the interpersonal conversations that followed news coverage, and in India the "news" that statues of Hindu deities were drinking milk on the morning of September 21, 1995, led to attempts by Indian Hindus all over the world to feed milk to religious statues as a consequence of the interpersonal conversations about the initial event (no mention is made of why milk was at hand in the original instance). The major point is that interpersonal sources can act as a major force in furthering media influence.

Social scientists continue to be surprised at the failure of the data to indicate persuasively that there is widespread "pocketbook voting," or the basing of support for candidates on one's own economic state and experiences. We agree with Mutz (1998) that the explanation for this failure is partly cultural, stemming from the American ideal of individualism. The result is "individualistic attributions of responsibility" (Mutz, 1998, p. 101). Individuals tend to point to their own agency when explaining their economic condition.

Economic conditions nevertheless have a major role in elections. The data indicate, however, that it is not one's own pocketbook that usually counts. Rather, it is the perception of the pocketbooks and piggy banks of the nation as a whole—as represented by collective experiences reported through media—that have a central role (Kiewiet, 1981; Kinder, 1998). Thus, support of presidential incumbents (or lack thereof) has been linked clearly with social-level judgments of economic health (Fiorina, 1981; Lau & Sears, 1981).

However, individualism is unlikely to be the complete answer. This is because the same disparity occurs on a wide range of topics in which individualism offers little in the way of explanation. Aggregated reports of the experiences and opinions of individuals often paint a different picture than their perceptions of collective experience. When individuals are asked in a survey to rate their own economic situation, and then asked to rate that of the nation as a whole, the aggregation of the responses of individuals to the first question regularly depicts a more optimistic picture than the replies to the second (Mutz, 1998). The same pattern applies to a wide range of topics. For example, in a *Washington Post* survey of a nationally representative sample in the mid-1990s, the average rating of the seriousness of nine social problems in the communities of the respondents was strikingly more positive or optimistic than the ratings by the same sample for the nation as a whole (Mutz, 1998). This disparity occurred for all the problems evaluated: racism in general, white racism toward blacks, black racism toward whites, poverty, violence, drug abuse, declining moral standards, crime, and unemployment. The inescapable conclusion is that societal-level judgments are made independently of personal-level judgments, and usually are more pessimistic.

What is responsible for the failure of personal-level and societal-level perceptions to match? A major factor that would also figure in economic judgments is biased optimism (Weinstein, 1980, 1989). There is a decided pattern of optimism apparent in aggregated individual experiences. Across 266 separate studies in a recent meta-analysis (Mezulis et al., 2004), perceptions by individuals of their state of well-being were consistently more positive and favorable than generalized perceptions of the experiences of others, and the average difference between individual and generalized perceptions was quite large. Individuals perceive themselves as less susceptible to negative impact and more likely to experience positive events than the general population (Weinstein, 1980, 1989). As we observed earlier, this is the third-person effect (Chapters 1 and 2). The explanation for biased optimism is two aspects of ego defensiveness. Individuals experience less threat when they perceive themselves as comparatively safe from harm, and experience some satisfaction—as well as a justification for experiencing less threat—by perceiving others as more vulnerable to risk (Perloff & Fetzer, 1986; Weinstein, 1980, 1989). These ego defensive maneuvers are supported by a tendency of individuals, when asked to conjure up vague others about whom they will speculate, to construct an abstraction of high-risk individuals (Kahneman & Tversky, 1973). This cognitive error, in which the group for comparison is incorrectly constituted, is joined by a number of other missteps that can produce an erroneous estimate of the status of others (Chambers & Windschitl, 2004), such as not making use of all available information, focusing on one or two prominent examples, and simply not paying enough attention to or giving enough thought to the estimate. These errors, when unmotivated by ego defense, can result in both over- and underestimates (Chambers & Windschitl, 2004). Thus, cognitive error often aids and abets ego defensiveness, but sometimes simply leads to errors.

B. News Values and Exemplars

The influence of news reports of the collective experiences of others underscores the importance of the accuracy of such accounts. Although objective statistical indicators appear in such reports (Tims, Freeman, & Fan, 1989), we agree with Mutz that three pervasive practices result in frequent distortions. They are (a) overemphasis on the negative, (b) highlighting of rarities, and (c) a focus on change. We would add a fourth that pertains primarily to television: reliance on personalized reporting that privileges individualistic explanations for events and issues over those more systemic. Reports of collective experiences of others—regardless of the medium in which they appear—are often supplemented by personalized accounts used as individual exemplars. We argue that in television news the tendency to focus on personalized news sources (e.g., an ordinary citizen commenting on the impact of a factory closing) is even more prevalent due to the visual nature of the medium. They make for good storytelling, supply a human element that may increase viewer identification, and because they generally represent figures well-integrated into existing schema—doctors, lawyers, truck drivers, factory workers, farmers, law enforcement officers—they increase learning of the particular point or message that they are employed to present (Comstock & Scharrer, 1999; Graber, 1990). However, as we shall soon argue, this very learning may lead to distorted perceptions because such personalized examples often take precedence in assessing the meaning and magnitude of events.

The emphasis on negativity in coverage of politics and social issues (Chapter 4) is apparent in the treatment of the economy (Nadeau, Niemi, & Fan, 1996), crime rates (Lowry, Nio, & Leitner, 2003), and threats to health (Singer & Endreny, 1987). As agenda setting informs us, such emphases guide public perceptions (Blood & Phillips, 1995; Nadeau, Niemi, & Fan, 1996) so there is reason to expect that impressions of the social world held by members of the news audience skew toward the negative.

News values promote the novel or unusual. Rare events often are given prominent display, which may translate into inaccurate public perceptions regarding their likelihood (Slovic, Fischoff, & Lichtenstein, 1987). Impersonal influence holds that such perceptions are more likely to influence societal views than personal expectations. For example, after September 11, 2001, polls produced average estimates of the likelihood of becoming the victim of a terrorist attack that were distinctly higher for others in general than for the respondents. The individual may assume inaccurately that a relatively rare condition or experience is actually common for collective others.

News values also favor "new" information. Fluctuations rather than stability in social statistics are more likely to be emphasized. A headline reading "HIV cases on the rise" is viewed as more newsworthy and more likely to capture the attention of readers than one that notes "Number of HIV cases stays the same" (Comstock & Scharrer, 1999). Inaccurate perceptions also stem from the interpretation of minor statistical fluctuations as "harbingers of things to come" (Mutz, 1998, p. 119).

There is also the powerful influence of exemplars made up of personalized accounts, a convention of reporting in all media but particularly prominent on television because of the newsworthiness in this medium of snapshots of the human condition (Comstock & Scharrer, 1999; Iyengar, 1990, 1991; Neuman, Just, & Crigler, 1992). Brosius and Bathelt (1994) and Zillmann and Brosius (2000) present convincing evidence that case studies of this kind take priority over base-rate information made up of statistics representing collective others—and therefore, in effect, constituting the facts of the case—in forming impressions and judgments. There is greater learning because of the vividness of the case, and cases are taken as representative of the general population of events rather than perhaps having been selected for their vividness (as is likely to be the case for television news), and statistics are much more easily forgotten or ignored (Zillmann & Brosius, 2000). We would extend the argument to include not just base-rate versus exemplar comparisons but also the many instances in which issues are discussed only by exemplar news sources without accompanying base-rate information. The reader or viewer has a difficult choice—accept the exemplar as representative or ignore it, a decision likely to be governed by the degree of credibility extended to the media. Most would opt for the former because an accurate picture of the world is the justification for the news and a major motive for attending to it. Crime coverage on nightly local newscasts may lead to an overestimation of the prevalence of crime that develops independently of news stories presenting statistics representing collective experience with crime.

The underlying significance of impersonal influence when applied to politics is that "when people perceive an issue to be a large-scale social problem, and not just an individual one, they are much more likely to hold government leaders responsible for it" (Mutz, 1998, p. 103). Mutz documents the pattern between societal-level perceptions and political evaluations succinctly in data drawn from rolling surveys with nationally representative samples in the late 1980s. Collective-level judgments of the "drug problem" were better indicators of performance evaluations of President Reagan than were individual-level judgments; that is, the belief that drugs were a national problem affected ratings of the president while the belief that drugs posed a problem for the individual—presumably through the community or family—did not affect ratings of the president. Furthermore, heavy coverage of the drug problem in the news media at the time of the survey increased the impact of collective-level judgments (but not personal-level judgments) on Reagan's favorability ratings. Thus, the media govern perceptions of societal problems, and perceptions of societal problems affect political judgments.

Decisions of news media personnel regarding what events and issues to cover take on importance because of the role of coverage in shaping perceptions of collective experiences. Perceptions of collective experiences, in turn, have the power to shape political judgments. Accuracy of those media reports matters because, by their very nature, the reports cannot be confirmed by personal observation or experience. Impressions of collective experience transmitted by the media suffer from the four biases toward inaccuracy and can also be manipulated by political figures themselves. As Mutz argues:

> Moreover, since candidates for office have obvious motives for trying to persuade citizens that it is 'morning in America' (in the case of incumbents) or that collective affairs have gone to hell in a handbasket (in the case of challengers), perceptions of collective well-being often may be targeted for purposeful manipulation. In short, media provide a thin basis for ensuring democratic accountability, whereas personal experiences seem solidly rooted in concrete aspects of the realities we live with on a day-to-day basis (p. 110).

C. When Pocketbooks Count

Pocketbook interests of a personal nature are not irrelevant to political judgments. They are simply subordinate to judgments about larger entities, and principally the nation. Mutz (1998) combines survey data and content analyses of news coverage (Mutz, 1992, 1994) to examine the interplay between personal experience and news coverage. Her analysis is deft and ingenious, testing two seemingly conflicting hypotheses about the role of personal information and media accounts. She drew on a state sample and a national sample, with the former providing better control of exposure to news coverage and the latter a more representative group. Thus, the replication employs samples with different strengths. One hypothesis, based on the well-established ability of the media to be more powerful in defining social circumstances than personal experience, held that media accounts would diminish the role of personal experience. The other held that media accounts would facilitate the application of personal experience to politics; pocketbooks would count when their interests were confirmed by sociotropic conditions. Thus, which of these hypotheses applied would depend on the divergence or convergence of personal experience and media accounts.

This facilitation hypothesis is rather elegantly attributed by Mutz (1998) to Tocqueville (p. 147) more than 165 years ago:

> . . . It frequently happens . . . in democratic countries that a great number of men who wish or who want to combine cannot accomplish it because, as they are very insignificant and lost amidst the crowd, they cannot see, and know not where to find, one another. A newspaper then takes up the notion or the feeling which had occurred simultaneously, but singly, to each of them. All are then immediately guided towards this beacon, and these wandering minds, which had long sought each other in darkness, at length meet and unite (Tocqueville, 1835: 203).

Mutz (1998) introduces contrast and consonance between personal experience and media accounts as the factors that govern which hypothesis applies. In this case, the specific focus was media coverage of unemployment and the economy and approval ratings of the president. She found:

1. When personal experience and the emphases of coverage contrast, ratings of the president are unaffected by personal experience.
2. When personal experience is reinforced by media coverage, this consonance with personal experience facilitates the influence of personal experience on ratings of the president.
3. Differences in vulnerability to being laid off, which is inversely associated with socioeconomic status, make "concern about unemployment" a more sensitive measure of political anxiety over the economy among those higher in socioeconomic status than personal experience with unemployment.
4. Those who have little information or knowledge about the societal-level state of affairs are particularly likely to draw on personal and interpersonal experience when making judgments about the state of the nation.
5. High news media use was associated with a more negative economic outlook, as would be expected from the negativity bias of news coverage.
6. Partisanship played a part, as we also would expect, with those of the opposition party (Democrats in this instance), giving lower approval ratings to the two Republican presidents (Reagan and the first Bush).

The exploration of the facilitation of class interests (which is what personal concerns become when widespread among a population segment) by media coverage raises the question of the role of group identity. As we will see (Chapter 7), the norms of a group generally have a decisive influence on evaluations and judgments. Mutz (1998; Mutz & Mondak, 1997) in her three-wave South Bend panel survey data examined a variety of possible group influences on the 1984 presidential vote. The principal independent variable was economic well-being, and the focus was on the vote for the incumbent (at the time, Ronald Reagan) as a consequence of perceptions or involvement with seven population segments (women, blacks, Hispanics, the poor, working men and women, the middle class, and the well-to-do).

Perceptions of economic improvement for blacks and the poor, two long-recognized subjects of social concern in regard to wages, employment, and living standards, promoted votes for the incumbent, while such perceptions about the well-to-do inhibited votes—an early hint at the important role of perceived fairness (Mutz, Table 4.3, p. 134). Voting was unaffected by membership in and perceived economic gains among groups; this was the case when membership was determined by objective criteria and when it was based on subjective declaration (Mutz, Table 4.4, p. 136). That is, blacks, Hispanics, the poor, working men and women, and the middle class (this analysis was confined to five groups) were unaffected in their vote by their perception of their own group's economic well-being. The entry of salient attachment—what we earlier (Chapter 1) called symbolic voting—did not make a difference; that is, identifying with or feeling close to a population group did not lead to an effect on the vote for the incumbent by the perceived economic well-being of the group (Mutz, Table 4.5, p. 138). Using the group as a standard to assess personal economic well-being ("relative deprivation" or "relative prosperity") also had no noteworthy connection to the vote (Mutz, Table 4.6, p. 140). However, the entry of fairness or equity—in this case, the degree to which economic outcomes across groups were judged to be similar or different—produced a marked effect (Mutz, Table 4.7, p. 141) that by the author's estimate amounted to " . . . a rather impressive 31-point swing in the estimated likelihood of voting for Reagan . . . " (Mutz, p. 141). Thus, perceptions of group well-being for groups of particular concern make a difference; group membership and identification with a group does not; neither does one's own well-being compared to that of one's group; but perceived equity (or lack thereof) has a powerful effect.

In contrast, Cohen (2003) experimentally has demonstrated that simply the priming (that is, introducing the name) of an esteemed political reference group (in his case, Democrats or Republicans) will shift the policy preferences of individuals not deeply interested or concerned about politics toward those of the reference group. This is very much in accord with the findings in general about the power of group norms (Chapter 7).

Our explanation for the difference in these two sets of outcomes invokes the articulation of standards of judgment. In the case of support for an incumbent president, the social entities that might inspire symbolic voting and could serve as references lack articulated, clear standards. Groups organized for political purposes, such as the two major parties, have them in abundance. As Huddy observes (2003), salience (which is represented here by membership and identification) is not enough for group influence; perceived norms and perceived fairness are major contingent variables.

Finally, Mutz (1998) examines the possibility that television functions differently than print media in evaluations of the president. Specifically, she focuses on the argument of Iyengar (1991) that television news, by promoting individualistic explanations for social malaise through personalized accounts and exemplars, insulates the president from accountability. The data demonstrate that Iyengar was inaccurate. Use of both television news and newspapers affects performance ratings, but use of television news in isolation from newspaper use is a less strong predictor than joint newspaper and television use. The case for a politically dysfunctional role for television rests upon whether, in the absence of the medium, those who use it as their principal source would turn to other media. Mutz thinks not, and we thoroughly agree—most of those who use television as their primary news medium would cease attending to the news at all rather than patronize other media with higher costs in terms both of effort and expense. Accountability in the sense of holding someone responsible, whether rightly or wrongly, is enhanced by newspaper use but it is also predicted by use of television news.

V. EMOTIONS AND SURVEILLANCE

Marcus, Neuman, and MacKuen (2000) extend political communication research importantly by drawing from recent advances in neuroscience to explain how cognitions and affect intersect in governing political behavior. They introduce their theory of "affective intelligence" [which has nothing to do with Goleman's (1995) "emotional intelligence" that deals with the strategic management of emotions in goal attainment] to describe the functions of emotion in the responses of individuals to political stimuli. The critical issue is whether the individual engages in focused cognitive processing of information. A basic premise is that individuals begin the process of responding to new stimuli with affect rather than conscious thought. Much of the time they rely on habitual responses and practices that do not require cognitive elaboration. These habits operate under the threshold of cognitive perception, because "affective reactions often arise before conscious—that is to say cognitive—awareness" (p. 9). This is what occurs when affect does not send a signal that something needs attending to. Occasionally, individuals' emotions tell them that a new stimulus is threatening or novel, and, rather than engage in habitual behavior, a neural pathway to a more reasoned cognitive response is activated. Affective intelligence is thus a dual-processing model analogous to the elaboration likelihood model of Petty and Cacioppo (1996) and the heuristic/cognitive model of Eagly and Chaiken (1993), with one path ("peripheral" or "heuristic") representing well-learned responses that are executed without much thought and the other representing the thoughtful review of options and their consequences ("central" or "cognitive").

They describe the prevailing emphases in past research and theory—to differentiate between affective and cognitive processes, and to assign cognition greater importance and higher value. The celebration of rational choice traces back to Greek mythology and established a consistent presence in psychology, sociology, and political science research (Marcus, 2003). Emotions, on the other hand, have been perceived as forces that need to be curtailed or that lead to pathologies if left unchecked, and their constructive role in human coping has been little understood. The lack of research attention to affect can be attributed to three factors: the difficulty in measuring emotions, their volatility, and their perceived idiosyncratic nature (Marcus, Neuman, & MacKuen, 2000).

The role of emotion in research regarding the political sphere has been most visible in the debate over the degree of sophistication and competence with which the typical member of the public goes about making voting decisions. Marcus and colleagues suggest that in this past research, emotion is seen in one of two ways. First, it is sometimes advanced as partly responsible for long-term attachment and loyalty to political parties, which is often seen as problematic because it inhibits reasoned shifts according to specific candidates and issues. Second, it is sometimes seen as responsible for short-term fluctuations in support for candidates and issues based on new bits of information, which is often viewed as problematic because of the fickleness and lack of basis in reason. Thus, most past research ascribes emotion a secondary role in explaining political behavior and views it as an obstacle to rational behavior and effective democratic participation.

A. Disposition

Marcus and colleagues—and the researchers whose findings they draw from—revolutionize understanding of emotion to include not only how individuals feel but also the role of emotions in managing what individuals think (cognition) and do (behavior). They conclude that "emotion is not the result of a single psychological process but rather the engagement of two physiological subsystems or pathways in the brain" (p. 28). One subsystem is referred to as the disposition system, responsible for overseeing habitual and previously learned behavior. The other subsystem is the surveillance system, responsible for identifying novel and threatening situations during which reliance on habit would be unwise. Neural pathways connect the two systems, so that the brain areas that are operating when behavioral routines are enacted are linked with the cortex region of the brain where conscious awareness occurs (Mishkin & Appenzeller, 1987). When the surveillance system signals a mismatch between incoming "sensory streams" (information gathered through the senses) and learned routines and habits, the routine behavior is halted and cognitive processing to determine an alternative plan is triggered. Frustration or anxiety ensues when routines and habits are deemed unsuitable. Marcus and colleagues caution that the pathways should not be interpreted as singular, one for cognition and one for affect. Rather, they show that affect is central—and primary—in both.

There are three main corollaries of the affective intelligence theory. First is the notion of affective primacy, or the finding that "emotional evaluations" of stimuli (people, events, groups, etc.) precede conscious awareness. Second is the assertion that the majority of the processing of incoming sensory stimuli via emotions never reaches the conscious level because it can be dealt with using subconscious habitual responses. Third, the usefulness of such habitual responses depends on the ability to link emotions with actions. These constitute the "match" or "mismatch" between new situations and previously learned routines that determines whether a routine behavior is fitting or whether a new strategy needs to be thought out. When emotional processing is made conscious, individuals experience feelings they can articulate. Yet, most habitual responses, managed by affect, will not result in conscious feelings unless the surveillance system creates a sense of enthusiasm or anxiety triggered by new stimuli. At the threshold between conscious and unconscious processing are fleeting emotions that are best expressed as "intuitions" or "hunches."

To support the first corollary, Marcus and colleagues introduce evidence regarding declarative memory and procedural memory. Declarative memory is that which individuals can express because it stems from conscious awareness. Procedural memory is evidence of memory or learning from stimuli that is manifested in behavior before it can be articulated by the individual. To demonstrate the primacy of procedural memory, Marcus and colleagues turn to Bechara's card game (Bechara, Damasio, Tranel, & Damasio, 1997). This is a strategy-detection task that permits the investigators to examine the role of feelings and hunches in uncovering the optimal strategy and becoming able to articulate it. There are several decks of cards, and rewards and penalties are accrued as cards are drawn. The subjects were instructed to draw their first card from a particular pair of decks, and the result was a substantial reward. Unbeknown to the subjects, repeated draws from those decks would gain substantial rewards but also accrue large penalties that ultimately would lead to a losing game. Draws from the other decks would result in smaller rewards but also much smaller penalties and ultimately a winning game. Subjects were queried repeatedly at intervals with such questions as "how do you feel about this game" and "what is going on in this game?" (Marcus, Neuman, & MacKuen, 2000, p. 31), and galvanic skin response (GSR) was continuously monitored.

After 20 trials, none of the subjects had figured out the game. As play progressed, most subjects began to report positive feelings about the decks that would provide a winning game. GSR readings confirmed that emotional responses had been elicited by drawing cards with heavier penalties. Cognitive understanding of the game, and the ability to articulate it, followed for the majority of subjects. But even those who could not articulate cognitive understanding improved their strategy in conjunction with emotional responses—good feelings toward the winning decks and GSR responses to higher penalties. On the other hand, patients whose brain damage inhibited use of procedural memory eventually understood the game cognitively but in the absence of emotional reactions identifying profitable moves did not apply a winning strategy. The implication is that emotion triggers shifts in behavior without conscious cognition and is an important part of everyday functioning (the authors offer the example of writing a postcard, with the routine task of forming letters triggered at each step without conscious thought by emotional reactions—procedural memory at work but easily defeated if we try the same task with our other hand, where each step has to be calculated).

B. Habit

Procedural memory occurs under the radar screen of conscious thought and is used to monitor habitual tasks. Such habits are fairly easy to perform and therefore do not spur consciousness about the behavior until individuals begin to fail at them or until something surprising occurs. Libet and colleagues (1983, 1985, 1991) used neuroscience techniques to study the amount of time the brain requires to represent data taken in by the senses in the form of conscious awareness, and arrived at an overall estimate of half a second. They also determined that the senses collect one million bits of information for every one bit that is displayed in conscious awareness. Thus, the reduction from one million to one occurs within half of a second, and, according to Marcus, Neuman, and MacKuen (2000), is a process that is managed by affect.

The application of affective intelligence to the political decision making of individuals, like impersonal influence (Mutz, 1998), can be thought of simultaneously as having the capacity to both facilitate and inhibit "ideal democracy." The application of habit and learned responses to manage incoming stimuli is efficient for an individual because it acknowledges the value of prior learning rather than making necessary constant, careful, and demanding processing of each new stimulus. Reliance on habit in the political realm takes form in general dispositions toward candidates that are based on a somewhat vague sense of enthusiasm (or lack thereof) rather than on cognitive elaboration of specific new information pertaining to campaigns. Such reliance may suffice when the candidates do not incite worry and political events do not warrant concern. Reliance on habit will become dysfunctional when circumstances change and a learned response is no longer appropriate. At novel or threatening times as detected by the surveillance system, routines would cease and a more reasoned, calculated assessment of the unfolding scenario would occur. When a candidate toward whom an individual is favorably disposed is involved in a scandal or a major misstep, for example, the routine disposition will be reevaluated and a new, cognitive assessment will be employed.

Marcus and colleagues (2000) present considerable empirical evidence. That the role of emotion in negotiating the political world can be perceived as both a trait (general disposition displayed in degree of enthusiasm toward a party) and a state (infrequent and short-term changes in degree of anxiety about candidates) is apparent in the data of Marcus and colleagues (1995, 1998). They exposed college students to either a negative (an attack ad) or a positive (a debate speech) message from Bob Dole's and Bill Clinton's presidential campaigns. They found that those exposed to the negative message of either candidate experienced an increase in distress compared not only to a control group but also to those exposed to a positive message. Only those exposed to the positive message of Clinton experienced an increase in enthusiasm, and especially among self-described Democrats. The data provide support for the variability of emotional responses to political campaign messages delivered by the media, and suggest that emotions are multidimensional and operate in complex ways. A positive emotional response, for instance, was limited to one candidate and interacted with the long-term emotional attachment of party allegiance. A negative response occurred more universally and was associated with viewing an anxiety-producing media stimulus.

Some have conceived of anxiety and enthusiasm as opposing indicators of the same emotion. The authors compare individuals' emotional responses to candidates (from the 1980, 1984, and 1988 National Election Studies) as a consequence of high-profile events (positive and negative) in candidate performance and disagree. Anxiety and enthusiasm fluctuated independently in response to real world events that impugned or favored the candidates (e.g., enthusiasm for Carter waned during the Iran hostage crisis). Levels of anxiety differed from levels of enthusiasm, with variations in the former generally less frequent than in the latter. Levels of enthusiasm for the challenger were typically more muted than those for the incumbent. The authors conclude that challengers are well advised to attempt to spark the surveillance system of voters so that the habitual, general support that an incumbent enjoys based on years in office is reassessed. Many challengers have inferred the efficacy of this strategy, as challengers are more likely to use negative ads than incumbents to attempt to chip away at the incumbent's advantage (Comstock & Scharrer, 1999). Finally, an example of a marked increase in anxiety regarding a candidate occurred in the wake of the famous commercial of the George H. Bush campaign featuring Willie Horton, a Massachusetts convict accused of raping and murdering a victim while on a weekend furlough from prison. Marcus and colleagues (2000) explain that a spike in anxiety about the candidacy of Michael Dukakis stemmed from the ad's assailing of his ability to ensure safety and order, and essentially his judgment, thereby stimulating the surveillance system through perception of threat.

Party affiliation is also a factor in determining whether anxiety will be ignited. Marcus, Neuman, and MacKuen (2000) reviewed National Election

Study (NES) data from four elections and determined that poor economic conditions predict anxiety about incumbents, and that anxiety is more profound among those who share the political party of the incumbent candidate. They contend (and we agree) that negative developments regarding one's preferred candidate are more anxiety-producing than those pertaining to a less-preferred candidate, because they are more surprising and would be more likely to engage the surveillance system. We would add that they are also more likely to produce anxiety because of the stakes involved. Supporters of a candidate who performs badly will worry about how others now perceive the candidate and about his or her chances for success. Their own self-interest (or group-interest defined by political party) is seen as threatened. Missteps for less-preferred candidates are both less surprising and less likely to cause concern.

The negativity bias of the news media is thus rooted in legitimate expectations of reader and viewer response, and is consistent with the findings of psychologists that negative stimuli are more quickly and readily attended to than positive stimuli (Dijksterhuis & Aarts, 2003; Dijksterhuis et al., 2004) and are more memorable (Fazio, Eiser, & Shook, 2004). In addition, as we argued earlier (Chapter 4), the news by the very nature of events is asymmetrical in its seeming consequences. A rise in the stock market simply signals the possibility of financial gain, were stocks to be sold; a downturn forecloses the opportunity of salvaging part of one's investment. The same holds in many political contexts. A positive occurrence signals the possibility of reward whereas a negative event makes an undesired outcome decidedly more likely.

Two extensive analyses of election data by Marcus, Neuman, and MacKuen (2000) provide considerable support for the operation of their theory in everyday life. One employs cross-sectional National Election Study (NES) data covering five elections, which minimizes the contribution of unique or unusual circumstances. We can think of this analysis as an electoral snapshot. The other employs panel data from the same respondents at three different times in the 1980 election, with the focus on changes in the responses of individuals during the campaign. We can think of this analysis as the emergence of the figures in a photo in chemical reaction to the developer; the first examines stable relationships, the second dynamic electoral shifts. Both statistically controlled for the influence of strength of partisanship, "habitual attentiveness" to politics, and education, each of which would be expected to be associated with the variables under scrutiny: anxiety over and enthusiasm for the candidates, interest in the campaign, and attention to the media.

In the five-election data, the pattern was consistent with emotional responses fostering greater interest and participation. Anxiety over and enthusiasm for candidates were both associated with interest in the campaign, caring about who wins or loses, following the campaign in the media, and participating in politics beyond voting. Anxiety, but not enthusiasm, was also correlated with the ability of voters to connect candidates with their stands on policies. In the panel data, changes on the part of voters during the campaign saw greater differentiation between enthusiasm and anxiety. Enthusiasm for candidates was a weak predictor of increases in both campaign interest and caring about the outcome of the election, whereas anxiety did not predict these outcomes at all. Conversely, anxiety was a moderate predictor of increases in media attention and the ability to associate policies with candidates, whereas enthusiasm did not predict media attention at all. Within these panel data, then, changes in campaign interest and caring who wins that took place between June and October were more a function of general enthusiasm or satisfaction than anything that was emotionally alerting. In contrast, fluctuations in the quest for information were explained by changes in the degree of concern or anxiety about the state of political affairs. Those who are pleased with their candidate and the campaign have little motive to seek out information in the media. Equipping oneself with more information is a strategy engaged in when one is agitated.

The data in our view support the two emotional processes proposed by Marcus and colleagues. General dispositions toward candidates lead to interest in elections and their outcomes. Individuals would like to see the candidates they favor do well, and will assign importance to the election based on their level of contentment with the participants. The arguably more cognitively taxing strategy of following campaign developments in the media and learning about the stands of candidates on issues and policies is motivated more by perceived threats attributable to a development in a campaign that is unfavorable or unwelcome. These situations pose "lurking dangers" (Marcus et al., 2000, p. 94) that jolt individuals away from routines toward a more reason-based strategy. However, following the same voters within an election produces somewhat different dynamics than the relationships found among voters across elections.

C. Rationality

Marcus and colleagues cite additional evidence that political judgments about events (rather than candidates) also are influenced by emotion. Using data drawn in a national survey in 1996, they discovered that support for the candidacy of Pat Buchanan among those anxious about him was significantly predicted by level of support for his position on NAFTA (North American Free Trade Agreement) rather than on a voter's long-standing political ideology. Among those who were relatively more complacent about Buchanan, ideology was a significant predictor but support of his NAFTA position was not. Marcus, Neuman, and Mackuen (2000) trace a causal chain from anxiety about the policy to anxiety about the candidate that leads potential voters to shrug off the habitual force of political ideology in favor of a more reasoned consideration of the policy itself when assessing their support for the candidate.

They find analogous support in NES data gathered at two points in time during the 1991 Gulf War (Kinder & D'Ambrosio, 1996). Among those with high anxiety about the war—indicated by reporting being upset, being afraid for troops, and being fearful that the fighting would spread—assessments of the outcome of the war predicted change in their support for President Bush. Among those with low anxiety about the war, the assessment of the outcome of the war had no bearing on changing support for the president. Again, the emotion of anxiety was a precursor to the formation of political judgments in evaluating a public figure, a process that is similar to the concept of priming (this chapter) but is more precise about the psychological mechanism by lodging it in emotion and the activation of the surveillance system.

The architects of the affective intelligence theory present a compelling case that once anxiety is sparked about politics, the traditional, habitual ways of engaging in political behavior will be suspended. A final claim derives from studies of "defecting" from one's party in votes cast in presidential elections from 1980 to 1996, as measured in NES data. Across those five elections, 20 percent of individual respondents with partisan identification reported voting in opposition to their party. The small minority demonstrates the relative strength of the force of habitual voting, while the defective voters supply an excellent opportunity to test the theory. Marcus and colleagues' analysis show that anxiety about the candidate representing one's own political party is a major factor in defecting. Those with anxiety about their own party's candidate who also preferred the policies of the opposing party's candidate were twice as likely to defect as were those complacent about their own party candidate who preferred the policies of the opposition. Policy positions of candidates make a difference, but the emotions in voters stirred by the candidates are the prevailing force.

The authors summarize, "The activation of the surveillance system goes a long way toward enabling people to choose rationally. Not only does it stimulate people to acquire more, and more accurate, information, but it also motivates them to use that information more decisively" (Marcus, Neuman, & MacKuen, 2000, p. 113). Anxiety spurred by the candidate from one's own political party (Will he do well? Is he the right person for the job? Does he have skeletons in the closet that are sure to be discovered?) rather than anxiety about opponents is the key scenario, because only the former is novel, surprising, and threatens the typical ways an individual manages vote decisions. Building a multivariate model from the 1980 to 1996 NES data using regression analysis, Marcus and colleagues show that the basis for voting differs for complacent and anxious voters. Voting decisions of those complacent with the candidate from their political party relied massively on partisanship (beta = .78), followed by policy stands (beta = .65) and the personal qualities of the candidate (beta = .34). Voting decisions of the anxious relied drastically less on partisanship (beta = .17) and the influence of policy and personal qualities of the candidates were twice as large (beta = .78 and 1.28, respectively). The analysis rules out emotional arousal in general rather than anxiety or complacency in the particular campaign as an alternative explanation and eliminates habitual attentiveness to politics as a factor.

The theory of affective intelligence, and the multifaceted supporting evidence, calls into question allegations that voters are characteristically lackadaisical, uninformed, and, for much of the electoral cycle, indifferent (Kinder, 1998). Rather, it suggests that conscientious and potentially complex reasoning about issues, policies, and the strengths and weaknesses of candidates occurs when it is most useful—when an unusual or threatening situation requires the voter to reject the "business as usual" stance that manages much human behavior, political and otherwise. When circumstances fail to alert voters, habitual responses are sufficient to proceed with political participation without fear of costly errors. Marcus, Neuman, and MacKuen explain:

> In the end, we see that emotions enhance citizen rationality because they allow citizens to condition their political judgment to fit the circumstances. . . . What makes citizen rationality possible is the dynamic attentiveness of affective intelligence: people alter the depth of their investment in political judgment in response to the character of the external political world. When the political environment demands real consideration, anxiety spurs the needed reassessment; when the political environment is relatively benign, emotional calm permits the reliance on voters' effective habits, their standing decisions guided by enthusiasm (p. 124).

VI. PRIMACY OF THE MEDIA

The five primary ways that individuals use media to take account of and participate in politics often do not involve great enthusiasm for or intense and consistent dedication to political affairs. Individuals do not pay the same amount of attention to politics and public affairs throughout the year. Rather, most direct their attention to public affairs when infrequent yet highly important political decisions are called for, as in the election of the president. Individuals do not ordinarily collect information and consider experiences from a variety of sources when they rank the most pressing issues of the day. Rather, they rely often and largely on the news media to inform them of what issues and topics to think about. In the same vein, individuals often do not consider the many aspects of a prominent person's character or performance when evaluating that person. Rather, they typically use the most cognitively accessible information to do so—the attributes of the person that are covered in the news. The same holds for the particular attributes of topics and issues—those that will be used in reaching judgments and forming opinions most often will be those primed by the media. Individuals rely on the news media to learn of the opinions of collective others and are occasionally swayed by the direction of those opinions. Similarly, individuals use the news media to inform themselves of the collective experiences of large numbers of others and they use that information to reach judgments about the state of the nation instead of drawing primarily on their personal experiences. Finally, most individuals most of the time employ habitual rather than cognitively demanding ways of responding to political stimuli. Only when their surveillance system alerts them to an unusual or potentially threatening situation do individuals devote considerable amounts of cognitive energy to manage (and potentially act on) incoming political information.

We return, briefly, to a review of the ways in which our population segments differ in response to the media (Table 6.3). We retain Klapper's (1960) concept of "reinforcement," but discard his "conversion" for shifts in opinion, which

TABLE 6.3 Role of Media by Population Segment

Segment	Percent Population	Use of Media
Nonvoters		
Actives	14	High in media use; open to influence because of favorable view of both parties and high levels of political efficacy and salience; high potential for voting in behalf of redress or remedy
Disenchanted	9	High in media use; low opinion of political parties, particularly Republicans, and politicians in general makes media influenced unlikely
Know-nothings	13	Modest use of media, with newspaper reading particularly low; lack of political knowledge and indifference to both parties results in little media influence
Disconnected	7	Very low media use with no newspaper reading; low scores on "officials care," efficacy and salience suggest little media influence between campaigns but favorable opinions of political parties, and especially Democrats, suggests some influence during campaigns
Alienated	6	Moderate in TV news viewing but almost nil in newspaper use; poor opinion of both parties and the political process inhibits persuasion or other media influence
Republicans		
Conservatives	6	High media use, especially newspapers and the Internet; follow news to identify issues and choose among party's candidates; strongly held views combined with cognitive skills to counter-argue minimizes any persuasive influence of media; media mostly reinforce

TABLE 6.3 Role of Media by Population Segment—Cont'd

Segment	Percent Population	Use of Media
Moderates	7	Moderate to high media use; use media to identify issues and select among candidates; media probably particularly important during campaigns; high levels of political knowledge and party allegiance promote counter-arguing – media largely reinforce, but openness toward Democrats makes some persuasive influence possible
Populists	6	Use media less than other Republican segments, although newspaper reading is about the same as the Moderates; use media for political decision-making, especially during campaigns, as evidenced from low support for Republican nominee; reinforcement less prominent, some persuasion likely
Democrats		
Liberals	5	High newspaper and Internet use; highly educated and politically knowledgeable; use media to identify issues, follow campaigns; counter-arguing minimizes persuasive influence of media; strong commitment to party and ideology means media largely reinforce
Social conservatives	8	Moderate to high in use of newspapers and TV news; use media to identify issues; average in political knowledge, but follow political news closely so campaign coverage particularly important; counter-arguing minimizes persuasive influence of media; media largely reinforce
New Democrats	5	Moderate in media use, but attend more than average to TV newsmagazines and specialized channels such as CNN; use media to identify issues and choose among party's candidates; strong support for Democratic nominee indicates that media largely reinforce
Partisan poor	6	Moderate newspaper use but low in use of TV news and the Internet; use media to identify issues and choose among candidates; strong support for Democratic nominee indicates that media largely reinforce
Independents		
New Prosperity	5	High use of newspapers and the Internet; use media to identify issues and choose among candidates and parties; highly open to media influence and persuasion as evidenced by divided vote and low proportions favoring one or the other of the two major parties; close attention to media during campaigns very likely
Disaffecteds	4	Low use of media, although open to influence and persuasion because of lack of party allegiance; nevertheless, low attention to news media confines them to a comparatively small role

we construe as having four dimensions: changes in a) interest in politics and public affairs, b) the salience of issues, topics and persons, c) degree of support for one or another policy, and d) allegiance to a candidate or party. As we scan across these segments, it is clear that the media serve the interests and motives of the highly involved, provide important guidance to the less involved, and especially during the election, but are largely ignored, as is politics and public affairs in general, by a sizable portion of the public.

Nevertheless, the patterns across these five areas of research and theory do point to a citizenry that operates in reasonable, rational ways. Individuals wisely conserve cognitive exertion for times when it is most needed, in electing a president or in dealing with surprising or troubling political information or developments. The readiness of the undecided voter to learn about candidates and issues through attention to the media, of persons with a high need for orientation to evaluate the importance of topics through exposure to the news, and of the individual to forego the less taxing habitual ways of dealing with political stimuli when there is an increased risk of an erroneous judgment or act nevertheless all point to the capacity and willingness of individuals to apply reason and high-order cognition when necessary. The findings also demonstrate that the news media are the main means through which these processes occur, and provide coverage that is useful and helpful to individuals who are motivated to apply that information to political ends.

The issue and topic agendas of individuals are set jointly by the media, personal experience and observation, and interpersonal sources. However, the media in most cases are the major and sometimes the sole source of information. This is a product of their authoritativeness, superior information gathering, and influence on interpersonal sources. It is from these latter circumstances that the psychology of media and politics draws its importance. In many respects, the media are a sole source for political information, and understanding how the human mind makes use of them for political purposes is essential to understanding modern politics in America. The collective and institutional aspects of public life of course have crucial roles. They are central in the defining and articulating of interests, the mobilizing of public opinion and voter support, and the framing of choices. Two grand and diverse parties present a quite different and more stable political context than is presented by a half-dozen or more militias, each marching beneath its particular unfurled banner. Nevertheless, they take on meaning only as they are confronted by individuals in reaching political decisions. This primacy of the media holds for all five of the processes we have examined. Even in the regularly recurring electoral cycle the media are preeminent (not many people mark their calendars with dates of elections as they do for vacations). Members of the public embrace the opportunity provided by the news media to expand their horizons and learn about things outside the confines of their own personal experience. They selectively attend to media in accord with their political goals, and attempt to act rationally using the media within the inevitable constraints of limited knowledge and limited accuracy in assigning accountability.

In Chapter 5 we set forth two assumptions necessary to accurate and effective political participation by individuals. Briefly, they were:

1. The coverage and emphases of the media are essentially accurate and valid.
2. Voter decision making is largely free of distorting biases.

Both are obviously out of reach. Nevertheless, we argue that voters make reasoned choices, and these choices typically serve fairly well; we accede here to the definition of Lupia, McCubbins, and Popkin (2000) that a "rational choice is one that is based on reason, irrespective of what those reasons may be" (p. 7). Our presidents, senators, representatives, governors, and lesser officials, and the propositions enacted or cast aside by ballot at the state or local level, largely function successfully, although often to the dissatisfaction of large minorities who are unhappy with the electoral results.

The explanation is that our assumptions represent the ideals of modern democratic government. Such a government is representative and does not depend on community deliberation; it travels by the media, as do its parties and politicians; and it assures continuity of governance by scheduled elections. In reality, deviations from our two assumptions fail to defeat the process of reasoned voter decision making in these circumstances. That process is resilient in the face of misinformation and biased reasoning, although hardly immune to them. Principal safeguards are the stability of the political system, the possibility of rectifying perceived errors, and the dominance of two parties whose victories—while typically requiring the support of their more radical wings—rest on the leadership of their more centrist elements.

Most citizens, during most of the presidential electoral cycle, are badly informed (Neuman, Just, & Crigler, 1992). They score low on what we have called "civic knowledge" (Comstock & Scharrer, 1999) such as the names of representatives and senators, the gist of pending legislation, recent events involving a world leader. Philip Converse, the political scientist, argued famously many years ago (1964) that most "public opinion" was conjured on the spot in response to a pollster's or survey researcher's questions. This undoubtedly remains largely true today, with ignorance, prejudices, and biases in cognitive processing distinguishing much of the voting public (Achen & Bartels, 2004; Kinder, 1998). Much has been made of the fact that repeated rephrasings or even repetition of questions in polls and surveys produce apparently contradictory results; a majority may endorse greater financial aid to the poor but favor reductions in welfare. However, this ignores the very real consequences for the voicing of individual opinion of the framing of a question. Such framing includes the order of questions, which may establish one or another politically relevant context, as well as the phrasing, which may differentially evoke thoughts and emotions that influence the response (Schwarz & Groves, 1998). It is not surprising, then, that seemingly similar questions are answered differently by the same person. At the aggregate level, however, opinions are quite stable. This is easily seen in *Public Opinion Quarterly*'s continuing "The Polls—Trends" feature, where the proportion favoring one or another position generally remains about the same across a decade or more and as a generalization receives stunning support from the well-known analysis of Page and Shapiro (1992) of 50 years of public opinion, where the opinions registered by the public are largely stable, and shifts typically reflect responses to changed national or world conditions (although neither of these sets of data would detect levels of opinion inconsistent with concrete facts; they document stability and responsiveness, not judiciousness).

We see the decision-making process evolving through a series of frames, each with its particular components. At the same time, we recognize, as is the case with many matters of cognition and affect, that these frames may be passed through simultaneously or in a different order. These frames include (a) the political context, (b) the process of choosing, and (c) the systemic and structural factors that give clarity and stability to politics.

The first frame that makes choice possible is the political context. There will be an inheritance of remembered events, such as the Vietnam war, that will serve as analogues in assessing current circumstances (Schuman & Rodgers, 2004). Events that are particularly well recalled often will have occurred in the voters' adolescence, when the momentous was being seriously encountered for the first time, and often will have benefited from cues that deter forgetting, such as being the subject of films, television entertainment, and retrospective news accounts, or having been initially cloaked in dramaturgy (Davis, 2004; Schuman & Rodgers, 2004). These are accompanied by impressions of the state of the nation that can be characterized variously as its mood, sense of well-being, or desire for change (Popkin & Dimock, 2000; Rahn, 2000). There is also the more concrete baggage of recent decisions and occurrences: war, the economy, a party's agenda for reforms. These will not only be the focus of attention for many individuals, but also there will be shared attributions of responsibility and achievement and these will further the process of political alignment (Denzau & North, 2000). Then there are a fairly stable set of political values, a philosophy, and a preference for the historic positions of one or another of the two major parties on the part of the individual (Alvarez & Brehn, 2002; Feldman, 2003). These are joined by the phenomenon of issue ownership, in which one or the other of the parties is supposedly ceded special expertise by the public on particular topics (Ansolabehere & Iyengar,

1994; Iyengar & Valentino, 2000), one or more of which may be prominent in the campaign at hand.

The result is a foundation, and much guidance in regard to direction, for choosing among candidates and deciding about ballot propositions. For some (those with a high interest in politics) evaluation of political figures and actions is continuous. For the majority, it largely waits upon the necessity of electoral choice. This means that the public's understanding of what has been taking place is constantly undergoing some change, but for most it remains for the electoral cycle to signal the campaign for the presidency or the off-year elections for the initiation of the process of choice (Lau, 2003). Potential voters now pay more attention to political news, and impressions form about candidates and issues, with these impressions depending to a considerable extent on imputed motives (McGraw, 2003)—public service, honesty, vision, and the like—for candidates, and perceived vested interests in regard to ballot propositions. Most of the public misses much in regard to civic details, but they will grasp the broad dimensions of the forces in collision. For example, very high proportions will accurately recognize one or the other of the two major party presidential candidates as more or less liberal or conservative (Hamilton, 2004).

The second frame consists of two processes that enable electoral choices to be reasoned, in the sense of representing a thoughtful process, and rational, in the sense of weighing a variety of factors. The first is the substitution of heuristics for deep and thorough knowledge—tactics or shortcuts that make cognitive processing in a situation feasible (Kuklinski & Quirk, 2000; Lau, 2003). These include the opinions of experts, gurus, and commentators in print and on television, the latest polls, the parties to which candidates belong, endorsements, familiarity, and signs of local enthusiasm for a candidate. These shortcuts are not quicker ways to reach a thoroughly reasoned decision; instead, they make a reasoned decision possible in the absence of thorough reasoning (and do not guarantee that the outcome will be the same). The second is the aggregation of individual choices in the final tally. This aggregation cancels out the influence of those voting with scant knowledge and little effective reasoning (who presumably would be equally divided between parties and on ballot issues), giving those who are at least somewhat better informed and more politically attuned a more decisive say (Kinder, 1998). The result is the weighting of decision making in favor of the more knowledgeable, and to some degree the attenuation of errors.

The third frame is made up of several diverse factors that supply a degree of stability to the system. These are structural and systemic elements, and provide the conditions for voter decision making. The institutional element in politics has an important role. Parties, advocacy groups, and collections of vested interests refine issues so that the public or their representatives are offered finite choices (Lupia & McCubbins, 2000). Choice is dependent on this process, where the option is between one or the other and not a multitude of outcomes, and it is this narrowing of options that makes possible the effective use of heuristics. In a similar process, each of the two parties usually advances a candidate representing the party's center. This is much maligned by critics for failing to offer voters real and dramatic alternatives, but it has the very real advantage of ensuring a degree of stability across changes in government and largely precludes the possibility that a "wrong" choice will have radical consequences.

Two additional factors further promise stability. One is the regular, inviolate scheduling of elections. Changes in the parties in power in the White House or Congress do not affect the political system that placed them there. Perceived errors can be readily rectified in the next election. The other is the malleability (we don't quarrel with "fickleness") of the voting public. A small proportion not adamantly aligned with one or the other parties or an ideology regularly shifts from one party to the other. The result is an alternating series of trials and flirtations with social solutions and political philosophies. Liberal administrations after a time are supplanted by conservative administrations. These are not random shifts. The evidence is clear in the power of length of time in office to predict presidential electoral victory (the longer in office, the less the chance of victory). It is one of three major variables for the projection of outcomes prior to the campaign (Holbrook, 1996); the others are the economy, and favorability of performance ratings before the campaign. In the aggregate, the voting public extends a semester or so of opportunity to a particular perspective, and then, as this particular course suffers from a perceived discount in effectiveness (if not quite bankruptcy), shifts to a different philosophy, approach, and party. The public pursues one plausible option, then rationally attempts to redress the inadequacies of that course of action.

In this context some of the distortions of the media are functional or at least not wholly detrimental. The emphasis on bad news may well imperil an administration, but also often serves to attract the attention of the public and signal that a review of options and priorities might be in order. The emphasis on personalities, while detracting from knowledge of issues, presents easily understandable alternatives that are not entirely divorced from issues—leadership and decisiveness in combating terrorism, vision and remedy in addressing the economy. The emphasis on the horse race, while again detracting from issues, provides important information on two fronts: normative opinion (who the public favors) and the probability of an unacceptable outcome.

Overall, the process of electoral choice provides a great deal to worry about while giving no reason for despair. Kuklinski and Quirk (2000) are probably correct that the basing of votes on inaccurate, inappropriate or irrelevant cues has increased with the diminution of party influence, but party—and ideology—still plays a major role only with a somewhat subordinate voice; most voters still have a preferred party although they are less likely to name it as their political identification than they once were (Kinder, 1998). Voters often do not accurately express their interests, desires, and values in their choice. They are often badly informed. They typically have only a vague understanding of how the government works, which agency or department does what, what federal policies on various topics are (or even what those topics might be); the novelist Jim Harrison (2004) put it nicely, " . . . I felt lucky that my capacity for the French language was limited to understanding only the gist of conversations—sort of the way the average American comprehends our government" (p. 82). The media may give wrong impressions; and interpersonal sources, who largely rely on the media, pass on the inaccuracies of the media. Minutiae and trivia often will figure in choices among candidates (Achen & Bartels, 2004; Menaud, 2004): the attempt to eat a tamale without removing the corn husk may arouse doubts among Hispanics (Gerald Ford); fall weather that is too wet or dry may raise animosity toward the current administration (Al Gore); amazement at an everyday device, such as a supermarket scanner, may call into question credentials as an everyman as well as knowledge of contemporary life (George H.W. Bush). The "fundamental attribution error" (psychology's term for attributing actions to personality and character rather than circumstance; Krull et al., 1999; Ross, 1977) certainly takes a toll as voters attempt to assemble a portrait of suitability rather than assess a record of responses to varying situations that may or may not be astute or honorable. That is, they think of the man (or woman) rather than the political actor. Voters certainly entertain a litany of cognitive biases. Kuklinski and Quirk (2000) name several: stereotyping, overconfidence in the rightness of their convictions (and often the belief that most others share their views), resistance to arguments in behalf of other perspectives, and a susceptibility to easy arguments in behalf of their partisanship.

Politicians and parties will attempt to employ these varied factors in manipulating opinion to their advantage. Nevertheless, all of these forces for disorder are constrained by the framework that fosters stability and order: clarity of choices, regular elections, two diverse parties usually led by centrist elements, and the shifting of the public between political philosophies and parties. It is a ship afloat, if occasionally beset by crosswinds and high waves.

Elections, of course, vary. We have tried, throughout, to depict prevailing patterns. There always will be exceptions. In 2004, conventional wisdom held that the partisanship and allegiance to one or the other party or candidate appeared earlier than usual. Kerry received no convention bounce (although we could make the pattern fit by substituting his primary victories) while Bush received a substantial one. Each faced particular challenges, which is always the case. Howard Moskowitz, a social psychologist noted for his consumer studies (a paradigm he applies to politics), was quoted as saying, "Bush has to harness a group of dogs basically pulling in the same direction. Kerry's got to harness a group of cats" ("Political Points," 2004).

Individuals use the media for political purposes in reasoning ways. Members of the public certainly differ according to the degree of involvement with and prior knowledge about politics and public affairs that they bring to their exposure to the media. However, those less informed and involved as well as those highly and consistently informed and involved achieve considerable political gains from media use.

CHAPTER 7

Beyond Politics

The readiness of individuals to look beyond their own experiences in seeking guidance about what they should think and how they should act applies outside the realm of politics. The media provide a lens through which an individual gains the opportunity to observe and learn about the opinions and experiences of others that he or she would not otherwise encounter. Practical use of what is observed on the part of others is a frequent circumstance of social life, and has two sequential components: the acquisition of information about others, often through the mass media, and the weighing of that information in adapting attitudes and choosing modes of behavior. By attitudes, we mean dispositions of all sorts—beliefs, perceptions, and values—and the types of behavior on which we will focus are consumption and two aspects of socialization: gender roles and aggression.

When asked to list major motives for watching television, a substantial number of individuals refer to the ability of the medium to help them learn about and keep up with the world around them (Albarran & Umphrey, 1993; Harwood, 1997). Yet, they do not refer to news and educational programs when reporting this gratification. Individuals apparently derive satisfaction from what we call the "surveillance function" of the media: learning about styles, fads, trends, fashion, popular expressions, and the like (Comstock & Scharrer, 1999). Appearance and behavior are observed. Attitudes and points of view are inferred. The result is a set of pictures of the social world that take on an edifying force when joined with the individual's own thoughts, attitudes, and actions. There is also a shift from large collectives to much smaller numbers that nevertheless derive much of their authority from their representation of norms. These norms endorse what is correct, worthy, and socially approved. The media provide audience members with the ability to monitor their culture—the good, especially, but also the bad, and the ugly—and construct a relationship with it.

The effects of the surveillance function of the media, and in particular television because of the combination of frequent and expansive use, graphic visual presentations, and the popularity of characters, personalities, and programs, represent the same type of impersonal influence that we have seen operating in the sphere of political decision making. In both cases, exposure to the thoughts and experiences of those with whom the individual has no first-hand relationship achieves some degree of influence, although now the emphasis shifts from the state of the polity to the instruction that may be derived from them, and thus the interest in the behavior rather than the experiences of others.

We begin our exploration of this process by examining two theories that share characteristics of our model of media influence and extend our discussion beyond politics. Social comparison theory and social identity theory, both describing the effect on individuals of impressions formed about others, are essential to the wider application of our model. Individuals view others in the media (as well as in "real life") and engage in a social comparison process (Festinger, 1954), comparing and contrasting themselves to those others. The social comparison process can result in a number of effects, including changes in mood (positive when the individual "wins" the comparison, negative when the individual does not) and behavior (such as purchasing a product or emulating a way of behaving). Comparisons with others also help to shape one's identity, as similarities and differences with those around us are taken into account in forming concepts about ourselves (Tajfel & Turner, 1979; Turner, 1999). Social identity theory explores the individual's construction of in-groups (with which the individual feels an affiliation, manifested in preference and loyalty) and out-groups (which are perceived as made up of individuals distinctly different from oneself—distrust and antipathy replace loyalty and preference), and the implications of those constructions for self and social behavior.

Next, we focus on two specific instances in which media-based information about others beyond politics has influence—consumer behavior and socialization. Both are affected by the surveillance function of the media and both entail a comparison of self to others. In neither case do the media provide the sole source of information about proper, acceptable, or popular behavior. The parents, teachers, and peers of a child or young person and the family members, friends, acquaintances, and coworkers of adults provide important guidance. Nevertheless, the media proffer a unique opportunity in consumer decision making and socialization by widening experiences and points of view beyond the inevitably narrow confines of personal experience. Furthermore, both consumer behavior and socialization derive from the development and expression of the social identity of the individual—the view of the self in relation to others.

We treat these two separately because consumer behavior represents the expression of the two processes of social comparison and social identity, whereas socialization constitutes their contribution to social structure. From the perspective of the individual, the former is concerned with means to particular ends, while the latter is concerned with the assumption of particular roles (Burke, 2004).

I. SOCIAL INFLUENCE

Social comparison theory and social identity theory are related to the processes of impersonal influence that we have outlined in regard to politics but they are also different in important ways. Chief among the common characteristics is the comparison of self to others, resulting in an influence on an individual's thoughts, attitudes, and behavior that has a social basis. In the theory of impersonal influence on decisions about politics, this comparison typically results in the assignment of greater weight to the opinions and experiences of others rather than to one's own. That is not necessarily the case in social comparison and social identity theories. Rather, as we will see, social comparisons can privilege either others (the comparison group) or the self, depending on the motivation for engaging in the comparison. Social identity formation, contrary to the direction of the comparisons made in impersonal influence (with the exception of those concerned with vulnerability, risk, or social dysfunction), tends to be driven by an ego-protection or biased optimism about the self, and therefore typically favors the self and groups to which the self belongs in comparisons of the self with others. Greater weight is given to self-interest. The selfless effect of impersonal influence (in which the individual's perception of the good of the group prevails) can be overturned in favor of self-interest or in-group interest in the contexts of social comparisons and social identity formation. This is because ego-gratification in the form of superior status and attributes is the driving force rather than satisfaction at having reached a just and accurate conclusion about the state of society. Self-esteem is a prevailing factor in the latter two theories (Maltby & Day, 2003), but plays (a smaller role) in impersonal influence in political decision making.

Another key difference between impersonal influence and the theories of social comparison and social identity is that the former is based on one's impressions of an anonymous, impersonal, large collective, whereas the latter two need not be. The power of the influence of information about impersonal others lies in their numbers as well as the absence of characteristics that would imperil the representativeness or credibility of their experiences and opinions (Mutz, 1998). Conversely, the groups of others employed for comparison in the other two theories do not necessarily share that anonymous and amorphous quality. In social identity theory, in-groups with which the individual associates are, by definition, known quantities. Out-groups, on the other hand, are not typically well known by the individual and therefore may take on a largely unspecified quality that is similar to impersonal others. In social comparison theory, the nature of the group used for comparison depends on the context of the situation and can vary from a single, well-known person in the individual's social network to a host of impersonal others presented to the individual via the media (Botta, 1999; Goethals, 1986; Jones, 2001). Thus, social comparison and social identity are more variable in the concreteness and singularity of the others who have an influence; these others in these two cases are frequently analogous to the exemplars that have such a powerful role in affecting the impressions of societal conditions based on news accounts.

Because the others in the impersonal influence model are largely nonspecified and heterogeneous, the model does not much concern itself with the relationship between the individual and those others. Both of the other two theories assign a central role to this relationship. In social comparison theory, the perceived status of the comparison group relative to the individual performs a critical role. In social identity theory, the perceived linkages between the self and in-group others—as well as the perceived disconnections between self and out-group others—are the pivotal force.

Despite these differences, however, a fundamental commonality across these three theories is the opening up of the perspective of the individual to encompass the social: the characteristics, opinions, and experiences of others. All three rest on the supplementation and transfiguration of individual thought processes and attitude formation in light of information about others. All three feature comparisons made between the personal—the individual's own thoughts, attitudes, and behavior—and the social. In all three theories, the individual bases decisions and attitude formation in large part on information acquired about others. And in all three, the media are an instrumental source in bringing that information to the attention of the individual, whether it is in the form of public opinion polls, public experience depicted in the news, or characters in entertainment programming modeling what is popular, acceptable, and successful.

A. Social Comparison

Social comparison theory has received a great deal of empirical support since Leon Festinger (1954) first laid out its preliminary conceptualization. It describes the tendency for individuals to compare themselves with others to arrive at an understanding of how others view them, how they stack up relative to others in regard to abilities and rewards, and how their thoughts, feelings, and behavior relate to those of others. For individuals, a primary means of discerning social reality (e.g., "How smart am I?") as opposed to physical reality (e.g., "What grade did I get on that standardized test?") is through social comparison. Physical reality can be determined through one's own observation of the manifest properties of information (e.g., the letter grade reported from an exam). Social reality is best deciphered through a process in which one engages in comparisons with others (e.g., "How well did I do compared to others?" "Do my friends think I'm smart?"). Individuals generally prefer objective, nonsocial criteria, but such criteria often are unavailable (there are usually no GREs on anxiety in the face of an impending volcanic eruption), and so they frequently turn to comparison with others (Taylor, 1998). Thus, the underlying motive is self-knowledge, which pursues the most efficient course.

There is some disagreement regarding those whom an individual chooses for social comparison. Festinger (1954) originally argued that people tend to compare themselves to those who are demographically similar because they would provide the most accurate benchmark. For instance, in a quest to determine how smart one is, it is logical to compare oneself to others of the same age and in the same situation (e.g., in college, or in a particular college class). Advancing a somewhat different reason for the primacy of comparisons made with similar others, Schachter (1959) concluded that perceptions of affiliation were a motivating force. When subjects awaiting participation in an experiment in which they expected to receive electric shocks were given the choice of waiting with fellow participants or with students merely waiting for their professors, they overwhelmingly chose the former. They had a choice between two similar groups of strangers, but they preferred those with whom they shared something transiently significant—an imminent anxiety-producing event. Presumably, this kind of situational similarity would enable the study participants to better assess their own mental state in comparison with others awaiting the same task.

Other psychologists have suggested that social comparison also can be motivated by the desire to feel better about oneself (Taylor & Lobel, 1989; Wills, 1981, 1991). Thus, social comparisons can be made with others based on their status on the issue at stake and can be used to strategically regulate one's self-concept, self-esteem, or self-motivation. Horizontal comparisons based on shared circumstances or status are replaced or complemented by comparisons with those perceived as superior or inferior to the individual.

Individuals engage in upward social comparisons (with those perceived as superior to the self on the issue in question) when looking for inspiration, motivation, or problem-solving strategies. An example is breast cancer patients seeking out others who have successfully coped with the disease, thereby making the patients feel more comfortable about their own circumstances and more optimistic over the likelihood of recovery (Taylor & Lobel, 1989). Downward social comparisons (with those perceived as inferior to the self) can help an individual to bolster self-esteem or improve feelings of well-being. An example is breast cancer patients comparing themselves to fellow patients who are worse off than themselves in order to enjoy comparative resiliency (Wood, Taylor, & Lichtman, 1985).

The population employed for comparison depends on the motivation for the comparison. As Lippa (1994) argues, "If we want accurate information about ourselves, we may seek out similar others who face our predicament; if we want inspiration, advice, and problem-solving skills, we may seek out better-off people who have faced our predicament successfully; and if we want to feel better about ourselves and reduce our anxiety, we may make 'downward comparisons' with people who are worse off than we are" (p. 379). Efficacy governs choice of population. The common element is evaluation, which may be served merely by similarity, a shared event or predicament, or an example that bolster's the individual's sense of well-being.

B. Social Identity

Social groups carry a degree of persuasive power over individuals in the formation of attitudes and behavior. Both groups varying in status and anonymous collectives have the potential to influence the thoughts and actions of the individual. With social comparison theory, we take into account an abstract relationship between the individual and the group that serves the individual's needs. In social identity theory, we turn to relationships between individuals and groups that assist the individual in self-definition.

A crude but instructive comparison of these two sources of influence is provided by the experiments of Ybarra and Trafimow (1998), who compared the roles of attitudes and norms in behavioral intention (Table 7.1). The process of social comparison includes determining what others think and assessing one's own dispositions (Heider, 1958; Hogg & Terry, 2000). Norms, in contrast, represent the individual's perceptions of the standards held by the social group to which the individual belongs or with which the individual claims some allegiance. The behavior in question was condom use, a volitional act that serves as a proxy for a wide range of behavior. A principal manipulation was whether the self ("private self") or the group ("collective self") was primed—that is, made relevant to the experimental subjects. As can be seen across three experiments, attitudes consistently provided a context for persuasion when the self was primed, but norms consistently provided a context for persuasion when the group was primed. These data neatly illustrate how social comparison and social identity affect behavior, as well as their susceptibility to the context that makes one or another relevant in a particular set of circumstances.

Decades of social psychological research tell us that the persuasive power of social groups is based in part on an individual's perceptions of membership or affiliation ("I am Korean" rather than "I am smart"). Theorists exploring social identity (Abrams & Hogg, 1990; Brewer, 1979; Hinkle & Brown, 1990; Tajfel & Turner, 1986) have shown that perceptions by individuals of the status of the in-groups to which they feel they belong and of the out-groups for which they entertain distrust and antipathy have a central role in the formation of self-concept. Such categorization by the individual of self and others into groups typically defines those groups according to demographics (e.g., by gender, race, class, political party, religion, occupation, place of residence, and the like) that the individual uses in self-definition or self-description.

Social identity theory posits that the self-concept is determined in part by membership in social groups and that the act of self-categorization into groups emphasizes perceived similarities between the self and some others while at the same time emphasizing perceived differences between the self and different

TABLE 7.1 Compliance as a Function of Attitudes, Norms, and Priming of Self and Collective

	(Beta Weights)	
Priming	Attitudes	Norms
Experiment 1		
Private self	.54**	.23
Collective self	.29	.53**
Experiment 2		
Private self	.65**	.28
Collective self	.14	.49**
Experiment 3		
Private self	.43*	.13
Collective self	.17	.66**

*$p < .05$; ** $p < .01$
Topic: Intention to use condom
Adapted from Trafimow, 2000.

others (Duck, Hogg, & Terry; 1999; Gunther & Mundy, 1993; Gunther & Thorson, 1992). These social identities produce a motive to make "intergroup comparisons that favor the in-group" (Duck et al., 1999, p. 1882) in order to maintain or enhance self-esteem. Maass and colleagues succinctly put it: "People tend to create or maintain a positive self-image by enhancing the status of their own group with respect to relevant comparison groups" (Maass, Cadinu, Guarnieri, & Grasselli, 2003, p. 854). When social comparison processes are engaged, the groups with which an individual identifies usually benefit from the exercise while out-groups suffer in comparison. Group members derive satisfaction from adhering to the norms of a group, and this satisfaction increases as identity with the group increases (Christensen et al., 2004); this effect is particularly frequent with injunctive norms, which specify what members should do, but descriptive norms similarly serve as means of attachment to a group when they differentiate an in-group from an out-group.

Tajfel (1978) has defined social identity as "that part of an individual's self-concept which derives from . . . knowledge of . . . membership of a social group (or groups) together with the value and emotional significance attached to that membership" (p. 63). The categories or groups of people so employed will differ according to their importance in relationship to the individual's self-concept. Cameron (2000; Cameron & Lalonde, 2001) has introduced a three-factor model of in-group determinants. *In-group ties* entail the degree to which the individual perceives a sense of belonging with or a bond with others. *Centrality* is the extent to which the group frequently comes to the individual's mind, or the cognitive accessibility of the group. *In-group affect* represents the degree to which the relationship produces positive feelings for the individual. These three factors describe the means by which groups become a salient feature in the identity of the individual (Cameron, 2001).

The persuasion experiment of Mackie, Gastardo-Conaco, and Skelly (1992) provides an excellent example of the power of the group in attitude formation (Figure 7.1). They defined an in-group source as a student from the same institution as the subjects, the University of California at Santa Barbara. An out-group source was defined as a student from an East Coast university. Subjects were either exposed to the views of an in-group or out-group source, after which they heard three pro and three con arguments (essentially, a balanced presentation), or they heard the same three pro and three con arguments before exposure to the views of an in-group or out-group source. The arguments were constructed to be strong or weak. They also differed in whether they supported or were counter to positions generally held initially by the subjects. The topics were the legalization of euthanasia (which the subjects generally opposed) and handgun control (which the subjects generally supported). The crux of interpretation is the influence of knowledge of group position versus the processing of the arguments without knowledge of group position. As can be seen, persuasion was substantial for both weak and strong arguments among those first exposed to the views of the in-group. In contrast, for those who processed the arguments without prior knowledge of the in-group position, only the strong argument had a noticeable persuasive effect among those exposed to an in-group source. These data point to the primacy of group authority in persuasiveness when an in-group position is known before arguments are processed.

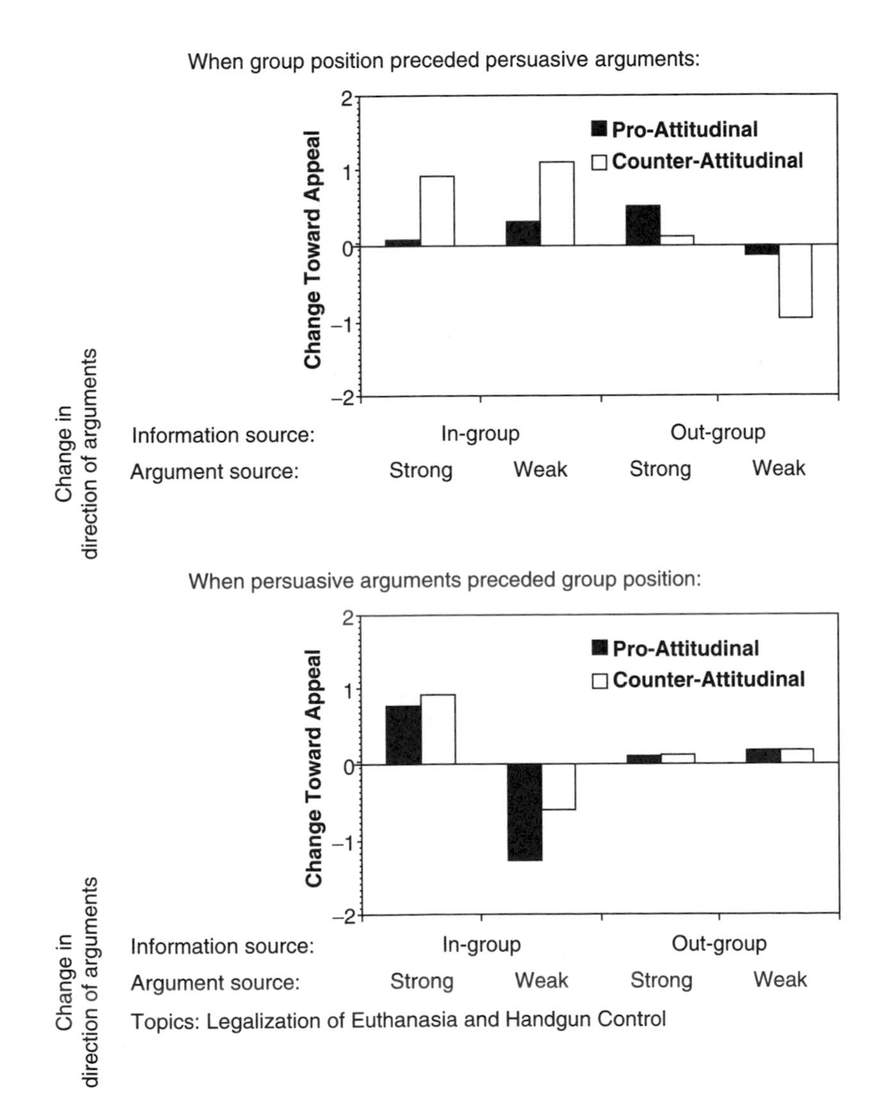

FIGURE 7.1 In-group influence on attitudes (adapted from Mackie and Queller, 2000).

The central role of links with others in the formation of individual identity means that in-groups must be viewed favorably to achieve positive self-esteem (Abrams & Hogg, 1988; Hornsey, 2003; Maltby & Day, 2003; Tajfel & Turner, 1986). One means of retaining a favorable view of the self is to perceive in-groups as impervious to negative influence but satisfyingly vulnerable to positive influence. Duck and colleagues argue "that perceptions of persuasive impact on self and other are also dependent on salient group memberships or social identities (e.g., gender identity, political identity, student identity)" (Duck et al., 2000, p. 266). This is the explanation for the frequent belief by individuals that they and their in-groups are persuaded in directions that are socially approved or carry a mantel of merit and deny that they are persuaded in directions that are socially disapproved or might be seen as injudicious. This again is the phenomenon labeled in regard to media as the third-person effect (Chapters 1 and 2). Self and in-group others are perceived to be positively influenced by the media (e.g., affected by public service announcements or learning from the news), whereas out-group others are perceived to be negatively influenced (e.g., affected by media violence or stereotypes) (Duck, 1999; Duck, Hogg, & Terry, 1999; Duck, Terry, & Hogg, 1995; Scharrer, 2002).

These processes involve three levels of social construction. Two rest firmly on networks of shared values and expectations (Burke, 2004). Group identity generally serves self-esteem because it places a positive value on membership in, loyalty to, and a favorable disposition toward the group. However, it is necessary that a number of people share in these convictions, or the very existence of the group will come into question. Similarly, role identity requires that numerous others reciprocate with complementary roles; mates require spouses, teachers need students, musicians and actors depend on audiences, femme fatales entrap vulnerable males, and thieves rely on victims. Thus, what we do and who we are depend on location within the social structure, and are products of social interaction. The third level, personal identity, evokes claims to certain special aspects of the self, such as distinct core of being, authenticity, and self-expression. These three processes sometimes collide or conspire: the force of group and role identities will be enhanced by larger numbers of people participating in the necessary social interaction, personal identity that draws heavily on group and role similarly will lead to their greater force in governing thought and behavior, and ill-defined roles and weak group ties will strand the individual in a sea of ambiguity over the proper port of call. Nevertheless, conflict between the three identities and the inevitable ambiguities of exactly what is required of an individual opens the way to some innovation and exploration. In this respect, the media can be quite liberating by supplying examples and models for thought and behavior that distinctly contrast with and remove the individual from his or her immediate and imminent social circumstances.

Group identity, when sought after to satisfy personal ambitions, achieve the desired definition of self, and cross social boundaries, typically requires the donning of mannerisms, rituals, and appearances that argue for the legitimacy of membership. The conversation between Dean Benedetti and Charlie Parker described by Ross Russell in *Bird Lives!* (1996) is a nice example.

> Benedetti steps across the threshold and is officially admitted . . . To Bird he says, "It don't kill me." The *don't* is deliberate. Errors in grammar and Dean's acquired, specialized, limited vocabulary are all part of the efforts he is making to become a white Negro. The high school education he received at Susanville, California, before entering the music profession, is an obstacle to his progress in the social group he esteems. In order to be in, it is necessary to master the argot of the black ghetto and jazz club. The musicians Dean has admired and seeks to emulate have all been black, and few of their generation have gone very far in school. The classes they attended met in other places—bars, cabarets, dance halls, pads, dressing rooms, and all-night cafeterias—where the chief object for study was the playing of jazz (p. 6).

Benedetti, of course, is famous in a small circle for clandestinely recording the alto saxophonist's club dates in the late 1940s (Russell, 1996). Our point is that group identity or the aspiration to membership in a group often drives everyday behavior in the direction of conformity to the group and the adoption of group coloration. Social comparison rests on self-evaluation; social identity rests on self-definition. The former asks, "What am I?" The latter, "Who am I?"

II. CONSUMER BEHAVIOR

Individuals consume goods and services daily. A prerequisite is a decision to purchase a product or begin a service transaction. Brands often will have a major role because they evoke perceptions of quality and suitability. Such decisions run the gamut from complex, protracted, and agonizing (e.g., buying a car) to simple, impulsive, and unthinking (e.g., picking up a pack of gum at the checkout register).

One popular model for categorizing the major practices employed to influence consumer behavior is the "four p's of marketing": price, product, placement, and promotion (McCarthy & Perreault, 1990). A reasonably priced product or a sale can facilitate a purchasing decision, as can an eye-catching, attractive package or product design. The placement of a product in a variety of retail outlets as well as strategically within those outlets (e.g., in a supermarket, at eye-level or on an "endcap" display) can make a purchase more likely. Promotion of a product or service—dominated by advertising but also including such various strategies as sponsorship of a sporting event or home mailings of a sample—is another technique that can increase consumers' awareness of a product or the degree to which they feel favorably disposed toward it.

We would argue for the addition to McCarthy and Perreault's (1990) model of a fifth "p." Our fifth "p" is "people." The modeling by people of the satisfying, pleasant, or effective use of a product or service—often but not always brought to the attention of the individual through the media—influences purchase decisions. The strength of modeling in shaping consumer behavior rests on three factors: the appeal or attractiveness of the product or service, the degree of favorableness in other people's response to the product or service, and the attitude of the individual toward those people. We would particularly emphasize the degree to which the first is affected by the second and third. An individual is likely to develop an approving orientation toward a product or service if the people seen using the product or service offer a favorable response and high level of satisfaction and if they are attractive to the individual (because they are handsome, fun-loving, sympathetic, or socially successful, for instance). Such figures can be either "real" people encountered in daily life or actors in the media who model product use. In either case, those observed will function as a standard that facilitates or impedes the purchase, depending on the credibility of their favorable disposition toward the purchase and their attractiveness.

Our viewpoint is informed by the theory of planned behavior (Ajzen, 1985, 1991), formerly the theory of reasoned action (Fishbein, 1967; Fishbein & Ajzen, 1975). The theory of planned behavior posits that behavioral intentions rest on three factors: attitude toward the behavior (which will be a function of the belief that the behavior will deliver certain returns and the value placed on those returns), subjective norms (which encompass both beliefs about how important others will evaluate the behavior and the individual's desire to comply with those others), and perception of the capacity to execute the behavior. It is the second factor that plays a particularly large role in our schema, because it recognizes the influence of social pressures. Such pressures take the shape of norms of acceptance, indifference, or rejection. However, the first and third also have importance. Perceptions of product attributes and the rewards they provide in part will be the result of observing others acquiring or using the product, and confidence in the capability to purchase a product will be partly the result of observing similar others; both are common techniques in advertising—expected product gratifications lead to purchase, and someone like us can use a credit card for a quick vacation.

Of course, the strategy of attractive models demonstrating a favorable reaction to a product or service is used incessantly by advertisers (e.g., Lin, 1997; Signorielli, McLeod, & Healy, 1994). The pairing of attractive models with products, services, and brand names is a banal example of classical conditioning (e.g., Stuart, Shimp, & Engle, 1987). The favorable response to the model (the "unconditioned response," in the language of psychology) presumably becomes elicited by the product, service, or brand name (the "conditioned response"). Our interest here is not in this common effect, but in the social influence exerted by these models.

We propose not only an important but a very broad and sweeping role for the media. The influence of the experiences and opinions of others who are observed in the media on consumer behavior can be equally substantial when the people are not characters in advertisements but rather model the use of products without the burden of directly selling them to the audience. Examples include the numerous characters in movies and television programs who use products or services seemingly naturally in the course of the story, now a calculated artifice called *product placement*. Then there are the tastes and preferences of celebrities and stars brought to us indirectly through their appearances on television or elsewhere in their principal roles and explicitly in the coverage devoted to them—interviews across the media, newspaper features, *TV Guide* profiles, entertainment news on television, and magazines such as *People*. The resistance to and annoyance with which many consumers respond to advertising appeals that are transparent and direct (Comstock & Scharrer, 1999) may make more circumscribed approaches that sidestep these obstacles even more likely to influence consumer behavior. Indeed, some individuals have a large degree of "persuasion knowledge" about the strategies of manipulation that makes them wary in their responses to persuasive attempts (Campbell & Kirmani, 2000; Friestad & Wright, 1994).

In our view, presentations in the media function analogously to the everyday, real-life comparisons that serve self-evaluation and self-concept. In addition to the concrete benefits they bestow, products and services have two roles: status achievement and symbolic usage. The first represents the role of social comparison in evaluating the usefulness to self-esteem of goods and services. The second represents the role of goods and services in distinguishing between in-groups and out-groups. In both instances, consumption turns on social relationships as well as the concrete utility of products and services.

A. Interpersonal Others

A number of studies in consumer psychology have found an important role for group norms and interpersonal influence in purchase intentions and behavior (Tybout & Artz, 1994). The presence of a social tie between the buyer and the seller of goods, for instance, has been found to facilitate purchasing (Frenzen & Davis, 1990). Other researchers have investigated group rather than one-to-one interpersonal influence, focusing attention on the role of groups, called reference groups, in setting consumer standards. Reference groups are well established as important criteria for the personal evaluation of the success, desirability, and feasibility of behavior and states of being, and the concept derives from sociological attempts to explain deviations from objective standards or the literal facts in making such evaluations (Merton, 1957). Bearden and Etzel (1982), for example, determined that the products and services that individuals select can be influenced by the reference groups employed, and that such influence depends on whether the consumption of that product or service would be conspicuous enough so that the user accrues the benefits of adhering to the standards of the group. They found that reference-group influence was stronger when products were consumed publicly, such as clothing, rather than privately, such as toothpaste or bath soap. In effect, social influence matters more when consumption occurs within the social sphere, although this should not be taken to mean that goods privately consumed may not sometimes involve the pleasures of loyalty to the standards of an esteemed group.

Fisher and Price (1992) similarly found that visible consumption of a high-status product in front of an esteemed group had a greater impact on future purchase intentions and expectations about the group's approval than consumption in private. The symbolic benefits of consumption in private apparently were not as rewarding to self-esteem and thus not as influential on purchase intentions as consumption within a social context. In contrast, Childers and Rao (1992) found that privately consumed goods and services were more susceptible to influence by family-based reference groups than by peer-based reference groups. Thus, the congruity between the sphere of consumption and the applicability of the reference group makes a difference.

The concept of opinion leadership provides a long-standing conceptualization of how social influence plays a part in individual consumer decision making (Arndt, 1967; Myers & Robertson, 1972; Reynolds & Darden, 1971; Summers, 1970). Members of interpersonal networks often act as sources of information that influence evaluations of products and individual purchase decisions (Brown & Reingen, 1987; Kiel & Layton, 1981). Persuasive influence here rests on information obtained rather than pressure to conform to group norms (Dawar, Parker, & Price, 1996). The individual turns to a friend, colleague, family member, or acquaintance who is thought to have expertise or information regarding goods or services—for example, audio and video electronic equipment, food, wine, home improvement, or fashion (Jacoby & Hoyer, 1981; Leonard-Barton, 1985; Thomas, 1982). The information obtained from that opinion leader (e.g., "Those pants are out of style," "Kosher, not table salt") influences product evaluations and purchase decisions.

The role of opinion leaders in individuals' responses to news about politics and public affairs has probably been much reduced by the enormously increased access to the mass media, as exemplified by television (Chapters 2 and 3). However, this same type of influence almost certainly continues with undiminished prominence in the area of consumption, where it was first advanced (Katz

& Lazarsfeld, 1955). The reasons are the enormously increased variety of media sources from which information might be drawn, which limits what the nonexpert can know; the resulting differences in knowledge that would make quite different people experts for particular kinds of consumption; and the technical complexities and the social nuances of many modern purchases.

Much research has sought to identify the characteristics of those who perform the role of opinion leaders. In addition to the seemingly requisite high levels of information, interest, or involvement with categories of products and services, associations have been found between opinion leading and education and income (Feick, Price, & Higie, 1986; Reynolds & Darden, 1971) as well as with the penchant for actually sharing opinions (Reynolds & Darden, 1971; Richins & Root-Shaffer, 1988; Summers, 1970). Furthermore, opinion leaders have been shown to both provide information and to seek it from both interpersonal and media sources (Feick & Price, 1987; Feick et al., 1986). Thus, opinion leaders are frequently high media users (Dawar et al., 1996), but probably should be thought of as information brokers rather than persuaders.

Other scholars have determined that the likelihood of influence by group or interpersonal forces also depends on both individual and cultural differences. Individuals vary in susceptibility, and cultures vary in the importance ascribed to group behavior.

At the forefront in the case of individual differences is the research of Bearden and colleagues. Bearden and Rose (1990) found individuals scoring high on a measure of susceptibility to interpersonal influence were more likely to conform to group pressure in making consumer purchasing decisions, using a scale developed by Bearden, Netermeyer, and Teel (1989). Rose, Bearden, and Teel (1992) found that individuals are more likely to resist the pressure to conform to groups if they entertain attributions that explain group behavior on grounds other than product quality. Thus, the mindset of the individual will vary in its amenability to interpersonal influence.

Cultures differ in the emphasis placed on the individual versus the collective, which will affect the strength of the role of group influence on the self. Some scholars have contended, for instance, that in an individualistic society such as the United States, the emphasis is largely placed on the self—manifested in the value assigned to such outcomes as self-sufficiency, self-accomplishment, and individual expression and determination (Hofstede, 1983; Hui, 1988; Markus & Kitayama, 1991). Other societies place greater emphasis on the collective, with individual behavior subordinated to the norms of close-knit ingroups or large collectives (Childers & Rao, 1992; Hui, 1988; Triandis, 1994, 1997; Yang, 1981). In collectivist compared with individualistic cultures, group norms are thought to be stronger determinants of individuals' behavior (Chiou, 2000; Triandis, McCusker, & Hui, 1990). Thus, the power of social influence is partly a function of cultural norms and conditions.

B. Mediated Others

Childers and Rao (1992) explain that "the pervasive use of spokespeople in product and service endorsements reflects the widely held belief that individuals who are admired or who belong to a group to which other individuals aspire can exercise an influence on information processing, attitude formation, and purchase behavior" (p. 198). Thus, advertisements provide a means of showing an individual audience member a highly admired spokesperson—or one who represents a "typical" or ordinary person—who is not likely to be personally known by the individual audience member.

The ordinary person as endorser embodies the concept of impersonal influence because this ordinary person is chosen to represent the common or typical. Celebrity rather than ordinary endorsers also fit our schema because the use of such people in advertising entails the transfer of cultural authority and status from celebrity to product and from product to consumer (McCracken, 1989). Again, we go beyond classical conditioning to social influence, although classical conditioning may help explain—along with the development of expectations of social approval—how this transfer occurs. That is, pairing the product (the "conditioned stimulus") with a positive stimulus (the "unconditioned stimulus") is likely to enhance the favorability of responses to the product (the "conditioned response"). Although they appear only one at a time rather than as a mass collective, and although they are more extraordinary than ordinary (although sometimes presented as so ordinary as to belie their actual status), the celebrity employed in ads is usually a surrogate for cultural values. They can be perceived as a weathervane, mapping shifts in the collective psyche, as do public opinion polls and reports of collective experience polls.

The use of both "ordinary" and celebrity endorsers and spokespersons in advertising is a popular persuasive technique. In a study of over 1,000 television commercials obtained from a copy-testing company, Laskey, Fox, and Crask (1994) found that the use of a celebrity endorser, typical person endorser, and spokesperson (a celebrity who reads the ad copy but does not directly endorse the product or service) were the top three most frequent "executional styles" in the sample, outnumbering such techniques as demonstrations, narration, and analogies. Using the copy-testing data, the authors found that both typical person endorsement and spokespeople techniques had a positive impact on recall of the ad; the typical person endorser strategy also led to greater message comprehension.

Chief among the factors that account for the effectiveness of endorsers and spokespersons is credibility. This derives from three elements; trustworthiness (Friedman & Friedman, 1979; Hovland & Weiss, 1951–52, McGinnies & Ward, 1980), knowledge or expertise (Chawla, Dave, & Barr, 1994; Wilson &

Sherrell, 1993), and attractiveness (Chaiken, 1979; Kamins & Gupta, 1994; Petroshius & Crocker, 1989). In one study, these three factors were found to be influential in the purchasing decisions of American and Korean consumers alike (Yoon, Kim, & Kim, 1998).

The research establishes the importance of the perceived similarity of the spokesperson to the audience member (Berscheid, 1966; Brock, 1965). Caballero, Lumpkin, and Madden (1989) found that a gender match between the spokesperson and the audience member was more effective than a mismatch in decisions to purchase soda and cheese. Deshpande and Stayman (1994) found that members of racial minority groups judged spokespersons from their own racial group to be more trustworthy than those outside their racial group, and that trustworthiness was associated with positive attitudes toward the brand. Basil (1996) found that degree of identification between audience member and on-screen actor—which often rests on perceived similarity—mediates the effects of celebrities appearing in advertisements. These data conform to the principles of social identity theory in the tacit assembly of an in-group.

In the mid-1990s, celebrity endorsers or spokespeople were estimated to appear in approximately 20 percent of all television ads and to account for 10 percent of total television advertising expenditures (Agrawal & Kamakura, 1995). Goldsmith, Lafferty, and Newell (2000) found evidence of the impact of celebrity endorsement as well as of "corporate credibility" or the sense of trust or confidence inspired by the organization. They exposed 152 adults to a fictitious print ad for Mobil Oil that contained an endorsement by Tom Brokaw (inserted by the researchers). They found that perceptions of the credibility of the endorser (Brokaw) influenced favorability toward the ad strongly whereas corporate credibility influenced attitude toward the brand.

The celebrity technique has been determined to be most effective when there is a perceived link between the celebrity and the product or service (Kamins & Gupta, 1994; Till, 1998). Kamins (1990), for instance, found that the use of a physically attractive celebrity (Tom Selleck) led to higher scores in spokesperson (or endorser) credibility and a more favorable attitude toward the ad compared to the use of a non physically attractive celebrity (Telly Savalas) when the ad was for an attractiveness-related product. When the product advertised was unrelated to physical attractiveness, there were no differences in spokesperson and ad-response dependent measures. In a uniquely designed study, Ohanian (1991) asked 40 graduate students to list celebrity names and requested a similar group to write down products they thought those celebrities could endorse. The hypothetical endorsements were then presented to a sample of survey respondents who were asked about their intentions to purchase the products. Intentions in this instance were based on the perceived expertise of the celebrity regarding the product or service rather than on their attractiveness or trustworthiness.

Of course, spokespeople and endorsers are not always effective. Among the factors that can limit effectiveness are distance from the observer and seeming promiscuity of endorsements. Bower (2001) found that the use of highly attractive female models can backfire if individual consumers experience negative affect when comparing themselves to these characters. This is an example of a contrast effect resulting from too great a gulf between the model and observers, and indicates that upward comparisons may not always serve self-esteem. Tripp, Jensen, and Carlson (1994) found that as the number of products endorsed by a celebrity grew, the perceptions of credibility dropped, likeability of the endorser declined, and the consumer's attitude toward the ad became less favorable. Wary consumers are skeptical of apparent greed or lack of a genuine affinity for the product.

C. Standards

Comparisons made by individuals to esteemed but similar others can create a "keeping up with the Joneses" situation in which purchases are made to perpetuate the perception of similarity and to protect their desire not to be left behind. They can influence purchases that vary from a teenager's choice in clothing to a homeowner's choice in paint color or brand. Exercise equipment, cures for headaches or other ailments, remedies for male sexual inadequacy, formulas for weight loss and other means to "self improvement" are other examples of these horizontal comparisons. Horizontal comparison invokes pertinence—the suitability of the behavior for the individual (Comstock & Scharrer, 1999).

Upward social comparisons can influence consumer behavior when the individual perceives the others to be more attractive, wealthier, or more successful than the self without experiencing envy or negative affect. This is the case when viewers compare themselves to glamorous television and film stars or magazine ad models and purchase products or services in an attempt to emulate those revered others. So Nicholas Cage has an Italian wood-burning oven at both his Malibu and Beverly Hills residences: modest needs lavishly met and a chance to join the stars. Upward comparisons may facilitate purchase decisions by giving the individual a means of looking or feeling more like a member of the desired group. Upward comparison invokes efficacy—the rewards to be enjoyed by the individual (Comstock & Scharrer, 1999).

The psychology of downward comparisons also can be used strategically by advertisers and marketers. Individuals are motivated by a desire to avoid the social problems that are modeled by "inferior" others. Commercials sometimes depict a problem experienced by a character—from bad breath to wrinkles to lonely Saturday nights or being able to "pinch an inch"—and present the product or service as a means of avoiding that problem. The individual is motivated to buy the product or service to escape the fate of unfortunate others.

Schor (1998) argues that individuals look to neighbors and coworkers in comparing possessions less frequently than once was the case because in an increasingly mobile society many individuals have little interaction with neighbors and coworkers. To replace these traditional reference groups, Schor argues that individuals turn more and more to the media to witness the products and services enjoyed by those on the screen or in the pages of magazines. This is Putnam's (2000) social isolation and immersion in television (Chapter 5) adapted to consumer psychology. Choices of products often rest on expectations of a favored group in the media that is likely to be legions beyond the individual's financial capacity and inaccessible socially. Comparisons in the past were likely to result in only modest economic discrepancies. The new wave of comparisons creates unrealistic aspirations because of the wide disparities in disposable income.

Media portrayals certainly meet our criteria for serving as standards for comparison. Celebrities and stars are generally appealing, although wistfully dissimilar in ways that the individual may perceive as superior. Social comparisons will be upward. The esteem to be gained is obvious. Their choices of what to wear, which car to drive, and what services to use are made apparent through media portrayals.

The consequences, according to Schor (1998), are lamentable. Use of celebrities and media characters as a frame of reference for the consumption of goods contributes to a tendency of Americans to spend beyond their means, to save less and become deeper in debt, to feel dissatisfied with what they have, and to define "the good life" as more and more opulent. This is an expression of the materialism that has become noticeable in the latter half of the twentieth century. Schor argues that individuals are in denial in regard to media influence. She presents data that show that friends are the number one reference group listed by those in public opinion polls (28 percent), followed by coworkers (22 percent) and relatives (12 percent), with neighbors listed by a scant few (2.2 percent). As Mutz (1998) notes, more than 70 years ago George Herbert Mead called attention to certain problematic features of reference groups in modern industrialized societies—they may not be groups of which the individual is a member, there may never have been participation in the group, and the group may not in fact exist as a distinct set of individuals other than in the imagination and yearning of the individual. In our view, these problematic aspects include a lack of verifiable knowledge, a constant threat of inaccuracy, and in the case of celebrities and figures in the media, a lack of realism in employing the group's supposed standards.

Schor (1998) finds support for her view that reference groups drive consumption in their relationship to savings (Table 7.2). Disparity between reference group and self in financial circumstances predicts savings, with the effect enhanced among those particularly susceptible to reference group influence. Using data drawn from 834 employees of a telecommunication company in the southeastern United States, she found evidence that downward social comparisons with those who serve as a reference group tend to raise the amount of money individuals save. Among those who reported a strong desire to emulate a reference group, each step up in financial status compared with the reference group was associated with an additional yearly savings of nearly $3,500. Even among those who did not acknowledge strong reference group pressure, a similar differential on the social comparison scale was associated with an increase of nearly $3,000 a year in savings.

She also tracked a negative relationship between exposure to the images of television and amount of savings, but only for some of the respondents. Among those low in self-described pressure to keep up with others, for each additional hour of television viewed per week, there was a reduction in annual savings of $225. Interestingly, no such television effect surfaced among those with high self-described pressure, perhaps because the stronger force of the reference group comparison suppressed it. Other data document an association between heavy television viewing and overestimation of wealth and of luxury activities—private planes, tennis courts, maid service (O'Guinn & Shrum, 1997). Schor's (1998) explanation is that "what we see on TV inflates our sense of what's normal" (p. 80). She points to a socialization process in which normativeness—the standards that define what is expected, has the approval of others, and thereby is within the confines of ready embrace (Comstock & Scharrer, 1999)—is defined in large part by television.

D. Fashion

Fashion and the purchasing of clothing, footwear, jewelry, and accessories are a billion-dollar industry that has historically constituted an example of the influ-

TABLE 7.2 TV Viewing and Other Predictors of Pressure "To Keep Up"

	Self-described pressure	
	Low	High
Constant term	$25,094.00 (2.57)	$16,451.00 (–0.56)
Household income	.106 (5.56)	.226 (3.85)
Age	–12,168.00 (–2.45)	572.00 (0.04)
Education level	–1,595.00 (–2.00)	733.00 (0.23)
Financial status compared to reference group	2,938.00 (3.31)	3,451.00 (1.70)
Hours per week watching TV	–225.00 (–3.36)	28.00 (0.16)

Adapted from Schor, J. (1998). *The overspent American: Why we want what we don't need*. New York: Basic Books.

ence of the surveillance function of the media. Viewers young and old watch television not only to relax, unwind, and be entertained, but also to witness and make note of trends in fashion. The same motive draws readers to many magazines, much magazine advertising, and theater movies. Fashion here extends beyond apparel to furniture, appliances, and interior design. It is not only the clothes on our backs but the floors under our feet that are subject to the influence of the media. The parade of logos and objects is extensive if not infinite: Prada, Fendi, Burberry, Coach, Polo, Gap, Banana Republic, and in our homes, Viking, Dualit, Sub-Zero, Jenn-Aire, Kitchen Aid, and Bosch. These observations become influential when individuals engage in social comparison—comparing themselves with others to determine how they measure up.

Certainly there are a number of forces that determine the fashion attitudes and behavior of the individual, including the numerous variables identified in the "four p" model (McCarthy & Perreault, 1990). Nevertheless, researchers have isolated the effect of several social- and individual-level factors. Group influence is of paramount importance, as are relationships and interactions between self and others. Media are central, because they serve as a vehicle for the former and establish the standards of exchange for the latter.

The association between fashion and identity is a fruitful path for such research (Guy & Banim, 2000). Choice of clothing styles constitutes means of self-expression often employed in the presentation of a preferred or idealized self to others. Such choices may follow from astute planning to achieve a specific end. Wearing a suit for a job interview can convey a sense of professionalism, experience, and success. Messages also can be sent about the self to others via clothing in less obvious and more haphazard ways. A choice of a particular color, for instance, can convey mood, and loose, comfortable clothing can suggest pragmatism. Likewise, individuals can choose to conform to or challenge social norms through apparel. Use of dress and self-presentation by teenagers exploring their identity and challenging "the establishment" is an example. A passage from the novel *Band Box* (a calculatedly breezy account of a circulation war between two men's magazines in the New York of the 1920s) by Thomas Mallon (2004) strikes an illustrative note:

> Seeing the ad for Interwoven Socks, he curled his own toes with satisfaction. He had in his suitcase one pair of that very product, purchased this afternoon in Indianapolis. What he'd really wanted from the window of Lazarus's Department Store was a Kuppenheimer trench coat, but he could hardly afford one of those and had settled on the socks as a bon voyage present to himself. An excellent choice! He now decided, noticing the ad copy at the bottom of the page. *Stepping forth in his ribbed Interwoven argyles, our "Bandbox" man is ready for any place his feet may carry him to* . . . (p. 63).

Personality variables, of course, play a part in fashion decisions. Stanforth (1995) provides an example in comparing "clothing individuality" scores with personality traits. Nearly 150 undergraduates completed self-report scales for innovativeness, sensation seeking, and clothing interest. Those classified as "fashion innovators" scored higher on sensation- and stimulation-seeking and using clothing to express individuality more than "fashion followers." However, such expression of individuality occurs within the context of the self compared to others, so this is essentially a social process.

Fashion is often employed as a sign of status, and individuals may make clothing choices as well as those for appliances, furniture, and interior design in pursuit of social standing (Coelho & McClure, 1993; Simmel, [1904] 1957). High prices can signify high quality or prestige (Gaedeke & Tootelian, 1983; McCarthy & Perreault, 1990), and "high fashion" goods by their very nature are thought to confer eminence (Coelho & McClure, 1993). Coelho and McClure argue that "the value consumers attach to a fashion good depends on the stock held by other consumers" (1993, p. 597). The individual's view of a product or service is shaped by his or her perception of the views of others. The relationship of self to others in this equation harbors a neat balance. For a fashion to be appealing it also must be appealing to others, yet the allure may diminish if too many people adopt a fashion because it will no longer set the individual apart. The Burberry lining and the L_V of Louis Vuitton are welcome only as exceptions—which is the primary reason that high fashion manufacturers war against knock-offs, rather than lost sales. In the words of Coelho and McClure (1993), "positional goods convey distinction, but the larger the number of people who claim it, the less distinction it confers" (p. 599).

This means that a strain between popular acceptance and prestige is inevitable, and there inevitably will be compromises. When items become popular, those who can afford to do so will turn elsewhere while others, financially not so well off, will adopt them because of their particular properties. We are not happy with a crowd of shoppers brandishing $10 Vuitton totes when we paid $600 for our original, but we may settle for a sofa from IKEA because the design is good and the price far more affordable than at B&B Italia or Roche Bobois. In both cases, however, the media have helped us make our choices, for where else will we learn of the status of Vuitton, which derives from its users, or the desirability of good design, which derives from its endorsement in the pages of magazines. The essential element in this process is the cultivation of social acceptability, a task at which the media excel; this unites the rarefied and exclusive with the popular, Prada with Eddie Bauer, Fendi with J.Crew.

In this "top-down" model of diffusion of apparel, early adopters are often wealthy individuals who attempt to be in the fashion vanguard. They will abandon a style as soon as there are signs of wide adoption (McCracken, 1985). As Coelho and McClure (1993) explain in their economic model of fashion:

> Fashion goods signal status. To be an effective signal the fashion good must be more costly to obtain for those who do not possess the status than for those who do [in the authors' context, this is perceived marginal cost—a dollar has less value to those of higher status]. If fashionable clothing is to be an effective signal of status, it must change. An unchanging fashion and a second-hand market would allow everyone to be "fashionable," negating the value of fashion as a signal (p. 601).

The top-down fashion model points to the persuasive power of group influences on the individual. Prestige for self resides in the eyes of others. The ideal circumstance is for a fashion to be coveted by a number of important others but not accessible to them. The individual who adopts such a fashion has the distinction of being the first or only one to do so, and gains in self-esteem. The media act as an aesthetic middleman in this process, bestowing significance, notoriety, and desirability on scarce goods.

Social identity theory also has a role. The individual may acquire and maintain a sense of inclusion with a group through fashion and clothing. An out-group may be identified by fashion as well. An example is the adolescent who proclaims identity with one group through attire while at the same time establishing distance from other groups who dress differently.

The Japanese American writer Garrett Hongo (2002) neatly captures these practices in his memoir of growing up in Los Angeles:

> Crazes of dress moved through our populations—for Chicanos: woolen Pendletons over thin undershirts and a crucifix; big low-top oxfords; khaki work trousers, starched and pressed; for the *bloods*: rayon and satin shirts in metallic "fly-ass" colors; pegged gabardine slacks; cheap moccasin-toed shoes from downtown shops in L.A.; and for us *Buddhas*: high-collar Kensingtons of pastel cloths, A1 tapered "Racer" slacks, and the same moccasin shoes as the bloods, who were our brothers. It was crazy. And *inviolable*. Dress and social behavior were a code one did not break for fear of ostracism and reprisal. Bad dressers were ridiculed. Offending speakers were beaten, tripped walking into the john, and set upon by gangs. They *wailed* on you if you fucked up . . . (pp. 831–832).

An alternative model of fashion diffusion envisions early adopters and fashion innovators as the young more than the wealthy (Field, 1970). In this "bottom-up" model, new styles originate among adolescents and young adults who constitute a subculture and who are often from lower rather than upper socioeconomic strata. Others learn of these styles through the media. Without the media, diffusion would be limited to a comparatively confined area—the neighborhood, city or region. The traditional apparel that still distinguishes many regions of the world, although often increasingly only on holidays, owes its provincial confinement to the absence of media attention and lack of participation in a large-scale market where there are powerful economic incentives for successful promotion and widespread dissemination. Adoption in the bottom-up model then occurs among those of different ages and economic means scattered across the globe (Polhemus, 1994).

In the top-down model in which styles are promulgated by the financially elite, the innovators are fashion designers, and the opinion leaders are fashion writers for major newspapers, editors of fashion magazines, and fashionable celebrities. In the bottom-up model in which styles are promulgated by the young, innovators are individuals from largely urban communities whose styles are "discovered" by and promoted in the media (Crane, 1999).

Sociologist Diana Crane (1999) argues for the inclusion of these two models within a larger, more global framework. While fashion designers in a number of countries still design clothing for various "small publics" located in specific markets, she observes that profits are now more dependent on product licensing. She argues that the fashion world that was previously conceived as centered in New York, London, Paris, and Milan has given way to a less centralized system that resembles a collection of far-flung but interconnected orbs. The defining element is the quick translation of innovation into marketable products. The essential link is between the manufacturer, who undertakes this translation, and the retail outlets that bring it to the attention of their customers. These outlets are somewhat stratified by gender and age, so that fashion becomes defined within social groups. Innovations come from a wide variety of sources. The manufacturers are continually searching for trends and developments. Shifts in retail sales and portrayals in the media are two signs. Crane argues that modern fashion trends are not exclusively set by either "elite" designers or by subcultures such as urban adolescents. In addition to these two sources, fashions also spring from various countries and other contexts. She also points out that the fashions of urban subcultures sometimes are adopted by elites. Finally, Crane contends that widespread adoption of fashion is no longer a feasible or even preferred outcome, and has been replaced by multiple diffusions within specific subgroups, such as those based on age or lifestyle. In an economic era increasingly defined in terms of global markets, industrial manufacturers of clothing and accessories are driven by consumer demand and interest, rather than by the fashion elite. Crane concludes that "fashion emanates from many sources and diffuses in various ways to different publics" (1999, p. 13).

In each of these models the media play a key role. The diffusion of the clothing styles of urban adolescents—the gangsta rap costume of the late 1990s—discussed by Crane (1999) is an example. The style originated in major cities in the United States but has since diffused beyond that milieu to adolescents in suburban and rural areas as well as to groups both somewhat younger and somewhat older. A major source of information was the media, and, specifically, the images that were displayed on television, in magazines, and by music videos. The media again demonstrate their power to instigate group influence by supplementing firsthand observations with an opportunity to view and therefore learn about impersonal others.

We believe that the role for popular media in the diffusion of high fashion products that are created by exclusive designers, modeled on the runways of world fashion capitals, and carry hefty price tags that put them out of the reach of most, is limited but important. The media are the means by which fashion writers and editors, who largely determine the success of annual offerings, make their views public and the media are the means by which the public in general gets a glimpse of these designs. This results, on the one hand, in the validation of the significance and merit of the line when the fashion writers and editors approve, and, on the other, the diffusion of the identity of the latest to a wider if vaguely defined public that will serve as a receptive circle of admirers for those who wear these fashions. The media also make it possible for the fashion designers to use their shows as sleight-of-hand conceits to establish the prestige and worthiness of their brands for the sale to a mass market of other clothes and other products. What you see is not what you get, but it is—in another guise—what you (they hope) will want.

Media accounts are the second lives of the runways. Nevertheless, immediate interest in these fashions is largely confined to the wealthy and their coverage in the media is short-lived and confined to magazines and a few newspapers in major cities. Long-term effects are another matter. The fashions annually on display at the great shows do not, themselves, penetrate the mass market. However, the trends implied and the directions taken are often translated by marketers into shifts that become expressed in mass consumption. Hemlines rise or fall, a particular part of the anatomy becomes more or less emphasized, colors and shadings glow, burn, and diminish, silhouettes change. As Bandura (1986) observes, innovation depends on incentives, and these are supplied in the case of fashion by profits to the suppliers on the one hand and by the rewards to the self-esteem of consumers on the other. The marketers have an interest in the obsolescence of current attire, and the customers for popular goods have an interest in publicly displaying adherence to the latest, thereby signifying at once knowledge, alertness, and financial well-being.

The media are also a major factor in the tendency for women consumers to borrow from or emulate a variety of sources, thus significantly reducing the ability of name fashion lines to sell complete or coordinated outfits (Agins, 2004). This diversification of sources—television and movie stars, celebrities, sports heroes and heroines, high fashion runways, unexpected fads (that $800 handbag), and the salacious disruptions of sartorial deference by the young—is a further embellishment in the global streams of unexpected convergence and departure described by Crane.

In contrast to the milieu of high fashion, the models and characters who appear in television, in the movies, and in advertisements demonstrate enviable financial success but not typically beyond the borders of attainment. Most of the models and characters encountered in the media are not blue collar, and paying bills and making ends meet are not ordinarily of concern, but the representation of the economic elite is rare. Their attractiveness for emulation rests on their not being beyond the horizons of most of those in the audience. This formula has been in place in prime time and daytime television drama since the inception of the medium, and similarly has long been pervasive in movies and advertising and is used effectively to appeal to the widest possible audience to translate into the highest possible advertising revenues. We agree with Schor (1998) that the lifestyles emulated by most media characters can contribute to a longing for personal wealth that is out of reach for most individual audience members. We also believe that the example of financial comfort set by media depictions is not so extravagant as to appear hopelessly unattainable. And that is precisely why their social influence is so effective.

III. SOCIALIZATION

Individuals gain a sense of what is acceptable and expected from observing others. We take our cues regarding what we perceive to be appropriate behavior—as well as that outside the boundaries of normativeness—from witnessing how others perform, behave, express their thoughts and display their attitudes, and the consequences ensuing from these acts. Signorielli (2001) has defined socialization as "the way people learn about their culture and acquire its values, beliefs, perspectives, and social norms" (p. 343). A number of institutions perform socializing functions for individuals. At the personal, informal level, these include parents, family members, care providers, friends, acquaintances, and peers. At the institutional, formal level, these include schools, churches, mosques, synagogues, and the media. These varied sources teach individuals—either directly through formal instruction or indirectly by example—how to interpret and respond to the world around them.

Socialization shares many characteristics of our general media model in which influence is exerted by others on the opinions, judgments, and subsequent behavior of the individual. As we have seen with social comparison theory, socialization is not restricted to the observation of others with whom the individual has a direct and personal relationship. Although learning about one's culture can and does occur through interpersonal means, understanding of the social world is also shaped by information acquired from the observation of impersonal others presented by the media. The platform of celebrity enjoyed by many characters appearing in the media carries with it a sense that such individuals embody cultural values. Even characters who are not celebrities but appear in commercials or on "reality-based" or news-oriented programming are often chosen because they reflect an "everyman" or "everywoman" quality, or because they represent a "type" (e.g., in "reality" programming, the boisterous clown, the pensive intellectual). Again, although they do not appear in the form of an impersonal mass as typifies public opinion polls or reports of collective experience, they achieve some of the qualities associated with those collectives in symbolic form. These characters exemplify a general cultural sensibility.

We believe that the media are powerful agents of socialization for many for three major and interrelated reasons. First, the media have an unparalleled ability to disseminate information about the culture, and especially information that can be expressed in the narratives of news, sports, and storytelling. Second, individuals typically spend a considerable amount of time attending to the narratives of the media. Third, there is discernible homogeneity in many of the media's stories, which results in a degree of consistency in what individual audience members can learn about the social environment. Just as direct learning can occur from media exposure—for example, preschoolers can learn the alphabet by watching *Sesame Street* and adults can learn names of world leaders from watching the news—media audience members also can be taught more indirectly about cultural values and social roles.

Recent estimates establish that young people in the United States spend approximately six-and-a-half hours per day with all forms of media (Roberts & Foehr, 2004). Patterns for adults are quite similar (with the qualification that socioeconomic differences are much greater, with those lower in SES much lower in use of media other than television in younger cohorts), as seen in their average daily television consumption of about three-and-a-half hours (Comstock & Scharrer, 1999). Although new media forms and a greater array of channels available to the television viewer have brought some variation in media content, a small number of themes continue to pervade the messages that media audiences receive. More than 50 years of experience with television, cable, satellite distribution, the VCR, and the DVD suggest strongly that this is a permanent state of affairs. We turn our attention now to two such patterns of media content, present and even prevalent in a variety of types of media: gender roles and aggression. In each case, we begin with an examination of the messages of the media, and then turn to the criterion of empirical evidence of a contribution by media exposure to thought and behavior.

A. Gender

Social identity theory (Heider, 1958; Tajfel, 1981, 1982; Tajfel & Turner, 1979) holds that one way individuals define themselves is through their "membership in larger, more impersonal collectives or social categories" such as those delineated by gender, race, age, or other social descriptors (Brewer & Gardner,

1996, p. 83). These collective identities are formed from the perception of similarities with members of an in-group as well as the perception of dissimilarities with members of out-groups. Parallel with impersonal influence, the others to which an individual compares herself or himself are impersonal collectives. The individual's own social group will be part of the in-group but the in-group may extend to a much larger population possessing the determining elements of race, age, gender, and socioeconomic status. There is constricted direct, face-to-face connection. The view of the self that derives from such intergroup comparisons is motivated by a drive to consider the self in favorable terms to boost or maintain self-esteem (Hogg & Abrams, 1988; Oaks & Turner, 1980).

The making of identity-related judgments about in- and out-groups depends in part on the salience of group membership. Certain conceptions of identity are chronically more salient than others. Those who are members of social groups that are marginalized by low status display a consistent tendency to have a more salient view of group membership (Lorenzi-Cioldi, 1988, 1993). Indeed, "members of dominated groups define themselves more, and are also defined more by others in terms of social categorizations imposed on them" (Doise, 1988, p. 105). Race and gender are two such categories. Salience is generally high, and minorities and females at times may feel marginalized. The salience of such identities can be triggered by environmental circumstances. Brewer and colleague (Brewer, 1991; Brewer & Gardner, 1996), for example, found that collective identities can be activated through the priming of the collective and can, in turn, affect proffered self-definitions and judgments of similarities and differences with others.

Perceived differences between the self and others can become manifest in negative stereotyping of out-groups (Brewer & Gardner, 1996). Loyalty to in-groups and the desire to view them favorably can encourage hostility toward or negative stereotypes of out-groups (Allport, 1979). Stereotyping is also promoted by ignorance, rationalizations for inequality, and competition for scarce resources (Coser, 1956; Horowitz, 1985; Kinder, 1998). Stereotypes are almost a necessity when there is limited information about the specific and varied qualities of members of an out-group (Macrae, Milne, & Bodenhausen, 1994). Those who enjoy greater social status may explain and justify the marginalized status of others by stereotype (Hogg & Abrams, 1988). Groups, when positioned in direct rivalry, often express negative views of rivals that occasionally become bristlingly hostile (Sherif et al., 1961; Sherif & Sherif, 1953).

One widely employed dichotomy for categorizing typical and persistent gender stereotypes is that women tend to be perceived as more expressive and men as more instrumental (Eagly & Kite, 1987; Lippa, 1994). Common traits long ascribed to men include logic, competitiveness, and assertiveness whereas common traits long ascribed to women include a nurturing nature, willingness to express emotions, and concern for the happiness of others (Lippa, 1994; Rosenkrantz et al., 1968). In addition to traits, stereotypes form regarding roles appropriate for men and women (Deaux & Lewis, 1984). Males are typically assigned the roles of aggressor in romance, breadwinner, and provider, and defender of property and honor, and females of sexual trophy, housework and child care provider, and nurturing supporter.

Social identity processes often encourage stereotypical views of gender. This is more attributable to loyalty, rationalization, and competition than to unfamiliarity because in its extreme forms unfamiliarity is not at issue in the case of gender. For a woman, a positive view of the in-group can result from a tendency to see women as more sensitive to the needs and emotions of others (Eagly, Mladinic, & Otto, 1991); thus, certain aspects of a stereotype may be employed in behalf of group identity and self definition. An example of rationalization and competition is the increasingly discredited view held by some males that a female should not hold high public office because women are not sufficiently rational to make tough decisions (Ashmore, Del Boca, & Wohlers, 1986).

Studies of television content reveal fairly narrow representations of men and women. This is perhaps partly due to the limited time allotted in many media formats—television programs, commercials, print ads—to character development, resulting in rather unidimensional and conventional depictions (Signorielli, 2001). Television programming emphasizes nonprofessional jobs for women, gender-stereotyped jobs for both genders, and gender-specific activities at the workplace (Signorielli, 1984, 1993; VandeBerg & Streckfuss, 1992). Men are more likely to be portrayed in network prime time drama as perpetrators or victims of serious, hurtful physical violence, while females specialize in leveling insults and telling lies (Potter & Ware, 1987). Over a 30-year period, males consistently appeared more often as major characters in new network prime time programs, and about a fourth of these males occupationally were professionals, such as doctors, lawyers, or accountants (Greenberg & Collette, 1997). A recent analysis shows some enhancement in the variety of occupational roles held by women and a significant increase in professional roles (e.g., Signorielli, 2001). Yet, this change is accompanied by a strict divide between female characters who are shown with marriage and family and the single, working woman, providing limited models for success at combining the mixed elements of many modern women's lives (Signorielli, 2001). On television, men are presented as inept fathers (Scharrer, 2001) and as infrequently doing household chores (Bartsch, Burnett, Diller, & Rankin-Williams, 2000). A meta-analysis of studies of gender representations in television programming (Herrett-Skjellum & Allen, 1996) concludes that "males are seen more often on television, appear more often in major roles, exhibit dominant behaviors and attitudes, and are represented outside the home in jobs of authority" (p. 171). Greater numbers of cable channels and new broadcast networks have brought no essential changes in the representation of gender (Eaton, 1997; Kubey, Schifflet, Weerakkody, & Ukeiley, 1995).

Similar representations predominate in advertising in all media: newspapers, magazines, and television (Comstock & Scharrer, 1999; Craig, 1992; Kaufman, 1999). Household tasks are assigned in traditional ways. Women are almost exclusively seen caring for children, attending to family health, cleaning, and cooking—with the occasional exceptions of a long way (baby) to tobacco equality and auto purchase. Gender roles in commercials still give males a particularly authoritative role through voice-overs, although the frequency of males and females appearing in commercials has become about equal compared with the mid-1970s when males were predominant (Comstock & Scharrer, 1999). Nevertheless, the emphasis on physical attractiveness is greater for females than males (Comstock & Scharrer, 1999).

Patterns for commercials directed at children resemble the rest of advertising. Commercials during Saturday morning television (a "child-friendly" time slot) have been found to overrepresent boys and convey stereotypical gender roles (Browne, 1998; Larson, 2001; Smith, 1994; Thompson & Zerbinos, 1997). Furnham, Abramsky, and Gunter (1997) found boys and men in children's television commercials more often were central characters and were presented as more authoritative. Browne (1998) determined that in both U.S. and Australian television commercials aimed at children, male characters were presented as more active, aggressive, and knowledgeable than female characters.

There is evidence that such media portrayals have consequences for audience members. Both Morgan (1987) and Signorielli and Lears (1992) found a link in survey data between television viewing and stereotypical notions of household chore distribution, the former among adolescents and the latter among fourth and fifth graders. A longitudinal panel study of young adolescents by Morgan (1982) also found that amount of earlier television viewing was associated with such gender-stereotypical ideas as "women are happiest at home raising children" and "men are born with more ambition than women." Signorielli (1989) found similar patterns among adults in an analysis of nationally representative surveys conducted from 1975 to 1986; greater amounts of television viewing were associated with increased stereotyping.

Experimental and quasi-experimental evidence adds importantly to the data provided by surveys. In one experiment, Tan (1979) found that adolescent girls exposed to commercials emphasizing beauty were more likely than control group members to believe that good looks were essential to be popular with men and that beauty was important for them, personally. In another, Geis, Brown, Walstedt, and Porter (1984) exposed one group of women to a gender-stereotypical commercial and another group to a counter-stereotypical commercial. After exposure, the women were asked to write an essay explaining what their lives would be like in the future. Those who had seen the gender-typed commercial were more likely to emphasize housewife duties. The outcomes of these two experiments would be paralleled daily because they exemplify exposure to the brief messages common to television commercials. Finally, the well-known quasi-experiment involving three small British Columbia communities (Williams, 1986), one of which was receiving television for the first time, provides evidence of a socialization effect in a real-life setting (Kimball, 1986). Those young people living in the two communities with no television and limited availability of television (only a Canadian public channel) were less likely to have gender-stereotyped views than those living in the multiple-channel community location (the Canadian channel and the three U.S. networks). Two years after the former no-television town began to receive television, the girls in that town had caught up to the multiple television community girls in the degree of gender stereotyping.

Two meta-analyses confirm a small but statistically significant relationship between media exposure and gender stereotyping. Herrett-Skjellum and Allen (1996) combined the findings of 19 surveys and 11 experiments. Morgan and Shanahan (1997), taking a cultivation theory perspective, combined the outcomes of 14 studies. In both cases, the effect size representing the association between television exposure and gender stereotyping was positive, although small, and about the same (+.10).

Media depictions clearly reinforce traditional gender roles (Mitchell-Kerman, 1982; Roberts & Bachen, 1981; Roberts & Maccoby, 1985). We base this conclusion on links found in surveys between television viewing and gender stereotyping, the outcomes of experiments and quasi-experiments, and the effect sizes reported in meta-analyses that aggregate the outcomes of many studies.

Past studies have also determined that media exposure has the ability to counter stereotypes. Early studies pointed to the viewing of *Sesame Street* in the reduction of racial and ethnic prejudice (Bogatz & Ball, 1971; Gorn, Goldberg, & Kanungo, 1976) and to the viewing of a specially designed series, *Freestyle*, in the widening of gender roles among preadolescent boys and girls (Johnston & Ettema, 1982). The effects of exposure are rooted in content. The socializing capacity of television and other media has the potential to teach viewers more liberating roles in addition to the traditional and narrow roles to which they have largely confined themselves throughout their histories.

B. Aggression

The behavior of models and characters in the media exemplify cultural norms. Individuals respond to these models much as they respond to public opinion polls and public reports of collective experience. Media characters are not anonymous impersonal others, yet they have the potential to signify many of the same qualities as those impersonal others because by their presence in the media they appear to represent either a common condition or an ideal. Their opinions and experiences, then, may take on a persuasive function.

Socialization of perceptions and attitudes by media exposure can translate into behavioral effects when what is observed is pertinent to the observer's life (Bandura, 1986; Comstock & Scharrer, 1999). Children and young audience members are especially likely to learn from the behavior of media characters because they are engaging in a developmental process in which they "try on" thoughts, attitudes, and ways of behaving (Comstock, 1991). The same influences that guide the learning of gender roles apply to the learning of aggression.

Media content has historically and consistently reserved a starring role for violence and aggression. Gerbner and colleagues (1994) have examined television violence, defined as "the overt expression of physical force against self or other, compelling action against one's will on pain of being hurt or killed, or actually hurting or killing" (Signorielli, Gerbner, & Morgan, 1995, p. 280) in broadcast network prime time and weekend programming for two decades beginning in the mid-1970s. The data fall neatly into two persisting patterns. First, children's programming consistently has had a great deal more violence than general audience prime time programming, as measured by the rate of violent acts per hour. Second, the amount of violence on television was quite stable over the two decades except for a slight decline in the final decade between the mid-1980s and mid-1990s (Comstock & Scharrer, 1999)—possibly in part because of the migration of viewers favoring violent entertainment to cable channels (Hamilton, 1998), and possibly in part because of increased scrutiny and expressions of concern from high officials and federal agencies combined with large majorities of the public endorsing the view in polls that there was too much violence on television and that television violence increased juvenile crime and misbehavior (Comstock & Scharrer, 1999). Short-lived oscillations in the number of violent acts on television occur from season to season, but the long-term pattern is one of stability.

The findings from the National Television Violence Study (National Television Violence Study, 1996, 1997, 1998) complement those of Gerbner and colleagues. The researchers studied the presence of violence, defined as "any overt depiction of a credible threat of physical force or the actual use of such force intended to physically harm an animated being or group of beings" (National Television Violence Study, 1998, p. 20) in over 10,000 hours of cable and broadcast programming—a truly comprehensive sampling. Cable television, and particularly the movie channels, presented more violence than broadcast channels. Cartoons once again were singled out for their high frequency of violent acts. Overall in the third year of analysis, about 60 percent of all programs contained violence and only a miniscule 3 percent had an antiviolence theme.

One of the strengths of the National Television Violence Study is close attention to the ways violence is portrayed. In many respects, the medium endorses violence. Socialization of an aggression-permissive outlook—once we grant the possibility of media influences—logically follows from television's infrequent attention to dire consequences of violent actions, emphasis on justified violence, depiction of appealing rewards for violent behavior, use of likeable characters as perpetrators of violence (e.g., "good guys"), portrayal of humor that makes light of violence, and display of exciting weapons. These are long-term, pervasive characteristics of televised violent entertainment; for example, the National Television Violence Study found virtually no changes in these aspects of portrayals over a three-year period. The same pattern was even more pronounced in children's programming. In children's television, specifically, long-term negative consequences were especially rare, violence was combined with humor more often, and unrealistically low levels of harm were portrayed more frequently compared to other television genres (National Television Violence Study, 1998).

The National Television Violence Study has calculated that 75 percent of violent acts on television are not punished, thereby sending the accommodating message to potential perpetrators that violence is free of social sanctions. Almost 40 percent of all violent acts on television are performed by attractive or appealing characters, thereby laying a claim to normativeness. Violence, then, is not exclusively the domain of "bad guys" who are presented as antisocial, unpopular, outlaws, or loners. Violence is often depicted as permissible and mainstream, performed by likeable characters designed to appeal to the vast majority of viewers. Research and theory demonstrate that viewers are more strongly influenced by the behavior of those whom they identity with and admire (Bandura, 1986; Huesmann & Eron, 1986). When perpetrators are appealing and attractive, violence is made to seem normative.

Much of what has been written about media violence has focused on its contribution to aggressive behavior (e.g., Anderson et al., 2003; Comstock & Scharrer, 1999; Potter, 1999). Our focus here is on the ways the media, and particularly television, facilitate such an outcome by affecting perceptions and attitudes. Our purpose, as with gender portrayals, is to emphasize the place of the media within the broad framework of socialization.

By modeling a great deal of violence—especially violence that is shown as justified, rewarded, and free of dire consequences and where setting, weapons, and targets are not too distant from the circumstances of the viewer—television and the media in general send the message that violence is acceptable. Viewing steady doses of violence suggests to viewers that violence and aggression are just a normal part of everyday life. Exposure to television violence has long been associated with acceptance of violence among children (Dominick & Greenberg, 1972; Drabman & Thomas, 1974a, 1974b; Thomas & Drabman, 1975). Indeed, Huesmann and Moise (1999) found that early childhood exposure to television violence leads to a greater acceptance of violence—an indication that violence is seen as normative—15 years later. Such acceptance has been shown to be an important precursor to aggressive behavior (Bushman & Huesmann, 2001; Huesmann & Guerra, 1997). We have elsewhere (Comstock & Scharrer, 1999) labeled these factors *efficacy*, representing the degree to which the behavior is portrayed as instrumental in obtaining rewards; *normativeness*, defined as the extent of portrayed social acceptability and conformity to the standards of peers and society; and *pertinence*, the portrayal of circumstances that imply relevance for the viewer, such as weapons that are readily obtainable, targets likely to be encountered, perpetrators resembling the viewer in gender and age or, at least, well liked, and settings that are similar, such as pedestrian spaces, parking structures, freeways and two-lane blacktops.

Social cognitive theory (Bandura, 1986) contends that individuals engage in "vicarious learning" of attitudes and behavior from media. Depictions of reward or reinforcement increase the likelihood of such learning, and particularly its expression in behavior. Thus, depictions in which perpetrators have a good reason for their aggression (e.g., self-defense, revenge) or in which violence goes unpunished or results in favorable circumstances (e.g., winning the love of a romantic interest or the praise of the local authorities) send the message that violence is natural, normal, understandable, and, ultimately, acceptable. The media instill social and cultural expectations about violence, and individuals apply them to their own circumstances. The conventions of television entertainment thus promote aggression.

Script theory (Huesmann, 1988, 1998) suggests that viewers learn "how to solve social problems" by observation of the media through the acquisition and development of "scripts" (mental routines that guide behavior) for aggression (Bushman & Huesmann, 2001, p. 237). Scripts learned from the media may be used by individuals to define and respond to real-life situations. This is especially the case when there are similarities between what is portrayed and real-life circumstances. Repeated exposure to violence in the media results in the practice and rehearsal of aggressive scripts and the creation and reinforcement of a worldview of aggression. Thus, viewers of media violence develop a belief system in which violence is considered a normal part of daily life.

Comstock (2004) has argued that these varied elements need not be consciously articulatable, but may function through their readier availability in the mind—because of their portrayal by the media—when a situation that conceivably requires such a response is assessed. Efficacy, normativeness, and pertinence on the surface would seem to operate through cognitions; in this view, violent portrayals would alter values and attitudes toward those more favorable to aggressive behavior. Comstock draws on the very large sample of 1,600 London male teenagers examined by Belson (1978). There was a clear link favoring the interpretation that the viewing of violent television entertainment causally contributed to seriously harmful antisocial behavior (such as rape and use in fights of knives and guns) among a subsample of delinquent youth. Values and attitudes favorable to aggressive behavior repeatedly did not appear in the causal chain; they failed to predict the behavior in question. Thus, conscious, articulatable values and attitudes cannot be said to be a necessary condition for media influence on behavior.

In Groebel's (1998, 2001) compass theory, media depictions similarly operate as a measure or a benchmark, providing a means of comparison between the individual and the larger culture as revealed in media content. Compass theory suggests that viewers develop a relative sense of what is right or wrong and what is acceptable and unacceptable about violence and aggression as they compare their own actions to the violence presented in the media. The theory also takes into account social control over antisocial behavior, such as that exerted by norms for violence in one's real-life environment (as measured by "low aggression" and "high aggression" neighborhoods), as well as the context in which violence is depicted in media content. Groebel (2001) explains:

> Depending on already existing experiences, social control, and the cultural environment, media content offers an orientation, a frame of reference that determines the direction of one's own behavior. Viewers do not necessarily adapt simultaneously to what they have observed, but they measure their own behavior in terms of distance to the perceived media models. If extreme cruelty is "common," for example, just kicking another seems to be innocent by comparison if the cultural environment has not established a working alternative frame of reference (e.g., social control, values) (p. 260).

Groebel (2001) presents evidence that a synergy between media violence and dispositions toward violence among the young is a global phenomenon. In a cross-cultural study of over 5,000 12-year-olds from 23 countries, he found an association between violence viewing and three attitudes toward aggression: that aggression is a good way to solve problems or conflicts, that it can award status, and that it can be fun. These three attitudes reflect normativeness, as each supports a view of violence as acceptable and even admirable. Despite the fact that there are important cultural variations in the 23 countries from which data were drawn, globalization of media dissemination has created a situation in which the normativeness ascribed by the media to violence can transcend borders. Groebel (2001) provides the example of Arnold Schwarzenegger, an actor (more recently governor of California) who has starred mostly in violent movies, and was known to 88 percent of the 12-year-olds in the sample from countries around the globe (including Angola, Croatia, Mauritius, India, and Ukraine). Schwarzenegger also was widely admired, as substantial proportions of respondents reported wanting to be like him—51 percent of those from high-aggression areas and 37 percent of those from low-aggression areas. Thus, prominent media figures enjoy widespread recognition, although culture provides a context that affects the degree to which the traits and behavior typically attributed to such a model will be admired.

Social cognitive, script, and compass theories at root are based on a social comparison process. Individuals observe others in the media. They compare themselves to those portrayed. They respond to real-life situations borrowing in part from what they have seen modeled in the media. This borrowing encompasses both ways of behaving and the perceptions and attitudes that support such ways of behaving. Similarities between media portrayals and real-life circumstances increase the likelihood of comparisons (Comstock & Scharrer, 1999). Often, audience members think of themselves as resembling media models and characters (Festinger, 1954; Schachter, 1959). Comparisons may also take place upward or downward (Taylor & Lobel, 1989; Wills, 1981, 1991). In upward social comparisons, the viewer may aspire to be like the media model and therefore would use that model to guide behavior in a real-life situation. In downward social comparisons, the viewer may be inspired to avoid the unfortunate circumstances or states modeled by a media character. The conventions of violence in media entertainment unhappily make this an infrequent occurrence in the case of violence.

Our criterion of an empirical link between media exposure and thought and behavior is more readily met than in the case of gender. Comstock and Scharrer (2003) examined seven different meta-analyses. In each case, effect sizes between exposure to media violence and aggressive thought or behavior were positive and statistically significant. The focus was quite varied among the meta-analyses: one was confined to erotic stimuli, including violent erotica (Allen, D'Alessio, & Brezgel, 1995); another examined only experiments in which the dependent variable was unconstrained aggression in naturalistic settings (Wood, Wong, & Chachere, 1991); and a third examined only studies in which the measure of exposure reflected everyday viewing but included a sweeping array of aggression-related dependent measures, such as hostile attitudes, personality variables supportive of aggression, and degree of violence in made-up stories, as well as aggressive behavior (Hogben, 1998). The consistent positive and significant effects sizes thus represent a very robust outcome observable for a wide range of measures of exposure and aggression-related thought and behavior. Effect sizes are clearly positive and significant for both experimental designs, which permit causal inference, and for survey designs, which describe the relationship between everyday television viewing and everyday aggression. In one of the most comprehensive efforts covering more than 200 empirical studies (Paik & Comstock, 1994), the overall effect size was in the medium range by Cohen's (1988) well-known criteria (+ 0.31). Other similarly comprehensive undertakings have produced similarly positive, statistically significant effect sizes (Bushman & Anderson, 2001; Hearold,

1986), with one analysis (Bushman & Huesman, 2001) reporting that the effect size of Paik and Comstock exceeds that for many recorded associations between putative causes and socially and personally undesirable, injurious outcomes.

Comstock and Scharrer (2003) interpret this pattern as constituting a strong case for a causal contribution by exposure to violent television entertainment to aggressive and antisocial behavior. They note (as we have argued here) that the positive association between exposure and behavior is extremely robust, extending to a wide range of paradigms involving different measures of exposure, different outcome measures, and different research methods. They also note that the meta-analyses encompass data from many hundreds of individuals. These factors strengthen the credibility of the pattern, but do not directly address the issue of causation. Comstock and Scharrer conclude that a strong case for causation rests on three factors: (a) the consistently positive outcomes for experiments, where causal inference is clearly justified; (b) the confirmation by survey designs that a positive association also occurs between everyday viewing and behavior; and, (c) the consistent failure to wholly account for, by some other variable or variables (although quite a few have been entered into the equation), the positive association between exposure and behavior.

Two other recent analyses strongly corroborate Comstock and Scharrer. The Surgeon General's report on youth violence concluded that a risk factor for felony teenage violence was earlier exposure to television violence (U.S. Department Health & Human Services, 2001), and although this factor was small by Cohen's (1988) criteria it was also about the same size as three-fourths of about 20 documented risk factors. Taking a broader view, the American Psychological Society series intended to present state-of-knowledge, critical analyses of bodies of socially significant research, *Psychological Science in the Public Interest*, concludes that television violence has a number of undesirable effects on young viewers, including the facilitation of aggressive and antisocial behavior (Anderson et al., 2003). These two analyses present impressive credentials, with the first insisting that only well-documented instances of contributions to serious criminal violence be included, and the second attempting, through the use of a panel of experts, to serve as a decisive arbiter.

Comstock (1991) identified normativeness as one of four factors that determines the strength and likelihood of an effect of exposure to violence in the media on viewers. The other three factors were efficacy (reward or punishment, or lack of punishment if the aggression is inherently satisfying), pertinence (similarity between the circumstances of the viewer and those of the portrayal), and susceptibility (frustration or anger on the part of the viewer). Normativeness embraced depictions of aggression as justified or intentional, because such portrayals imply social acceptance, and as without consequences, because such portrayals suggest that no social taboo has been violated. We continue to think that such distinctions are useful in more carefully and precisely delineating the conditions on which media effects on aggression and antisocial behavior are contingent. However, in the present larger context of socialization we also argue that efficacy and pertinence, through the portrayal of reward and a link with the viewer, promote a heightened state of acceptability of the portrayed behavior. Efficacy and pertinence on the larger stage serve in behalf of the norm of aggression and antisocial behavior.

C. Self and Society

In contemporary society, the mass media provide the dominant means of representing the opinions and experiences of collectives. No other information source matches the media in furnishing the individual with information about society. Individuals tune in to television, scan print media, listen to the radio, and search the Internet to gain a sense of what others think, feel, and experience in their lives. Social observations on a wide scale would not be possible without the media.

The primary contribution of such information, as contrasted with direct, personal observation or interpersonal sources, is its perceived generalizability. By literally representing collectives, the reports of public opinion and social experience in the media become benchmarks for the individual. The essential element is the representativeness of the information. The reports become standards by which to assess one's own well-being, the propriety of one's thoughts, and the advisability of action or inaction. As a result, the models and characters that appear in the media outside the context of news gathering serve a similar function because they exemplify cultural norms. The search for social identity and the motivations for social comparison make the impersonal influence of the media pervasive.

Reflection of the culture is a central element in the use of the media for surveilling the social landscape. Representativeness bestows utility on media exposure. Individuals look to the media for information regarding trends and styles, popular points of view and expressions: in short, cultural conditions (Albarran & Umphrey, 1993; Comstock & Scharrer, 1999; Harwood, 1997). They then engage in a social comparison process in which they assess themselves in relation to the depictions observed in the media. These comparisons are often motivated by a desire to achieve or maintain positive self-esteem, as suggested by social comparison theory (Festinger, 1954; Taylor & Lobel, 1989; Wills, 1981, 1991).

The desire to feel good about oneself is also an underlying mechanism behind the influence on consumer behavior exerted through social comparisons with reference groups. Reference groups can be comprised of those encountered in daily life (Tybout & Artz, 1994) as well as of those observed daily in the media, such as spokespeople and endorsers in advertising (Chawla, Dave, & Barr, 1994; Kamins & Gupta, 1994; Wilson & Sherrell, 1993). In both cases, attitudes about products and services as well as purchase decisions are shaped in part by the norms, preferences, and points of view demonstrated by others.

Self-esteem also governs the perception of identity. Social identity theory suggests that identity takes shape, in part, from comparisons made with others that identify those others as either similar or dissimilar to the self (Abrams & Hogg, 1988; Brewer, 1979; Hinkle & Brown, 1990; Tajfel & Turner, 1986). The media provide information directly through information-oriented programming and sports but also indirectly through the representation and characterization of social groups. These groups are primarily defined by gender, race, class, age, or sexual orientation. Individuals use such information to develop thoughts and attitudes regarding in-groups, often motivated by preference and loyalty for those they perceive as similar to themselves, and out-groups, from which they distance themselves. Stereotypes of out-groups support the superiority of the in-group, and such stereotypes may be learned from or modified by depictions in the media (Allport, 1979; Brewer & Gardner, 1996; Macrae, Milne, & Bodenhausen, 1994).

The impersonal influence of media depictions rests on the perception that they represent a norm. Our two examples in regard to socialization have been gender roles and aggression. Depictions of gender roles typically emphasize the conventional; the conventions of violent entertainment assign aggression an important and sometimes exalted role. Once individuals perceive media characters and content as representing collective conditions, they have a tendency to compartmentalize personal experiences (Mutz, 1998). Information about the collective is potentially persuasive because of its representative nature, whereas the potential power of the personal in attitude formation is weakened because it is perceived as unique and idiosyncratic.

We don't dismiss the importance of interpersonal influences on consumer behavior and socialization. Parents, peers, neighbors, teachers, and other significant people in an individual's life often exert major, important influences. There is nevertheless reason to suspect that a number of social changes have begun to restrict the strength of interpersonal sources. These include the increased mobility and more frequent changes in jobs that constrain interaction with neighbors and coworkers (Schor, 1998), the factors that have reduced memberships in associational organizations and seemingly lowered the levels of civic participation and interaction with others (Putnam, 2000), and the increasing amount of time spent with media (Roberts & Foehr, 2004). Comparisons between self and others will increasingly supplement information gained from the traditional reference groups (parents, family, friends, peers, coworkers) with that gained from the mass media. The transformation of the world of politics and public affairs into a universe of media depictions, and the central role of the media in the relationship between the individual and the polity in modern democratic America, are paralleled by a more central place for the media wherever the self is at issue.

REFERENCES

Abrams, D., & Hogg, M. (1988). Comments on the motivational status of self-esteem in social identity and intergroup discrimination. *European Journal of Social Psychology* 18, 317–334.

Achen, C., & Bartels, L. (2004). Blind retrospection: Electoral responses to droughts, flu, and shark attacks. Working paper [revised]. Princeton University.

Adair, B. (2004, November 5). Bush unveils his new agenda. *St. Petersburg Times*, p. 1A.

Adatto, K. (1990). *Sound bite democracy: Network evening news presidential campaign coverage, 1968 and 1988*. Joan Shorenstein Barone Center on the Press, Politics, and Public Policy, Research Paper R-2, Cambridge, MA: John F. Kennedy School of Government, Harvard University.

Agins, T. (2004, September 8). As consumers mix and match, fashion industry starts to fray. *Wall Street Journal* pp. 1, A6.

Agrawal, J., & Kamakura, W. A. (1995). The economic worth of celebrity endorsers: An event study analysis. *Journal of Marketing* 59(3), 56–63.

Ajzen, I. (1991). The theory of planned behavior. *Organizational Behavior and Human Decision Processes* 50, 179–211.

Ajzen, I. (1985). From intentions to actions: A theory of planned behavior. In J. Kuhl & J. Beckmann (Eds.), *Action control: From cognition to behavior* (pp. 11–39). New York: Springer-Verlag.

Albarran, A. B., & Umphrey, D. (1993). An examination of television motivations and program preferences by Hispanics, blacks, and whites. *Journal of Broadcasting and Electronic Media* 37(1), 95–103.

Allen, M., D'Alessio, D., & Brezgel, K. (1995). A meta-analysis summarizing the effects of pornography II: Aggression after exposure. *Human Communication Research* 22(2), 258–283.

Allport, G. W. (1979). *The nature of prejudice*, 25th Anniversary Ed. Reading, MA: Addison-Wesley.

Almond, G. A., & Verba, S. (1989a). *The civic culture*. Newbury Park, CA: Sage.

Almond, G. A., & Verba, S. (1989b). *The civic culture revisited*. Newbury Park, CA: Sage.

Altheide, D. L. (2002). *Creating fear: News and the construction of crisis*. New York: Aldine de Gruyter.

Altheide, D. L. (1976). *Creating reality: How TV news distorts events*. Beverly Hills, CA: Sage.

Alvarez, R. M., & Brehm, J. (2002). *Hard choices, easy answers: Values, information, and American public opinion*. Princeton, NJ: Princeton University Press.

American Enterprise Institute for Public Policy Research (2001). Accessed 12/16/04 at http://www.aei.org/news/news ID.13175/news_detail.asp.

Anderson, C. A., Berkowitz, L., Donnerstien, E., Huesmann, L. R., Johnson, J. D., Linz, D., Malamuth, N. M., & Wartella, E. (2003). The influence of media violence on youth. *Psychological Science in the Public Interest* 4 (3), 81–110.

Anderson, R., & Engledow, J. (1977). A factor analytic comparison of U.S. and German information seekers. *Journal of Consumer Research* 3, 185–196.

Ansolabehere, S., & Iyengar, S. (1994). Riding the wave and claiming ownership over issues: The joint effects of advertising and news coverage in campaigns. *Public Opinion Quarterly* 58(3), 335–357.

Arndt, J. (1967). Role of product-related conversations in the diffusion of a new product. *Journal of Marketing Research* 4, 291–295.

Aronson, E., Wilson, T. D., & Brewer, M. B. (1998). Experimentation in social psychology. In D. T. Gilbert, S. T. Fiske, & G. Lindzey (Eds.), *The Handbook of Social Psychology*. Vol. I, 4th Ed. (pp. 99–142). New York: McGraw-Hill.

Asch, S. E. (1956). Studies of independence and conformity: A minority of one against a unanimous majority. *Psychological Monographs* 70(9) (Whole No. 416).

Asch, S. E. (1952). *Social psychology.* Englewood Cliffs, NJ: Prentice-Hall.

Asch, S. E. (1951). Effects of group pressure upon the modification and distortion of judgments. In H. Guetzkow (Ed.), *Groups, leadership and men.* Pittsburgh, PA: Carnegie Press.

Ashmore, R. D., Del Boca, F. K., & Wohlers, A. J. (1986). Gender stereotypes. In R. D. Ashmore & F. K. Del Boca (Eds.), *The social psychology of female-male relations.* Orlando, FL: Academic Press.

Atkin, C., Hocking, J., & McDermott, S. (1977). Home state viewer response and secondary media coverage. In Kraus, S. (Ed.), *The great debates: Carter vs. Ford, 1976* (pp. 429–436). Bloomington: Indiana University Press.

Atwood, L. E., & Major A. M. (1996). *Good-bye Gweilo: Public opinion and the 1997 problem in Hong Kong.* Cresskill, NJ: Hampton Press.

Atwood, L. E., & Major, A. M. (1991). Applying situational communication theory to an international political problem: Two studies. *Journalism Quarterly* 68(1/2), 200–210.

Bagdikian, B. H. (1987). *The media monopoly*, 2nd Ed. Boston: Beacon Press.

Bandura, A. (1986). *Social foundations of thought and action: A social cognitive theory.* Englewood Cliffs, NJ: Prentice-Hall.

Baran, S. J., & Davis, D. K. (2000). *Mass communication theory*, 2nd Ed. Belmont, CA: Wadsworth.

Barnhurst, K., & Mutz, D. C. (1997). American journalism and the decline in event-centered reporting. *Journal of Communication* (47), 27–53.

Bartels, L. M. (1993). Messages received: The political impact of media exposure. *American Political Science Review* 87(2), 267–285.

Bartsch, R. A., Burnett, T., Diller, T. R., & Rankin-Williams, E. (2000). Gender representation in television commercials: Updating an update. *Sex Roles* 43(9/10), 735–743.

Basil, M. D. (1996). Identification as a mediator of celebrity effects. *Journal of Broadcasting & Electronic Media* 40(4), 478–496.

Bauer, R. A. (1971). The obstinate audience: The influence process from the point of view of social communication. In W. Schramm & D. F. Roberts (Eds.), *The process and effects of mass communication*, Rev. Ed. (pp. 326–346). Urbana: University of Illinois Press.

Bearden, W. O., & Etzel, M. J. (1982). Reference group influence on product and brand purchase decisions. *Journal of Consumer Research* 9, 183–194.

Bearden, W. O., Netemeyer, R. G., & Teel, J. E. (1989). Measurement of consumer susceptibility to interpersonal influence. *Journal of Consumer Research* 15, 473–481.

Bearden, W. O., & Rose, R. L. (1990). Attention to social comparison information: An individual difference factor affecting consumer conformity. *Journal of Consumer Research* 16, 461–471.

Bechara, A., Damasio, H., Tranel, D., & Damasio, A. (1997, 28 February). Deciding advantageously before knowing the advantageous strategy. *Science* 1293–1295.

Becker, L., & McCombs, M. E. (1978). The role of the press in determining voter reaction to presidential primaries. *Human Communication Research* 4, 301–307.

Becker, S. L., Pepper, R., Wenner, L. A., & Kim, J. K. (1979). Information flow and the shaping of meanings. In S. Kraus (Ed.), *The great debates: Carter vs. Ford, 1976* (pp. 384–397). Bloomington: Indiana University Press.

Bedy, Z. (1996). Couch potatoes and the indifferent electorate: Television viewing, voting, and responsible citizenship. Ph.D. dissertation. Syracuse, NY: Syracuse University.

Belson, W. A. (1978). *Television violence and the adolescent boy.* Westmead, England: Saxon House, Teakfield.

Bem, D. J. (1972). Self-perception theory. In L. Berkowitz (Ed.), *Advances in experimental social psychology*, Vol. VI (pp. 1–62). New York: Academic Press.

Bennett, W. L. (1983). *News: The politics of illusion.* New York: Longman.

Benoit, W. L., Hansen, G. J., & Holbert, R. L. (2004). Presidential campaigns and democracy. *Mass Communication & Society* 7(2), 177–190.

Benoit, W. L., Hansen, G. J., & Verser, R. M. (2003). A meta-analysis of the effects of viewing U.S. presidential debates. *Communication Monographs* 70(4), 335–351.

Berelson, B. R., Lazarsfeld, P. F., & McPhee, W. N. (1954). *Voting: A study of opinion formation in a presidential campaign*. Chicago: University of Chicago Press.

Berry, G., & Mitchell-Kerman, C. (Eds.). (1982). *Television and the socialization of the minority child*. New York: Academic Press.

Berscheid, E. (1966). Opinion change and communicator-communicatee similarity and dissimilarity. *Journal of Personality and Social Psychology* 4(6), 670–680.

Bimber, B., & Davis, R. (2003). *Campaigning online: The Internet in U.S. elections*. New York: Oxford University Press.

Bineham, J. L. (1988). A historical account of the hypodermic model in mass communication. *Communication Monographs* 55, 230–246.

Blass, T. (2000a). The Milgram paradigm after 35 years: Some things we now know about obedience to authority. In T. Blass (Ed.), *Obedience to authority: Current perspectives on the Milgram paradigm* (pp. 35–39). Mahwah, NJ: Erlbaum.

Blass, T. (Ed.). (2000b). *Obedience to authority: Current perspectives on the Milgram paradigm*. Mahwah, NJ: Erlbaum.

Blood, D. J., & Phillips, P. C. B. (1995). Recession headline news, consumer sentiment, the state of the economy and presidential popularity: A time series analysis 1989–1993. *International Journal of Public Opinion Research* 7, 2–22.

Bogart, L. (2000). *Commercial culture: The media system and the public interest*. New Brunswick, NJ: Transaction Publishers.

Bogart, L. (1989). *Press and public: Who reads what, where, when, and why in American newspapers?* Hillsdale, NJ: Erlbaum.

Bogatz, G. A., & Ball, S. (1971). *The second year of* Sesame Street: *A continuing evaluation,* Vols. 1 & 2. Princeton, NJ: Educational Testing Service.

Borgida, E., & Brekke, N. (1981). The base rate fallacy in attribution and prediction. In J. Harvey, W. Ickes, & R. Kidd (Eds.), *New directions in attribution research,* Vol. 3 (pp. 63–95). Hillsdale, NJ: Erlbaum.

Botta, R. (1999). Television images and adolescent girls' body image disturbance. *Journal of Communication* 49(2), 22–41.

Bowen, L. (1994). Time of voting decision and use of political advertising: The Slade Gorton-Brock Adams senatorial campaign. *Journalism Quarterly* 71(3), 665–675.

Bower, A. B. (2001). Highly attractive models in advertising and the women who loathe them: The implications of negative affect for spokesperson effectiveness. *Journal of Advertising* 30(3), 51–62.

Bower, R. (1985). *The changing television audience in America*. New York: Columbia University Press.

Bower, R. (1973). *Television and the public*. New York: Holt, Rhinehart, and Winston.

Braungart, R. G. (1971, July). Family status, socialization, and student politics: A multi-variate analysis. *American Journal of Sociology* 77, 108–130.

Brehm, J., & Rahn, W. (1997). Individual-level evidence for the causes and consequences of social capital. *American Journal of Political Science* 41(3), 999–1023.

Brewer, M. (1979). In-group bias in the minimal group situation: A cognitive-motivational analysis. *Psychological Bulletin* 86, 307–324.

Brewer, M. B. (1991). The social self: On being the same and different at the same time. *Personality and Social Psychology Bulletin* 17, 475–482.

Brewer, M. B., & Gardner, W. (1996). Who is this "we"? Levels of collective identity and self-representations. *Journal of Personality and Social Psychology* 71, 83–93.

Brock, T. C. (1965). Communicator-recipient similarity and decision change. *Journal of Personality and Social Psychology* 1(6), 650–654.

Brosius, H., & Bathelt, A. (1994). The utility of exemplars in persuasive communication. *Communication Research* 21, 48–78.

Brosius, H. B, & Engel, D. (1996). The causes of third-person effects: Unrealistic optimism, impersonal impact, or generalized negative attitudes towards media influence. *International Journal of Public Opinion Research* 8(2), 142–161.

Brosius, H. B., & Kepplinger, H. M. (1990). The agenda-setting function of television news. *Communication Research* 17(2), 183–211.

Brown, J. J., & Reingen, P. H. (1987). Social ties and word-of-mouth referral behavior. *Journal of Consumer Research* 14, 350–362.

Browne, B. A. (1998). Gender stereotypes in advertising on children's television in the 1990s: A cross-national analysis. *Journal of Advertising* 27(1), 83–97.

Bryant, J., & Thompson, S. (2002). *Fundamentals of media effects*. Boston: McGraw-Hill.

Bryant, J., & Zillmann, D. (Eds.). (1994). *Media effects: Advances in theory and research*. Hillsdale, NJ: Erlbaum.

Bucy, E. P., & D'Angelo, P. (2004). Democratic realism, neoconservatism, and the normative underpinnings of political communication research. *Mass Communication & Society* 7(1), 3–28.

Burke, P. J. (2004). Identities and social structure: The 2003 Cooley-Mead award address. *Social Psychology Quarterly* 67(1), 5–15.

Bushman, B. J., & Anderson, C. A. (2001). Media violence and the American public: Scientific facts versus media misinformation. *American Psychologist* 56, 477–489.

Bushman, B. J., & Huesmann, L. R. (2001). Effects of televised violence on aggression. In D. G. Singer & J. L. Singer (Eds.), *Handbook of children and the media* (pp. 223–254). Thousand Oaks, CA: Sage.

Caballero, M. J., Lumpkin, J. R., & Madden, C. S. (1989). Using physical attractiveness as an advertising tool: An empirical test of the attraction phenomenon. *Journal of Advertising Research* 29(4), 16–23.

Cameron, J. E. (2001, December). Social identity, modern sexism, and perceptions of personal and group discrimination by women and men. *Sex Roles: A Journal of Research*, 45(11/12), 743–767.

Cameron, J. E. (2000). A three-factor model of social identity. Manuscript submitted for publication, cited in Cameron, 2001.

Cameron, J. E., & Lalonde, R. N. (2001). Social identification and gender-based ideology in women and men. *British Journal of Social Psychology* 40, 59–77.

Campaign 2000 highly rated. (2000). Pew Research Center for the People and the Press. Accessed 6/12/03 at http://people-press.org/reports/display.php3?ReportID=23.

Campbell, A., Converse, P. E., Miller, W. E., & Stokes, D. E. (1960). *The American voter.* New York: Wiley.

Campbell, A., Gurin, G., & Miller, W.E. (1954). *The voter decides*. Evanston, IL: Row, Peterson.

Campbell, D.T. (1990). Asch's moral epistemology for socially shared knowledge. In I. Rock (Ed.), *The legacy of Solomon Asch: Essays in cognition and social psychology*. Hillsdale, NJ: Erlbaum.

Campbell, J. E., Cherry, L., & Wink, K. (1992). The convention bump. *American Politics Quarterly* 20(3), 287–307.

Campbell, M. C., & Kirmani, A. (2000). Consumers' use of persuasion knowledge: The effects of accessibility and cognitive capacity on perceptions of an influence agent. *Journal of Consumer Research* 27(1), 69–82.

Cappella, J. N., & Jamieson, K. H. (1997). *Spiral of cynicism: The press and the public good.* New York: Oxford University Press.

Cappella, J. N., & Jamieson, K. H. (1994). Broadcast adwatch effects: A field experiment. *Communication Research* 21(3), 342–365.

Center, A. H., & Jackson, P. (1995). *Public relations practices: Managerial case studies and problems,* 5th Ed. Englewood Cliffs, NJ: Prentice-Hall.

Chaffee, S. H. (1987). Media election research without party identification. *Mass Communication Review* 14(1/2), 36–42.

Chaffee, S. H., & Frank, S. (1996). How Americans get political information: Print versus broadcast news. *Annals of the American Academy of Political and Social Science* 546, 48–58.

Chaffee, S. H., & Hochheimer, J. L. (1985). The beginnings of political communication research in the United States: Origins of the "limited effects" model. In E. M. Rogers & F. Balle (Eds.), *The media revolution in America and in Western Europe* (pp. 267–296). Norwook, NJ: Ablex.

Chaffee, S. H., Zhao, X., & Leshner, G. (1994). Political knowledge and the campaign media of 1992. *Communication Research* 22(3), 305–324.

Chaiken, S. (1979). Communicator physical attractiveness and persuasion. *Journal of Personality and Social Psychology* 37(8), 1387–1397.

Chambers, J. R., & Windschitl, P. D. (2004). Biases in social comparative judgments: The role of nonmotivated factors in above-average and comparative-optimism effects. *Psychological Bulletin* 130(5), 813–838.

Chan, S. (1997). Effects of attention to campaign coverage on political trust. *International Journal of Public Opinion Research* 9(3), 286–296.

Chanley, V. A., Rudolph, T. J., & Rahn, W. M. (2000). The origins and consequences of public trust in government: A time series analysis. *Public Opinion Quarterly* 64(3), 239–256.

Charters, W. W. (1933). *Motion pictures and youth: A summary*. New York: Macmillan.

Chawla, S. K., Dave, D. S., & Barr, P. B. (1994). Role of physical attractiveness in endorsement: An empirical study. *Journal of Services Marketing* 10(2), 203–215.

Childers, T. L., & Rao, A. R. (1992). The influence of familial and peer-based reference groups on consumer decisions. *Journal of Consumer Research* 19, 198–211.

Chiou, J. S. (2000). Antecedents and moderators of behavioral intention: Differences between U.S. and Taiwanese students. *Genetic, Social, and General Psychology Monographs* 126(1), 105–119.

Christensen, P. N., Rothgerber, H., Wood, W., & Matz, D. C. (2004). Social norms and identity relevance: A motivational approach to normative behavior. *Personality and Social Psychology Bulletin* 30(10), 1295–1309.

Cialdini, R. B., & Trost, M. R. (1998). Social influence: Social norms, conformity, and compliance. In D. T. Gilbert, S. E. Fiske, & G. Lindzey (Eds.), *Handbook of social psychology,* Vol. 2, 4th Ed. (pp. 151–192). Boston: McGraw-Hill.

Clancey, M., & Robinson, M. J. (1985). General election coverage in campaign '84: Part 1. *Public Opinion* 7, 49–54, 59.

Clayman, S. E. (1995). Defining moments, presidential debates, and the dynamics of quotability. *Journal of Communication* 45(3), 118–146.

Clinton's the one. (1992, November). Media monitor, (p. 2). Washington, DC: Center for Media and Public Affairs, Washington, DC.

Coelho, P. R. P., & McClure, J. E. (1993). Toward an economic theory of fashion. *Economic Inquiry* 31(4), 595–609.

Cohen, B. C. (1963). *The press and foreign policy*. Princeton, NJ: Princeton University Press.

Cohen, G. L. (2003). Party over policy: The dominating impact of group influences on political beliefs. *Journal of Personality and Social Psychology* 85(5), 808–822.

Cohen, J. (1988). *Statistical power analysis for the behavioral sciences*, 2nd Ed. Hillsdale, NJ: Earlbaum.

Cohen, J., & Davis, R. G. (1991). Third person effects and the differential impact in negative advertising. *Journalism Quarterly* 68(4), 680–688.

Cohen, J., Mutz, D. C., Price, V., & Gunther, A. (1988). Perceived impact of defamation: An experiment on third-person effects. *Public Opinion Quarterly* 52(2), 161–173.

Comstock, G. (2004). Paths from television violence to aggression: Reinterpreting the evidence. In L. J. Shrum (Ed.), *The psychology of entertainment media.* Mahwah, NJ: Erlbaum.

Comstock, G. (1991). *Television and the American child.* San Diego, CA: Academic Press.

Comstock, G. (1989). *The evolution of American television*. Newbury Park, CA: Sage.

Comstock, G., Chaffee, S., Katzman, N., McCombs, M., & Roberts, D. (1978). *Television and human behavior*. New York: Columbia University Press.

Comstock, G., & Rubinstein, E. A. (Eds.) (1972). *Television and social behavior:* Vol. 3. Television and adolescent aggressiveness (pp. 314–335). Washington, DC: U.S. Government Printing Office.

Comstock, G., & Scharrer, E. (2003). Meta-analyzing the controversy over television violence and aggression. In D. Gentile (Ed.), *Media violence and children* (pp. 205–226). Westport, CT: Praeger.

Comstock, G., & Scharrer, E. (1999). *Television: What's on, who's watching, and what it means*. San Diego: Academic Press.

Conover, P. J., Feldman, S., & Knight, K. (1986). Judging inflation and unemployment: The origins of retrospective evaluations. *Journal of Politics* 48, 565–588.

Converse, P. E. (1966). Information flow and the stability of partisan attitudes. In A. Campbell, P. Converse, W. Miller, & D. Stokes (Eds.), *Elections and the political order* (pp. 212–242). Madison, WI: University of Wisconsin Press.

Converse, P. E. (1964). The nature of belief systems in mass publics. In D. E. Apter (Ed.), *Ideology and discontent* (pp. 206–261). New York: Free Press.

Cook, T. E. (1998). *Governing with the news: The news media as a political institution*. Chicago: University of Chicago Press.

Coser, L. A. (1956). *The functions of social conflict*. Glencoe, IL: Free Press.

Craig, R. S. (1992). The effect of television day part on gender portrayals in television commercials: A content analysis. *Sex Roles* 26, 197–211.

Crane, D. (1999). Diffusion models and fashion: A reassessment. *The Annals of the American Academy of Political and Social Science* 566, 13–25.

Cranston, P. (1960). Political convention broadcasts: Their history and influence. *Journalism Quarterly* 37(2), 186–194.

Crespi, I. (1997). *The public opinion process*. Mahwah, NJ: Erlbaum.

Crespi, I. (1989). *Public opinion, polls, and democracy*. Boulder, CO: Westview Press.

Crouse, T. (1974). *The boys on the bus*. New York: Ballantine.

D'Alessio, D., & Allen, M. (2000). Media bias in presidential elections: A meta-analysis. *Journal of Communication* (4)50: 133–156.

Dautrich, K., & Hartley, T. H. (1999). *How the news media fail American voters: Causes, consequences, & remedies*. New York: Columbia University Press.

Davis, J. A. (2004). Did growing up in the 1960s leave a permanent mark on attitudes and values? Evidence from the general social survey. *Public Opinion Quarterly* 68(2), 161–183.

Davis, R. (1999). *The web of politics: The Internet's impact on the American political system*. New York: Oxford University Press.

Davison, W. P. (1983). The third-person effect in communication. *Public Opinion Quarterly* 47(1), 1–15.

Dawar, N., Parker, P. M., & Price, L. J. (1996). A cross-cultural study of interpersonal information exchange. *Journal of International Business Studies*, 27, 497–517.

Dayan, D., & Katz, E. (1992). *Media events: The live broadcasting of history*. Cambridge, MA: Harvard University Press.

Dearing, J., & Rogers, E. (1996). *Agenda setting*. Thousand Oaks, CA: Sage.

Deaux, K., & Lewis, L. L. (1984). The structure of gender stereotypes: Interrelationships among components and gender label. *Journal of Personality and Social Psychology* 46, 991–1004.

DeCoster, J., & Claypool, H. M. (2004). A meta-analysis of priming effects on impression formation supporting a general model of informational biases. *Personality and Social Psychology Review* 8(1), 2–27.

Delia, J. G. (1987). Communication research: A history. In C. R. Berger & S. H. Chaffee (Eds.), *Handbook of communication science* (pp. 20–98). Newbury Park, CA: Sage.

DeLuca, T. (1995). *The two faces of political apathy*. Philadelphia, PA: Temple University Press.

Dennis, J., Chaffee, S. H., & Choe, S. Y. (1979). Impact on partisan, image, and issue voting. In S. Kraus (Ed.), *The great debates: Carter vs. Ford, 1976* (pp. 314–330). Bloomington: Indiana University Press.

Denzau, A. T., & North, D. C. (2000). Shared mental models: Ideologies and institutions. In A. Lupia, M. D. McCubbins, & S. L. Popkin (Eds.), *Elements of reason: Cognition, choice, and the bounds of rationality* (pp. 23–46). New York: Cambridge University Press.

Deshpande, R., & Stayman, D. M. (1994). A tale of two cities: Distinctiveness theory and advertising effectiveness. *Journal of Marketing Research* 31(1), 57–65.

Devlin, L. P. (1997). Contrasts in presidential campaign commercials of 1996. *American Behavioral Scientist* 40(8), 1058–1084.

Devlin, L. P. (1993). Contrasts in presidential campaign commercials of 1992. *American Behavioral Scientist* 37(2), 272–290.

DeVries, W., & Tarrance, L., Jr. (1972). *The ticket-splitter: A new force in American politics.* Grand Rapids, MI: Eerdmans.

Dijksterhuis, A., & Aarts, H. (2003). On wildebeests and humans: The preferential detection of negative stimuli. *Psychological Science* 14(1), 14–18.

Dijksterhuis, A., Corneille, O., Aarts, H., Vermuelen, N., & Luminet, O. (2004). Yes, there is a preferential detection of negative stimuli: A response to Labiouse. *Psychological Science* 15(8), 571–572.

Doise, W. (1988). Individual and social identities in intergroup relations. *European Journal of Social Psychology* 63, 754–763.

Dominick, J. R., & Greenberg, B. S. (1972). Attitudes toward violence: The interaction of television exposure, family attitudes, and social class. In G. A. Comstock & E. A. Rubinstein (Eds.), *Television and social behavior: Vol. 3. Television and adolescent aggressiveness* (pp. 314–335). Washington, DC: U.S. Government Printing Office.

Domke, D., Fan, D. P., Fibison, M., Shah, D. V., Smith, S. S., & Watts, M. D. (1997). New media, candidates and issues, and public opinion in the 1996 presidential campaign. *Journalism and Mass Communication Quarterly* 74(4), 718–737.

Doob, L. W. (1950). Goebbels' Principles of Propaganda. *Public Opinion Quarterly* 14, 419–442. In D. Katz et al. (Eds.), *Public opinion and propaganda* (pp. 508–522). New York: Holt.

Doppelt, J. C., & Shearer, E. (1999). *Nonvoters: America's no-shows.* Thousand Oaks, CA: Sage.

Downs, A. (1972). Up and down with ecology: The issue-attention cycle. *Public Interest* 28, 38–50.

Downs, A. (1957). *An economic theory of democracy*. New York: Harper.

Drabman, R. S., & Thomas, M. H. (1974a). Does media violence increase children's tolerance of real-life aggression? *Developmental Psychology* 10, 418–421.

Drabman, R. S., & Thomas, M. H. (1974b). Exposure to filmed violence and children's tolerance of real life aggression. *Personality & Social Psychology Bulletin* 1(1), 198–199.

Drew, D. G., & Weaver, D. (1991). Voter learning in the 1988 presidential election: Did the debates and the media matter? *Journalism Quarterly* 68(1/2), 155–164.

Dreyer, E. C. (1971–72, Winter). Media use and electoral choices: Some political consequences of information exposure. *Public Opinion Quarterly* 35, 544–553.

Driscoll, P. D., & Salwen, M. B. (1997). Self-perceived knowledge of the O. J. Simpson trial: Third-person perception and perceptions of guilt. *Journalism & Mass Communication Quarterly* 74(3), 541–556.

Duck, J., & Mullin, B. (1995). The perceived impact of the mass media: Reconsidering the third-person effect. *European Journal of Social Psychology* 25, 77–93.

Duck, J., Terry, D., & Hogg, M. (1995). The perceived influence of AIDS advertising: Third-person effects in the context of positive media content. *Basic and Applied Social Psychology* 17, 305–325.

Duck, J. M. (1999). Gender identity and the perceived impact of commercial advertising. Manuscript submitted for publication.

Duck, J. M., Hogg, M. A., & Terry, D. J. (2000). The perceived impact of persuasive messages on "us" and "them." In D. J. Terry & M. A. Hogg (Eds.), *Attitudes, behavior, and social context: The role of norms and group membership* (pp. 265–291). Mahwah, NJ: Erlbaum.

Duck, J. M., Hogg, M. A., & Terry, D. J. (1999). Social identity and perceptions of media persuasion: Are we always less influenced than others? *Journal of Applied Social Psychology* 29, 1879–1899.

Eagly, A. H., & Chaiken, S. (1993). *The psychology of attitudes*. Orlando, FL: Harcourt Brace.

Eagly, A. H., & Kite, M. E. (1987). Are stereotypes of nationalities applied to both women and men? *Journal of Personality and Social Psychology* 53, 457–462.

Eagly, A. H., Mladinic, A., & Otto, S. (1991). Are women evaluated more favorably than men? An analysis of attitudes, beliefs, and emotions. *Psychology of Women Quarterly* 15, 203–216.

Easton, D., & Denis, J. (1969). *Children in the political system: Origins of political legitimacy*. New York: McGraw-Hill.

Eaton, B. C. (1997). Prime-time stereotyping on the new television networks. *Journalism and Mass Communication Quarterly* 74(4), 859–872.

Edwards, B., & Foley, M. W. (1998). Civil society and social capital beyond Putnam. *American Behavioral Scientist* 42(1), 124–139.

Elliott, W. R., & Sothirajah, J. (1993). Post-debate analysis and media reliance: Influences on candidate image and voting probabilities. *Journalism Quarterly* 70(2), 321–335.

Eveland, W. P., McLeod, D. M., & Signorielli, N. (1995). Actual and perceived U.S. public opinion: The spiral of silence during the Persian Gulf War. *International Journal of Public Opinion Research* 7, 91–109.

Eveland, W. P., Jr., Nathanson, A. I., Detenber, B. H., & McLeod, D. M. (1999). Rethinking the social distance corollary: Perceived likelihood of exposure and the third-person perception. *Communication Research* 26(3), 275–302.

Fabrigar, L. R., & Krosnick, J. A. (1995). Attitude importance and the false consensus effect. *Personality and Social Psychology Bulletin* 21(5), 468–479.

Fazio, R. H., Eiser, J. R., & Shook, N. J. (2004). Attitude formation through exploration: Valence asymmetries. *Journal of Personality and Social Psychology* 87(3), 293–311.

Feick, L. F., & Price, L. L. (1987). The market maven: A diffuser of marketplace information. *Journal of Marketing* 51, 83–97.

Feick, L. F., Price, L. L., & Higie, R. A. (1986). People who use people: The other side of opinion leadership. In R. J. Lutz (Ed.), *Advances in consumer research* (13, 301–305). Provo, UT: Association for Consumer Research.

Feldman, S. (2003). Values, ideology, and the structure of political attitudes. In D. O. Sears, L. Huddy, & R. Jervis (Eds.), *Oxford handbook of political psychology* (pp. 477–508). New York: Oxford University Press.

Festinger, L. (1954). A theory of social comparison processes. *Human Relations* 7, 117–140.

Field, G. A. (1970, August). The status float phenomenon: The upward diffusion of innovation. *Business Horizons* 13, 45–52.

Fields, J., & Schuman, H. (1976). Public beliefs about the beliefs of the public. *Public Opinion Quarterly* 40, 427–448.

Fiorina, M. P. (1981). *Retrospective voting in American national elections*. New Haven, CT: Yale University Press.

Fishbein, M. A. (1967). *Readings in attitude theory and measurement*. New York: Wiley.

Fishbein, M. A., & Ajzen, I. (1975). *Belief, attitude, intention and behavior: An introduction to theory and research*. Reading, MA: Addison-Wesley.

Fisher, R. J., & Price, L. L. (1992). An investigation into the social context of early adoption behavior. *Journal of Consumer Research* 19, 477–486.

Fishman, M. (1980). *Manufacturing the news*. Austin: University of Texas Press.

Flanagan, A. J., & Metzger, M. J. (2001). Internet use in the contemporary media environment. *Human Communication Research* 27(1), 153–181.

Foley, M. W., & Edwards, B. (1997). Escape from politics? Social capital and the political economy of our discontent. *American Behavioral Scientist* 40(5), 669–678.

Freedman, E., & Fico, F. (2004). Whither the experts? Newspaper use of horse race and issue experts in coverage of open governor's races in 2002. *Journalism & Mass Communication Quarterly* 81(3), 498–510.

Frenzen, J. K., & Davis, H. L. (1990). Purchasing behavior in embedded markets. *Journal of Consumer Research* 17, 1–12.

Friedenberg, R. V. (1997). Patterns and trends in national political debates: 1960–1996. In Friedenberg, R. V. (Ed.), *Rhetorical studies of national political debates—1996*. Westport, CT: Greenwood Press.

Friedman, H. H., & Friedman, L. (1979). Endorser effectiveness by product type. *Journal of Advertising Research* 19(5), 63–71.

Friend, R., Rafferty, Y., & Bramel, D. (1990). A puzzling misinterpretation of the Asch conformity study. *European Journal of Social Psychology* 20, 29–44.

Friestad, M., & Wright, P. (1994). The persuasion knowledge model: How people cope with persuasive attempts. *Journal of Consumer Research* 21, 1–31.

Fuchs, D. A. (1966). Election day radio-television and Western voting. *Public Opinion Quarterly* 30(2), 226–236.

Funkhouser, G. R. (1973a). The issues of the sixties: An exploratory study in the dynamics of public opinion. *Public Opinion Quarterly* 37(1), 62–75.

Funkhouser, G. R. (1973b). Trends in media coverage of the issues of the sixties. *Journalism Quarterly* 50(3), 533–538.

Furnham, A., Abramsky, S., & Gunter, B. (1997). A cross-cultural content analysis of children's television advertisements. *Sex Roles* 37(1/2), 91–99.

Gaedeke, R. M., & Tootelian, D. H. (1983). *Marketing*. Saint Paul, MN: West Publishing.

Gans, H. J. (1979). *Deciding what's news: A study of* CBS Evening News, NBC Nightly News, Newsweek, *and* Time. New York: Pantheon.

Garramone, G. M., Atkin, C. K., Pinkleton, B. E., & Cole, R. T. (1990). Effects of negative political advertising on the political process. *Journal of Broadcasting and Electronic Media* 34(3), 299–311.

Gaziano, C., & Gaziano, E. (1996). Theories and methods in knowledge gap research since 1970. In M. Salwen & D. Stacks (Eds.), *An integrated approach to communication theory and research*. Mahwah, NJ: Erlbaum.

Geis, F. L., Brown, V., Walstedt, J. J., & Porter, N. (1984). TV commercials as achievement scripts for women. *Sex Roles* 10(7/8), 513–525.

Gerbner, G., Morgan, M., & Signorielli, N. (1994). Television violence profile no. 16. Working paper, The Annenberg School of Communication, University of Pennsylvania, Philadelphia.

Gerth, H., Merton, R. K., & Mills, C. W. (1964). Character and social structure: The psychology of social institutions. San Diego, CA: Harvest.

Gigerenzer, G., & Goldstein, D. G. (1999). Betting on one good reason: The take the best heuristic. In G. Gigerenzer, P. M. Todd, & The ABS Research (Eds.), *Simple heuristics that make us smart* (pp. 75–95). New York: Oxford University Press.

Gitlin, T. (1980). *The whole world is watching: Mass media in the making and unmaking of the new left*. Berkeley: University of California Press.

Gitlin, T. (1978). Media sociology: The dominant paradigm. *Theory and Society* 6, 205–253.

Glynn, C. J., Hayes, A. F., & Shanahan, J. (1997). Perceived support for one's opinions and willingness to speak out: A meta-analysis of survey studies on the "spiral of silence." *Public Opinion Quarterly* 61(3), 452–463.

Glynn, C. J., & McLeod, J. M. (1984). Implications of the spiral of silence theory for communication and public opinion research. In K. R. Sanders, L. L. Kaid, & D. Nimmo (Eds.). *Political communication yearbook, 1984* (pp. 43–65). Carbondale: Southern Illinois University Press.

Goethals, G. R. (1986). Social comparison theory: Psychology from the lost and found. *Personality and Social Psychology Bulletin* 12(3), 261–278.

Goldenberg, E. N., & Traugott, M. W. (1987). Mass media in U.S. congressional elections. *Legislative Studies Quarterly* 12(3), 317–339.

Goldsmith, R. E., Lafferty, B. A., & Newell, S. J. (2000). The impact of corporate credibility and celebrity credibility on consumer reaction to advertisements and brands. *Journal of Advertising* 29(3), 43–51.

Goleman, D. (1995). *Emotional intelligence: Why it can matter more than I.Q.* New York: Bantam.

Goodhardt, G. J., Ehrenberg, A. S. C., & Collins, M. A. (1987). *The television audience: Patterns of viewing,* 2nd Ed. Westmead, England: Gower.

Gorn, G. J., Goldberg, M. E., & Kanungo, R. N. (1976). The role of educational television in changing the intergroup attitudes of children. *Child Development* 47, 277–280.

Graber, D. A. (2001). *Processing politics: Learning from television in the Internet age.* Chicago: University of Chicago Press.

Graber, D. A. (1997). *Mass media and American politics*, 5th Ed. Washington, DC: Congressional Quarterly Press.

Graber, D. A. (1990). Seeing is remembering: How visuals contribute to learning from television news. *Journal of Communication* 40(3), 134–155.

Graber, D. A. (1988). *Processing the news*, 2nd Ed. New York: Longman.

Graber, D. A. (1987). Framing election news broadcasts: News content and its impact on the 1984 presidential election. *Social Science Quarterly* 68(3), 552–568.

Greenberg, B. S., & Collette, L. (1997). The changing faces on TV: A demographic analysis of network television's new seasons 1966–1992. *Journal of Broadcasting and Electronic Media* 41(1), 1–13.

Greenstein, F. I. (1960, December). The benevolent leader: Children's images of political authority. *American Political Science Review* 54, 934–943.

Groebel, J. (2001). Media violence in cross-cultural perspective: A global study on children's media behavior and some educational implications. In D. G. Singer, & J. L. Singer (Eds.), *Handbook of children and the media* (pp. 255–268). Thousand Oaks, CA: Sage.

Groebel, J. (1998). *The UNESCO global study on media violence.* A joint project of UNESCO, the World Organization of the Scout Movement, and Utrecht University. Paris: UNESCO.

Gunther, A. (1995). Overrating the X-rating: The third-person perception and support for censorship of pornography. *Journal of Communication* 45(1), 27–38.

Gunther, A., & Thorson, E. (1992). Perceived persuasive effects of product commercials and public service announcements. *Communication Research* 19(5), 574–596.

Gunther, A. C. (1998, October). The persuasive press inference: Effects of mass media on perceived public opinion. *Communication Research* 25(5), 486–504.

Gunther, A. C., & Chia, S. C.-Y. (2000). Predicting pluralistic ignorance: The hostile media perception and its consequences. *Journalism & Mass Communication Quarterly* 78(4), 688–701.

Gunther, A. C., Chia, S. C., & Liebhart, (2001). Predicting pluralistic ignorance: The hostile media perception and its consequences. *Journalism & Mass Communication Quarterly* (78)4, 688–701.

Gunther, A. C., Christen, C. T. Liebhart, J. L., & Chia, S. C.-Y. (2001). Congenial public, contrary press, and biased estimates of the climate of opinion. *Public Opinion Quarterly* 65(3), 295–321.

Gunther, A. C., Hwa, A. P. (1996). Public perceptions of television influence and opinions about censorship in Singapore. *International Journal of Public Opinion Research* 8(3), 248–266.

Gunther, A. C., & Mundy, P. (1993). Biased optimism and the third-person effect. *Journalism Quarterly* 70, 58–67.

Guy, A., & Banim, M. (2000). Personal collections: Women's clothing use and identity. *Journal of Gender Studies* 9(3), 313–328.

Hallin, D. C. (1992). Soundbite news: Television coverage of elections, 1968-1988. *Journal of Communication* 42(2), 5–24.

Halpern, D. H. (1996). Media marginalization of political parties and candidates: The focus on fringe issues and the lack of consistent coverage in both print and broadcast. Paper presented at the annual meeting of the International Communication Association, Chicago.

Hamilton, J. T. (2004). *All the news that's fit to sell: How the market transforms information into news.* Princeton, NJ: Princeton University Press.

Hamilton, J. T. (1998). *Channeling violence.* Princeton, NJ: Princeton University Press.

Harris, R. J. (2004). *A cognitive psychology of mass communication*, 4th ed. Mahwah, NJ: Erlbaum.

Harrison, J. (2004, September 6). A really big lunch. *New Yorker*, 78–82.

Hart, R. (1999). *Seducing America: How television charms the modern voter.* Thousand Oaks, CA: Sage.

Harwood, J. (1997). Viewing age: Lifespan identity and television viewing choices. *Journal of Broadcasting and Electronic Media* 41(2), 203–213.

Hearold, S. (1986). A systhesis of 1043 effects of television on social behavior. In G. Comstock (Ed.), *Public communication and behavior,* Vol. 1 (pp. 65–133). New York: Academic Press.

Heider, F. (1958). *The psychology of interpersonal relations.* New York: Wiley.

Henriksen, L., & Flora, J. A. (1999). Third-person perception and children: Perceived impact of pro- and anti-smoking ads. *Communication Research* 26(6) 643–665.

Hernson, P. S. (1995). *Congressional elections: Campaigning at home and in Washington, D.C.* Washington, DC: Congressional Quarterly.

Herrett-Skjellum, J., & Allen, M. (1996). Television programming and sex stereotyping: A meta-analysis. In B. R. Burelson (Ed.), *Communication yearbook 19* (pp. 157–185). Thousand Oaks, CA: Sage.

Hess, R. D., & Easton, D. (1960, Winter). The child's changing image of the President. *Public Opinion Quarterly* 24, 632–644.

Hess. R. D., & Torney, J. (1967). *The development of political attitudes in children.* Chicago: Aldine.

Himmelstein, H. (1994). *Television myth and the American mind.* Westport, CT: Praeger.

Hinkle, S., & Brown, R. (1990). Intergroup comparisons and social identity: Some links and lacunae. In D. Abrams & M. Hogg (Eds.), *Social identity theory: Constructive and critical advances* (pp. 48–70). Hemel Hempstead, England: Harvester Wheatsheaf.

Hoffner, C., Buchanan M., Anderson, J. D., Hubbs, L. A., Kamigaki, S. K., Kowalczyk, L., Pastorek, A., Plotkin, R. S., & Silberg, K. J. (1999). Support for censorship of television violence: The role of the third-person effect and news exposure. *Communication Research* 26(6),726–742.

Hofstede, G. (1983, Fall). The culture relativity of organizational practices and theories. *Journal of International Business Studies* 14, 75–89.

Hofstetter, C. R. (1976). *Bias in the news: Network television coverage of the 1972 election campaign.* Columbus: Ohio State University Press.

Hogben, M. (1998). Factors moderating the effect of television aggression on viewer behavior. *Communication Research* 25, 220–247.

Hogg, M. A., & Abrams, D. (1988). *Social identifications: A social psychology of intergroup relations and group processes.* London: Routledge.

Hogg, M. A., & Terry, D. J. (2000). Social contextual influences on attitude-behavior correspondence, attitude change, and persuasion. In D. J. Terry & M. A. Hogg (Eds.), *Attitudes, behavior, and social context: The role of norms and group membership* (pp. 1–9). Mahwah, NJ: Erlbaum.

Holbrook, T. M. (1996). *Do campaigns matter?* Thousand Oaks, CA: Sage.

Hollander, B. A. (1993). Candidate discrimination and attention to the news. *Mass Communication Review* 20(1/2), 76–85.

Hongo, G. (2002). From Volcano. In D. L. Ulin (Ed.), *Writing Los Angeles: A literary anthology* (pp. 827–835). New York: The Library of America.

Hoorens, V., & Ruiter, S. (1996). The optimal impact phenomenon: Beyond the third person effect. *European Journal of Social Psychology* 26, 599–610.

Hornsey, M. J. (2003). Linking superiority bias in the interpersonal and intergroup domains. *Journal of Social Psychology* 143(4), 479–492.

Horowitz, D. P. (1985). *Ethnic groups in conflict*. Berkeley: University of California Press.

Hovland, C., Lumsdaine, A. & Sheffield, F. (1949). *Experiments in mass communication: Studies of social psychology in World War II* (pp. 287–291). Ann Arbor, MI: Association for Consumer Research.

Hovland, C. I., & Weiss, W. (1951-52). The influence of source credibility on communication effectiveness. *Public Opinion Quarterly* 15, 635–650.

Huckfeldt, R., & Sprague, J. (1995). *Citizens, politics, and social communication: Information and influence in an election campaign*. New York: Cambridge University Press.

Huddy, L. (2003). Group identity and political cohesion. In D. O. Sears, L. Huddy, & R. Jervis (Eds.), *Oxford handbook of political psychology* (pp. 511–558). New York: Oxford University Press.

Huesmann, L. R. (1998). The role of social information processing and cognitive schemas in the acquisition and maintenance of habitual aggressive behavior. In R. G. Geen & E. Donnerstein (Eds.), *Human aggression: Theories, research, and implications for policy* (pp. 73–109). New York: Academic Press.

Huesmann, L. R. (1988). An information processing model for the development of aggression. *Aggressive Behavior* 14, 13–24.

Huesmann, L. R., & Eron, L. D. (1986). *Television and the aggressive child: A cross-national comparison*. Hillsdale, NJ: Erlbaum.

Huesmann, L. R., & Guerra, N. G. (1997). Normative beliefs about aggression and aggressive behavior. *Journal of Personality and Social Psychology* 72(2), 408–419.

Huesmann, L. R., & Moise, J. (1999, September). The role of cognitions in mediating the effect of childhood exposure to violence on adult aggression: A 15-year comparison of youth in four countries. Paper presented at the European Conference on Developmental Psychology, Spetses, Greece.

Hui, C. H. (1988). Measurement of individualism-collectivism. *Journal of Research in Personality* 22, 17–36.

Hunt, M. (1997). *How science takes stock*. New York: Russell Sage.

Hyman, H. (1959). *Political socialization*. Glencoe, IL: Free Press.

Innes, J. M., & Zeitz, H. (1988). The public's view of the impact of the mass media: A test of the "third person" effect. *European Journal of Social Psychology* 18, 457–463.

Internet election news audience seeks convenience, familiar names. (2000). Pew Research Center for the People and the Press. Accessed 6/12/03 at http://peoplepress.org/reports/display.php3?ReportID=21.

Internet sapping broadcast news audience. (2000). Pew Research Center for the People and the Press. Accessed 6/12/03 at http://people-press.org/reports/display.php3?ReportID=36.

Iyengar, S. (1991). *Is anyone responsible? How television frames political issues*. Chicago: University of Chicago Press.

Iyengar, S. (1990). Framing responsibility for political issues: The case of poverty. *Political Behavior* 12, 19–40.

Iyengar, S., & Kinder, D. R. (1987a). More than meets the eye: TV news, priming, and public evaluations of the President. In G. A. Comstock (Ed.), *Public communication and behavior,* Vol. 1 (pp. 135–171). San Diego, CA: Academic Press.

Iyengar, S., & Kinder, D. R. (1987b). *News that matters: Television and American opinion*. Chicago: University of Chicago Press.

Iyengar, S., & Valentino, N. A. (2000). Who says what? Source credibility as a mediator of campaign advertising. In A. Lupia, M. D. McCubbins, & S. L. Popkin (Eds.), *Elements of reason: Cognition, choice, and the bounds of rationality* (pp. 108–129). New York: Cambridge University Press.

Jacobs, R. C., & Campbell, D. T. (1961). The perpetuation of an arbitrary tradition through several generations of a laboratory microculture. *Journal of Abnormal and Social Psychology* 62, 649–658.

Jacoby, J., & Hoyer, W. D. (1981). What if opinion leaders don't know more? A question of nomological validity. In K. B. Monroe (Vol. Ed.), *Advances in consumer research*, Vol. 8, (pp. 31–34). Ann Arbor, MI: Association for Consumer Research.

Jamieson, K. H. (1992). *Packaging the presidency,* 2nd ed. New York: Oxford University Press.

Jamieson, K. H., & Waldman, P. (2003). *The press effect: Politicians, journalists, and the stories that shape the political world.* New York: Oxford University Press.

Jennings, M. K., & Niemi, R. C. (1983). *Generations and politics.* Princeton, NJ: Princeton University Press.

Johnson, N. R., (1973, Autumn). Television and politicization: A test of competing models. *Journalism Quarterly* 50, 447–455, 474.

Johnson, T. J. (1993). Filling out the racing form: How the media covered the horse race in the 1988 primaries. *Journalism Quarterly* 70(2), 300–310.

Johnson, T. J., Boudreau, T., & Glowacki, C. (1996). Turning the spotlight inward: How five leading news organizations covered the media in the 1992 presidential election. *Journalism & Mass Communication Quarterly* 73(3), 657–671.

Johnston, J., & Ettema, J. S. (1982). *Positive images: Breaking stereotypes with children's television.* Newbury Park, CA: Sage.

Jones, D. C. (2001, Nov.). Social comparison and body image: Attractiveness comparisons to models and peers among adolescent girls and boys. *Sex Roles* 645–665.

Jones, E. E. (1998). Major developments in five decades of social psychology. In D. T. Gilbert, S. T. Fiske, & G. Lindzey, (Eds.), *The handbook of social psychology*, Vol.1, 4th ed. (pp. 3–57). New York: McGraw-Hill.

Just, M., Crigler, A., & Wallach, L. (1990). Thirty seconds or thirty minutes: What viewers can learn from spot advertisements and candidate debates. *Journal of Communication* 40(8), 120–133.

Kahn, K. F. (1993). Gender differences in campaign messages: The political advertisements of men and women candidates for the U.S. Senate. *Political Research Quarterly* 46(3), 481–502.

Kahneman, D., Slovic, P., & Tversky, A. (1982). *Judgment under uncertainty: Heuristics and biases.* Cambridge: Cambridge University Press.

Kahneman, D., & Tversky, A. (1973). On the psychology of prediction. *Psychological Review* 80, 237–251.

Kaid, L. L., Gobetz, R., Garner, J., Leland, C., & Scott, D. (1993). Television news and presidential campaigns: The legitimization of televised political advertising. *Social Science Quarterly* 74(2), 274–285.

Kaid, L. L., Leland, C. M., & Whitney, S. (1992). The impact of televised political advertisements: Evoking viewer response in the 1988 presidential campaign. *Southern Communication Journal* 57(4), 285–295.

Kamber, V. (1993). Television big winner of '92 election, '93 presidency. *Public Relations Quarterly* 38(2), 26.

Kamins, M. A. (1990). An investigation of the "match-up" hypothesis in celebrity advertising: When beauty may be only skin deep. *Journal of Advertising* 19(1), 4–14.

Kamins, M. A., & Gupta, K. (1994). Congruence between spokesperson and product type: A matchup hypothesis perspective. *Psychology & Marketing* 11(6), 569–586.

Katz, E. (1996). Diffusion research at Columbia. In E. Dennis and E. Wartella (Eds.), *American communication research: The remembered history* (pp. 61–70). Mahwah, NJ: Erlbaum.

Katz, E. (1971, Summer). Platforms and windows: Broadcasting's role in election campaigns. *Journalism Quarterly* 48, 304–314.

Katz, E., & Lazarsfeld, P. (1955). *Personal influence: The part played by people in the flow of mass communications*. New York: Free Press.

Kaufman, G. (1999). The portrayal of men's family roles in television commercials. *Sex Roles* 41(5/6), 439–458.

Kaufmann, H., & Kooman, A. (1967). Predicted compliance in obedience situations as a function of implied instructional variables. *Psychonomic Science* (7)6, 205–206.

Keenan, K. (1986). Polls in network newscasts in the 1984 presidential race. *Journalism Quarterly* (63)3, 616–618.

Kennamer, J. D. (1990a). Comparing predictions of the likelihood of voting in a primary and general election. *Journalism Quarterly* 67(4), 777–784.

Kennamer, J. D. (1990b). Self-serving bias in perceiving the opinions of others. *Communication Research* 17(3), 393–404.

Kennamer, J. D. (1987). How media use during campaign affects the intent to vote. *Journalism Quarterly* 64(2/3), 291–300.

Key, V. O., Jr. (1966). *The responsible electorate*. Cambridge, MA: Harvard University Press.

Key, V. O., Jr. (1961). *Public opinion and American democracy*. New York: Knopf.

Kiel, G. C., & Layton, R. A. (1981). Dimensions of consumer information seeking behavior. *Journal of Marketing Research* 18, 233–239.

Kielbowicz, R. B. (1989). *News in the mail: The press, post office, and public information, 1700–1860s*. Westport, CT: Greenwood.

Kiewiet, D. R. (1981). Policy-oriented voting in response to economic issues. *American Political Science Review* 75, 448–459.

Kimball, M. M. (1986). Television and sex-role attitudes. In T. M. Williams (Ed.), *The impact of television: A natural experiment in three communities*. New York: Academic Press.

Kinder, D. R. (2003). Communication and politics in the age of information. In D. Sears, L. Huddy, & R. Jervis (Eds.), *Oxford handbook of political psychology* (pp. 357–393). New York: Oxford University Press.

Kinder, D. R. (1998). Opinion and action in the realm of politics. In D. T. Gilbert, S. T. Fiske, & G. Lindzey (Eds.), *Handbook of social psychology*, 4th ed. (pp. 778–867). Boston: McGraw-Hill.

Kinder, D. R. (1981). Presidents, prosperity, and public opinion. *Public Opinion Quarterly* 45, 1–21.

Kinder, D. R., & D'Ambrosio, L. (1996). War, emotion, and public opinion. Working manuscript, University of Michigan at Ann Arbor.

King, P. (1997). The press, candidate images and voter perceptions. In M. E. McCombs, D. L. Shaw, & D. Weaver (Eds.), *Communication and democracy: Exploring the intellectual frontiers in agenda setting* (pp. 29–40). Mahwah, NJ: Erlbaum.

Kiousis, S., Bantimaroudis, P., & Ban, H. (1999). Candidate image attributes: Experiments on the substantive dimension of second-level agenda setting. *Communication Research* 26, 414–428.

Klapper, J. T. (1960). *The effects of mass communication*. New York: Free Press.

Kobland, C. E. (1999). Talking about the news: News discussion panels. Ph.D. dissertation. Syracuse University.

Korn, J. H. (1997). *Illusions of reality: A history of deception in social psychology*. Albany: State University of New York Press.

Kraus, S. (2000). *Televised presidential debates and public policy,* 2nd ed. Mahwah, NJ: Erlbaum.

Kraus, S. (Ed.). (1979). *The great debates: Carter vs. Ford, 1976.* Bloomington: Indiana University Press.

Kraus, S., & Davis, D. (1976). *The effects of mass communication on political behavior.* University Park: Pennsylvania State University Press.

Krosnick, J., & Kinder, D. R. (1990). Altering the foundations of support for the president through priming. *American Political Science Review* 84, 497–512.

Krueger, J., & Clement, R. W. (1994). The truly false consensus effect: An ineradicable and egocentric bias in social perception. *Journal of Personality and Social Psychology* 67(4), 596–610.

Krull, D. S., Loy, M. H., Lin, J., Wang, C., Chen, S., & Zhao, X. (1999). The fundamental attribution error: Correspondence bias in individualist and collectivist cultures. *Personality & Social Psychology Bulletin* 25(10), 1208–1219.

Kubey, R., Shifflet, M., Weerakkody, N., & Ukeiley, S. (1995). Demographic diversity on cable: Have the new cable channels made a difference in the representation of gender, race, and age? *Journal of Broadcasting and Electronic Media* 39(4), 459–471.

Kuklinski, J. H., & Quirk, D. (2000). Reconsidering the rational public: Cognition, heuristics, and mass opinion. In A. Lupia, M. D. McCubbins, & S. L. Popkin (Eds.). *Elements of reason: Cognition, choice, and the bounds of rationality* (pp. 153–182). New York: Cambridge University Press.

Lang, G. E., & Lang, K. (1983). *The battle for public opinion: The president, the press and the polls during Watergate.* New York: Columbia University Press.

Lang, G. E., & Lang, K. (1968). *Politics and television.* Chicago: Quadrangle Books.

Lang, K., & Lang, G. E. (1953). The unique perspective of television and its effects: A pilot study. *American Sociological Review* 18, 3–12.

Lanoue, D. J. (1991). The "turning point": Viewers' reactions to the second 1988 presidential debate. *American Politics Quarterly* 19(1), 80–95.

Larson, M. S. (2001). Interactions, activities and gender in children's television commercials: A content analysis. *Journal of Broadcasting & Electronic Media* 45(1), 41–56.

Laskey, H. A., Fox, R. J., & Crask, M. R. (1994). Investigating the impact of executional style on television commercial effectiveness. *Journal of Advertising Research* 34(6), 9–17.

Lasorsa, D. L. (1989). Real and perceived effects of "Amerika." *Journalism Quarterly* 66(2), 373–378, 529.

Lasswell, H. D. (1935). *World politics and personal insecurity.* New York: McGraw-Hill.

Lasswell, H. D. (1930). *Psychopathology and politics.* Chicago: University of Chicago Press.

Lau, R. R. (2003). Models of decision-making. In D. O. Sears, L. Huddy, & R. Jervis (Eds.), *Oxford handbook of political psychology* (pp. 19–59). New York: Oxford University Press.

Lau, R. R., & Sears, D. O. (1981). Cognitive links between economic grievances and political responses. *Political Behavior* 3, 279–302.

Lau, R. R., Sigelman, L., Heldman, C., & Babbitt, P. (1999). The effectiveness of negative political advertisements: A meta-analytic assessment. *American Political Science Review* 93(4), 851–875.

Lavrakas, P. J., & Traugott, M. W. (2000) *Election polls, the news media, and democracy.* New York: Seven Bridges Press.

Lazarsfeld, P. F., Berelson, B., & Gaudet, H. (1948). *The people's choice,* 2nd ed. New York: Columbia University Press.

Lazarsfeld, P. F., Berelson, B., & Gaudet, H. (1944). *The people's choice: How the voter makes up his mind in a presidential campaign.* New York: Duell, Sloan and Pearce.

Lazarsfeld, P. F., & Menzel, H. (1963). Mass media and personal influence. In Wilbur Schramm, (Ed.), *The science of human communication* (pp. 94–115). New York: Basic Books.

Lazarsfeld, P. F., & Merton, R. K. (1948). Mass communication, popular taste, and organized social action. In L. Bryson (Ed.), *The communication of ideas* (pp. 95–118). New York: Harper.

Leonard-Barton, D. (1985). Experts as negative opinion leaders in the diffusion of a technological innovation. *Journal of Consumer Research* 11, 914–926.

Libet, B. (1985). Unconscious cerebral initiative and the role of conscious will in voluntary action. *Behavioral and Brain Sciences* 8, 529–566.

Libet, B., Gleason, C., Wright, E., & Pearl, D. (1983). Time of conscious intention to act in relation to onset of cerebral activity (readiness-potential). *Brain* 106, 623–642.

Libet, B., Pearl, D., Morledge, D., Gleason, C., Morledge, Y., & Barbaro, N. (1991). Control of the transition from sensory detection to sensory awareness in man by the duration of a thalamic stimulus. *Brain* 114, 1731–1757.

Lichter, S. R., Amundsen, D., & Noyes, R. E. (1989). Election '88 media coverage. *Public Opinion* 11, 18–19, 52.

Lichter, S. R., Rothman, S., & Lichter, L. S. (1986). *The media elite*. Bethesda, MD: Adler and Adler.

Lichty, L. W. (1982). Video vs. print. *Wilson Quarterly* 6(5), 49–57.

Lin, C. A. (1997). Beefcake versus cheesecake in the 1990s: Sexist portrayals of both genders in television commercials. *Howard Journal of Communication* 8(3), 237–249.

Linz, D., Donnerstein, E., Land, K. C., McCall, P. L., Scott, J., Shafer, B. J., Klein, L. J., & Lance, L. (1991). Estimating community standards: The use of social science evidence in an obscenity prosecution. *Public Opinion Quarterly* 55(1), 80–112.

Lippa, R. A. (1994). *Introduction to social psychology*. Belmont, CA: Wadsworth.

Lipset, S., & Schneider, W. (1983). *The confidence gap: Business, labor, and government in the public mind*. New York: Free Press.

Littlejohn, S. W. (1999). *Theories of human communication*, 6th ed. Belmont, CA: Wadsworth.

Lorenzi-Cioldi, F. (1993). They all look alike, but so do we sometimes: Perceptions of in-group and out-group homogeneity as a function of sex and context. *British Journal of Social Psychology* 32, 111–124.

Lorenzi-Cioldi, F. (1988). Self-other discrimination and social categorization. *Revue Internationale de Psychologie Sociale* 1(2), 239–256.

Lowry, D. T., Bridges, J. A., & Barefield, P. A. (1990). Effects of television "instant analysis and querulous criticism" following the first Bush-Dukakis debate. *Journalism Quarterly* 67(4), 814–825.

Lowry, D. T., Nio, T. C. J., & Leitner, D. W. (2003). Setting the public fear agenda: A longitudinal analysis of network TV crime reporting, public perceptions of crime and FBI crime statistics. *Journal of Communication* (53)1, 61–73.

Lucas, W. A., & Adams, W. C. (1978). Talking TV and voter indecision. *Journal of Communication* 28(4), 120–131.

Lukewarm interest in presidential debates. (2000). Pew Research Center for the People and the Press. Accessed 6/12/03 at http://people-press.org/reports/display.php3?ReportID=31.

Lupia, A., & McCubbins, M. D. (2000). The institutional foundations of political competence: How citizens learn what they need to know. In A. Lupia, M. D. McCubbins, & S. L. Popkin (Eds.), *Elements of reason: Cognition, choice, and the bounds of rationality* (pp. 47–66). New York: Cambridge University Press.

Lupia, A., McCubbins, M. D., & Popkin, S. L. (2000). *Elements of reason: Cognition, choice, and the bounds of rationality.* New York: Cambridge University Press.

Maass, A., Cadinu, M., Guarnieri, G., & Grasselli, A. (2003). Sexual harassment under social identity threat: The computer harassment paradigm. *Journal of Personality and Social Psychology* 85(5), 853–870.

Maccoby, E. E., Matthews, R. E., & Morton, A. S. (1954–55). Youth and political change. *Public Opinion Quarterly* 18, 23–39.

Mackie, D. M., Gastardo-Conaco, M. C., & Skelly, J. J. (1992). Knowledge of the advocated position and the processing of in-group and out-group persuasive messages. *Personality and Social Psychology Bulletin* 18, 145–151.

Mackie, D. M., & Queller, S. (2000). The impact of group membership on persuasion: Revisiting "Who says what to whom with what effect?" In D. J. Terry & M. A. Hogg (Eds.), *Attitudes, behavior, and social context: The role of norms and group membership* (pp. 135–155). Mahwah, NJ: Erlbaum.

Macrae, C. N., Milne, A. R., & Bodenhausen, G. V. (1994). Stereotypes as energy-saving devices: A peek inside the cognitive toolbox. *Journal of Personality and Social Psychology* 66, 37–47.

Major A. M. (2000). Correlates of accuracy and inaccuracy in the perception of the climate of opinion for four environmental issues. *Journalism & Mass Communication Quarterly* 77(2), 223–242.

Major, A.M. & Atwood, L. E. (1997). Changes in media credibility when a predicted disaster doesn't happen. *Journalism and Mass Communication Quarterly* 74(4), 797–813.

Mallon, T. (2004). *Bandbox*. New York: Pantheon Books.

Maltby, J., & Day, L. (2003). Applying a social identity paradigm to examine the relationship between men's self-esteem and their attitudes toward men and women. *Journal of Social Psychology* 143(1), 111–127.

Mann, T. E., & Orren, G. R. (1992). *Media polls in American politics*. Washington, DC: The Brookings Institution.

Marcus, G., Sullivan, J., Theiss-Morse, E., & Wood, S. (1995). With malice toward some: How people make civil liberties judgments. In J. Kuklinski (Ed.), *Political psychology*. New York: Cambridge University Press.

Marcus, G., Wood, S., & Theiss-Morse, E. (1998). Linking neuroscience to political intolerance and political judgment. *Politics and the Life Sciences* 17(2), 165–178.

Marcus, G. E. (2003). The psychology of emotion and politics. In D. O. Sears, L. Huddy, & R. Jervis (Eds.), *Oxford handbook of political psychology* (pp. 182–221). New York: Oxford University Press.

Marcus, G. E., Neuman, W. R., & MacKuen, M. (2000). *Affective intelligence and political judgment*. Chicago: University of Chicago Press.

Marks, G., & Miller, N. (1987) Ten years of research on the false-consensus effect: An empirical and theoretical review. *Psychological Bulletin* 102(1), 72–90.

Markus, H. R., & Kitayama, S. (1991). Culture and the self: Implications for cognition, emotion, and motivation. *Psychological Review* 98, 224–253.

Marsh, C. (2000). A science museum's exhibit on Milgram's obedience research: History, description, and visitor's reactions. In T. Blass, (Ed.), *Obedience to authority: Current perspectives on the Milgram paradigm*. Mahwah, NJ: Erlbaum.

Martinelli, K., & Chaffee, S. H. (1995). Measuring new-voter learning via three channels of political information. *Journalism & Mass Communication Quarterly* 72(1), 18–32.

Mazur, A. (1987). Putting radon on the public risk agenda. *Science, Technology, and Human Values* 12, 86–93.

Mazur, A., & Hall, G. S. (1990). Effects of social influence and measured exposure level on response to radon. *Sociological Inquiry* 60, 274–284.

McCarthy, E. J., & Perreault, W. D., Jr. (1990). *Basic marketing*, 10th ed. (p. 37) Homewood, IL: Irwin.

McClosky, H., & Dahlgren, H. E. (1959). Primary group influence on party loyalty. *American Political Science Revue* 53(3), 757–776.

McCombs, M. E., Gilbert, S., & Eyal, C. H. (1982). The State of the Union address and the press agenda: A replication. Paper presented to the International Communication Association, Boston.

McCombs, M. E., Llamas, J. P., Lopez-Escobar, E., & Rey, R. (1997). Candidate images in Spanish elections: Second-level agenda-setting effects. *Journalism & Mass Communication Quarterly* 74, 703–717.

McCombs, M. E., & Reynolds, A. (2002). News influence on our pictures of the world. In J. Bryant and D. Zillmann, (Eds.), *Media effects*, 2nd ed. (pp. 1–16). Mahwah, NJ: Erlbaum.

McCombs, M. E., & Shaw, D. L. (1972). The agenda-setting function of mass media. *Public Opinion Quarterly* 36, 176–187.

McCracken, G. (1989). Who is the celebrity endorser? Cultural foundations of the endorsement process. *Journal of Consumer Research* 16(3), 310–322.

McCracken, G. D. (1985). The trickle-down theory rehabilitated. In M. R. Solomon (Ed.), *The psychology of fashion*. Lexington, MA: D.C. Heath, Lexington Books.

McDonald, M. P., & Popkin, S. (2001). The myth of the vanishing voter. *American Political Science Review* 95, 963–974.

McGinnies, E., & Ward, C. D. (1980). Better liked than right: Trustworthiness and expertise as factors in credibility. *Personality and Social Psychology Bulletin* 6(3), 467–472.

McGraw, K. M. (2003). Political impressions: Formation and management. In D. O. Sears, L. Huddy, & R. Jervis, (Eds.), *Oxford handbook of political psychology* (pp. 394–432). New York: Oxford University Press.

McLeod, D. M., Eveland, W. P., Jr., & Nathanson, A. I. (1997). Support for censorship of violent and misogynic rap lyrics: An analysis of the third-person effect. *Communication Research* 24(2), 153–174.

McLeod, J., Becker, L. B., & Byrnes, J. (1974). Another look at the agenda-setting function of the press. *Communication Research* 1, 131–166.

McLeod, J. M., & Becker, L. B. (1974). Testing the validity of gratification measures through political effects analysis. In J. G. Blumler & E. Katz (Eds.), *The uses of mass communications: Current perspectives on gratifications research* (pp.137–164). Beverly Hills, CA: Sage.

McQuail, D. (2000). *Mass communication theory*, 4th ed. Thousand Oaks, CA: Sage.

Media seen as fair, but tilting to Gore. (2000). Pew Research Center for the People and the Press. Accessed 6/12/03 at http://people-press.org/reports/display.php3?ReportID=29.

Menaud, L. (2004, August 30). The unpolitical animal. *New Yorker* 92–96.

Mendelsohn, H. A. (1966). Election day broadcasts and terminal voting decisions. *Public Opinion Quarterly* 30(2), 212–225.

Mendelsohn, H. A., & Crespi, I. (1970). *Polls, television and the new politics*. San Francisco: Chandler.

Mendelsohn, H. A., & O'Keefe, G. J. (1976). *The people choose a president: Influences on voter decision-making*. New York: Praeger.

Merton, R. K. (1957). *Social theory and social structure*. Glencoe, IL: The Free Press.

Merton, R. K. (1949). Patterns of influence. In P. F. Lazarsfeld & F. N. Stanton (Eds.), *Communication research*. New York: Harpers.

Meyer, J. R. (2001). Effect of request type and situational features on negative politeness in requests. *Communication Research Reports* (18)2, 158–165.

Mezulis, A. H., Abramson, L. Y., Hyde, J. S., & Hankin, B. L. (2004). Is there a universal positivity bias in attributions? A meta-analytic review of individual, developmental, and cultural differences in the self-serving attributional bias. *Psychological Bulletin* 130(5), 711–747.

Milgram, S. (1974). *Obedience to authority*. New York: Harper & Row.

Milgram, S. (1965). Some conditions of obedience and disobedience to authority. *Human Relations* 18, 57–76.

Milgram, S. (1963). Behavioral study of obedience. *Journal of Abnormal and Social Psychology* 67, 371–378.

Miller, A. G. (1995). Constructions of the obedience experiments: A focus upon domains of relevance. *Journal of Social Issues* 51(3), 33–53.

Miller, A. G. (1986). *The obedience experiments: A case study of controversy in social science*. New York: Praeger.

Miller, K. I., & Monge, P. R. (1987). The development and test of a system of organizational participation and allocation. In McLaughlin, M. L. (Ed). *Communication yearbook 10* (pp. 431–455). Newbury Park, CA: Sage.

Mishkin, M., & Appenzeller, T. (1987). The anatomy of memory. *Scientific American* 256, 80–89.

Mixon, D. (1971, April). Behaviour analysis treating subjects as actors rather than organisms. *Journal for the Theory of Social Behaviour* (1)1, 19–31.

Mohn, E. L. (1991). Opinion and affect: An experimental investigation of the "fear of isolation" in the spiral of silence theory of public opinion formation and change. Doctoral dissertation, Syracuse University, Syracuse, NY.

Moral values: How important? Voters like campaign 2004, but too much 'mudslinging.' (2004). Pew Research Center for the People and the Press. Accessed 12/22/04 at http://people-press.org/reports/display.php3?ReportID-233.

Morgan, M. (1987). Television, sex-role attitudes, and sex-role behavior. *Journal of Early Adolescence* 7(3), 269–282.

Morgan, M. (1982). Television and adolescents' sex-role stereotypes: A longitudinal study. *Journal of Personality and Social Psychology* 43, 947–955.

Morgan, M., & Shanahan, J. (1997). Two decades of cultivation research: An appraisal and meta-analysis. In B. R. Burelson (Ed.), *Communication yearbook 20* (pp. 1–46). Thousand Oaks, CA: Sage.

Morris, D., & Gamache, M. E. (1994). *Handbook of campaign spending: Money in the 1992 congressional races.* Washington, DC: Congressional Quarterly.

Moscovici, S. (1985). Social influence and conformity. In G. Lindzey and E. Aronson (Eds.), *Handbook of social psychology,* Vol. 2. New York: Random House.

Mouw, T. (2003). Social capital and finding a job: Do contacts matter? *American Sociological Review* 68(6), 868–898.

Moy, P., & Pfau, M. (2000). *With malice toward all? The media and public confidence in democratic institutions.* Westport, CT: Praeger.

Moy, P., & Scheufele, D. A. (2000). Media effects on political and social trust. *Journalism and Mass Communication Quarterly* 77(4), 744–759.

Moy, P., Scheufele, D. A., & Holbert, R. L. (1999). Television use and social capital: Testing Putnam's time displacement hypothesis. *Mass Communication & Society* 2(1/2), 27–45.

Mullen, B., Atkins, J. L., Champion, D. S., Edwards, C., Hardy, D., Story, J. E., & Vanerklok, M. (1985) The false consensus effect: A meta-analysis of 115 hypothesis tests. *Journal of Experimental Social Psychology* 21, 262–283.

Mutz, D. C. (1998). *Impersonal influence: How perceptions of mass collectives affect political attitudes.* Cambridge, UK: Cambridge University Press.

Mutz, D. C. (1994). The political effects of perceptions of mass opinion. In M. X. Delli Carpini, L. Huddy, & R. Y. Shapiro (Eds.), *Research in micropolitics: New directions in political psychology,* Vol. 4. Greenwich, CT: JAI Press.

Mutz, D. C. (1992). Mass media and the depoliticization of personal experience. *American Journal of Political Science* 36, 483–508.

Mutz, D. C., & Mondak, J. J. (1997). Dimensions of sociotropic behavior: Group-based judgments of fairness and well-being. *American Journal of Political Sciences* 41, 284–308.

Myers, J. H., & Robertson, T. S. (1972). Dimensions of opinion leadership. *Journal of Marketing Research* 9, 41–46.

Nadeau, R., Niemi, R. G., & Fan, D. P. (1996). Elite economic forecasts, economic news, mass economic expectations, and presidential approval. Paper presented at the Annual Meeting of the Midwest Political Science Association, Chicago.

National Television Violence Study. (1998). *National Television Violence Study*, Vol. III. Santa Barbara, CA: Center for Communication and Social Policy, University of California.

National Television Violence Study. (1997). *National Television Violence Study*, Vol. II. Santa Barbara, CA: Center for Communication and Social Policy, University of California.

National Television Violence Study. (1996). *National Television Violence Study: Executive summary, 1994–1995.* Studio City, CA: Mediascope.

Neuman, W. R. (1990). The threshold of public attention. *Public Opinion Quarterly* 54(2), 159–176.

Neuman, W. R. (1986). *The paradox of mass politics.* Cambridge, MA: Harvard University Press.

Neuman, W. R., Just, M., & Crigler, A. (1992). *Common knowledge: News and the construction of political meaning.* Chicago: University of Chicago Press.

Newhagen, J. E., & Nass, C. (1989). Differential criteria for evaluating credibility of newspaper and television news. *Journalism Quarterly* 66(2), 277–284.

Nie, N. H., Verba, S., & Petrocik, J. R. (1976). *The changing American voter.* Cambridge, MA: Harvard University Press.

Nimmo, D., & Combs, J. E. (1983). *Mediated political realities.* New York: Longman.

Noelle-Neumann, E. (1993). *The spiral of silence: Public opinion—our social skin*, 2nd ed. Chicago: University of Chicago Press.

Noelle-Neumann, E. (1984). *Spiral of silence.* Chicago: University of Chicago Press.

Noelle-Neumann, E. (1974). The spiral of silence: A theory of public opinion. *Journal of Communication* 34, 43–51.

Norris, P. (2000). *A virtuous circle: Political communication in postindustrial societies.* New York: Cambridge University Press.

Oakes, O. J., & Turner, J. C. (1980). Social categorization and intergroup behavior: Does minimal intergroup discrimination make social identity more positive? *European Journal of Social Psychology* 10, 295–301.

O'Guinn, T. C., & Shrum, L. J. (1997). The role of television in the construction of consumer reality. *Journal of Consumer Research* 23, 278–294.

Ohanian, R. (1991). The impact of celebrity spokespersons' perceived image on consumers' intention to purchase. *Journal of Advertising Research* 31(1), 46–55.

Page, B. I., & Shapiro, R. Y. (1992). *The rational public: Fifty years of trends in Americans' policy preferences.* Chicago: University of Chicago Press.

Paik, H., & Comstock, G. (1994). The effects of television violence on antisocial behavior: A meta-analysis. *Communication Research* 21(4), 516–546.

Paisley, W. (1989). Public communication campaigns: The American experience. In R. E. Rice & C. K. Atkin (Eds.), *Public communication campaigns,* 2nd ed. (pp. 15–41). Newbury Park, CA: Sage.

Paletz, D. L., & Guthrie, K. K. (1987). The three faces of Ronald Reagan. *Journal of Communication* 37(4), 7–23.

Patterson, T. E. (2002). *The vanishing voter: Public involvement in an age of uncertainty.* New York: Knopf.

Patterson, T. E. (1993). *Out of order.* New York: Random House.

Patterson, T. E. (1980). *The mass media election: How Americans choose their president.* New York: Praeger.

Patterson, T. E., & McClure, R. D. (1976). *The unseeing eye: The myth of television power in national elections.* New York: Putnam.

Peer, L., & Chestnut, B. (1995). Deciphering media independence: The Gulf War debate in television and newspaper news. *Political Communication* 12(1), 81–95.

Peiser, W., & Peter, J. (2000). Third-person perception of television-viewing behavior. *Journal of Communication* 50(1), 25–46.

Perloff, L. S., & Fetzer, B. K. (1986). Self-other judgments and perceived vulnerability to victimization. *Journal of Personality and Social Psychology* 50(3), 502–510.

Perloff, R. M. (1989). Ego-involvement and the third person effect of televised news coverage. *Communication Research* 16(2), 236–262.

Perse, E. M. (1990). Media involvement and local news effects. *Journal of Broadcasting and Electronic Media* 34(1), 17–36.

Petrocik, J. R. (1996). Issue ownership in presidential elections, with a 1980 case study. *American Journal of Political Science* 40, 825–850.

Petroshius, S. M., & Crocker, K. E. (1989). An empirical analysis of spokesperson characteristics on advertisement and product evaluations. *Journal of the Academy of Marketing Science* 17(3), 217–226.

Petty, R. E., & Cacioppo, J. T. (1996). *Attitudes and persuasion: Classic and contemporary approaches*. Boulder, CO: Westview.

Pew Internet and American Life Project (2004). Accessed 12/16/04 at http://www.pewinternet.org/PPF/r/121/report_display.asp.

Pew Research Center for the People and the Press. (Nov. 11, 1999). *Retropolitics: The political typology: Version 3.0*. Washington, DC.

Pfau, M., & Burgoon, M. (1989). The efficacy of issue and character attack message strategies in political campaign communication. *Communication Reports* 2(2), 53–61.

Pinkleton, B. (1997). The effects of negative comparative political advertising on candidate evaluations and advertising evaluations: An exploration. *Journal of Advertising* 26(1), 19–29.

Pinkleton, B. E., Austin, E. W., & Fortman, K. K. J. (1998). Relationships of media use and political disaffection to political efficacy and voting behavior. *Journal of Broadcasting and Electronic Media* 42(1), 34–49.

Polhemus, T. (1994). *Street style: From sidewalk to catwalk*. London: Thames & Hudson.

Popkin, S. L., & Dimock, M. A. (2000). Knowledge, trust and international reasoning. In A. Lupia, M. D. McCubbins, & S. L. Popkin (Eds.), *Elements of reason: Cognition, choice, and the bounds of rationality* (pp. 214–238). New York: Cambridge University Press.

Potter, W. J. (1999). *On media violence*. Thousand Oaks, CA: Sage.

Potter, W. J. (1994). A methodological critique of cultivation research. *Journalism Monographs* 147.

Potter, W. J., & Ware, W. (1987). Traits of perpetrators and receivers of antisocial and prosocial acts on television. *Journalism Quarterly* 21(3), 382–391.

Price, V., Huang, L. N., & Tewksbury, D. (1997, Autumn). Third-person effects of news coverage: Orientations toward media. *Journalism & Mass Communication Quarterly* 74(3), 525–540.

Price, V., & Tewksbury, D. (1996). Measuring the third-person effect of news: The impact of question order, contrast and knowledge. *International Journal of Public Opinion Research* 8(2), 120–141.

Price, V., Tewksbury, D., & Huang, L. N. (1998, Spring). Third-person effects on publication of a Holocaust-denial advertisement. *Journal of Communication* (48) 2, 3–26.

Putnam, R. D. (2000). *Bowling alone: The collapse and revival of American community*. New York: Simon & Schuster.

Putnam, R. D. (1995). Tuning in, tuning out: The strange disappearance of social capital in America. *PS: Political Science & Politics* 28(4), 664–683.

Rahn, W. M. (2000). Affect as information: The role of public mood in political reasoning. In A. Lupia, M. D. McCubbins, & S. L. Popkin (Eds.), *Elements of reason: Cognition, choice, and the bounds of rationality* (pp. 130–150). New York: Cambridge University Press.

Ranney, A. (1977). *Participation in American presidential nominations*. Washington, DC: American Enterprise Institute.

Ratzan, S. (1989). Comments made at the Conference on Polling, (p. 28) Cambridge, MA: Joan Shorenstein Barone Center on the Press, Politics, and Public Policy, John F. Kennedy School of Government, Harvard University.

Reese, S. D., & Danielian, L. (1989). Intermedia influence and the drug issue: Converging on cocaine. In P. Shoemaker (Ed.), *Communication campaigns about drugs* (pp. 29–46). Hillsdale, NJ: Erlbaum.

Reese, S. O., & Buckalew, B. (1995). The militarism of local television: The routine framing of the Persian Gulf War. *Critical Studies in Mass Communication* 12(1), pp. 40–59.

Reynolds, F. D., & Darden, W. R. (1971). Mutually adaptive effects of interpersonal communication. *Journal of Marketing Research* 8, 449–454.

Rhee, J. W., & Cappella, J. N. (1997). The role of political sophistication in learning from news: Measuring schema development. *Communication Research* 24(3), 197–233.

Richins, M. L., & Root-Shaffer, T. (1988). The role of involvement and opinion leadership in consumer word-of-mouth: An implicit model made explicit. In M. Houston (Ed.), *Advances in consumer research* (pp. 15, 32–36). Provo, UT: Association for Consumer Research.

Roberts, D. F., & Bachen, C. M. (1981). Mass communication effects. *American Review of Psychology* 32, 307–356.

Roberts, D. F., & Foehr, U. G. (2004). *Kids & media in America.* Cambridge, UK: Cambridge University Press.

Roberts, D. F., & Maccoby, N. (1985). Effects of mass communication. In G. Lindzey & E. Aronson (Eds.), *Handbook of social psychology,* 3rd ed. Reading, MA: Addison-Wesley.

Robinson, J. P. (1974). The press as king-maker: What surveys from last five campaigns show. *Journalism Quarterly* 56, 587–595, 606.

Robinson, J. P. (1971). The audience for national TV news programs. *Public Opinion Quarterly* 35(3), 403–405.

Robinson, J. P., & Godbey, G. (1997). *Time for life: The surprising ways Americans use their time.* University Park: Pennsylvania State University Press.

Robinson, J. P., & Levy, M. R. (1986a). Interpersonal communication and news comprehension. *Public Opinion Quarterly* 50(1), pp. 160–175.

Robinson, J. P., & Levy, M. R. (1986b). *The main source: Learning from television news.* Beverly Hills, CA: Sage.

Robinson, M. J., & Clancey, M. (1985). Teflon politics. In M. J. Robinson and A. Ranney (Eds.), *The mass media in campaign '84.* Washington, DC: American Enterprise Institute.

Robinson, M. J., & Sheehan, M. A. (1983). *Over the wire and on TV: CBS and UPI in campaign '80.* New York: Russell Sage.

Roddy, B. L., & Garramone, G. M. (1988). Appeals and strategies of negative political advertising. *Journal of Broadcasting and Electronic Media* 32(4), 415–427.

Rogers, E. M. (2002). Intermedia processes and powerful media effects. In J. Bryant, & D. Zillmann (Eds.), *Media effects: Advances in theory and research.* Mahwah, NJ: Erlbaum.

Rojas, H., Shah, D. V., & Faber, R. J. (1996). For the good of others: Censorship and the third-person effect. *International Journal of Public Opinion Research* 8(2), 163–186.

Roper Center. (2001, November/December). War on innocents. *Public Perspective Magazine.*

Roper Center. (1997). *America at the polls 1996.* Storrs: Roper Center for Public Opinion Research, University of Connecticut.

Roper Starch. (1995). *America's watching: Public attitudes toward television.* New York: Roper Starch Worldwide.

Rose, R. L., Bearden, W. O., & Teel, J. E. (1992). An attributional analysis of resistance to group pressure regarding illicit drug and alcohol consumption. *Journal of Consumer Research* 19, 1–13.

Rosenkrantz, P., Vogel, S., Bee, H., Broverman, I., & Broverman, D. M. (1968). Sex-role stereotypes and self-concepts in college students. *Journal of Consulting and Clinical Psychology* 32, 286–295.

Ross, L. (1977). The intuitive psychologist and his shortcomings: Distortions in the attribution process. In L. Berkowitz (Ed.), *Advances in experimental social psychology,* Vol. 10 (pp. 173–220). Orlando, FL: Academic Press.

Ross, L., Bierbrauer, C., & Hoffman S. (1976). The role of attribution processes in conformity and dissent: Revisiting the Asch situation. *American Psychologist* 31, 148–157.

Ross, L., Greene, D., & House, P. (1976). The "false consensus effect": An egocentric bias in social perception and attribution process. *Journal of Experimental Social Psychology* 13, 279–301.

Ross, M. H. (1992). Television news and candidate fortunes in presidential nominations campaigns: The case of 1984. *American Politics Quarterly* 20(1), 69–98.
Rubin, R. (1980). *Press, party, and president*. New York: W. W. Norton.
Rucinski, D. (2004). Community boundedness, personal relevance, and the knowledge gap. *Communication Research* 31(4), 472–495.
Rucinski, D., and Salmon, C. T. (1990). The "other" as the vulnerable voter: A study of the third-person effect in the 1988 campaign. *International Journal of Public Opinion Research* 2(4), 345–369.
Rudd, R., & Fish, M. J. (1989). Depth is issue coverage in television news: Campaign '84. *Journal of Broadcasting & Electronic Media* 33(2), 197–202.
Rusk, J. G., & Weisberg, H. J. (1972, August). Perceptions of presidential candidates: Implications for electoral change. *Midwest Journal of Political Science* 16, 388–410.
Russell, R. (1996). *Bird lives!: The high life and hard times of Charlie (Yardbird) Parker.* New York: Da Capo Press.
Sabato, L. J. (1991). *Feeding frenzy: How attack journalism has transformed American politics*. New York: Free Press.
Salmon, C. T., & Kline, F. G. (1985). The spiral of silence ten years later. In D. R. Sanders, L. L. Kaid, & D. Nimmo (Eds.), *Political communication yearbook 1984* (pp. 3–30). Carbondale, IL: Southern Illinois University Press.
Salwen, M. B. (1998, June). Perceptions of media influence and support for censorship: The third-person effect in the 1996 presidential election. *Communication Research* (25)3, 259–285.
Salwen, M. B., & Dupagne, M. (1999). The third-person effect: Perceptions of the media's influence and immoral consequences. *Communication Research* 26(5), 523–550.
Schachter, S. (1959). *The psychology of affiliation*. Stanford, CA: Stanford University Press.
Scharrer, E. (2002). Third-person perception and television violence: The role of out-group stereotyping in perceptions of susceptibility to effects. *Communication Research* 29(6), 681–704.
Scheufele, D. A. (2002). Examining differential gains from mass media and their implications for participatory behavior. *Communication Research* 29(1), 46–65.
Scheufele, D. A., & Shah, D. V. (2000). Personality strength and social capital. *Communication Research* 27(2), 107–131.
Schoenbach, K. (1991). Agenda-setting effects of print and television in West Germany. In D. L. Protess & M. E. McCombs (Eds.), *Agenda-setting: Readings on media, public opinion, and policymaking* (pp. 127–129). Hillsdale, NJ: Erlbaum.
Schoenbach, K., & Becker, L. B. (1995). Origins and consequences of mediated public opinion. In C. Salmon & T. Glasser (Eds.). *Public opinion and the communication of consent* (pp. 323–347). New York: Guilford.
Schor, J. B. (1998). *The overspent American: Why we want what we don't need.* New York: Harper Collins.
Schramm, W., & White, D. M. (1960). Age, education, and economic status as factors in newspaper reading. In W. Schramm (Ed.), *Mass communication* (pp. 438–450) Urbana: University of Illinois Press.
Schudson, M. (1998). *The good citizen: A history of American civic life*. New York: The Free Press.
Schudson, M. (1978). *Discovering the news: A social history of American newspapers*. New York: Basic.
Schuman, H., & Rodgers, W. L. (2004). Cohorts, chronology, and collective memories. *Public Opinion Quarterly* 68(2), 217–254.
Schwarz, N., & Groves, R. M. (1998). Survey methods. In D. T. Gilbert, S. T. Fiske, & G. Lindzey (Eds.), *The handbook of social psychology,* 4th ed. Vol. 1 (pp. 143–179). New York: McGraw-Hill.
Searing, D. R., Schwartz, J. J., & Lind, A. E. (1973, June). The structuring principle: Political socialization and belief systems. *American Political Science Review* 67, 415–432.

Sears, D. O., & Chaffee, S. H. (1979). Uses and effects of the 1976 debates: An overview of empirical studies. In S. Kraus (Ed.), *The great debates: Carter vs. Ford, 1976*. Bloomington: Indiana University Press.

Shah, D. V. (1998). Civic engagement, interpersonal trust, and television use: An individual-level assessment of social capital. *Political Psychology* 19(3), 469–496.

Sherif, M. (1947). Group influences upon the formation of norms and attitudes. In T. M. Newcomb & E. L. Hartley (Eds.), *Readings in social psychology* (pp. 77–980). New York: Henry Holt.

Sherif, M. (1936). Group influences upon the formation of norms and attitudes. In M. Sherif (Ed.), *The psychology of social norms*. New York: Harper.

Sherif, M., Harvey, O. J., White, B. J., Hood, W. R., & Sherif, C. W. (1961). *Intergroup conflict and cooperation: The Robbers Cave experiment*. Norman: University of Oklahoma Book Exchange.

Sherif, M., & Sherif, C. W. (1953). *Groups in harmony and tension: An integration of studies on intergroup relations*. New York: Octagon Books.

Shoemaker, P., & Reese, S. D. (1991). *Meditating the message: Theories of influence on mass media content*. New York: Longman.

Shyles, L. (1984). The relationships of images, issues and presentational methods in televised spot advertisements for 1980's American presidential primaries. *Journal of Broadcasting* 28(4), 405–421.

Sigelman, L., & Bullock, D. (1991). Candidates, issues, horse races, and hoopla: Presidential campaign coverage, 1888–1988. *American Politics Quarterly* 19(1), 5–32.

Signorielli, N. (2001). Television's gender role images and contribution to stereotyping: Past, present, future. In D. G. Singer & J. L. Singer (Eds.). *Handbook of children and the media* (pp. 341–358). Thousand Oaks, CA: Sage.

Signorielli, N. (1993). Television and adolescents' perceptions about work. *Youth & Society* 24, 314–341.

Signorielli, N. (1989). Television and conceptions about sex roles: Maintaining conventionality and the status quo. *Sex Roles* 21(5/6), 341–360.

Signorielli, N. (1984). The demography of the television world. In G. Melischek, E. Rosengren, & J. Stappers (Eds.), *Cultural indicators: An international symposium*. Vienna, Austria: Osterreichischen Akademie der Wissenschaften.

Signorielli, N., Gerbner, G., & Morgan, M. (1995). Violence on television: The cultural indicators project. *Journal of Broadcasting & Electronic Media* 39(2), 278–283.

Signorielli, N., & Lears, M. (1992). Children, television, and conceptions about chores: Attitudes and behaviors. *Sex Roles*, 27, 157–170.

Signorielli, N., McLeod, D., & Healy, E., (1994). Gender stereotypes in MTV commercials: The beat goes on. *Journal of Broadcasting & Electronic Media* 38(1), 91–101.

Signorelli, N., & Morgan, M. (Eds.). (1990). Cultivation analysis: New directions in media effects research.

Sills, D. L. (1996). Stanton, Lazarsfeld, and Merton: Pioneers in communication research. In E. Dennis, and E. Wartella (Eds.), *American communication research: The remembered history* (pp. 105–116). Mahwah, NJ: Erlbaum.

Simmel, G. [1904] (1957). Fashion. *American Journal of Sociology* 62, 541–548.

Simon, D. M., & Ostrom, C. W., Jr. (1989). The impact of televised speeches and foreign travel on presidential approval. *Public Opinion Quarterly* 53(1), 58–82.

Simpson, C. (1996). Elisabeth Noelle-Neumann's "spiral of silence" and the historical context of communication theory. *Journal of Communication* 46(3), 149–175.

Singer, E., & Endreny, P. M. (1987). Reporting hazards: Their benefits and costs. *Journal of Communication* 37(3), 10–26.

Slovic, P., Fischhoff, B., & Lichtenstein, S. (1987). Behavioral decision theory perspectives on protective behavior. In N. D. Weinstein (Ed.), *Taking care: Understanding and encouraging self-protective behavior*. New York: Cambridge University Press.

Smith, K. A., & Ferguson, D. A. (1990). Voter partisan orientations and use of political television. *Journalism Quarterly* 67(4), 864–874.

Smith, L. (1994). A content analysis of gender differences in children's advertising. *Journal of Broadcasting & Electronic Media* 38(3), 323–337.

Smith, S. A., & Roden, C. D. (1988). CBS, the *New York Times*, and reconstructed political reality. *Southern Speech Communication Journal* 53(2), 140–158.

Smith, T. J., Lichter, S. R., Harris, L., et al. (1997). *What the people want from the press*. Washington, DC: Center for Media and Public Affairs.

Some final observations on voter opinions. (2000). Pew Research Center for the People and the Press. Accessed 6/12/03 at http://people-press.org/reports/display.php3?ReportID=20.

Stamm, K., Johnson, M., & Martin, B. (1997). Differences among newspapers, television, and radio in their contribution to knowledge of the Contract with America. *Journalism & Mass Communication Quarterly* 74(4), 687–702.

Stanforth, N. (1995). Fashion innovators, sensation seekers, and clothing individualists. *Perceptual and Motor Skills* 81(3), 1203–1211.

Starr, K. (2004). *Coast of dreams: California on the edge, 1990–2003*. New York: Knopf.

Starr, P. (2004). *The creation of the media: Political origins of modern communications*. New York: Basic Books.

Statistical Abstract of the United States, 2003. Accessed 12/16/04 at http:www.census.gov/prod/2004pubs/03statab/inforcomm.pdf.

Stempel, G. H., III, & Windhauser, J. W. (Eds.). (1991). *The media in the 1984 and 1988 presidential campaigns*. Westport, CT: Greenwood Press.

Stephens, M. (1989). *A history of news: From the drum to the satellite*. New York: Viking.

Stevenson, R. L., Eisinger, R. A., Feinberg, B. M., & Kotok, A. B. (1973). Untwisting the news twisters: A replication of Efron's study. *Journalism Quarterly* 50(2), 211–219.

Stonecash, J. M. (2003). *Political polling: Strategic information in campaigns*. Lanham, MD: Rowman & Littlefield.

Stovall, J. G., & Solomon, J. H. (1984). The poll as a news event in the 1980 presidential campaign. *Public Opinion Quarterly* 48, 619–627.

Strachan, J. (2003). *High-tech grass roots*. Lanham, MD: Rowman & Littlefield.

Stuart, E. W., Shimp, T. A., & Engle, R. W. (1987). Classical conditioning of consumer attitudes: Four experiments in an advertising context. *Journal of Consumer Research* 14, 334–350.

Summers, J. O. (1970). The identity of women's clothing fashion opinion leaders. *Journal of Marketing Research* 7, 178–185.

Tajfel, H. (1982). *Social identity and intergroup relations*. Cambridge, England: Cambridge University Press.

Tajfel, H. (1981). *Human groups and social categories*. Cambridge, England: Cambridge University Press.

Tajfel, H. (Ed.). (1978). *Differentiation between social groups: Studies in the social psychology of intergroup relations*. London: Academic Press.

Tajfel, H., & Turner, J. C. (1986). The social identity theory of intergroup behavior. In S. Worchel & W. G. Austin (Eds.), *Psychology of intergroup relations* (pp. 7–24). Chicago: Nelson Hall.

Tajfel, H., & Turner, J. C. (1979). An integrative theory of social conflict. In W. Austin & S. Worchel (Eds.), *The social psychology of intergroup relations*. Monterey, CA: Brooks/Cole.

Tan, A. S. (1979). TV beauty ads and role expectations of adolescent female viewers. *Journalism Quarterly* 56(2), 283–288.

Tannenbaum, P. H., & Kostrich, L. J. (1983). *Turned-on TV/Turned-off voters*. Beverly Hills, CA: Sage.

Tarfimow, D. (2000). A theory of attitudes, subjective norms, and private vs. collective self-concepts. In D. J. Terry & M. A. Hogg (Eds.), *Attitudes, behavior, and social context: The role of norms and group membership* (pp. 47–65). Mahwah, NJ: Erlbaum.

Taylor, D. G. (1986). *Public opinion and collective action: The Boston school desegregation conflict.* Chicago: University of Chicago Press.

Taylor, S. E. (1998). The social being in social psychology. In D. T. Gilbert, S. T. Fiske, & G. Lindzey, (Eds.), *The handbook of social psychology*, 4th ed., Vol. I (pp. 58–95). New York: McGraw-Hill,.

Taylor, S. E., & Lobel, M. (1989). Social comparison activity under threat: Downward evaluation and upward contacts. *Psychological Review* 96, 569–575.

Terror coverage boosts news media's images. (2001). Pew Research Center for the People and the Press. Accessed 6/12/03 at http://people-press.org/reports/display.php3?ReportID=143.

Thomas, M. H., & Drabman, R. S. (1975). Toleration of real life aggression as a function of exposure to televised violence and age of subject. *Merrill-Palmer Quarterly* 21, 227–232.

Thomas, R. J. (1982). Correlates of interpersonal purchase influence in organizations. *Journal of Consumer Research* 9, 171–181.

Thompson, T. L., & Zerbinos, E. (1997). Television cartoons: Do children notice it's a boy's world? *Sex Roles* 37(5/6), 415–432.

Thorson, E., Christ, W. G., & Caywood, C. (1991). Effects of issues-image strategies, attack and support appeals, music, and visual content in political commercials. *Journal of Broadcasting and Electronic Media* 35(4), 465–486.

Tichenor, P. J., Donohue, G. A., & Olien, C.N. (1980). Conflict and the knowledge gap. In P. J. Tichenor, G. A. Donohue, & C. N. Olien, *Community conflict and the press* (pp. 175–203). Beverly Hills, CA: Sage.

Tiedge, J. T., Silverblatt, A., Havice, M. J., & Rosenfeld, R., (1991). Discrepancy between perceived first-person and perceived third-person mass media effects. *Journalism Quarterly* 68(1/2), 141–155.

Tierny, J. (2004, May 30). Political points. *New York Times,* p. 14.

Till, B. D. (1998). Using celebrity endorsers effectively: Lessons from associative learning. *Journal of Product & Brand Management* 7(5), 400–409.

Tims, A. R., Freeman, J. R., & Fan, D. P. (1989). The cultivation of consumer confidence: A longitudinal analysis of news media influence on consumer sentiment. *Advances in Consumer Research* 16, 758–770.

Tinkham, S. F., & Weaver-Lariscy, R. A. (1995). Incumbency and its perceived advantage: A comparison of 1982 and 1990 congressional advertising strategies. *Political Communication* 12(3), 291–304.

Tinkham, S. F., & Weaver-Lariscy, R. A. (1993). A diagnostic approach to assessing the impact of negative political television commercials. *Journal of Broadcasting and Electronic Media* 37(4), 377–400.

Tinkham, S. F., & Weaver-Lariscy, R. A. (1990). Advertising message strategy in U.S. congressional campaigns: Its impact on election outcome. *Journal of Current Issues and Research in Advertising* 13(1/2), 207–226.

Tocqueville, A. (1835). *Democracy in America.* R. D. Heffner (Ed). (1956). New York: Mentor.

Tolbert, C. J., & McNeal, R. S. (2003). Unraveling the effects of the Internet on political participation. *Political Research Quarterly* 56(2), 175–185.

Tolman, E. C. (1948). Cognitive maps in rats and men. *Psychological Review* 55, 189–208.

Tolman, E. C. (1932). *Purposive behavior in animals and men.* New York: Appleton-Century-Crofts.

"Track talk." (October 4, 2003). The Blood-horse, p. 5308.

Traugott, M. W. (1992). The impact of media polls on the public. In T. E. Mann and G. R. Orren (Eds.), *Media polls in American politics.* Washington, DC: Brookings Institute.

Triandis, H. C. (1997). A cross-cultural perspective on social psychology. In C. McGarty & S. A. Haslam (Eds.), *The message of social psychology: Perspectives on mind in society* (pp. 342–354). Oxford, England: Blackwell.

Triandis, H. C. (1994). *Culture and social behavior*. New York: Praeger.

Triandis, H. C., McCusker, C., & Hui, C. H. (1990). Multimethod probes of individualism and collectivism. *Journal of Personality and Social Psychology* 59, 1006–1020.

Tripp, C., Jensen, T. D., & Carlson, L. (1994). The effects of multiple product endorsements by celebrities on consumers' attitudes and intentions. *Journal of Consumer Research* 20(4), 535–548.

Trumbo, C. (1995). Longitudinal modeling of public issues: An application of the agenda-setting process to the issue of global warming. *Journalism & Mass Communication Monographs*. Columbia, SC: AEJM.

Tuchman, G. (1978). *Making news: A study in the construction of reality*. New York: Free Press.

Tuchman, S., & Coffin, T. E. (1971). The influence of election night television broadcasts in a close election. *Public Opinion Quarterly* 35(3), 315–326.

Turner, J. C. (1999). Some current issues in research on social identity and self-categorization theories. In N. Ellemers, R. Spears, & B. Doosje (Eds.), *Social identity: Context, commitment and content* (pp. 6–34). Oxford, England: Blackwell.

Tybout, A. M., & Artz, N. (1994). Consumer psychology. *Annual Review of Psychology* 45, 131–150.

Tyler, T. R. (1984). Assessing the risk of crime victimization: The integration of personal victimization experience and socially-transmitted information. *Journal of Social Issues* 40(1), 27–38.

Tyler, T. R. (1980). The impact of directly and indirectly experienced events. The origin of crime-related judgments and behaviors. *Journal of Personality and Social Psychology* 39(1), 13–28.

Tyler, T. R., & Lavrakas, P. J. (1985). Cognitions leading to personal and political behaviors: The case of crime. In S. Kraus & R. M. Perloff (Eds.), *Mass media and political thought*. Beverly Hills: Sage.

Tyler, T. R., & Lavrakas, P. J. (1983). Support for gun control: The influence of personal, sociotropic, and ideological concerns. *Journal of Applied Social Psychology* 13, 392–405.

U.S. Department of Health and Human Services. (2001). *Youth violence: A report of the Surgeon General*. Rockville, MD: U.S. Department of Health and Human Services, Centers for Disease Control and Prevention, National Center for Injury Prevention and Control, Substance Abuse and Mental Health Services Administration, Center for Mental Health Services, National Institutes of Health, National Institute of Mental Health.

Vallone, R., Ross, L., & Lepper, M. (1985). The hostile media phenomenon: Biased perception and perceptions of media bias in coverage of the Beirut massacre. *Journal of Personality and Social Psychology* 49(3), 577–585.

Vande Berg, L. R., & Streckfuss, D. (1992). Prime-time television's portrayal of women and the world of work: A demographic profile. *Journal of Broadcasting & Electronic Media* 36(2), 195–208.

Vincent, R. C., & Basil, M. D. (1997). College students' news gratifications, media use, and current events knowledge. *Journal of Broadcasting and Electronic Media* 41(3), 380–392.

"Voter news service: What went wrong?" (2003). *Baseline*, January 13. Ziff-Davis Media.

Wanta, W. (1997). *The public and the national agenda: How people learn about important issues*. Mahwah, NJ: Erlbaum.

Wanta, W. (1992). The influence of the president on the news media and public agendas. *Mass Communication Review* 19(1/2), 14–21.

Wanta, W., & Chang, K. (1999). Priming and the second level of agenda setting: Merging two theoretical approaches. Paper presented to the International Communication Association, San Francisco, CA.

Wanta, W., & Foote, J. (1994). The president-news media relationship: A time series analysis of agenda setting. *Journal of Broadcasting and Electronic Media* 38(4), 437–448.

Wanta, W., & Ghanem, S. (forthcoming). Effects of agenda-setting. In J. Bryant & R. Carveth (Eds.), *Meta-analyses of media effects*. Mahwah, NJ: Erlbaum.

Wanta, W., & Hu, Y. W. (1994). The effects of credibility, reliance, and exposure on media agenda-setting: A path analysis. *Journalism Quarterly* 71(1), 99–109.

Wartella, E. (1996). The history reconsidered. In E. Dennis & E. Wartella (Eds.), *American communication research: The remembered history* (pp. 169–180). Mahwah, NJ: Erlbaum.

Wattenberg, M. P. (1996). *The decline of American political parties, 1952–1994*. Cambridge, MA: Harvard University Press.

Weatherford, M. S. (1983). Evaluating economic policy: A contextual model of the opinion formation process. *Journal of Politics* 45, 866–888.

Weaver, D., & McCombs, M. E. (1978). Voters' need for orientation and choice of candidate: Mass media and electoral decision making. Paper presented to the American Association for Public Opinion Research, Roanoke, VA.

Weaver, D. H., & Wilhoit, G. C. (1992, November 12). *The American journalist in the 1990s*. Preliminary report released at the Freedom Forum World Center, Arlington, VA.

Weinstein, N. D. (1989). Optimistic biases about personal risks. *Science* 246, 1232–1233.

Weinstein, N. D. (1980). Unrealistic optimism about future life events. *Journal of Personality and Social Psychology* 39, 806–820.

Whitney, D. C., & Becker, L. (1982). "Keeping the gates" for gatekeepers: The effects of wire news. *Journalism Quarterly* 59, 60–65.

Williams, T. M. (Ed.). (1986). *The impact of television: A natural experiment in three communities*. New York: Academic Press.

Williams, W., Jr., Shapiro, M., & Cutbirth, C. (1983). The impact of campaign agendas on perceptions of issues in the 1980 campaign. *Journalism Quarterly* 60(2), 226–231.

Willman, L. (1996). Mass media and political outspokenness in Hong Kong: Linking the third-person effect and the spiral of silence. *International Journal of Public Opinion Research* 8(2), 187–212.

Willnat, L. (1996). Mass media and political outspokenness in Hong Kong: Testing the interaction of the third-person effect and the spiral of silence. *International Journal of Public Opinion Research* 8, 187–212.

Wills, T. A. (1991). Similarity and self-esteem in downward comparison. In B. Seidenberg & A. Snadowski (Eds.), *Social psychology: An introduction*. New York: Free Press.

Wills, T. A. (1981). Downward comparison principles in social psychology. *Psychological Bulletin* 90, 245–271.

Wilson, E. J., & Sherrell, D. L. (1993). Source effects in communication and persuasion research: A meta-analysis of effect size. *Journal of the Academy of Marketing Science* 21(2), 101–112.

Winter, J. P., & Eyal, C. H. (1981). Agenda-setting for the civil rights issue. *Public Opinion Quarterly* 45(3), 376–383.

Wood, J. V., Taylor, S. E., & Lichtman, R. R. (1985). Social comparison in adjustment to breast cancer. *Journal of Personality and Social Psychology* 49, 1169–1183.

Wood, W., Wong, F., & Chachere, J. (1991). Effects of media violence on viewers' aggression in unconstrained social interaction. *Psychological Bulletin* 109(3), 371–383.

Yang, K. S. (1981). Social orientation and individual modernity among Chinese students in Taiwan. *Journal of Social Psychology* 113, 159–170.

Ybarra, O., & Trafimow, D. (1998). How priming the private self or collective self affects the relative weights of attitudes and subjective norms. *Personality and Social Psychology Bulletin* 24, 362–370.

Yoon, K., Kim, C. H., & Kim, M.S. (1998). A cross-cultural comparison of the effects of source credibility on attitudes and behavioral intentions. *Mass Communication and Society* 1(3/4), 153–165.

Zaller, J. R. (1992). *The nature and origins of mass opinion*. New York: Cambridge University Press.

Zhao, X., & Bleske, G. L. (1995). Measurement effects in comparing voter learning from television news and campaign advertisements. *Journalism & Mass Communication Quarterly* 72(1), 72–83.

Zhao, X., & Chaffee, S. H. (1995). Campaign advertisements versus television news as sources of political issue information. *Public Opinion Quarterly* 59(1), 41–65.

Zhu, J., Milavsky, J. R., & Biswas, R. (1994). Do televised debates affect image perception more than issue knowledge? A study of the first 1992 presidential debate. *Human Communication Research* 20(3), 302–333.

Zillmann, D., & Brosius, H. B. (2000). *Exemplification in communication: The influence of case reports on the perception of issues*. Mahwah, NJ: Erlbaum.

EPILOGUE

The sun had little to do with the quality of the dawn on November 3, 2004. There was a rosy glow for supporters of George W. Bush and a gray portent for those of John Kerry. The story of the election has been told and retold, and will continue to be told and retold. We will not add to this catalogue. Our intent is to filter the campaign through the lens we have constructed here.

The most striking aspect was the increase in turnout over the previous two presidential elections, which validated the view that there are large numbers in American elections who are quite prepared to vote—in the sense of having both knowledge of the process and confidence in their choice—when a particular outcome is sufficiently unwelcome. This circumstance in turn dovetails in this instance with a substantial role for the review of alternatives driven by the arousal of affect and threat. Thus, for some, "affective intelligence" was spurred when the usual, habitual monitoring of the political situation was overthrown in favor of greater activity and involvement in response to feelings of potential peril.

The surge in voter turnout for the presidential election of 2004 was, perhaps, explained by a feeling of "moral risk" experienced by some. Postelection polls showed that 27 percent of respondents chose "moral values" from an itemized list of issues and topics that mattered most in their vote (22 percent cited Iraq and 21 percent jobs or the economy). When those individuals listing moral values as one of their two most important issues were asked to say what the term brought to mind, 29 percent mentioned gay marriage, 28 percent abortion, 23 percent candidate qualities, and 18 percent religious preferences. (They were able to list more than one.) ("Moral values: How important? Voters like campaign 2004, but too much 'mudslinging,' " 2004).

The debates, presidential and vice presidential, as usual did not play a clearly decisive role in the outcome (unless you wish to indulge the tautology that whoever wins the election must have done well enough). However, Bush's comments made for better sound bites ("It's hard work.") while Kerry's strong performance changed the shape of the campaign and left most pollsters with a race they thought too close to call. On Election Night the networks struck a cautious tone as states were slowly declared blue or red, the memory of the miscues in 2000 seemingly fresh in the minds of news personnel. Bush enjoyed the usual postconvention bounce; Kerry did not, although the attention given him after his surprise victories in the early causes and primaries may have bestowed the transient benefits usually reserved for the nominating convention.

Three long-term trends reasserted themselves: campaign expenditures again reached new heights (about 30 percent more than in 2000), with most as usual going to television advertising; the emphases of these commercials was often quite negative, focusing on supposed flaws of the opponent; and, the advertising and other campaign resources, such as visits by the candidates, were concentrated in the so-called battleground states that supposedly could go either way. The campaign began very early, as has become customary and, because the major issues on which it would turn, the war in Iraq and the terrorist attacks of September 11, 2001, already dominated the public landscape, partisanship and decision making among voters seemingly began earlier than usual.

The Internet played a fairly significant role, as both a source of information and a forum for posting or discussing views. Indeed, "bloggers" (those keeping online journals, discussions, and analyses) were among those calling Dan Rather to task for airing one source's unsubstantiated claims that Bush avoided National Guard service. With both Rather and Tom Brokaw having covered the final presidential election of their long careers, commentators ever alert to the uses of symbols began to herald the end of the three-network dominated news era—a bit tardily perhaps in terms of audience drift and certainly premature in terms of the remaining substantial audiences for the nightly weekday reviews of the day's events.

Finally, the emphasis of the media on the character of the candidates, rather than the policies and proposals they espouse, was evident in the usual echoing of continuing motifs. In 2004, the most prominent was the accusation of flip-flopping leveled against Kerry, which appeared again and again in coverage of the Bush campaign. We are not snarling bias, or dismissing the charge. Our point is that the need of the media for easily graspable concepts, and their penchant for the tactics of the horse race, inevitably subject campaign coverage to the sovereignty of the easy conceit.

AUTHOR INDEX

SUBJECT INDEX